Let Us Make Men

Let Us Make Men

The Twentieth-Century Black Press and a
Manly Vision for Racial Advancement

· ·

D'WESTON HAYWOOD

The University of North Carolina Press   Chapel Hill

This book is published with appreciation for Susan and Rusty Carter and their generous support of the University of North Carolina Press.

The University of North Carolina Press has been a member of the Green Press Initiative since 2003.

Library of Congress Cataloging-in-Publication Data
Names: Haywood, D'Weston, author.
Title: Let us make men : the twentieth-century black press and a manly vision for racial advancement / D'Weston Haywood.
Description: Chapel Hill : University of North Carolina Press, [2018] | Includes bibliographical references and index.
Identifiers: LCCN 2018008895| ISBN 9781469643380 (cloth) | ISBN 9781469643397 (pbk) | ISBN 9781469643403 (ebook) Subjects: LCSH: African American newspapers—History—20th century. | African American newspapers—Political activity. | African Americans in mass media—History—20th century. | Men in mass media—History—20th century. | African Americans—Civil rights—History—20th century.
Classification: LCC PN4882.5 .H39 2018 | DDC 071/.308996073—dc23
LC record available at https://lccn.loc.gov/2018008895

Cover illustration: *Three Black Men Reading by Fireplace* (1920) by Lewis W. Hine. Courtesy of the George Eastman Museum.

To Temple. Thank you for everything.

Contents

Acknowledgments

In examining the lives, ideas, and efforts of the black men who constitute this study, subjecting them to piercing questions that probed very personal sides of their thoughts and lives, I have tried to be critical. Yet my subjects refused to let me do this freely. I have taken stock of the relationships they held to their work and some of the people in their lives, and they have often expected me to do the same, to think critically about who helped "make" me and this project.

I am deeply grateful to a number of people whose critical insights and support helped me produce this book. Thank you to Martha Biondi, Dylan Penningroth, and Darlene Clark Hine for their brilliance and guidance. Professor Biondi's charge to "just plunge" into the sources was a welcome challenge I have carried with me. Thank you for being an incredible mentor and resource.

I would also like to thank Deborah Gray White, Mia Bay, Walter Rucker, Donna Murch, Rachel Devlin, and Marisa Fuentes for their encouragement and feedback during my time as a Postdoctoral Fellow in Race and Gender History at Rutgers, the State University of New Jersey. The intellectual, financial, and scholarly support the fellowship provided this project was invaluable.

Many thanks are also due to my editor at the University of North Carolina Press, Brandon Proia, as well as my anonymous readers for their time and insightful comments that helped strengthen the book.

No amount of thanks is enough for my family. Whenever the book appeared to send me on a very isolating and personal journey, I always discovered that the journey was a shared one. To my mother, Dante Haywood, and late father, David Haywood Jr.; sisters, Davida Haywood and DeVon H. Grant; grandparents, Hattie and Weston Butler and Norma and the late David Haywood Sr.; aunt, Audrey Wall; nephews, Kenneth Culbreth Jr. and Kole Culbreth; my second family, Treva Cunningham and Walter Cunningham III, Treasur and Walter Cunningham IV, Ruth McClellan, and the late Marian Huffman, I say thank you. It is my mother who has always maintained since my youth that no matter the size of the task, all one ever needs is the "faith of a mustard seed." Thank you for that life lesson.

I want to thank my wife, Temple—my best friend, resident scholar, sounding board, and life vest in a sea of words. I deeply appreciate you walking with me through every step of this journey. I look forward to future journeys we will take together. I could never pay you back for all I owe. But I will try.

Finally, and most of all, I must thank God, my ultimate source. I asked a lot of God in order to complete this journey. And God always answered, showing me that the greatest strength is earned—not granted.

Let Us Make Men

Introduction

What a Man Sees in Life He Sees in the Newspaper

· ·

Cato Anderson likely read the June 4, 1927, edition of the *Pittsburgh Courier* with great excitement. That day the *Courier* published his editorial "'Newspapers Should Take Up Race Leadership.'" The piece explained what he saw as the deeper role of black newspapers. Of course, its most basic function was to provide news and "first hand knowledge of conditions." But its deeper role, shaping "public opinion," "plays a most important part in the life of a people." "Where the school, church, the chautauqua and other agencies have given up the fight," the black press was "about the only agency" truly successful in molding public opinion and ensuring real racial uplift. For Anderson, "the newspaper is the mirror of public opinion. What a man sees in life he sees in the newspaper." Because the "crying need of our complex life is leadership, that type of leadership that will lead us out of the wilderness . . . I would delegate to the newspaper the task of taking that leadership," he affirmed. "The editor of the newspaper . . . occupies a most important position in our modern life."[1] Clearly, Anderson had an appreciation for black newspapers, shaped in large part by his own life experiences. Anderson obtained his education at Syracuse University, taught European History at Douglas High School in Baltimore, Maryland, and was a member of several black civic organizations, including a male beneficial society, a Negro civic league, and Omega Psi Phi Fraternity, a black Greek-letter fraternity. These experiences helped him recognize currents of racial leadership and uplift even in a newspaper. In many ways, he could see himself in the black press. He turned to it to express himself at a time when many black men in particular and black people in general felt they could not do so freely in any other public forum. Yet Anderson elevated the black press above other important, long-standing black social institutions. It would seem that Anderson's educational and professional experiences gave him a perspective that would have been lost on the masses, but the widespread popularity of the black press suggests that many readers would have agreed with him. Certainly, black male publishers would have agreed too.

In fact, Anderson's editorial only reiterated several points many of them had realized decades ago when they inaugurated the modern black press. They saw something similar in the newspaper page.

Let Us Make Men: The Twentieth-Century Black Press and a Manly Vision for Racial Advancement reinterprets the twentieth-century black press as a tool of black men's leadership, public vocalization, gender and identity formation, and space for the construction of ideas of proper black masculinity that shaped the twentieth-century black freedom struggle to wage a fight for racial justice *and* black manhood. The book draws its title from the words of another reader, Reverend J. C. Austin, whose editorial argued for the redemption of black manhood, and referenced Genesis 1:26 to help make the point. In it God says "Let us make man in our image, after our likeness."[2] Using Austin's words as a guide, this study takes "us" to represent the black male publishers of certain papers, who did not see themselves as God, to be sure, but did see themselves as powerful agents, who used their positions as publishers to build up black men through certain images and likenesses, or visions in their papers, and even through exemplifying parts of those visions themselves. The expressed intent of black newspapers was to report news and cover issues important to black people. Yet, by moving from the rise of the modern black press at the dawn of the twentieth century to the emergence of black radicalism in the 1960s, this study shows that certain issues prompted black male publishers to interpret and present those issues through a gendered lens that signaled moments in the black freedom struggle in which black men should stand up and be "men." The black press is a well-known and oft-used source by scholars, but has remained vastly underanalyzed in terms of gender. The growing digitization of black papers within the last decade has opened up new vistas for scholars to analyze black newspapers within this rich category of identity, among others.[3] Conducting a close, gendered reading of black newspaper articles and black male publishers' manuscript collections reveals that for Robert S. Abbott and John Sengstacke's *Chicago Defender*, W. E. B. DuBois's *Crisis*, Marcus Garvey's *Negro World*, Robert F. Williams's the *Crusader*, and Malcolm X's *Muhammad Speaks*, issues of black migration, New Negro politics, Depression-era economic challenges, civil rights protest, and urban renewal were fraught with tremendous implications for black men. The issues these pivotal moments raised signaled crises in black manhood, and, as a result, opportunities for its redemption. The reasons for this had much to do with the publishers of these papers, who shaped their columns to reflect a racial and personal quest for proper black manhood.

Focusing especially on these publishers and their newspapers, this study examines the black press at a time when it was the most powerful and popular form of mass print media in black communities. Yet this book construes black newspapers broadly to account for the diverse breadth of black print media during the twentieth century, ranging from national and prominent black weeklies to monthly journals to small local newsletters to organizational publications. The book uses the terms "newspaper," "paper," "publication," and "black press" interchangeably, though it also distinguishes between their differences when necessary. The particular publishers and papers this study examines were selected because they led the black press in circulation, influence, and/or relevancy at particular moments in the long black freedom struggle, while also leading it in articulating a vision for racial advancement that promised the redemption of black manhood. Putting these papers and the men behind them at the complex intersections of race, gender, identity, urbanization, black institutional life, and the black public sphere, *Let Us Make Men* argues that black people's ideas, rhetoric, and strategies for black protest and racial advancement during the twentieth-century black freedom struggle grew out of a quest for proper black manhood led by black newspapers. These publishers were shaped by their own gendered subjectivities and the gendered ideologies of their historical moment as they sought ways to assert and insert a carefully constructed masculine public self before an influential black public sphere that their papers helped solidify. They were convinced of the power of newspapers to shape public opinion *and* processes of gender identity formation among the masses. Here, black male publishers used their newspapers to instruct black people on what they thought were the proper models of black manhood. Black and nonblack communities perceived manhood to be natural and normative, but also believed it required the careful instruction and application of "proper" models, which were usually thought to be embodied already by the instructor. Black male publishers embraced this role and deployed their papers to help make black men "men," that is, to restore and maintain their access to the proper prerogatives, privileges, and rights to which men were believed to be entitled as men. From this, it was believed that ideologically, psychologically, socially, politically, and economically, current and future generations of black men would become the right kind of men the race needed in order to advance. This is what redeeming black men and black manhood fundamentally meant.

The particular historical developments that precipitated the rise of the modern black press motivated black men's use of black newspapers in these ways. The modern black press emerged amid the consolidation of the Jim Crow regime in the 1890s, and the determined efforts of black leaders and activists to respond by organizing and protesting initially in the urban North. Segregation and racial discrimination became law. Racial violence against individual black people or whole black communities was widespread. Scientific racism became entrenched in the country's legal, political, educational, and social institutions, promoting pseudoscientific theories of black mental and bodily inferiority through mainstream intellectual circles and popular culture.[4] These injustices were present too in the patently racist pages of white newspapers. Indeed, this age of capricious and brutal physical violence to black bodies and juridical violence to black people's citizenship rights also included discursive violence to black people's public image. These varied forms of violence were actually imbricated, all intended to dehumanize black people, literally and figuratively, while buttressing the false logics of white supremacy. The white press at this time was either uninterested in black people's affairs, removing them from the public record and serious public thought, or fixated on reporting black criminal activity and discussing black people as a perennial societal problem. Occasional accounts of outstanding black entertainers became the only exceptions to this practice.[5] In the main, white papers were guilty of constructing and operationalizing what Walter Lippmann's 1922 study of public opinion might have identified as a "system of stereotypes." "Prejudices are so much easier and more interesting," he wrote.[6] As the *Kansas City Call*, a black paper, editorialized, black people were "denied what other men are freely granted." "Oh, if you could see the story of your struggles honestly and fairly related in the newspapers . . . if your aspirations were met with applause as are those of your neighbors, this would be a wonderful world! But no!"[7]

This multifaceted attack on black people also had gendered implications that solidified a gendered and sexual racism in which whites held that black men were incapable of being real men and black women incapable of being real women. As one black paper pointed out, whites considered blacks a race in its "infancy," a "child race" not yet fully grown as mature men and women.[8] These ideas provided yet another way for whites to deny black humanity and uphold the structures of white supremacy. Jim Crow laws and the social etiquette they dictated reinforced this, making the meaning and practice of racial proscription deeply gendered.[9] But black people resisted. The right to be a "man" or "woman" was regarded by many, black and white, as rights in and of themselves. And black and nonblack men commonly expressed the language of rights, political and otherwise, in gendered terms of manhood and masculinity, a gendered vocabulary derived from centuries-old Enlightenment concepts of the nation, citizenship, and property ownership.[10] Many black people resisted by asserting their humanity and gendered selves in schools, churches, and fraternal societies, usually exclusively black social institutions independent of major white influence.[11] The racial violence that enforced Jim Crow had helped foreclose the spaces in which blacks could exert an appreciable public influence, confining their efforts to claim human value to these mostly private spaces. Black churches, educational institutions, and fraternities had been engaged in building up black men for decades, and had seen many black men and their communities through real and perceived crises and opportunities, both personal and racial.[12] Yet some of the men involved in these institutions came to publish newspapers and transferred elements of this private side of black resistance directly to the public.[13]

Indeed, the newspaper page represented one of the few spaces with a public function that black men could shape, if not control, at this time. That it was a white space might have made publishing even more attractive. Black male publishers approached this space deliberately and joined the public side of black resistance that openly organized and offered vocal social critique of racial injustice. Following on the heels of nineteenth-century black activists and publishers, the modern black press emerged to provide incisive analyses and build a culture of protest among readers that might help actualize a fight for racial justice on the ground, along with a dedicated readership. Concretizing a deep dialogic relationship with readers that at once reflected and shaped the issues that were important to black people, black newspapers became not the alternative media for black Americans, but the mainstream media.[14] For black male publishers, fighting white supremacy and its proponents, though discursively, was not only necessary but also appealing in a time when doing so literally could end abruptly inside of a noose tied together by the hands of a mob.[15]

The names of some papers, such as the *Defender, Challenge, Protector, Contender, Sentinel,* and *Crusader,* indicated this fight. Other names, such as the *Whip, Blade,* and *Broad Ax,* were even more dramatic in signaling a discursive black armed resistance. However, some papers' names, such as the *Negro Spokesman, Messenger, Crisis, Opportunity, People's Elevator, Journal and Guide,* and *Negro World,* pointed to black newspapers' crucial role in shaping black public opinion, signaling racial challenges and uplift, building racial consciousness, and envisaging a better physical space for black people.[16] Black men's fights from a printed page may have seemed insufficient against the behemoth of white supremacy. But their discursive fights were enough to enrage opponents and state authorities, attracting federal surveillance and threats of mob violence at different times. As an ordinance from Somerville, Tennessee, declared in 1919, "White people of this city . . . have issued an order that no 'colored newspapers' must be circulated in this town . . . in order to keep the 'nigger from getting besides himself, and to keep him in his place.'"[17] Government officials read black papers too, especially during periods of national crisis, though for reasons different from those of the typical black reader. Government officials instead read black newspapers in order to surveil them and their publishers.[18] The space that newspapers provided black publishers did not always offer a completely safe space, to be sure, especially for black publishers in the South.[19] Still, many black male publishers grew more determined to fight in the face of opposition, efforts that for them took on gendered tones. That white resistance sometimes emerged against black papers' protests, which sometimes revolved around redeeming black men, is interesting.

Let Us Make Men argues that when real or perceived moments of racial crisis emerged and unleashed profound changes in black people's political, social, economic, and cultural status in the United States, black male publishers interpreted them in masculine terms, a lens they applied in their papers and intended to appeal to readers' own gendered subjectivities in hopes that readers would embrace a proper black manhood for the benefit of the race. Black readers, who turned to these papers for information and inspiration, came to find this gendered framework shaping the issues of the day. Through this framework, black publishers and their presses promoted essentially five things. First, they promoted black newspapers as a tool of black men's public vocalization. Second, they promoted the idea that the right to be a "man" for black men was just as important as civil rights, and in fact constitutive of civil rights and full citizenship. Third, they promoted black leadership, rhetoric, and protest strategies that elevated black male leadership, masculinized rhetoric, strategies of resistance that displayed manliness, and the redemption of black manhood as a priority for racial advancement. Fourth, they promoted a vision for racial advancement that had a central gendered component that equated the advancement of the race with the advancement of black men. Fifth, they promoted discourses of racial advancement expressed within rhetorics of masculinity that came to be effective in mobilizing black activism. The black press became one of the most widely accessed black social institutions of the twentieth century. In fact, it had the greatest reach among the black masses, influence on the black public sphere, and power to elevate positive ideas, ideals, and images of black manhood to the largest numbers of the black public. Altogether, the constructions of black manhood that resulted were supposed to be applied literally in black communities with black men at the helm, mobilizing the race to protest racial oppression, using rhetoric and strategies of resistance that displayed a proper black manhood. With issues of racial advancement interpreted in this masculine frame, black men's issues became instrumental to the issues black people mobilized around, making the fight for racial justice a fight for manhood as well.

Why did a fight for black manhood go hand in hand with the fight for racial justice? Why and how did ideas about what black men needed as "men" get wrapped up in the claims black people made on citizenship rights? And why did black men choose newspapers to elevate these points to the race? *Let Us Make Men* pursues these questions, among others. Many historians of American manhood and masculinity have shown that "manhood" was a social and historical construct, and quite the capacious concept and term that Americans of all races constructed, contested, and infused with a variety of consonant and conflicted meanings depending on the historical moment. Black men, like other men in America, understood manhood, despite the concept's historical construction and malleability in a particular moment or over time, as something that could actually be attained and possessed, as well as lost.[20] These points about the construction, historical contingency, and malleability of manhood are essential to this book's gendered reinterpretation of the black press and black freedom struggle. That these processes took place in the blank white spaces of newspaper pages was useful to black male publishers and in broader discourses on racial uplift and black people's rights. With the page, publishers and their staffs could rework and retool ideas and ideals as malleable as manhood.[21] That most black papers remained weeklies with a few exceptions by midcentury, writers, editors, and publishers had time to do this, to analyze an issue, decide how to interpret it, present it on the page, and adapt it to any changes that might have arisen in that span of time. This process often took place alongside the framing and reframing of other categories of identity like race, class, and sexuality. But this process often produced contradictions, especially during the real and perceived moments of racial crisis and opportunity in which black papers mobilized. These real and perceived moments were crucial to black newspapers' discourses on black manhood because they helped produce and shape conceptions of black masculinity and shifts in them that often elevated one model of black manhood over others or sometimes rejected models once seen as proper at other times.[22] Thus, black male publishers' understandings and articulations of black masculinity were historically contingent, as well as regionally based, changing over time and sometimes with multiple definitions from different sources competing at the same times. Indeed, competing models of black manhood often emerged simultaneously, though one model might become dominant due to the traction it gained within the public sphere. The emergence of these competing models, and their appeal or lack thereof, was a process in which the black press was instrumental. But in spite of differences in publishers, papers, region, or time, what remained constant was that their constructions of black manhood were always intended to promote black men's access to the things to which men were believed to be entitled as "men." But because new real or perceived crises could reverse what seemed to be the restoration of black manhood at a previous point, underscoring the fluid and untenable nature of gendered ideologies, redeeming black men remained an ongoing process throughout the twentieth century that permeated the ongoing fight for racial justice.

By foregrounding black men, who published prominent and distinct publications during the twentieth century and used those publications to promote different models of black manhood, *Let Us Make Men* makes several crucial historiographic interventions, particularly in histories of black manhood, the black press, and the twentieth-century black freedom struggle. First, historical scholarship on black manhood has largely investigated the political and social arenas in which black men have had opportunities to formulate and enact ideas of masculinity. Theaters of war and military involvement, opportunities for sustainable and autonomous work, and private spaces of home, church, fraternal organizing, and community typify the sites probed by this scholarship.[23] Yet, in its observation of the arenas so central to the construction of black manhood, this scholarship has overlooked black newspapers as a critical arena involved in its construction. Treating the black press as such a site does more to reveal the contested processes through which black men discovered ways to articulate, represent, represent, and "market" (to borrow from Marlon B. Ross) themselves and other black men before different publics, and then exert some degree of influence on those publics.[24] This study shows that newspapers served as tools for black men's pursuit of personal and racial manhood, racial leadership, public vocalization, public influence, and manly public performances in order to help the race and black men themselves resist racist and emasculating forces in America. This use of newspapers motivated them to frame issues thought to be critical to racial progress in a masculine vein that promoted what they saw as proper black manhood.[25] Along these lines, the reader will find that this study does not directly engage black men's experiences during America's wars, as scholarship on this history and its importance to shaping black men's conceptions of manhood does so wonderfully.[26] Instead, in its effort to examine the gendered subjectivities and ideologies of black male publishers, this book considers the wars they saw themselves fighting for different causes and against different enemies at different times, waging these battles in print and before the black public sphere.

Second, the gender ideologies of black male publishers permeated their use of newspapers. Here, this book expands studies on the black press. Modern scholarship on the black press has argued that black newspapers helped forge a racial consciousness and collective racial identity among black people through influential protest campaigns during the twentieth century. This scholarship has also emphasized that black newspapers maintained a pronounced ethic of protest.[27] This study builds on these points, but rethinks the black press through a close gendered analysis that shows that the racial consciousness, identities, and protests black newspapers promoted were deeply gendered, and that black male publishers built a corresponding sense of racial and gender identity for themselves and the race. As real and perceived attacks on black people motivated many papers to be vocal about racial injustice, black male publishers were as vocal about redeeming black manhood, often expressing both in the same breath.[28] With the exception of a few recent works on black women journalists, this point about gender ideologies shaping black papers has gone largely unacknowledged by black press scholarship, however.[29] Drawing on media studies, discourse theory, and examinations of public spheres, black publics, and black counterpublics, this study reveals that as ideas and ideals of black manhood motivated black male publishers, these publishers helped make the black press instrumental to socializing people to think and act in terms of a gender identity. Accordingly, black newspapers were instrumental to engendering racial solidarity, black public opinion, and the political orientations of black Americans.[30] Along these lines, this study departs in significant ways from the typical history of the black press by examining not only the gendered discourses published by black papers but also what lay behind the printed page, the integrationist and black nationalist goals of the black press, the successes *and* limits of black papers' editorial campaigns, and how black male publishers' gendered subjectivities and political ideologies shaped their papers in ways that helped and hampered the black freedom struggle. Coming to terms with these contested sides of the black press, in addition to its gendered discourses, calls scholars to reevaluate black newspapers as more influential and more problematic than had been previously assumed.

Third, this analysis argues a far broader presence of black newspapers in promoting discourses, rhetorics, and strategies of black manhood to the goals and direction of the twentieth-century black freedom struggle. Many scholars of the "long civil rights movement," or what some scholars are increasingly calling the twentieth-century black freedom struggle as a more fitting term, have examined the long roots of black people's political organizing around issues of citizenship rights and racial justice across the South and urban North and West, for example.[31] Building on this work and its exploration of black social and protest movements and protest thought, this study shows that black people's conceptions of citizenship and justice, and their activism in the name of both, were deeply rooted in ideas of gender, particularly the redemption of black manhood. This scholarship has done well exploring the significance of gender and discourses of black masculinity to Black Nationalism and Black Power, for example. But through a close gendered analysis of certain black newspapers and their publishers beginning with the inception of the modern black press, this study illuminates how the Black Nationalists and Black Power radicals of the 1960s were not the progenitors of robust masculine rhetoric but the inheritors of it through an influential masculinized discourse constructed in the black press over the course of decades. This discourse on black manhood carried tremendous implications for black people's long fight for racial progress and justice. Scholars of black women's history have rightly asked why black leadership and issues of racial progress have been historically and socially gendered as male.[32] This book shows the instrumental role of black male publishers and their papers in shaping why and how this came to be. Indeed, black newspapers helped make the quest to redeem black manhood fundamental to black Americans' quest for racial justice during the twentieth century. Through black newspapers, both quests came to shape one another. If a real or perceived crisis erupted in one, it usually impinged on the other, deeply connecting the two in an ebb and flow in which the quest for one entailed a quest for the other.

Cut off from certain spaces in broader society, black male publishers dramatically transformed the white spaces of blank pages in order to influence the boundless space of the black public sphere with visions for racial advancement that promoted proper black manhood. Indeed, "the newspaper, printers ink and white paper," as the *Kansas City Call* put it, "are the best lever to win a fair deal from the world."[33] As if artists before an open canvas, publishers and their staffs stood before white paper with their black bodies and seized the chance to control some form of white space, something otherwise inconceivable in public life. Inserting themselves into the space and asserting themselves through it, they applied black ink and worked to rewrite the race.[34] Black male publishers saw themselves as leaders, intellectuals, and activists, working in these capacities through newspapers as a medium.[35] Indeed, in the heyday of the black press, many black newspapermen and newpaperwomen were convinced that leadership, literature, and literacy went hand in hand. Scientific racism and civiliza-tionist discourses had linked race and reading, insisting upon a relationship between racial progress and literacy. The more literate people were, the more civilized, cultured, and modern they and their racial group were thought to be. The figuring of race with reading was a problematic equation, to be sure, for reducing racial progress to reading obscured the legal and struc-tural processes necessary to create real progress for black Americans. But for those who believed blacks needed to first satisfy certain basic but arbi-trary requirements, such as literacy, before acquiring full citizenship, the presence of the black press helped black people battle real and alleged il-literacy.[36] It also helped them battle perceptions that they were mentally inferior, incapable of learning and independent thought, unless with the help of white people.[37] Black newspapers helped turn these notions on their head by producing a vibrant black print culture and public sphere in which racial, class, and gender identities, and ideas of racial progress, pro-test, community, and citizenship, were constructed and contested.[38] Where there were limited opportunities for aspiring black journalists and writing talent, black writers often sought publication in the black press.[39]

And it was no coincidence that virtually every major black male leader during the twentieth century published a paper, wrote for one regularly, or contributed to one periodically in order to disseminate their ideas and pro-mote their leadership. Some black male leaders, who did not write for them, such as Booker T. Washington and Martin Luther King Jr., still found ways to make use of the black press. In fact, part of the reason government of-ficials surveilled the black press was to follow the activities of some of these black male leaders. But we can imagine that the leadership potential of newspapers motivated black male publishers to brood over blank pages, methodically considering how to manipulate the space in order to ar-ticulate their vision in the best ways. Their editors and writers usually determined how to position type and images, arrange layouts, craft headlines, and then place it all strategically on the page to elevate certain stories and attract readers and sales.[40] Yet when this page reached finished form, it reflected the gendered ideologies of the people involved, which were rooted in their personal quests to redeem black manhood for themselves and other black men.

There were black women publishers and many women reporters and writers, as well as black women activists who contributed to and contested these developments throughout the twentieth century, to be sure.[41] But by and large, black men dominated the twentieth-century black press, whether as publishers, editors, or writers. The majority of black newspapers were owned by black men, and even their writers and personnel constituted a largely male workforce. This book in part explains why. During the twentieth century, black newspapers provided black men the means to assert a public voice and public masculine identity, and as a mass-circulated article of popular consumption, the papers made these assertions visible to a vast audience. Some of the men behind the black press earned little pay, if at all, especially at the inception of the modern black press. But as Enoch P. Waters, a writer for several black papers, reasoned, "it might have been that the times produced qualified men so angry about how they were treated as Negroes that they were more eager for a means of expressing their rage than in personal prosperity." Robert S. Abbott of the *Defender* stood out here, becoming one of the few publishers to make his press a tremendous commercial success, however.[42] There were women staff members, Waters remembered, or as he put it, "young girls," his language here disclosing some of the patriarchal gendered politics of the newsroom, who were "always looking for better paying jobs," he said.[43] Charlotta Bass and Mildred Brown, for example, represented the few black women who owned and edited a major black newspaper in the twentieth century. Bass owned the *California Eagle* and Brown, the *Omaha Star*.[44] Yet few black women journalists ascended to these kinds of positions, largely because many of their roles in the black press were circumscribed by gender. In many cases, black women journalists were paid less than their male counterparts and often assigned to a "Woman's Page," or what was considered women's news as papers explicitly divided their coverage along gendered lines in these ways. This remained the case well into the 1960s and 1970s, though these pages were important and wildly popular among readers as they showcased black society life and black women's efforts in racial uplift. Black men journalists, unlike many of their female colleagues, usually covered a wider range of news and had more opportunities to comment on the major political issues of the day. Here, black male writers were typically projected as more serious, cerebral, and political, overshadowing black women in many ways in this media-inflected black intellectual tradition.[45]

This study shows how discourses on black manhood took precedence in black newspapers, and as a consequence, the public sphere in part. Black newspapers' constructions of black manhood were not divorced from conceptions and articulations of a proper black womanhood, to be sure, but their coverage of black women's issues often served to support constructions of proper black manhood.[46] As a result, black women's issues were usually subsumed or rendered secondary, but thought to be elevated by default as black newspapers' quest to redeem black manhood was thought to benefit the entire race.[47] This further confirms many of the points that black feminist scholars have shown regarding the tremendous toll the privileging of black men's plight over that of black women has levied not only on black women but also on black people's fights for racial justice. Here, black male publishers' roles in shaping racial advancement, not unlike parts of the broader black freedom struggle, turned on notions of black liberation that were at once democratic and patriarchal, radical and conservative, liberating and limiting. That redeeming black manhood remained an ongoing process throughout the twentieth century, one always essentially incomplete because different real and perceived crises appeared to undermine black manhood, therefore requiring another quest for its restoration, helps explain why, at different times throughout the long black freedom struggle, some black women continued to confront varying strains of patriarchy, sexism, misogyny, machismo, hypermasculinity, secondary leadership roles, and/ or highly masculinized rhetoric and politics.

Black male publishers helped link the redemption of black manhood and a manly vision for racial advancement to the fight for racial justice, helping the black press cultivate a reputation for aggressive protest that attracted a great deal of scholarly interest for decades.[48] When this interest emerged in full beginning in the 1920s, just as the modern black press was crystallizing, some observers were fascinated, while others were alarmed. In one of the first studies to appear, Robert T. Kerlin's 1920 examination announced that the modern black press was the "voice of the Negro, and his heart and mind. Here the Negro race speaks as it thinks on the question of questions for America—the race question." Kerlin argued that the black press was "freer than the pulpit," actually foremost above it in his estimation because there was "a peculiar authority in printer's ink." "Those who would honestly seek to know the Negro must read his papers," he wrote.[49] Frederick G.

Detweiler was impressed to find that of the 705 news items and 174 editorials he examined in sixty-four black papers, nearly 21 percent of the items and 40 percent of the editorials were dedicated to addressing racial injustice. Issues of race progress constituted about 18 percent of the items and 7 percent of the editorials. And this content thrilled most readers, he discovered. Detweiler pointed out that some version of "Please allow me space in your paper" was a common refrain from readers, who wrote in to papers seeking a public forum to express themselves. It indicated "not only a ritual of dignity attaching to the highly honored newspaper, but also an urgent desire to get an audience for group achievements."[50] But other observers could not believe what they were reading. "Few white people realize that there are more than four hundred and fifty newspapers and other publications in America devoted exclusively to the interests of colored people, nearly all edited by Negroes," one observer noted. "The utter ignorance of the great mass of white Americans as to what is really going on among the colored people of the country is appalling—and dangerous."[51] The comment pointed to the degree to which blacks and whites were segregated even in public discourse. Scholar Jerome Dowd thought that black newspapers protested too much, bordering on an obsession with racial injustice. "The Negro, to be sure, has real grievances and plenty of them," he conceded, "but harping upon them has become such a habit of the Negro press that very often the Negro editor writes in vague generalities about injustices and outrages of which he has no real knowledge, and which in fact do not exist. . . . A man who shouts at the top of his voice will find that it will only squeak when the occasion comes for it to thunder."[52] Dowd's critique noticeably accused black male publishers of being whiny men.

Observers like Dowd charged the black press with having an explicit bias, though critics tended to overlook white newspapers that also had one against black people.[53] But many black male publishers took the stance that they had to be essentially partisan, given the mountain of injustices arrayed against black people and, as they thought, black men. C. F. Richardson of the *Houston Informer*, for example, recalled that he "saw that the pulpit and the teacher could not do all the work of bettering, advancing, enlightening and solidifying our racial group; I also saw the potent factor of the white press . . . in the development, progress and expansion of their race." He "finally dedicated and consecrated myself to the task" of publishing, even as "many of my class and school mates have apparently made better headway, financially." His gratification instead came from the "poor and downtrodden members of my race," who approached him "to shake my hands and compliment me on my position."[54] Black publishers and writers, who were formally educated in journalistic methods, usually received their training at black colleges.[55] These schools were already crucibles of racial uplift and were oftentimes the only schools offering training in printing and journalism to black people.[56] Some–nonformally educated black newspapermen and newspaperwomen received on-the-job-training from publishers themselves, a training that likely involved the publisher inculcating them with their ideals.[57] Others simply trained themselves in the art of publishing, prompted to do so by critical issues in the twentieth-century black freedom struggle, using at the time whatever resources they had available to turn out even small sheets. Indeed, black male publishers were not entirely objective. And the decidedly black commercial market to which they appealed virtually demanded that they not be.

But in addition to using newspapers to protest racial injustice, black male publishers used their papers to make men. To emphasize both points, many black papers used sensationalism as a literary device and strategy to signal the masculine implications of a critical racial moment through bold, provocative rhetoric and imagery. Many critics of the black press, and even some supporters, decried its sensationalism, what they argued was its tendency to appeal to the most rank and base tastes of consumers with lurid stories of crime, sex, and violence.[58] Indeed, some papers did this, as Enoch P. Waters admitted. "To hype newsstand sales that were relied upon to bring in revenue," Waters recalled, "the paper also needed unusual crime stories and those dealing with sexual misconduct. We, therefore, courted criminal and divorce lawyers."[59] Some papers like the *Defender* gained incredible influence and commercial power, as well as attracted much criticism, in part from publishing crime stories to encourage sales.[60] Some critics insisted that this kind of racy content did nothing to aid black people's public image or the cause of racial advancement, though these sensationalized reports ran alongside sensationalized stories of black achievement. As one writer for the *Courier* put it, "the dimes which have been paid for its papers by those interested in the more sordid reading have financed the reading which is inspiring and the material which effectively serves the cause of group progress."[61] This study argues, as historian Kim Gallon notes, that sensationalism in black newspapers had a practical goal intended to sell papers as well as arouse the ire and action of readers by dramatizing important issues with thrilling rhetoric and imagery, sometimes in ways that related to discourses revolving around sex and crime.[62] As black male publishers sought to waste no amount of space in their paper, especially that which could be used for advertisers, the life-blood of any paper that was a constant struggle for many black publications, a reader could find in stark relief politically charged discussions about redeeming black manhood followed at some point by an ad for "Revivo" or "Vigor Treatment," for example. These were sexual enhancements for men that promised to return "Lost Manhood!"[63] *Let Us Make Men* considers these complex layers of black papers' sensationalism. The book emphasizes particularly the striking language and imagery black papers deployed to forge the fight for racial justice and black manhood, while at times accounting for the criticism some publishers faced from observers and even from other black male publishers, who only saw content that seemed to them to undermine the vision for racial advancement.

But black newspapers deployed sensationalism to attract consumers to their take on important issues, distinguishing their paper from others because they knew patrons were quite the discriminating readers. Some observers of the black press wrongly assumed and feared that readers imbibed virtually everything papers printed, reinscribing prevailing racist ideologies that cast black people as simpletons and empty vessels.[64] But the most influential and commercially successful black publishers did not make the costly mistake of underestimating the agency of black readers. One publisher did unfortunately. "When we failed to print the news we lost popularity," he admitted.[65] One early study of the black press pointed out that readers could well discern the "charlatans and fakes, the self-seekers and false leaders, the political opportunists and race traitors," and their papers would "rarely survive for more than a year or two."[66] Even Abbott of the *Defender*, whom many scholars and observers regarded as the standard-bearer for the modern black press, faced critical readers. Samuel Piggsford, for example, wrote Abbott personally to tell him that his articles "lack punch." "You should study English grammar, master it. . . . What good are you to a people as a leader in a chosen field if you are not qualified and efficient. Just bla, bla, bla in [your] paper because it is yours simply wont go. I cant take your place and do better. I am not supposed to. I will critique though because I want the best and I want to keep learning." Piggsford recognized his role as the critical reader and recognized too the role of the influential publisher whose paper he patronized, cognizant of the discursive relationship they shared. The didactic value of Abbott's paper was key for Piggsford, owing to his scathing criticism. "You know as well as I that ninety-nine per cent of our race haven't the money to go to high school or college. We all have a dime or a nickel for your paper."[67]

As Piggsford, and Cato Anderson, illustrated, readers were nothing like the blank pages publishers transformed. Readers brought their own life experiences and corresponding set of values, including gendered ideologies, to black newspapers. Yet, at the same time, reading black newspapers helped reinforce, refine, and/or expand their ideas, values, and subjectivities in what reader-response theorists have called a "transaction" of ideas with the text. Here, both the text and the reader worked together in shaping the reading experience.[68] Readers made deliberate choices about what papers to purchase; they decided to embrace and/or contest the choices made by the people producing the papers, and still recognized the incredible influence black newspapers could have on their own lives and the public. Published editorials like Anderson's have provided scholars one of the few windows into what readers actually thought about pressing issues and the papers that reported them. This study accounts for the voices of readers where sources permit.

Black male publishers strove to meet readers' expectations by constructing particular visions for racial advancement, visions intended to promote racial justice and proper black manhood as they saw it. What this study calls the *vision for racial advancement* speaks to two things primarily. First, it refers to what media scholars have identified as the "agenda-setting capacity" of the press, its ability to influence, if not determine, what issues get elevated over others, framed as a priority before the public, and then linked with ideas of and actual efforts toward societal progress. Included in this is the press's ability to both mobilize during a crisis and sometimes mobilize the crisis itself.[69] It was not uncommon for black publishers, knowing that they needed to encourage readers to align their values with that of their paper's, to print a creed or platform for their paper, which might be published regularly or occasionally somewhere on the front page. This creed or platform espoused the ideological viewpoints of the paper and/or the leading issues that it insisted needed to be addressed for the good of the race. Their platforms instantiated an agenda that grew out of the news items they presented as the most salient, featured prominently under banner headlines, returned to week after week to analyze and discuss, sensationalized to attract attention and action, mobilized editorial campaigns around, and sometimes joined with other papers in something of a national front to make demands on society and the state. Papers constructed and proposed different agendas at different times depending on different issues. They could revise and update them. Agendas might coincide or contend with some organization's or leader's particular agenda. And because black newspapers were bulwarks of protest *and* businesses, their agendas could help distinguish their paper from competitors, especially if another paper was at odds with certain racial ideals, attracting sales and therefore public support that might supplant the competition. Indeed, intense competition among black publishers over readers moved some of them to produce some of their most sensationalized language, stories, images, and editorial campaigns. When parts of their agenda were accomplished through the efforts of some leader, group of activists, politician, or the paper itself, the publication could then declare how much it had led the way in advancing the race. This book highlights publishers' expressed agendas in order to consider the efforts papers took to distill complex political, social, racial, class, ideological, and gendered issues into pithy, provocative phrases or bullet-pointed formats encapsulating and delineating what publishers thought should be the priorities of the racial struggle.[70]

Second, the *vision for racial advancement* invokes the imagined future many black leaders and activists conceptualized and worked to operationalize at different times in the black freedom struggle in order to secure a desired and/or ideal destiny for black Americans on a number of fronts. This proceeded under the guise of many names throughout the twentieth century, as several historians have shown.[71] Building on their work, this study employs the *vision for racial advancement* in particular to foreground the role of black male publishers in mobilizing their papers to promote what they imagined the contours of real racial progress to be, and the importance of agenda-setting in projects of racial uplift that needed specific rally points to mobilize the race. For black male publishers, real racial progress in part hinged on the redemption of black manhood. Altogether, the right agenda mobilized behind the right vision could promote ideas of black manhood against others, edge out competing papers, and secure the right future for black people, so black male publishers thought. Shaped by their own gendered subjectivities, political ideologies, and historical moment, they promoted manly visions for racial advancement that were both empowering and problematic for the twentieth-century black freedom struggle.

Robert T. Kerlin's 1920 study announced that the black press represented the "voice" of black people.[72] The assertion was telling, but a metaphor, of course. One person could not speak for an entire group of people, and neither could a newspaper, an inanimate object, for that matter—or could they? Robert S. Abbott, W. E. B. DuBois, Marcus Garvey, John Sengstacke, Robert F. Williams, and Malcolm X believed they and their papers actually could. Chapter 1 examines how Abbott's *Defender* and DuBois's *Crisis* helped establish newspaper publishing as a pathway to black manhood and racial leadership, and how Abbott in particular inaugurated the modern black press by issuing a call to manhood that helped invigorate the Great Migration. Chapter 2 examines the proliferation of black newspapers during the New Negro era that helped lead to a war of words fought by Garvey and his *Negro World* with rival black male leaders over whose vision of New Negro masculinity was going to win control of the black public sphere. Chapter 3 examines the ways in which the production of black newspapers involved the "production" of proper Race Men as Abbott worked to groom his nephew John Sengstacke to take over the *Defender* during the Depression era. Their exchange helped raise major implications for the broader black press. Chapter 4 examines how Robert F. Williams heralded a new kind of black male publisher with a new kind of black publication, the *Crusader*. His paper ended up helping call into question the meaning of black militancy and black manhood within the black press and the civil rights movement. Chapter 5 reinterprets the rise of black radicalism through the rise of several contending black voices that were transmitted through a variety of mass media, signaling rapid changes in both the black freedom struggle and media landscape of the 1960s. Malcolm X founded *Muhammad Speaks* to capitalize on these developments, though his efforts in this regard both challenged and reaffirmed the role of the black press as the "voice" of the race. The book closes with John Sengstacke looking out on the future of a weathered black press and new generation of black male publishers.

Ultimately, the "voice" these black men asserted through the black press was largely masculine and spoke in masculine tones, using masculinized and gendered language to articulate a manly vision for racial advancement. Black male publishers and their readers shared attacks on black people's humanity, citizenship, bodies, and gendered selves, while they also shared certain aspirations for the race. Like Anderson, the civic-minded fraternity man, black male publishers had turned to black newspapers to assert and express their most pressing concerns and critiques at a time when there were few public forums in which black men could do so freely. These shared experiences and ideas might have been what Anderson meant when he insisted that black newspapers served as "the mirror of public opinion," that "what a man sees in life he sees in the newspaper."[73] The pages that follow contain a compelling and complicated history of black manhood, the black press, and the black freedom struggle, mostly from the side of the mirror that black male publishers saw, sides that readers like Anderson also saw, but sometimes did not see, as they read these publishers' efforts to make black men "men."

1 Go to It, My Southern Brothers

The Rise of the Modern Black Press, the Great Migration, and the Construction of Urban Black Manhood

. . . .

William Edward Burghardt (W. E. B.) DuBois marked his twenty-fifth birthday with a journal entry. "I am striving to make my life all that life may be," he wrote, setting several goals for himself that would shape the rest of his life. It was February 23, 1893. At the time, he was in a highly privileged position, pursuing a PhD at Harvard University and studying abroad in Europe. Still, his birthday came down to penetrating questions about his future, particularly the role he would play as a black man, hoping to use his education and talents to advance his race. "God knows I am sorely puzzled. I am firmly convinced that my own best development is not one and the same with the best development of the world and here I am willing to sacrifice. . . . I therefore . . . work for the rise of the Negro people." "These are my plans," he determined, "to make a name in science, to make a name in literature and thus to raise my race."[1] Around the same time, Robert S. Abbott, a student studying printing at Hampton Institute, wrestled with a similar masculine crisis.[2] He considered himself "blessed with a spirit that knew no defeat and a body that knew no fatigue," but " it was not uncommon for me to spend sleepless nights wondering how I would fit in the outside world where prejudice and discrimination dogged every step a black man took." While he faced some financial struggles, probably concerning payments for his room and board, questions about his future prospects as a man and aspiring professional plagued him, though he remained "much more concerned with the plight of my people." He tried "to develop in my immature intellect some concept which would solve some of the major difficulties of my race."[3] Abbott's introspection led him, like DuBois, to a self-discovery that convinced him to put his life and training in the service of the race. The two men did not yet know each other, but along with many other black men of their era, they shared in common a deep concern for the future of the race that they linked to a concern for their own manhood. For many black men of their generation, the prospects of racial advancement and a proper masculinity were bound together amid an apparent crisis in black manhood.[4] Many of them imagined that through their individual success, even in achieving their own manhood, they could help the race confront the onslaught of racial injustice that had begun to crystallize by the turn of the century.[5] Over time, DuBois and Abbott found ways to resolve their personal crises and render the service they imagined providing the race. Abbott founded the *Chicago Defender* in 1905. DuBois founded the *Crisis: A Record of the Darker Races* in 1910. Indeed, one of the ways they overcame their struggles to be men committed to serving the race was by founding their own newspapers.

This chapter examines how DuBois's and Abbott's founding and publication of their own newspapers helped fulfill their quests to achieve a proper role as black men who served the race in an effective and far-reaching fashion while also giving many black men grappling with the crisis in black manhood a manly movement by which to achieve theirs too. By 1917, their goals materialized at the height of the Great Migration. It was then that virtually every weekly edition of black newspapers was afire with the leading story of the time: the extraordinary exodus of black people from the rural South.[6] With the migration fully underway, pages of the black press were full of anxious discussions about the record numbers of blacks leaving. Reactions varied by region, however. One of the leading black papers of the South, the *Norfolk Journal and Guide*, cautioned blacks against it. "South Views with Alarm Negro Exodus," "Dangerous Phases of the Migration Movement," and other foreboding headlines underscored the position of publisher P. B. Young. He believed that black people should remain planted where they were, for there were "Great Opportunities for Negro Labor in the South."[7] The *North Carolina Star of Zion* remarked, "While I concede the Negro man's right to go where he likes . . . I doubt the wisdom of such wholesale exodus from the South."[8] Some other black southern newspapers also discouraged the migration but insisted that white southerners mend their ways soon and stop oppressing the race, or face losing black labor to the North. "This is our home and we do not want to leave . . . unless we are driven by want and a lack of freedom. . . . We appeal to the white man . . . not to drive us away but to open the doors of the shops, of the industries and the fields to our genius and push," the *Atlanta Independent* pleaded.[9]

The response of the northern black press was far different. Situated in the North where it was somewhat safer to assail Jim Crow and rally for political and social change, black papers such as the *Christian Recorder, New York News,* and *New York Age* fully endorsed the exodus.[10] Others, such as the *Crisis* and the *Defender,* took that endorsement a step further. For

DuBois's *Crisis*, the migration was "the greatest thing that has happened for the Negro since emancipation."[11] Abbott's *Defender* urged a rapid departure: "Go to it, my Southern Brothers, the North needs you."[12] Abbott's particular approach to covering the migration helped fuel the movement and ultimately turned the black press into a leading force in the urban struggle for racial advancement. Abbott, himself a former migrant, assumed an editorial stance and a rhetorical strategy that made the paper the most successful one at galvanizing black southerners. Though initially slow to endorse the migration, Abbott was shaped by his own racial and gendered ideologies, which motivated him to demonstrate manly racial leadership. He was eventually able to outstrip other black papers because he chose to promote the migration as a pathway to individual and racial uplift, as well as individual and racial manhood.

Abbott's approach appealed directly to the gendered ideologies and subjectivities of readers amid a palpable crisis in black manhood. Jim Crow legislation reversed the political gains blacks achieved during Reconstruction, destroyed multiracial democracy in the South, expelled black male officeholders, and ushered in segregation. Happening too was the consolidation of scientific racism, the spread of exploitative labor arrangements in the countryside, the rise of lynching, and the growth of extralegal and violent intimidation of black male voters.[13] These developments effectively crushed nascent black political power and participation, and the postemancipation hopes of black Americans, concretizing what historian Rayford Logan called the "nadir of race relations."[14] As Jim Crow laws stripped many black men of their right to vote and control their own labor, rights considered sacred for men in a patriarchal society, this nadir touched off another nadir, one of gender relations in which whites considered black people less than human and less than real men and real women.[15] Many black men spoke out against these injustices, as did black women, particularly those who were part of the sweeping black women's club movement.[16] Many black men registered feelings of emasculation, even in regard to black women's activism and racial leadership, their speaking out on behalf of the race, and growing influence in the black public sphere.[17]

Attempting to resist the solidification of Jim Crow regimes, racial violence, pseudoscientific discourses, and these dual nadirs, many black people organized through a number of civic groups and social institutions, one of which was the black press.[18] The press became an organizing tool that many black leaders of the early twentieth century used to protest attacks on the rights and bodies of black Americans. As this tool, the press became the most vocal, visible, consistent, and influential proponent of black equality and racial advancement. With formal access to the political process impeded for many blacks, if not cut off completely, the press as a medium of black political expression became especially important. For black rights activists like Ida B. Wells, William Monroe Trotter, T. Thomas Fortune, and DuBois, newspaper publishing became indispensable to their political organizing. In fact, it became their most reliable means of raising a public voice of resistance against racial injustice.[19] As activism against racial oppression crystallized in the urban North, the modern black press did also. Growing institutionalized assaults on black humanity and autonomy in the South convinced many black southerners that migration out of the South was the best available solution. And this was a point that the northern press came to encourage.[20] With the critical voice and public platform that newspapers could provide newspapermen at this time, many black men in search of proper manhood, manly leadership, and a way to make a valuable contribution to the race emerged as publishers.

In many ways, DuBois and Abbott led the way in this regard. Yet when the migration transformed into a massive exodus in 1915, Abbott and his *Defender* made their endorsement of the migration the first successful black newspaper campaign of the twentieth century. To be sure, both the *Crisis* and the *Defender* articulated the significance of the migration in terms of a broader vision for racial advancement, promoting it as a much-needed response to racial oppression. In fact, their promotion helped foreground the debate over and fight for immediate black political rights. Their endorsement also helped frame the discussion of the migration by social analysts and migrants alike as self-help and racial uplift in action: the first major step by black people toward individual and collective progress. But reflecting popular beliefs among black people that the loss of political rights was emasculating, both men construed state-sanctioned racial oppression in the South as a double-edged sword that cut off blacks' political rights and black men's rights as men. The *Defender* especially amplified this point, promoting migration as the first step any black man could take to begin restoring his manhood. Accordingly, a migrant's journey was part of a larger manly movement, the last step of which was promised to end in the urban North with a newfound masculinity rooted in an urbanized black manhood. This framing of the migration as a movement toward manhood likely appealed to the majority male demographic of the World War I–era migration.[21] The paper deployed gendered terms that gained wide traction, terms that the black press would continue to use for the analysis of pressing racial issues, black men's public vocalization, and mobilizing the race to action.

Abbott, the aspiring businessman, departed from his nineteenth-century predecessors and many contemporaries by inaugurating a new style of race journalism that used sensationalism to dramatize news stories and mobilize readers to activism. Along with DuBois and others, Abbott helped continue a spirit of journalistic militancy established by nineteenth-century black publishers.[22] Yet Abbott heralded a new era for the black press that would advance this kind of militancy in distinctly new ways through sensationalism. Unlike the nineteenth-century press, the modern black press used sensationalism to help build a deep dialogical relationship with readers as the press responded to and shaped the social and political transformations African Americans would undergo during the twentieth century. The *Defender*'s use of sensationalism modeled for other black papers how to utilize language, images, ideas, and discourse in ways that engaged readers on personal, emotional, intellectual, and psychological levels so that they became faithful customers, as well as actors in building a racial movement.

Shaped by growing anxieties over political and social challenges to black men and the race, the *Defender* became the most sanguine paper in promoting the migration. Abbott dramatically deployed masculinist language and imagery to disparage the South, extol the North, and encourage black southerners to migrate. Invoking ideas of the North as the land of freedom, an idea that had been popular among black people since slavery, the *Defender* discursively split the United States into two opposed regions: the North, where absolute freedom for blacks reigned, and the South, where freedom did not exist for blacks at all. The *Defender*'s bifurcation of the United States into free and unfree regions proceeded along gendered lines of manly and emasculating spaces. In what would become its characteristic sensational tone, the *Defender* painted the North as a land of boundless opportunity where blacks enjoyed immense freedoms and black men could freely assert and experience their manhood. Through this rhetorical strategy, Abbott and the *Defender* helped gender the first major social movement of black Americans in the twentieth century as a movement for individual and racial manhood, in addition to political and economic freedom. The *Defender*'s strategy of deploying sensational editorials laced with gendered language sought to incite black people to action, as well as elevate the redemption of manhood as key to this movement and the greater push for racial advancement.[23] The *Defender*'s promotion of the migration issued a call to manhood. For black men who answered, the paper promised a new racial and masculine identity that abandoned southern models rooted in land ownership for an urbanity that represented the new marker and maker of proper black manhood. This construction would help set into motion developments that elevated manly black leadership before the black public sphere.

Publically supporting black migration was a defining political statement, especially as black leaders increasingly debated the proper course for achieving racial advancement, political rights, and individual autonomy.[24] In the late nineteenth century and early part of the twentieth century, many intellectuals and leaders, black and white, saw the city as a morally destructive space with harsh demands that black people were unprepared to confront.[25] Mary White Ovington, a white Socialist reformer, published *Half a Man* in 1911, a study of black urban life in New York. She argued that "race prejudice often proves a bar to complete success, to full manhood" for the working black man. His female counterpart "meets with severer race prejudice than the colored man" and "needs her full status as a woman."[26] Motivated by Progressive reform ideas in the later nineteenth and early twentieth centuries, some blacks and liberal whites worked to ameliorate the real and imagined deleterious effects of urbanization on blacks. DuBois was among them, pioneering the study of urban black people in his 1899 tome *The Philadelphia Negro.*[27] In addition to being a scholar, DuBois was a civil rights activist and an ambitious journalist. As an activist, DuBois was among the founding members of the Niagara movement in 1905, an organized effort to protest segregation and black people's loss of political rights. Though short lived, collapsing in four years partly due to personality struggles, as well as the resistance of Booker T. Washington, who worked to undermine the fledgling movement, it nonetheless helped herald a new tide of black civil rights activism. This tide would achieve its most persistent expression in the founding of the National Association for the Advancement of Colored People (NAACP) in 1909.[28] Prompted by the 1908 race riot in Springfield, Illinois, DuBois, white reformers such as Ovington, and other civil rights activists, including Ida B. Wells, started the organization to regain the rights black Americans achieved after the Civil War. The NAACP helped lead this period of greater civil rights leadership, a role that black newspapers like the *Crisis* would assume too and deepen during the twentieth century.

Indeed, for DuBois, journalism was another form of his civil rights activism. As historian Herbert Aptheker has written, "An important feature of [his] lifelong struggle against racism and for democracy was his editorship or magazines. . . . [They] were frankly instruments aimed at advancing these purposes."[29] Yet publishing was crucial to DuBois's masculinity, as well as his activism. DuBois felt he was not a "natural leader of men." But what he felt he lacked in innate leadership skills nonetheless came through in his manipulation of words on the printed page. "It had always been my ambition to write," Dubois recalled, "to seek through the written word the expression of my relation to the world and of the world to me."[30] In fact, publishing his ideas in newspaper form was what started him upon his literary career, having published his first "printed words" around 1882 or 1883 as a correspondent for the New York *Age*.[31] And through writing, DuBois cultivated his leadership skills. It was when he was active in the Niagara movement that he first realized that his "career as a scientist was to be swallowed up" in his "role as master of propaganda." He "refused to give up the idea that a critical periodical for the American Negro might be founded."[32] In 1905 in Memphis, Tennessee, he began the *Moon*. The weekly lasted two years. The *Moon* was followed by the *Horizon: A Journal of the Color Line* in 1907, the propaganda organ of the Niagara movement. In the first two years of its publication, *Horizon* was a pocket-sized magazine, five and a half inches by four and a half inches and twenty-eight pages in length, seemingly portable for the mobile reader. In 1909, the monthly grew to eight inches by eleven inches with twelve double-columned pages. Despite growth in its size, the *Horizon* struggled financially. DuBois and a small team of editors received no salary, and they had to finance the magazine using their own meager earnings in other lines of work. Publication stopped after July 1910. With the NAACP founded in January 1910, DuBois was appointed director of publicity and research. He started the *Crisis*, a monthly political journal, in November, and the aspiring scientist, writer, and leader of the race inched closer to his goals. Former subscribers to the *Horizon* now received the propaganda organ of the NAACP.[33]

The names of his first two magazines suggested optimism under a guiding light, glowing in a realm of possibilities toward racial advancement. The name, *Crisis*, was suggested to DuBois by his associate William English Walling, a Socialist and eventual newspaper publisher too.[34] DuBois indeed felt that "the Negro race in America is today in a critical condition. Only united concerned effort will save us from being crushed," he wrote. "To this end there is needed a high class journal to circulate among the intelligent Negroes, tell them of the deeds of themselves and their neighbors, interpret the news of the world to them and inspire them toward infinite ideals."[35] The word "crisis" invoked something grave, something that spoke to the urgency of the historical moment at the time of the magazine's founding.[36]

As DuBois put it, the news magazine was so named because its "editors believe that this is a critical time in the history of the advancement of men."[37] The name also reflected many black men's anxieties over contemporary political and social challenges to their manhood.

Within the context of some black people's growing advocacy for immediate black political rights and improved race relations, and his ongoing forays as a writer and journalist, DuBois launched the *Crisis*. "With *The Crisis*, I essayed a new role of interpreting to the world the hindrances and aspirations of American Negroes," he affirmed.[38] It became, as he put it, a "phenomenal business success," especially given his first two tries. And the publication was under his direct control as editor, the one thing that he not only prized but also absolutely required in any of his journalistic ventures, no matter the cost.[39] Within a year of its founding, "the need for a magazine devoted to the manhood rights of the Negroes was shown by the instant demand for this publication," the Association recognized in its second annual report.[40] Within five years, the magazine was self-supporting, a fact that was a "source of great pride" to DuBois.[41] "With this organ of propaganda," among the NAACP's many efforts, the organization "was able to organize one of the most effective assaults of liberalism upon prejudice and reaction that the modern world has seen," DuBois insisted. In addition to the organization itself, the *Crisis* provided a means to "place consistently and continuously before the country a clear-cut statement of the legitimate aims of the American Negro and the facts concerning his condition."[42] Interested in documenting the "important happenings and movements in the world which bear on the great problem of interracial relations, and especially those which affect the Negro American," the *Crisis* functioned as an extension of both the NAACP's political agenda and DuBois's academic and activist mind.[43] DuBois regarded it as his "soul-child," an "expression of myself."[44] And as a child might mirror its parents, the *Crisis* reflected, as historian David Levering Lewis has put it, the "expression, in monthly installments, of its editor's intellectual and moral personality."[45] Here, DuBois also intended to demonstrate the intelligence, refinement, and respectability of black men, consciously countering widely circulating negative images and ideas of black men in popular culture and scientific discourse as uncivilized and animal-like.[46] In one of his seminal essays, he wrote that the race would be "saved by its exceptional men." This manly vision likely included himself.[47]

Films such as *Dancing Nig* (1907), *How Rastus Got His Pork Chops* (1908), *Coon Town Suffragettes* (1914), and *Old Mammy's Charge* (1914), as well as literary characters present in works like *Uncle Tom's Cabin* (1852), popularized stereotypical representations of blacks as hapless, slave-like creatures incapable of morality and thinking independently. Some of these movies were made by D. W. Griffith, the innovative filmmaker who would produce in 1915 the controversial, yet widely popular, film *The Birth of a Nation*. The NAACP and the *Crisis* vehemently protested the film and tried to stop its showing.[48] But through his carefully constructed black masculine public persona as the quintessential, restrained "man of letters," whose manhood was cut from the tempered and erudite sensibilities and masculinity of the Victorian era, DuBois transferred his frustrations with racial oppression and desires of representing manly racial leadership into the pages of the NAACP's media organ.[49] He hoped that the monthly political journal would become popular and influential enough to help counter these pervasive destructive images of black people, among other things. Uniting his scholarship, activism, journalism, and desire to ensure proper manhood, the inaugural editorial of the *Crisis* said that the organ was dedicated to presenting "facts and arguments" that would "stand for the rights of men, irrespective of color or race."[50]

Scholars usually do not credit the *Crisis* for its part in covering the migration because the role of the *Defender* later overshadowed its contributions.[51] But the *Crisis* was important to situating the migration on scholarly terms. Striving to "put into concrete form such knowledge as we have of this movement," as DuBois said, it provided analyses complete with detailed data, statistical figures, information about the origins of migrants and their destinations, and in-depth reports on the proportions of the migration.[52] The growth of the *Crisis*'s circulation became tied to the migration, reaching upward of 100,000 paid subscribers by 1919. In fact, the magazine's circulation numbers exceeded the organization's membership, testifying to its growing influence.[53] With DuBois as editor, the *Crisis* channeled the emergence of social science as a growing credible field of scholarly investigation to explain the causes of the movement and justify it before the public. In particular, *Crisis* readers included many educated and middle-class blacks and white liberals, some of whom had missionary and philanthropic interests along with some connections to charitable institutions and progressive policy makers. Reaching this audience especially shaped the appeals of the *Crisis*. At DuBois's urging, they may have found their next cause in helping the migrants.[54]

The *Defender*'s growth would also become tied to the migration, though supporting it was a move that Abbott was initially hesitant to make, despite having been a migrant. Abbott was born on St. Simons Island off the coast of Georgia, the son of former slaves. Abbott's father, Thomas Abbott, died shortly after his birth, and his mother later married John Hermann Henry Sengstacke, the son of a slave woman and a German immigrant. Sengstacke was a congregational minister and publisher of the *Woodville Times*, a small newspaper that he founded in 1889.[55] Abbott's stepfather had a strong influence on him, especially in terms of exposing him to publishing. In 1897, Abbott moved to Chicago, not long after completing Hampton. His move was part of the migration of the "Talented Tenth," the professional out-migration of black southerners in the late nineteenth century and first decade of the twentieth century, which preceded the larger out-migration by a decade.[56] In Chicago, he hoped to become an attorney or a businessman of some sort. In 1899, he earned a law degree from Chicago's Kent College of Law, but racial discrimination in Chicago stymied his efforts at a successful practice. Having encountered difficulties in what he thought was going to be one route to professional success, Abbott fell back on his studies in printing at Hampton. But he faced difficulties here too. He began work in a printers' union and again encountered racial discrimination. "Many months some time would pass without my being called," he remembered. "I would go hungry. . . . I did not earn money enough to pay back rent, repay the loans and eat three meals, too. Consequently, I was always broke." People discouraged him. "Their argument was that I was wasting my time in a trade that wasn't lucrative. . . . They said I would never be able to have a shop of my own and that I would have to spend the rest of my days searching for a job or working for somebody else."[57] And like DuBois, his early attempts at publishing did not go well. A paper he started in Gary, Indiana, failed after three issues.[58]

Abbott's luck eventually changed with the *Defender*, his signal entrepreneurial and publishing venture. But it would take some time before it resembled anything like the "World's Greatest Weekly," as its masthead later proclaimed. While he was determined "to accomplish one thing, that was to give my people a newspaper that would champion fearlessly the cause of the Race," he had to borrow from his landlord twenty-five cents to print its first 300 copies. After he printed them in the landlord's kitchen, the *Chicago Defender* was born, and he sold the paper himself on the corners of Chicago.[59] The publication's name signaled black retaliation against whites' attacks on blacks' bodies, citizenship rights, and public image, as well as an assertion of a perceived paternal and patriarchal duty for men to protect one's dependents, in this case the race. The first edition was four pages, sixteen by twenty inches.[60] Like many black businessmen and women of his generation, Abbott believed that entrepreneurship and self-employment exemplified self-help, granted one economic independence, and therefore provided pathways to freedom and autonomy.[61] But by 1908, he was exhorting readers to do as much as they could to support his paper. Abbott insisted that, as a "one-man newspaper," he had successfully brought his weekly to readers on time consistently for one year, a feat few other newspapers could match, he contended. And if "one man alone, by his work, earnest efforts and untiring energy" could accomplish this for a year straight, it made the paper not only a "remarkable" one but also one deserving their support, so Abbott argued.[62]

Abbott's early struggles in Chicago, especially with unions, shaped his initial response to the migration. He reasoned that the racial bar to industrial work present in so many unions precluded gainful job opportunities for prospective migrants, and thus he hesitated to endorse the migration.[63] But another reason Abbott hesitated had to do with Booker T. Washington's advocacy of the idea that black people should work out their destiny in the South. Abbott vacillated between the influential president of Tuskegee's philosophy and his own racial militancy.[64] Railing against racial violence in the South, Abbott took stances that were radical for the time, such as encouraging blacks to defend themselves against white mobs: "Arise Members of the Race, Gird Your Armor about Your Loins. . . . If You Must Die, Take One with You."[65] Because of these stances, the paper developed a reputation for militant rhetoric that endorsed black self-defense. Still, he was insisting here that black people defend themselves and stand their ground in the South. Indeed, as late as mid-1915, with the migration well underway, Abbott stressed that black southerners should not be hasty in leaving, for "the southland is rich and fertile, and it requires brains first and brawn afterward to make farming pay."[66] Abbott's reticence on the subject mirrored the stance of the southern black press. This stance resulted in part from Washington's powerful influence, as well as the racially violent climate of the South.[67]

Following Washington's leadership, some southern black leaders and black newspaper publishers urged black people in the South to abandon the quest for political rights, at least for the immediate future. Instead, black people should focus on individual and collective thrift, hard work, and morality, qualities these leaders believed would demonstrate black people's fitness for citizenship and eventually earn them political rights.[68] When Washington became the de facto national spokesman for this approach around 1896, the same year that the Supreme Court's decision in *Plessy v.*

Ferguson upheld segregation under the Fourteenth Amendment, many black leaders, businessmen, and clergymen in the South echoed this approach. Part of their support for this approach was because their own social influence and economic stability depended on Washington's patronage.[69] This was the case too for some prominent members of the southern black press, for whose publications Washington was a critical benefactor, such as P. B. Young's *Norfolk Journal and Guide*.[70] By influencing the editorial policies of the southern black press, if not controlling them through financial support and political appointments, Washington exercised considerable power in the South. This was a point that black critics of Washington, namely, Du-Bois, termed the "Tuskegee Machine," a pejorative reference to corrupt political patronage.[71] In fact, DuBois argued in 1903 that Washington's vision for racial advancement added yet another emasculating policy to an existing sharp crisis in black political rights and black manhood. Washington's "propaganda" "counsels a silent submission to civic inferiority such as is bound to sap the manhood of any race in the long run."[72] And "Negro newspapers were definitely showing their reaction" to DuBois's criticisms of Washington, he remembered, "publishing jibes and innuendoes at my expense." DuBois even "published in the *Guardian* a statement concerning the venality of certain Negro papers which I charged had sold out to Mr. Washington." He eventually felt that because of this criticism, Washington and his affiliates may have stopped other ventures DuBois had tried to pursue.[73] For DuBois, his belief that the race would be "saved by its exceptional men" did not necessarily include Washington.

But white repression through the threat and use of violence in the South also curtailed the potential for a militant southern black press that might have otherwise endorsed black migration. Vocal newspapermen, such as Jesse Max Barber of the *Voice of the Negro* in Atlanta, were far from safe. Whites had destroyed the presses of Eugene N. Bryant's *Brookhaven People's Relief* in Mississippi and Jesse C. Duke's *Montgomery Herald* in Alabama for their outspokenness on racial matters, for example.[74] In 1904, the inaugural issue of the *Voice of the Negro* proudly announced it was "the herald of the Dawn of the Day," "the first magazine ever edited in the South by Colored Men." Two years later, Barber fled Atlanta after he criticized white mobs involved in the Atlanta Riot of 1906, accused white politicians and white newspaper publishers of helping foment the riot with racially incendiary rhetoric, and telegraphed his inflammatory account of the riot to the *New York World*.[75] Perhaps the best-known instance of racial violence in the South descending on a black publisher was the case of Ida B. Wells.

In the spring of 1892, she investigated the causes of lynching after the lynching of three of her friends. When she published several statements in her *Memphis Free Speech and Headlight*, accusing some white women of consenting to sexual affairs with black men and white men lynching black men because of it, a white mob destroyed her press. Wells fled Memphis for Chicago, and at a somewhat safer distance from the South, joined others, such as T. Thomas Fortune, publisher of the outspoken *New York Age*, and DuBois to organize and use journalism to protest racial violence and the Jim Crow regime.[76]

But around 1915, the scale of the migration changed dramatically, exploding due to a number of "push" and "pull" factors that soon included the northern black press. In 1910, nearly 440,000 blacks migrated. By 1920, this figure would double.[77] Escalating racial violence and terrorism, poor wages, declining economic opportunities, deteriorating agricultural conditions due to the boll weevil, and few, if any, legal rights pushed hundreds of thousands of black southerners out of the South. Greater demands for labor in the North brought on by the war and restrictions on European immigration, and better economic, educational, and political opportunities drew them northward.[78] The *Crisis* interpreted the explosion of the movement as a watershed moment for black people. This compelled DuBois to outline his most ringing endorsement of black migration yet: "The Immediate Program of the American Negro." In this agenda for racial advancement, he declared that the "American Negro demands equality—political equality, industrial equality and social equality," the "right of a human being to be a man even if he does not wear the same cut of vest, the same curl of hair or the same color of skin." DuBois explained that the migration signaled that there was a "more clearly recognized minimum of opportunity and maximum of freedom to be, to move and to think, which the modern world denies to no being which it recognizes as a real man." But DuBois warned that "first of all before taking steps the wise man knows the object and end of his journey. There are those who would advise the black man to pay little or no attention to where he is going so long as he keeps moving. This is arrant nonsense." "Conscious self-realization and self-direction is the watchword of modern man," he continued, "and the first article in the program of any group that will survive must be the great aim, equality and power among men." The opportunity for black people to have freedom, political rights, manhood, and a better racial destiny made the "systematic migration from mob rule and robbery" a necessity in bringing about the advancement of the race.[79] In announcing this defining program for racial advancement that marked "the urban," at once an actual environment and an idealized space constructed by the black press, as the new site for building black political power and a concerted civil rights struggle, DuBois was encouraging the migration, serving the race, and staking a claim to manly racial leadership.

When Abbott finally endorsed the migration in mid-1916, not too long after the death of Booker T. Washington in 1915, the *Defender* distinguished itself from other papers by shifting into an all-out crusade to bring black southerners to Chicago in particular, and the North in general. Abbott began to frame migration as essential to achieving freedom and manhood, an editorial change that would make the *Defender* the unofficial but lead propagandist of the migration.[80] Like DuBois, Abbott's masculine identity was shaped by Victorian sensibilities. But Abbott's model of masculinity hinged not on the restrained man of letters but another, equally influential ideal of the time: that of the self-made man in search of financial success in the marketplace.[81] When Abbott founded the Chicago-based *Defender*, he had not yet devised a strategy to build a national circulation and acquire national influence. The migration changed this, opening vast opportunities for him and his paper. Abbott's response exemplified the adaptability of the press in reacting to changes in the social conditions of black Americans, along with the power of the press to shape those changes. Around 1910, Abbott began taking a number of editorial cues from major white newspapers, particularly the tabloid style of publishers William Randolph Hearst and Joseph Pulitzer. Abbott had even borrowed his "World's Greatest Weekly" slogan from the *Chicago Tribune*'s "World's Greatest Newspaper."[82] But in the late 1890s, Hearst's and Pulitzer's popular papers especially featured salacious and sometimes concocted news coverage that came to be known notoriously as yellow journalism, even as they helped build a very influential and competitive print culture in America.[83] Like Hearst and Pulitzer, Abbott laced his columns with flamboyant mastheads, headlines, and print in order to garner more sales.[84] And unlike the *Crisis*'s readership, Abbott's paper was intended for a mass black audience.

During the migration, Abbott began to capitalize on the changing cultural tastes and racial outlook of the black masses, publishing a weekly that would earn more revenue by being political and popular, educational and entertaining for black readers.[85] On one level, when it became clear that employment opportunities and industrial unions were opening up to blacks, Abbott became convinced that the droves of migrants heading north meant a chance for black people to prove their mettle as industrial workers and hopefully reduce racial antagonism through increased contact between the races. "Only by a commingling with other races will the bars be let down and the Black man take his place in the limelight beside his white brother," the *Defender* asserted. But on another level, Abbott, the aspiring self-made man, realized that more blacks in Chicago and more content with vernacular and mass appeal meant more sales for the *Defender.*[86] "Farewell Dixie Land," "Come Up North. Why Stay Down South," and other headlines announced the change.[87] At the behest of *Defender* writer Lucius C. Harper, Abbott began to use black railroad porters to distribute and sell the paper in the South, helping spur the *Defender*'s national circulation, and most importantly, its influence among black southerners.[88] In 1916, the paper reached seventy-two towns and had a circulation of at least 50,000. Two years later, its circulation numbered 125,000, with two-thirds of its readers living outside Chicago. It became the first northern black newspaper to have a mass following in the South. Abbott had achieved circulation rates and popularity heretofore unseen by any other black newspaper.[89] By this time too, having observed and appropriated the successful printing methods of Hearst and Pulitzer, Abbott began using sensationalism to promote his paper, compete with other papers, and politicize important racial issues. And much like DuBois through the *Crisis*, Abbott also worked to serve the race, as well as stake a claim to manly racial leadership by asserting the leading role in encouraging the migration.

The *Defender*'s focus on the migration launched Abbott's turn to sensationalism, establishing the stylistic approach of the modern black press for the next several decades. The paper's sensationalism employed flamboyant text and images and focused on crime, especially sex crimes or violent crimes: "White Gentleman Rapes Colored Girl" and "100 Negroes Murdered Weekly in United States by White Americans" were just a few examples.[90] Before this shift to sensationalism, black newspapers typically reported weddings, births, deaths, and church and business affairs. In the age of yellow journalism many black publishers initially eschewed it as crass and irresponsible, failing to appreciate some of its potential to elevate important political points. "He, typically, was a man of one idea, the Afro-American journalist," publisher T. Thomas Fortune of the *New York Age* said, "who cleaved close to the line of race rights and loyalty." A leader of the nineteenth-century black press, Fortune held that "the old journalism was a fighting machine which feared no man or combination of men"; "it refused to print anything that would damage the good name or morals of the race, and kept all scandal and personalities, however sensational the news might be, in the background," a nostalgic Fortune complained.[91] But Abbott's contemporary DuBois resisted sensationalism too. Determined to present fact-driven arguments, and probably motivated to avoid offending the middle-class sensibilities of *Crisis* readers, he refused to print crime stories.[92] At one point, he even commented that many black newspapers were not "worth reprinting or even reading."[93]

But Abbott saw the immense commercial *and* political potential of this new style for black papers, helping instantiate an important feature of the modern black press. His use of sensationalism helped draw numerous readers, as well as elevate his ideas of black manhood, vision for racial advancement, and promotion of the migration over other papers. Indeed, Emmett J. Scott, former secretary for Booker T. Washington and at the time secretary-treasurer of Howard University, recognized the *Defender*'s ascendance. He found in his 1920 study of the migration, *Negro Migration during the War*, "conditions most distasteful to negroes were exaggerated and given first prominence [in the *Defender*]. In this the *Defender* had a clear field, for the local colored newspapers dared not make such unrestrained utterances." Scott credited the *Defender* for being one of the most influential causes in "stimulating" the migration.[94]

But at the same time, and more importantly, this journalistic style was often put in the service of racial protest and advocacy by the paper's editors and writers. As historian Kim Gallon has argued, sensationalism within the black press had a political content that was intended to emphasize the importance of particular issues and attract the attention of readers in order to shape racial consciousness and mobilize the black public to action, a process that was also influenced by gender constructions.[95] As some contemporaries criticized the *Defender*'s sensationalism as opportunistic and pandering, Abbott, and later other black newspapermen and newspaperwomen, still used it to humanize and dramatize the news and signal the importance of racial issues. Indeed, as he would write years later, "I have been accused of [tabloid] journalism, of insincerity," but "I have faithfully and diligently striven to make known and alleviate the suffering of my people. I have endeavored to bring to the attention of the reading public all the inhuman treatment, discrimination, segregation, disfranchisement, peonage and all other injustices directed at my people."[96] However, the *Defender* tended to frame its sensationalism in gendered terms, couching the discourse on black masculinity in riveting language that helped accentuate the need for black manhood. The *Defender*'s sensationalism became widely influential in entertaining and politicizing readers, and positioning Abbott as a cultural taste-maker for emerging New Negro sensibilities that valued mobility, urbanity, and performing black manhood.[97] While the *Crisis* helped define and support the migration through social science, the mass-driven *Defender*, more than any other black paper, helped define the migration as a movement of men to gain manhood before an overwhelmingly male demographic of migrants. For black men in the South, who were disfranchised and felt left out of black women's growing racial leadership as activists in the women's club movement, the call for a figurative and literal manly movement had powerful appeal.[98]

The *Defender*'s new campaign struck right at the heart of the matter, characterizing the South as a place that stripped blacks of their rights as human beings and as men. "From their point of view," the *Defender* declared, "the colored man has no right or privilege that they are bound to respect, and what little law that is in vogue is meted out to the white man and Black man differently."[99] Paraphrasing Chief Justice Roger B. Taney's explanation for the Supreme Court's decision in *Dred Scott v. Sanford*, the paper strove to inflame readers by reminding them of this crucial racial ideology that undergirded the Jim Crow South.[100] Jim Crow laws were designed to destroy not only the citizenship and humanity of black people but also their gender identities. The emasculation of black men and denial of true womanhood to black women had a deep and long history in the South, and in the United States in general. The southern Jim Crow system stood on a racial and sexual order that intended to bind black labor to cotton plantations, protect the white planter class from losing black labor and the white working class from economic competition with blacks, and ensure the racial subordination of black people, rendering them as less than human and lacking in the morals and virtues of manhood and womanhood.[101] Jim Crow laws enforced this, stripping many black men of their right to vote and/or control their own labor, rights considered sacred for men in a patriarchal society.[102] In her crusade against lynching, Ida B. Wells found that white supremacy was both a racial and sexual regime that codified sexual racism in law.[103] Daily racial interactions in the South enforced this too.[104] The *Defender* called these flagrant abuses of black humanity "the South's crime against the Negro," crimes "Of 'peonage.' . . . Of its hangings—THOUSANDS OF THEM! Of its 'gun parties' in the dark and in the open day—THOUSANDS OF THEM! . . . Of its debauchment and ruination of Colored women—THOUSANDS OF THEM! Of sweet faced, helpless girls destroyed . . . buds of womanhood. . . . Of the rule . . . that compels the Negro to enter the presence of a white man with his HAT UNDER HIS ARM: to step in the gutter, WHEN MEETING HIM ON THE SIDEWALK; or take his life in his hand if he dares to . . . address in terms of familiarity [a white woman]."[105]

Yet, for the *Defender*, perhaps nothing illustrated the systematic emasculation of black men in the South more than lynching. Lynching had risen sharply since the end of Reconstruction and had become a ritualistic practice of terrorism intended to enforce the racial order against any black person's real or perceived violation of the Jim Crow regime. Motivated by myths of black criminality and black male sexuality that emphasized a rapacious appetite for white women, lynchers made black men their most common targets. The actions of lynchers not only were unpunished but were applauded by other whites who saw lynch mobs as defenders of white womanhood and the prerogatives of white manhood.[106] Whites' castration of lynched black male victims exemplified the pervasiveness of these myths, as whites were determined to destroy black masculinity at the very site of biological maleness.[107] Wells called this systematic violent emasculation of black men the "subjugation of the young manhood of the race." In fact, she eventually gained a sympathetic international audience to the cause of racial justice in part by highlighting the horrors of lynching in her journalism.[108] Capitalizing on growing civil rights organizing against lynching led by such organizations as the NAACP, as well as migrants' own desires to escape racial violence in the South, the *Defender* argued that lynching was an outright attack on black men, their ability to protect themselves, black women, their families, and property.[109] Similar to Wells, Abbott in his *Defender* dramatized reports of lynchings, drawing special, descriptive attention to the suffering of black male victims and the "dirty outrages" of attackers.[110] After the lynching of a black man in Tennessee, the *Defender* reported, for example, that the victim was "bound to an iron post. . . . Scott stood one-half hour, while men heated pokers . . . until they were white with heat . . . and the holder began to bore out the prisoner's eyes. Scott moaned. . . . The smell of burning flesh permeated the atmosphere."[111] But the *Defender* made some of its most powerful protests against lynching without words. Poignantly illustrated cartoons sometimes said it all. One cartoon displayed the lifeless body of a black man hanging from a tree as his killers marched away triumphantly. The paper told readers to "Remember This Scene" when they decided to vote in the "solid South." Such vivid depictions were designed to illustrate the *Defender*'s overall point that in the South a black man was not considered "a man with all equality according to the law and constitution of the United States."[112]

Lynchings and racial violence raised the *Defender*'s campaign to a fever pitch, sparking some of its most sensational rhetoric. The *Defender* insisted that "every Negro man for the sake of his wife and daughters especially, should leave even at a financial sacrifice every spot in the south where his worth is not appreciated enough to give him the standing of a man and a citizen in the community."[113] On December 2, 1916, the paper issued "The Race's Magna Charta." Similar to DuBois's "Immediate Program for the American Negro," the *Defender* outlined its own agenda for racial advancement. The manifesto demanded the immediate end to Jim Crow segregation, unequal education, police brutality, lynchings, disfranchisement, and the sexual abuse of black women by white men. In fact, the manifesto went as far as calling for white men to marry the black women with whom they had improper sexual relations and support the children that resulted from those relationships, a controversial idea meant to underscore the virtue of black women.[114] To heighten the appeal of leaving, the *Defender* printed train schedules, publicized housing offers and help-wanted announcements, reported job wages, and advertised the activities and locations of labor agents recruiting black workers.[115] At a time when civil rights activism was on the rise, and black male leaders were looking for an issue or movement that would show their leadership and proper gender identities just as the Woman's Era had done for many black women, Abbott urged in one searing appeal that black southerners leave right away:

> It is time to act, and every man that has a spark of manhood or Race loyalty about him will join this national movement to better conditions for our people. . . . Remember it means liberty for you and yours. . . . Let every man and woman who reads this message carry it into each nook and corner of this broad but not free land. It is now or never. We are counting on you to do your bit. Let your voice join in the chorus of the thousands who answer "I WILL." Mail a copy of this issue with this appeal to every Race man throughout the south as well as the north. . . . Walk out from any job that robs you of manhood or womanhood. . . . Be Men; quit your job. . . . Make your own destiny.[116]

Here, Abbott stressed that leaving was not a cowardly retreat but a bold assertion of manhood. Here also the *Defender* sought to bolster the position of black men in the struggle for rights. While black clubwomen worked to defend the purity, morals, and character of black women against racist stereotypes that they were lascivious, Abbott's approach argued for a more robust role in black men defending black women's reputation and bodies.[117] Taking black women out of the South was the best way to show this manly assertion of defending black women. One article cautioned migrating men against leaving black women behind, even if the man intended to return for her. "When a whole people, by one unchecked impulse, acting as one man, inaugurate a crusade for change," unanticipated consequences were sure to follow, one of which was the abandonment of a "daughter here, a sister, wife or mother there, helpless and unprotected in this modern Sodom and Gomorrah, as far as the honor and virtue of Colored women is concerned."[118] It was possible for black men to make such a manly assertion because the extremes of white supremacy had stimulated a counteraction that propelled black men to act, the *Defender* argued. "A little rough usage toughens one up, strengthens the nerves and stiffens the backbone, essentials that perhaps we sadly lacked."[119] These "essentials" would help black men muster the will to leave. One cartoon, entitled "Backbone," showed two black men, one representing "The South" and receiving a spinal injection of "Backbone Tonic" by the other man, who was dressed as a doctor and represented "The Defender."[120] *Defender* writers were determined to help provide the manly mettle black men needed to leave the South, and thereby elevate their leadership.

The *Defender*'s gendered emphasis on moving heightened the appeal of mobility, a cherished freedom that for many blacks, north and south, was sacrosanct and had a long history of being challenged and proscribed by whites.[121] Yet this cherished freedom posed a threat to the racial, social, and economic order because it quite literally crossed the color line in the minds of whites, who wanted blacks to stay in their place, literally and figuratively, a place of forced labor, economic dependency, and racial subordination. Because of restrictions on black mobility during and after slavery, the ability to move about freely resonated for blacks as a powerful act of freedom, opportunity, equality, modernity, citizenship, and manhood. The *Defender* insisted that any other race of men forced to live under the same conditions would not hesitate to leave, and the "Colored man" should be no exception: "The man who travels is the man who learns most. . . . Go everywhere there is found an opportunity." Surely, in order to garner attention and drive the point home, the paper questioned in striking capital letters: "THE WHITE MAN SEEKS THE FARTHEST CORNERS OF THE GLOBE IF HE THINKS HE CAN BETTER HIMSELF, WHY SHOULD WE NOT DO LIKEWISE?"[122] Maintaining the relationship between mobility and freedom, as well as helping solidify one between mobility and masculinity, the *Defender* affirmed that through migration, the black man took "his place along other races of men, not as an object of pity, but as a man, striving to the end that he may be one of them, a man among men. And the exodus of Negroes to the North means just that."[123]

The paper's clarion calls to abandon the South for the sake of protecting black women from sexual violence may have motivated not only black men but also black women already determined to go north for reasons also connected to their gender identities. Many of these reasons included better economic prospects, as well as ensuring their own safety and the safety of their children from racial and sexual violence. Life in the South subjected black women to innumerable indignities that included the exploitation of their labor and sexual violence at the hands of both white and black men, all of which made the stakes of staying in the South just as high for black women as for black men, if not more. As historian Darlene Clark Hine has shown, black women were as motivated as black men to leave the South because of factors particular to their gendered experiences, what she has called the "gender dimension" of the migration.[124] The *Crisis*, for its part, examined and politicized many of the issues that concerned black women.[125] One extensive analysis of the employment status of black women in the urban North at the height of the migration argued that some black women had "made good," while others still faced enormous challenges in pay, equality with white women in the workplace, and acceptance by unions. In one cartoon, the *Crisis* depicted a black woman, working as a domestic in the South, about to be sexually assaulted by a white man, presumably her male employer, who was grabbing her arm. To the *Crisis*, this was "New Education in the New South: Domestic Science for Colored Girls Only."[126] Yet, reflecting popular concern among black people about job opportunities for black men in particular, the *Crisis* also asserted, and quite problematically, that "women are undercutting men in wages," and "every precaution must be taken to avoid it."[127] Indeed, as a result of the link between breadwinning and masculinity, and the perceived need to restore both for black men—points that the *Crisis* and the *Defender* reinforced—discussions about work for black men took precedence over that for black women for many black leaders and the black press.[128]

Helping restore black manhood through the migration and gainful employment resonated as a priority for some black women too, however. To illustrate, Emmett J. Scott found in his study of the migration one black woman from Mississippi who shared her concerns about the emasculating treatment of black men in the South. She commented that she would not let her son, who left for the North, return home because "for him to accept the same abuses to which we, his parents, are accustomed, would make him much less than the man we would have him to be."[129]

Indeed, the promise of the urban North as a place and space of opportunity appealed to both black men and women, though the *Defender* fantastically characterized it particularly as a manly space that redefined notions of black manhood to center on urbanity. Scholars have written extensively on how the *Defender*, more than any other paper of the era, was largely responsible for promoting Chicago as the ideal destination for migrants. This led the city to receive the greatest number of migrants to the Midwest.[130] "Conditions Good in North," the land of "liberty and freedom," the "Promised Land," and other similar captions helped attract throngs of migrants to Chicago.[131] Here, the *Defender* resembled the booster papers of the mid-nineteenth century, enticing prospective residents to settle in a particular city on the frontier with the promise of land and unprecedented opportunities.[132] In many ways, Chicago was such a frontier for black southerners, who had yet to explore the city but learned about it through relatives, rumors, and the *Defender*.[133] In describing the allure of Chicago—its jobs, homes, leisure life, educational institutions, culture, upwardly mobile black residents, and entertainment districts, among many other exciting attractions, opportunities, and luxuries—the paper was perhaps its most sensational. It portrayed Chicago as a "hypercity," an urban space that was far more than the sum of its parts, something greater than the city itself.[134] The *Defender* was promoting Chicago as a symbol of the urban ideal, the best of the urban that took on, as historian Allan Spear put it, a "mythical quality."[135] One white newspaper in the South complained, "The greatest disturbing element which has yet entered Georgia is the circulation of a Negro newspaper known as the CHICAGO DEFENDER, which has agitated the Negroes to leave the south on the word picture of equality with the whites, the freedom of hotels, theaters, and other places of public amusement on an equal basis with white people, and 'equality in citizenship.'"[136] The *Defender*'s descriptions of the "Stroll," the cluster of black businesses and entertainment venues in the Black Belt bounded by Twenty-Sixth Street and Thirty-Ninth Street, convinced one reader of the paper in Mississippi that the strip was "heaven itself."[137]

Within this space of freedom and possibility was a gendered geography in which black male migrants were to embrace the new marker and maker of black manhood. In the urban, they could find a better, more definitive manhood that would become the crux of New Negro identity and masculinity.[138] In addition to being a space for concerted black political struggle, as DuBois argued, the urban offered black men the chance to assert a new masculinity that hinged not on old, southern models of manhood connected to land ownership and self-produced commodities, as black leaders like Booker T. Washington had promoted. Indeed, P. B. Young's *Norfolk Journal and Guide,* the paper that Washington used to subsidize, was still promoting many of Washington's notions of black manhood during the height of the migration.[139] Instead, the new black masculinity was predicated on leisure, consumerism, and material consumption, along with having greater political rights. These were values that, as historian Davarian Baldwin has argued, became immensely important to New Negro consciousness and culture.[140] Black southerners' values and desires for ownership over their labor, income, body, time, mobility, and sexuality, things denied them in the South, might be realized more easily in the urban, where "the black man is indispensable because immigrant labor cannot be had," and "manhood and fair play for them is assured," the *Defender* maintained.[141] Through this framing, the paper helped shape the vision of these values and desires among black southerners before they arrived in urban centers. As historian Wallace Best has argued, black migrants brought to the urban a cultural calculus rooted in black southern culture that helped shape the city even as the city shaped them.[142] Over the course of its campaign, the *Defender* became a part of black southern culture. The paper helped stoke the desires for freedom, upward mobility, and manhood that migrants shared before their arrival and realized in ways that ultimately helped make the New Negro movement and its models of manhood possible.

The *Defender*'s published testimonies of successful black male migrants confirmed that black men in the urban North gained access to the political, economic, and social privileges and rights to which men were entitled, or as the *Defender* put it, "their manhood with the ballot . . . equal protection in the courts . . . [and] . . . all of the rights and privileges accorded to other American citizens."[143] One young man from Alabama proclaimed, "I find that a fellow can be a man in this section, and there is so much satisfaction on that account alone that it would be impossible for me to return to the section I came from even for a temporary stay." He continued that he was now making "first class wages" and advised others to "take my case as a sample of the progress a move north means, and come to the part of the country where [you] will at least be looked upon as human beings."[144] One editorial even thanked Abbott for his role in spurring the migration: "Editor Chicago Defender: I take the liberty to thank you for your bold and manly editorials concerning the exodus of the Race to the north. I hope and pray that the blessings of Almighty God may ever rest upon you . . . for the noble part your paper is playing to help the Race throughout the country. . . . In every pulpit and place I chance to speak I will cry aloud for the Defender. . . . I am now in the north and have no hesitancy in speaking out."[145]

The offer of unbridled freedom in the urban North contradicted the reality of racial tensions and increasing segregation there, but the *Defender*'s inaccuracy was intentional. African Americans faced intense racial discrimination in employment, wages, labor unions, housing, and public accommodations.[146] Indeed, Abbott had once faced the same discriminatory climate practicing law and working in a printers' union in Chicago. The *Defender* disclosed that the urban North was no racial utopia, that it was "far from being ideal and the demon [of racial discrimination] is seen stalking about here and there, only more masked than in the southland."[147] But these admissions were by and large rare. In fact, the *Defender*'s promotion of exuberant black life on the stroll and flamboyant consumerism and consumption that became popular among New Negro readers betrayed Abbott's own personal model of masculinity, which was still connected to Victorian and old-settler sensibilities of thrift and proper public deportment.[148] Abbott was a shrewd businessman, and painting the urban as a space of unbridled freedom, despite reality, was precisely the point of the *Defender*'s campaign, and it furthered Abbott's goal of becoming the leading black publisher of the day.[149] Through sensational graphics and writing, the paper exaggerated claims about the urban North as a paradise in order to disparage the South, motivate black migration, and capitalize on the cultural changes that heralded the New Negro era. However flawed, the urban remained the bastion of manhood for black men in the pages of the *Defender*. Its fantastical construction of the urban as a space of unbridled freedom for blacks may have also appealed to black southerners, who did not make the journey north but left the countryside to migrate to southern cities to take advantage of emerging industrial opportunities in the South.[150]

The *Crisis* and other papers supported the *Defender*'s lead in elevating the urban as the new location of black progress. Publisher of the *Pittsburgh Courier* and former migrant from North Carolina Robert L. Vann insisted that the migration "placed the race in the limelight," "on an equal industrial footing with other peoples."[151] The *Crisis* affirmed that the "migration . . . continues as it should. . . . The demand for black workers in the North is unprecedented. . . . Honest colored laborers are welcome in the North at good wages, just as they are lynched in the South for impudence. Take your choice!"[152] Not to be outdone, though, the *Defender* went a step further. In its characteristic sensational fashion, its efforts to convince black southerners to migrate culminated in the "Great Northern Drive," set for May 15, 1917. This was supposed to be the day when black southerners everywhere were to meet at train stations and leave the South in a dramatic mass departure. "Thousands have left for the north and thousands are still leaving, and a million will leave with the Great Northern Drive," the paper declared.[153] This was the most popular date the paper set, though it proposed others that, as Emmett J. Scott observed at the time, were set according to the most common paydays for people.[154] Promoted for three months, the event mushroomed into rumors that excited would-be migrants and led many of them to think that the "Drive" was going to offer special trains with discounted fares. This was not so. Still, as historian James Grossman has pointed out, the impact of the Great Northern Drive showed how migrants came to construe their actions in terms of a mass movement, terms the *Defender* was instrumental in shaping.[155] Indeed, as Scott wrote, "the setting of a definite date was another stimulus. . . . This date, or the week following, singularly corresponds with the date of the heaviest rush to the North."[156]

Abbott's campaign helped galvanize not only black migration but also white resistance from white publishers and the state. Southern white papers attempted to combat the *Defender*'s influence by trying to undermine its utopian images of the urban North. The "southern propagandists," as the *Defender* labeled them, erroneously claimed that black migrants were dying from the cold weather of the North.[157] "Aged Negro Frozen to Death," "Dies from Exposure," and "Coldest weather in the last four years claimed a [Negro] Victim" were common headlines and captions alleging that black southerners were not surviving and could not survive the cold weather of the North. These were all canards trumped up to scare blacks from migrating so that they would stay planted in the South and contain the critical source of cheap labor.

The *Crisis* and the *Defender* dispelled their myths of northern winters killing black people. "Southern white papers are filled with contradictory statements; to-day . . . ridiculing the exodus," the *Crisis* railed, "painting fearsome pictures of the awful conditions of the emigrants. . . . Tomorrow come editorials bewailing the loss of labor and crying for drastic measures to enslave the black peons."[158] But the *Defender* transformed the threat of the cold North into a natural test of masculinity. It assured black southerners that they *would* survive the weather of the North and argued that while it had found no actual evidence of a black person dying from the cold, "the able-bodied men of our Race" would have nothing to worry about.[159] To provide more assurance, the *Defender* affirmed that various branches of the Urban League were working in cities, such as Chicago, New York City, Philadelphia, Detroit, Nashville, Atlanta, and Louisville, to help migrants adjust to urban life, socially and otherwise.[160] Perhaps there was no greater assurance than God, for the North was "God's country," the paper insisted, drawing on powerful religious and biblical imagery to inspire the migration as a modern-day "Exodus." This led some supporters to call Abbott a "black Joshua."[161] Still, no matter how low temperatures tended to drop in the North, the *Defender* asserted that to "die from the bite of frost is far more glorious than at the hands of a mob. I beg you, my brother, to leave the benighted land. You are a free man." Such terms were intended to inspire male migrants in particular. "If you can freeze to death in the North and be free," the *Defender* continued, "why freeze to death in the South and be a slave, where your mother, sister and daughter are raped and burned at the stake; where your father, brother and sons are treated with contempt and hung to a pole. . . . The Defender says come."[162]

White publishers' opposition to the *Defender*'s tremendous influence continued. In November 1918, opposition even became a legal matter. Famous publisher William Randolph Hearst sued the paper for copying the masthead of two of Hearst's Chicago papers, the *Herald-Examiner* and the *Evening American*. To Hearst's organization, the outstretched wings of an eagle perched over a shield of stars and stripes at the top of the *Defender*'s front page, proclaiming the "World Greatest Weekly," too closely resembled Hearst's own eagle. Hearst representatives claimed that the reading public was being duped into thinking that they were buying a Hearst paper. In fact, the similarities in sensational style and layout between Hearst's papers and the *Defender* led some members of the public to think that Hearst owned the *Defender*, a charge that had haunted Abbott for years.[163] Some segments of the public simply thought it impossible that a black man could own such a well-financed, well-produced, militant paper.[164] Abbott's response to these insulting perceptions in 1916 was a clear, emphatic statement that not only dispelled the misperceptions but also defined his position as a new race leader:

The CHICAGO DEFENDER is owned, edited and published by
Robert Sengstacke Abbott. . . . The staff is composed entirely of race
men . . . founded May 6, 1905 by Editor Robert S. Abbott . . . owned
exclusively by him and is edited and published by him. The entire
staff, editorial writers . . . delivery men are all members of the race.

There is nothing about this paper that is connected with William Randolph Hearst. . . . There is not a white man connected with the management of the paper or the ownership thereof. The paper stands for the race. . . . If any doubt the above statements, go to the post office files and ask for the sworn statement of the editor.[165]

Hearst's case two years later actually served to corroborate Abbott's point, finally authenticating his ownership before the reading public, though it prompted the publishing of one more statement: "Chicago Defender Entirely Owned by R. S. Abbott."[166] Abbott also rushed to have the image of his front page masthead redesigned before the case went to trial. After the new design jettisoned the eagle for a sphinx, the case was dropped.[167] Unlike the white southern press, the Hearst organization was probably more concerned with getting a share of Abbott's lucrative campaign than undermining its influence among black readers, however. But the case testified to how effective Abbott had become at appropriating the printing methods of Hearst and Pulitzer, and how financially successful and influential the campaign was as a result.[168]

Repression of the *Defender* demonstrated the new importance of the black press, alarming white southerners, northern publishers, and government authorities. Southern white politicians reacted swiftly to the migration, passing legislation designed to stop the exodus of black laborers by enforcing vagrancy laws that arrested "idle" blacks and made it illegal to "abandon" one's work. Arrests often forced the convicted into work through the convict lease system, the southern penal system's use of prisoner labor for private citizens and corporations.[169] By 1918, some southern towns made it illegal to read or carry the *Defender*, now synonymous with the migration.[170] The chief of police in Meridian, Mississippi, for example, ordered the paper confiscated.[171] Yet the *Defender*'s collaboration with black railroad porters, themselves symbols of black masculine mobility, circumvented these challenges to the paper's distribution in the South.[172] Federal authorities posed another challenge, though Abbott managed to get around them too. Some white southerners wrote federal officials, charging that the paper's campaign was hurting the war effort because it was stealing away black labor and encouraging blacks to be unpatriotic. Along these lines, and as a part of federal anxieties over alleged domestic subversives during the war, the *Defender*, the *Crisis*, and other black newspapers vocal against racial injustice came under federal surveillance. DuBois remembered, for instance, the barrage of questions from federal officials who invaded the offices of the *Crisis*. "Just what, after all, were our objectives and activities?" they demanded to know.[173]

But federal officials especially targeted the *Defender* as the "most dangerous of all Negro Journals." In April 1917, agents of the Justice Department interrogated Abbott to determine his loyalties to the nation. He insisted his paper did support the war effort, that he had personally contributed $12,000 to the Liberty Loan, and that the paper was not indicting the entire country but speaking out against the "injustices done our race" in the South.[174] Abbott affirmed his support, though he had privately written Emmett J. Scott, now the special assistant to the secretary of war, in May 1918 to ask Scott to help protect his staff members from the war draft. Abbott knew that he was "asking a great deal," but "in defense of my publication and the good it is doing our race, I am forced to speak out. There are several men on my staff . . . who will come within the limit of the draft law, and it is my earnest desire to retain these men." It had been a "trial" for him to "find competent, reliable and trustworthy newspapermen among our people. I have for the past eight years battled unceasingly for such a group of men as I now have surrounding me." Losing them "would mean a severe blow to my publication" and "the field of journalism as affecting our race," especially since the *Defender* had recently gained a great deal of "influence," he argued. He requested Scott to "use your good influence" to spare "his highly trained newspapermen."[175] Agents returned in the summer of 1918, but Abbott remained within the bounds of acceptable public discourse, and the government never pressed charges against the publisher. But white resistance to Abbott's campaign only buttressed the militant reputation of his paper and stiffened his resolve to urge blacks northward.

On February 2, 1918, Abbott wrote an article that seemed to shore up his support for the war effort before federal officials as much as he shared plans for expanding the *Defender* in light of its lucrative campaign:

The Chicago Defender is preparing to give the reading public a
greater paper than it is now publishing. A full 16-page, up to date
newspaper, carrying a full page of news interesting to women,
two of sports, theatrical news, a column for children, fashions,
a good live editorial page, cartoons excelled by none, pictorial
history or world events pertaining to the Race, a soldiers' page, and
a regular page on the war, written by a Defender reporter who
will be with the troops. We will attempt something new, also set a
precedent for journals, by sending one of OUR REPORTERS with the

boys "over there" in France and by giving to the public its FIRST 16-PAGE WEEKLY paper issued every week instead of on Christmas and during business-boosting campaigns. It must be conceded that we have not only excelled in the field of journalism, but have always been in the lead in matters of public import, the first to speak out fearlessly and truthfully in the interest of the people without regard to whom it hurts. We wait only upon Washington and the proposed zone system. . . . We wish to thank the public for their loyal support in the past, and promise them that The Chicago Defender shall continue to be "The World's Greatest Weekly" in the future, striving its utmost to serve all the people, both black and white.[176]

The federal government's efforts to gain support from black newspapers for the war culminated in a June 1918 conference between black publishers and federal officials. Emmett J. Scott convened the group to discuss black people's grievances against the war and devise ways to build black morale. Among the forty-one black leaders called to attend, thirty-one of them were newspapermen, including Abbott and DuBois. DuBois drafted resolutions that attendees adopted, one of which demanded an end to lynching.[177]

Abbott and DuBois would continue to find themselves in positions of racial leadership. As for other black men, they could find something similar in the urban, the new marker and maker of manhood. The urban offered black men a "livelihood and a place where a man can be a man" though this ideal environment was not without requirements and responsibilities.[178] The urban promised to elevate only industrious, self-initiating men and women.[179] If there was any doubt about the necessity and utility of these qualities in the North, one need only turn to the *Defender*'s regular coverage of certain notable black Chicagoans for examples of the potential migrants could have in achieving success. Madame C. J. Walker, a former washerwoman from Louisiana–turned–beauty culture millionaire, or as the *Defender* put it, "the Richest Woman of the Race," exemplified what "a struggling woman could do who had no assistance and the possibilities that await her."[180] The most well-known example and possibly most covered black Chicagoan in the *Defender* was Jack Johnson, the first black world heavyweight champion.[181] Johnson, a migrant from Galveston, Texas, had become not only a wealthy athlete but also the premier symbol of a resistant, self-assertive black masculinity that, through the defeat of white opponents and controversial public displays of his wealth and lifestyle, inspired growing New Negro racial consciousness, particularly the public performance of New Negro masculinity.[182] "Jack Johnson as a self-made man," the *Defender* would editorialize, "stands out as the greatest individual in his lines that America has produced, regardless of color or creed. . . . Jack Johnson started out in life alone to be the world's greatest man in the art of self-defense."[183]

Even Abbott, the Georgia native who moved to Chicago to start a life of enterprise that became the founding of the "World's Greatest Weekly," was another example of a migrant-turned-mogul. "Every Race man should do homage to R. S. Abbott," said one reader, "for only now and then . . . do we see men that have the nerve and brain to publish a journal like the Chicago Defender, fearing none and giving justice to all."[184] Another reader appreciated Abbott's service to the race, suggesting that he "insert [his] photograph in the paper so that [readers] may really get a glimpse of a man who has the courage of his conviction, and whose single motive is the uplift of the race." "I think that every man and woman with higher aims in life should become a reader of [the *Defender*]. It gives strength to the weak and encourages thrift and ambition. It is a summons to the race to be up and doing," another reader shared enthusiastically.[185] Even some of the people, who discouraged Abbott during the *Defender*'s fledgling years, now "came to my office, into my home, saying the proverbial, 'I told you so,' and 'I knew you could do it,'" he recalled with an air of vindication.[186]

In public too, readers could see firsthand just how successful Abbott had become in the urban, due largely to the paper's lucrative campaign, of course. One contemporary observer of the black press lamented how "the old [black] journalism had few readers and advertisers, and payday was always a deathless agony to the editor."[187] In the early years of his career, Abbott would have been quick to agree with this statement. But this was no longer the case. With certain material accoutrements, he demonstrated the merits of his beliefs that entrepreneurship exemplified self-help and granted one economic independence and autonomy.[188] His projections of his success in public were displays and performances of the very model of entrepreneurship, leisure, and consumer-based urban black manhood that his paper was promoting.[189] Abbott had gone from struggling to feed himself and pay his rent and borrowing money from his landlord to start the paper to owning at some point an elegant fleet of cars. Archival records indicate that he owned a limousine, which bore a monogram of his initials on the door. He also owned a Rolls-Royce, which, as historian Christopher Robert Reed points out, was "pea green."[190] In 1919, Jasper Ross, a writer for the *Fraternal Advocate*, another black newspaper in Chicago, published a few words about one of Abbott's cars, and the symbol of black proprietary success he had become:

> In the years past I knew a man who essayed to edit a Race journal. But he was POOR AND UNKNOWN, and the people looked unkindly on his efforts. HARSH things were said of him, and he was TURNED AWAY from many doors. FEW were the meals he ate, SCANTY were the clothes that he wore. And the things of life that make one GROW SICK AT HEART and weary of the struggle were in truth HIS OWN. But the man WAS persistent AND stubborn AND determined to have his way, AND HIS NAME WAS ABBOTT. Yesterday I looked out upon a crowded thoroughfare, and noted the different types of cars as they wormed their way down the street. Among those moving palaces, its highly polished sides GLISTENING IN THE SUNLIGHT, silently and majestically, came one of a PALE GREEN VARIETY. "WHAT a magnificent car!" said a friend. "And to whom DOES IT BELONG?" questioned I. "And he answered: "Abbott—ABBOTT OF THE DEFENDER." And THEN, as it glided away, I saw, Dancing on its top, SHINING on its sides, REVOLVING in its wheels, SUCCESS, SUCCESS.[191]

Abbott's pea-green Rolls-Royce was probably the car Ross was describing. Some public observers thought that Abbott was ostentatious with displays of his wealth in public, though he sometimes instructed the black masses to be thrifty. As Metz P. Lochard, an editor for the *Defender*, wrote years later, some, "especially whites and upper-class Negroes, thought him a pompous, conspicuous spender, having a baronial home with a corps of servants and three automobiles." Enoch P. Waters, who would become a writer for the *Defender* years later, wrote that only Madame C. J. Walker rivaled him in wealth.[192] Altogether, as Walker, Johnson, and Abbott exemplified in their personal success, the *Defender* maintained that no one should go north without the intent of "making good," or being members of the "ambitious, hard working class . . . [who] had enough get-up about them to seek newer and greener fields."[193]

Walker, Johnson, and Abbott were national figures of black success that were exemplars of the *Defender*'s "Race Man" and "Race Woman," the novel signifiers for black men and women that Abbott deployed in the *Defender* in lieu of the word "Negro." Abbott considered "Negro" a pejorative term. "Race Man" and "Race Woman" had served as the *Defender*'s nomenclature for black people since 1910, and the migration reinvigorated and reshaped their usage.[194] At once, the terms' coupling of "man" and "woman" with "race" united blackness with masculinity and femininity, markers of identity that minstrelsy and racist stereotypes in popular culture and science denied. Abbott used the terms to give blacks the dignity their race, color, and gender identities deserved. Within the framework of this racial construct, as well as growing perceptions promoted by black leaders, cultural taste-makers, and the press that the urban offered the new means for racial advancement, black people left the South as "Negroes" and arrived in the North reborn into a publicly respected, self-assertive, and positive racial identity. This was part of what gave New Negroes their "newness." The terms "Race Man" and "Race Woman" remained popular signifiers for black men and black women for decades, even well after the term "New Negro" was en vogue.[195] Emphasizing that the urban North required migrants to do and be their best helped the *Defender* distinguish the North for valuing black people's ambition, mental ingenuity, and character above their physical abilities, a stark contrast to the South, which had only used black people for the labor their bodies produced.[196] But emphasizing requirements also prompted the *Defender* to advise migrants not to loaf, become burdens on northern society, or fulfill stereotypes of black people as lazy and shiftless. These dictates mirrored the class tensions earlier migrants like Abbott tended to exhibit toward newcomers. Abbott and the *Defender* never quite reconciled encouraging migrants with exuberant images of Chicago's black leisure and consumer life while emphasizing that they practice thrift and proper public comportment. The *Crisis*, as well as black uplift organizations and other black newspapers, also stressed proper public conduct for migrants in often condescending, class-specific terms intended to discipline their public behavior and physical appearance along lines of respectability.[197]

The *Defender* also conferred responsibilities on black northerners, black churches, and social organizations in the North to be their "brother's keeper" and help migrants adapt to their new environs.[198] This responsibility "every Race Man" owed to himself and to the migrants, for, as the *Defender* argued, "what affects one affects all." "Whether the colored man's condition will be improved or not depends in a great measure upon our own actions. . . . It is the duty, therefore, of every Northern organization, every pastor and every good citizen to guide and direct these newcomers," the *Defender* exhorted.[199] As an exemplary Race Man of the migration era, Abbott apparently took these words to heart. In one reported instance, he personally helped one migrant, Robert A. Wilson, after he "landed in Chicago . . . with one nickel and a Lincoln penny." Following a talk with the publisher, Wilson left instructed to "make good," and he eventually did, acquiring "a little bank account, a house and lot."[200] For many black leaders and the northern black press, the plight and future of black southerners and northerners were inextricably tied. To them, the exodus increased the numbers of black people in the North, thereby increasing their voting and economic power in terms of political representation and presence in labor unions, drawing the destinies of the newcomers and the natives ever closer. Historian and social critic Carter G. Woodson remarked in his 1918 study on the migration that the exodus "will doubtless prove to be the most significant event in our local history since the Civil War." Woodson was sure that the movement to the North promised black people's "best chance in the economic world of which he must emerge a real man with power to secure his rights as an American citizen."[201] Likewise, in the *Defender*'s optimistic estimation, the drawing together of native and newcomer signaled that "a great change is about to take place in the status of the Black man of this country."[202]

In 1919, things did change for black people, but in ways that few would have wanted. Beginning in April to early October of 1919, a series of race riots erupted across the country, ripping through twenty-five towns and cities.[203] The riots became known as the "Red Summer," a metaphor for the blood flowing in the streets as whites attacked returning black veterans and migrants.[204] Racial hostilities familiar to them in the South played out just as violently in their new settings, illustrating that racism and racial violence were not a regional phenomenon but national in character. In May, the *Crisis* published "Returning Soldiers," welcoming black soldiers back from Europe and celebrating their service in the war. But in the piece, DuBois announced, "We return from fighting. . . . We return fighting." He was right.[205] On July 27, a riot broke out in Chicago after white swimmers stoned and killed Eugene Williams, a fourteen-year-old black boy, for swimming in Lake Michigan across the "line" that segregated black and white swimmers. Black people, in turn, retaliated, but were outmatched by rampaging whites and their armed police allies. The Chicago riot raged for eight days. Thirty-eight people were killed in the Chicago riots, twenty-three of whom were black men and boys. Of the 542 people injured, 342 were black.[206]

The violence abruptly ended the *Defender*'s campaign to bring black southerners north. There was virtually no way Abbott and *Defender* writers could maintain their utopian images of Chicago and the North after the riots. But the *Defender*'s calls to black manhood remained powerful as the violence put its vision of black masculinity in the urban to the test. Indeed, the *Defender* construed the riots as an opportunity for black men to put their newfound manhood to even greater use, points that the paper suggested through some of its sensationalized coverage. The *Defender* ostensibly offered objective coverage of the riot, even cautioning blacks against getting involved, stating, "Do your part to restore quiet and order"; it was "no time to solve the race question!"[207] Still, the paper's biases in favor of manly self-assertion and resistance burst through the pages as it reported attacks on black people's attempts to defend themselves.[208] Lacing the coverage with the side of its sensationalism that highlighted crime, the paper even appeared to keep score by recording a tally of how many whites and blacks were reported dead day by day. Detailing vivid depictions of white violence, the *Defender* reported an attack on a black woman. She and her "3 month old baby were found dead on the street. . . . She had attempted to board a car . . . when the mob seized her, beat her, slashed her body into ribbons and beat the baby's brains out. . . . One rioter severed her breasts, and a white youngster bore it aloft on a pole, triumphantly, while the crowd hooted gleefully. All the time this was happening, several policemen were in the crowd, but did not make any attempt to make rescue." Such sensational reports likely inflamed readers, especially black men, with images of brutal attacks on black women by mobs of lawless white men. The story, according to historian William M. Tuttle, was not actually true—but the fabricated story of the murdered woman served as an arresting gendered appeal to incite black men to militantly stand up and defend themselves and other black people in the midst of the riot.[209] In one explanation of black self-defense at this critical moment, the *Defender* asserted that "men were within their rights when they refused at the point of a shotgun to allow their homes to be bombed or burned by the mob. They were defenders, not aggressors, and did only what all red-blooded men do, stand by their colors."[210]

Following the Chicago riot, Illinois governor Frank O. Lowden organized the Chicago Commission on Race Relations to investigate its causes and suggest means to prevent future racial problems in the city. In part testifying to his new standing in the community, Abbott was among the fifteen people appointed by the governor to the commission. Published three years after the riot, the final report of the commission opposed segregation, called for equal opportunities in the North, and offered a number of recommendations. It praised "the propriety and social values of race pride among Negroes," but warned "that thinking and talking too much in terms of race alone are calculated to promote separation of race interests and thereby to interfere with race adjustment." The *Defender* had played a significant role in shaping both these points, using sensationalism. But its sensationalism was implicated in the report. The report in part blamed Abbott's paper for helping to incite the riot with exaggerated stories of racial conflict. Abbott biographer Roi Ottley insisted that Abbott was "ambivalent" on how he should cover the riot, whether he should report responsibly or encourage blacks to retaliate, arguing for the visions of black self-defense the paper had repeatedly raised.[211] Indeed, invoking black self-defense was in part the paper's namesake. The report admonished the "Negro press" to consider "greater care and accuracy in reporting incidents involving whites and Negroes, the abandonment of sensational headlines and articles on racial questions, and more attention to educating Negro readers as to the available means and opportunities of adjusting themselves and their fellows into more harmonious relations with their white neighbors." It is significant that the report recognized sensationalism as a new tool shaping the tenor of the black press, though negatively. Abbott signed the final report.[212] His signing angered his editorial staff, whose innovative work had helped him transform the paper, and the black press.[213]

DuBois was angered too. He decried the commission. It "consists of colored men who apparently have a much too complacent trust in their white friends and of enemies of the Negro race who under the guise of impartiality and good will are pushing insidiously but unswervingly a program of racial segregation," he said, asserting his role as the analytical scholar and race leader.[214] The *Crisis*'s coverage on the riots partly reflected DuBois's anger. The horror of the Red Summer prompted the paper to condemn the violence, as well as encourage black people, in a sensational, gendered tone of its own, to defend themselves. "Brothers . . . for three centuries we have suffered and cowered," the *Crisis* contended. "Today we raise the terrible weapon of self-defense. . . . When the mob moves, we propose to meet it with bricks and clubs and guns."[215] The *Crisis*'s call to black self-defense not only conveyed DuBois's frustration but also exemplified a defining shift to manly, militant black politics. This heralded the dawn of the New Negro movement, greater assertions on the part of black men in physically and rhetorically defending black people, and the shift of racial leadership to black men away from black women.[216] Poet Claude McKay, who would become a leading literary figure of the Negro Renaissance in the 1920s, announced this shift best in his poem "If We Must Die," published in September 1919 in the *Messenger*, a Socialist black paper based in Harlem

that would come to speak to New Negro consciousness. "If we must die—
let it not be like hogs / Hunted and penned in an inglorious spot," McKay
declared, calling black men to aggressive action, even if it meant self-
sacrifice. "Like men we'll face the murderous, cowardly pack / Pressed to
the wall, dying but fighting back!"[217] One *Crisis* reader, a black woman, was
overjoyed to the point of tears by the new, manly assertion of this moment.
"At last our men had stood like men," she wrote. "Oh, I thank God, thank
God!"[218] Scholar Robert T. Kerlin recognized this new mood among black
people and their papers, prompting him to publish one of the first studies
on the modern black press, *The Voice of the Negro 1919*.[219]

This new black militancy reflected the gendered rhetorics that shaped
the inaugural editorial campaign that launched the modern black press.
Indeed, the migration and its aftermath had irreversibly transformed
black people, their culture, politics, and press. Coinciding with increasing black activism against Jim Crow, especially in the urban North, the
Crisis and the *Defender* assumed a role of black newspaper–led civil rights
protest during an apparent crisis in black manhood. Their publishers responded by transforming the migration into a manly movement and rede-
fining the urban along these lines. Using sensationalism, the *Defender* in
particular issued a resounding call to manhood, which helped move models of black masculinity away from land ownership to the urban, the new
marker and maker of proper black manhood. And rhetorical expressions
and actual demonstrations of black self-defense during the riots was the
culmination of this, the *Defender* argued. "It is conceded even by our
enemies," the paper rejoiced four months after the Chicago riots, "that the
Negro of today is not the Negro of yesterday. . . . It is safe to assume then
that we will fight to the last ditch any attempt to abridge our constitutional
rights," acknowledging DuBois's point that the urban now served as the
crucible of black political struggle. Celebrating black men's assertion of
self-defense, while anticipating the shift to a New Negro outlook, the
Defender continued that "THE CRINGING, subservient spirit of those dark
yesterdays has been transformed into one of self-assertion, one that brings
the full measure of manhood to the fore." "When the curtain is finally
rung down on the tragedy 'Colorphobia-Americanus,' the world will applaud when it finds the hero who is standing erect . . . with his heel on the
head of the serpent prejudice, is a black man."[220]

These masculinized assertions helped elevate black men to racial leadership before the black public sphere, arguing for and producing a politics
of black manhood that would justify a manly vision for racial advancement,

influencing the rhetoric, strategies, and leadership of the black freedom struggle for decades to come. DuBois and Abbott had demonstrated that newspapers could be effective tools in shaping black people's social movements and gender ideologies, as well as effective tools in helping black men assert a public voice and manly racial leadership. In fact, it would be this particular public function that helped make the black press crucial to other black men, offering them a pathway to manhood. In the wake of the migration, the riots, the rise of the modern black press, and their own papers' climbing circulation rates, DuBois and Abbott succeeded in serving the race by helping black men achieve their manhood. They also set into motion developments that helped them achieve theirs too. Anxieties they had expressed over their futures and manhood in the 1890s subsided. DuBois had desired to achieve recognition in science and literature, and thereby serve the race. The *Crisis*, "where most of my writing was done," provided the means to do this. Writing in 1920, an older DuBois had "emerged into full manhood. . . . I found myself suddenly the leader of a great wing of people fighting against another and greater wing." Leading was a role he "hated," preferring to "serve and follow and think." But one part of this role he found especially satisfying. "I dreamed of being an editor myself some day. I am an editor. In the great, slashing days of college life I dreamed of a strong organization to fight the battles of the Negro race. . . . I planned a time when I could speak freely to my people and of them interpreting between two worlds. I am speaking now. . . . My salary even for a year was not assured, but it was the 'voice without reply.' The result has been the National Association for the Advancement of Colored People and the *Crisis*." Other papers, including white ones, recognized DuBois's leadership in this regard. The New York *Sun*, for example, considered him the "leading factor in the race question."[221] As for Abbott, he now emerged the leading publisher of his day. He "was not interested merely in printing as a trade," he later wrote; "I wanted to create an organ that would mirror the needs, opinions and the aspirations of my race." One of those needs, opinions, and aspirations rested on manhood for black men, and for himself, the two reflecting one another in the *Defender*. "I should be among countless black men whose ambitions and optimism having been punctured by the arrows of prejudice, leave them prostrate without dreams and without hopes." "My very soul had been singed by the flame of prejudice to a far greater degree and intensity than has been the lot of most black men." But Abbott "was determined to see the principles of democracy extended to all areas of our social, political and economic life. To that end I dedicated my paper."[222]

2 Garvey Must Go

The Black Press and the Making and Unmaking of
Black Male Leadership

. . . .

Like DuBois, Abbott, and thousands of black men making their way out of
the South, migration, manhood, and militancy were on the mind of Marcus
Garvey. In fact, they had been for some time. Experiences as a youth in his
native Jamaica impressed these ideas upon him early on. He remembered
that his "father was a man of brilliant intellect and dashing courage" and
"unafraid of consequences. He took human chances in the course of Life,
as most bold men do," but "failed at the close of his career." Still, he was
"severe, firm, determined, bold and strong, refusing to yield even to superior forces if he believed he was right." Garvey's mother was "the direct
opposite," "always willing to return a smile for a blow, and ever ready to
bestow charity upon her enemy." Young Garvey grew up playing with
other boys, black and white. They "wanted to whip me," he recalled, but
never succeeded. "I was never whipped by any, but made them all respect
the strength of my arms. . . . I was not made to be whipped. It annoys me to
be defeated." As a youth, he started apprenticing under a printer, and by
the age of fourteen had gained "enough intelligence and experience to manage men. I was strong and manly, and I made them respect me. I developed
a strong and forceful character, and have maintained it still." By the age of
eighteen, the "aggressive" Garvey managed a printing establishment, but
during that time became greatly concerned about issues of racial injustice
in Jamaica and abroad. He then began traveling to parts of South America,
Central America, the West Indies, and Europe to observe the extent of racial problems. In each place he "found the same situation . . . the stumbling
block—'You are black.'"[1] In the course of his travels, Garvey applied the
skills he had acquired in printing and published newspapers to report on
local racial conditions, as well as mark his journeys, share his ideas, and
make his presence felt wherever he sojourned. In Jamaica he published
Garvey's Watchman; in Port Limón, Costa Rica, it was *La Nación*; in Colón,
Panama, *La Prensa*.[2] Garvey was working in London on the *African Times
and Orient Review*, published by the Black Nationalist and journalist Duse

Mohammed Ali, when he learned about racial conditions in America, and read Booker T. Washington's autobiography, *Up from Slavery*. It was then that "my doom—if I may so call it—of being a race leader dawned upon me," he said.[3] Garvey, the diasporic traveler, had not yet visited the United States. This soon changed. Like tens of thousands of black people migrating from the American South, Garvey joined the wave of West Indians leaving the global south for the United States. Garvey arrived in Harlem, New York, the destination of many black migrants, in March 1916. He had previously founded a racial uplift organization, the Universal Negro Improvement Association (UNIA), in Jamaica in 1914, but brought it with him to the United States and headquartered it in Harlem. And as he had done in other countries, he founded and published a paper, the *Negro World*, the UNIA's official news organ. The paper debuted in 1918, as the Great Migration in which Garvey had been swept up was helping catalyze a sea change for black America that heralded the New Negro era. Unlike his previous papers, however, the *Negro World* helped Garvey make his mark and presence felt like never before.

This chapter examines how the *Negro World* championed the racial consciousness of the New Negro era, promoted New Negro manhood and Garvey as the era's manly New Negro leader, but came to be at the center of an unprecedented war of words waged in the columns of an expanding black press with growing influence over an expanding black public sphere. By the 1920s, the role and reach of the black press were transformed greatly. Migrants' settlement in urban centers across the United States, the opportunities and challenges of urban life, and dramatic changes that had been unleashed in the aftermath of World War I irreversibly altered the social, political, economic, and cultural outlook of black Americans. These changes imbued black people with a vibrant urbanity, new radicalism, and greater intraracial complexity that greatly reshaped the political and racial consciousness of black people. These changes and black people's resulting new outlook helped generate the Harlem Renaissance and its cultural figure, the "New Negro." Amid these seismic changes, the black press proliferated, growing in influence to both reflect and help drive these changes. In 1919, for example, Claude Barnett founded the Associated Negro Press (ANP), a newswire service that provided members of the black press national and international news copy. This helped in many ways to provide the black press a consistent line of coverage on the changing black condition.[4] A wide array of black leaders used the press to address this condition, while also using it as a tool to spread their ideas and promote themselves as leaders.

Perhaps no paper capitalized on the new mood of black America, and the new power of the black press, more than Garvey's *Negro World*.

Yet Garvey sensed a brewing crisis in this moment, as did many other black leaders, though the crisis they perceived would eventually actually erupt among themselves. Initially, they thought that there was a crisis emerging from the effects of the migration, despite its part in having helped positively transform black people.[5] Given the Red Summer and social upheavals resulting from the migration, many black leaders and their organizations were concerned about the prospects of the migrants, how they would fare in the urban, and what postwar society would mean for racial advancement. Consequently, some black leaders increasingly saw the race as a loosed, leaderless mass of people without proper guidance, even as they also thought that this historical moment offered the race tremendous, unprecedented opportunities.[6] Indeed, some periodicals emerged at this time from this context, assuming a role intended to help adjust the race to this juncture and the potential, consciousness, and processes of modernization it was increasingly thought to confer. For instance, the National Urban League, the organization founded in 1911 to help acclimate black migrants to urban environments, started the *Opportunity* in 1923.[7] In a short matter of time, though, the *Negro World* became perhaps the leading paper of the day as the organization it spoke for became the largest membership-based black organization in U.S. history, and a touchstone for the anticolonial movement around the world.[8] Garvey believed himself a seasoned, first-rate journalist, having made a career of it for many years. Before a black public seemingly without proper guidance, Garvey used the *Negro World* as a tool of propaganda intended to direct the race toward his vision for racial advancement. He thought that he and his organization and paper could not simply help adjust the race to the promises of urban life, as many other leaders were trying to do. Instead, he thought he should adjust the race to the prospects of something greater: building an independent African empire. But other leaders still worked to guide the masses to their programs too, using newspapers. And the widespread use of the press by black male leaders as a tool for racial advocacy and self-promotion ultimately put them at loggerheads. When criticism of Garvey's program for racial uplift erupted, he and his critics became rival leaders and rival newspapermen, who ignited a media-based crisis in black male leadership. Anxieties over the proper course for racial advancement for the masses deepened as Garvey and his critics engaged in a vicious battle for influence, if not control, over the black public sphere.

Many of these contending black male leaders and newspaper publishers were based in Harlem. The city became a hub of New Negro thought and activity, as well as the epicenter of intense jockeying for racial leadership among black male leaders through the papers to which they were connected. A number of thinkers, activists, and leaders with opposing viewpoints were in close contact, and so were their papers, making Harlem a deeply contested space as much as it was a space for reimagining and promoting racial unity. Garvey and critics had the press immediately at their disposal to air their ideological differences. Their differences played out publicly in the black press, and typically in caustic and highly gendered terms, particularly from Garvey's side of things. Through bitter attacks and counterattacks, Garvey and other black leaders endorsed a resistant and militant black man as the ideal type of racial leader, though Garvey did this especially by deploying emasculating gendered language against critics. As some scholars have noted, Garvey rose to prominence in part because he articulated so well the militancy of returning black soldiers disappointed that they remained second-class citizens despite their service to the country. This militancy became expressed by many within rhetorics of black manhood during the era.[9] Indeed, Garvey embraced the resistant, militant ethic of New Negro manhood as his model of masculinity. But with the gendered language that came to signify it, Garvey also performed a rhetorical emasculation of his opponents in the *Negro World*, a strategy intended to defend the UNIA, promote his vision for racial advancement, distinguish himself as the only real manly leader of the era, and delegitimize the leadership of critical black male leaders.[10] This strategy of rhetorical emasculation would remain useful to black male leaders for decades in constructing contests of masculinity that helped delegitimize real and perceived rival black men. As black male leadership became tied to print media, their battles in print transformed the press into both a tool for the promotion of black male leadership and a tool for its destruction. In other words, the black press became influential enough to make *and* break black male leaders. Black newspapermen responded to Garvey's attacks with an editorial crusade intended to undermine him and oust him from the country. It became an editorial crusade like other editorial campaigns the black press would wage. This editorial campaign has been less often acknowledged by scholars of the black press, possibly because the contentious intraracial conflict it pointed up counters the traditional celebratory historical narrative of the black press coming together to rail against racial oppression and promote racial unity.[11] But this was "racial unity," at least in the sense of the united front members of the black press formed against Garvey to bring the full brunt of their papers down upon him.[12] Capitalizing on the new power of black newspapers, Garvey and his critics fought to see which leader the black press was going to make or break first.

When Garvey arrived in Harlem, he stepped into a crucible of black intellectual and radical activity, a social landscape dominated by New Negro politics and papers.[13] Harlem attracted massive numbers of southern migrants and black immigrants, as well as aspiring leaders and political agitators. Black artists, poets, writers, activists, and intellectuals involved in the movement heralded a reimagining and reconstruction of blackness, race, community, and self that figured black Americans as modern agents and purveyors of civilization and a unique black culture.[14] By the 1920s, Harlem would become the "de facto capital of black America," as historian Jeffrey O. G. Ogbar phrased it and as many other historians have shown.[15] While the Black Renaissance exploded in other cities across the country, much of the black artistic, political, literary, and intellectual production of the movement emanated from Harlem.[16] In part because of its heavy political activism and influx of blacks throughout the diaspora who, like black Americans, were affected by white supremacy, particularly colonialism, Harlem became a deeply constructive and contested space of cultures, ideas, and ideologies.[17] Here, the black press became especially important because it was a vehicle for channeling political discourse, promoting protest, and building black leadership on racial issues. Many leaders in Harlem led organizations that offered a publication, typically a newspaper, magazine, or newsletter that promoted the ideas of the leader and the agenda of their organization. To illustrate, the NAACP's *Crisis*, A. Phillip Randolph and Chandler Owen's *Messenger*, Cyril Briggs's *Crusader*, William Bridges's *Challenge Magazine*, Garvey's *Negro World*, and many other papers offered competing visions for racial advancement that varied from conservative lines of integrationist uplift to radical subversion inspired by the recent Socialist Revolution. Garvey came to the United States intent on building the UNIA, bringing with him a deeply informed perspective on racial uplift, especially in transnational contexts, gained from his travels throughout the black diaspora.[18] Garvey fell into an orbit of Harlem intellectuals and organizers, working initially with Black Nationalist and Socialist Hubert Harrison, and Socialist journalist A. Phillip Randolph, among others.[19] In fact, Randolph introduced Garvey to his first Harlem audience in the spring of 1917.[20]

By 1919, Garvey had become a major figure on the Harlem scene: membership in his UNIA grew rapidly, and circulation of the *Negro World* reached new heights.[21] His reputation as an effective agitator had also reached governments in the United States, Europe, and the West Indies. A colonial secretary, for example, sent the consul of the United States a letter, suggesting that they should investigate and consider restricting the circulation of several anticolonial black publications. The *Negro World* and Cyril Briggs's *Crusader* were included among the four newspapers listed.[22] The Bureau of Investigation (BOI, later renamed the Federal Bureau of Investigation) began following Garvey in November 1918, sending agents to UNIA meetings in search of evidence of sedition.[23] Authorized by the postwar Red Scare that generated intense anti-immigrant sentiment and a sharp increase in the deportations of foreign-born alleged subversives, the BOI deemed many black leaders in Harlem a threat to national interests.[24] The federal government had censored many black newspapers that were critical of the United States and the federal government during the war. The anticolonial and racially militant editorials of Garvey and other black leaders, in addition to their organizing efforts, made the black press a continued cause for federal concern even after the Red Scare.[25]

But black radical literature was everywhere to be found in Harlem, although Garvey's weekly may have been the most successful. As Amy Jacques Garvey, Garvey's second wife, would put it, the "paper was destined to play a leading part in the Negro Renaissance."[26] In just a few years, it helped transform his organization into the largest black mass movement. Garvey edited the paper, though he had ample help from leading black intellectuals, many of whom also had Caribbean connections. His editors and contributors included W. A. Domingo, Hubert Harrison, William H. Ferris, and John Edward Bruce.[27] These men ran in overlapping intellectual circles in Harlem. A radical Socialist and journalist, Domingo edited the *Negro World* while he also wrote for the *Messenger*.[28] Harrison was a radical Socialist, journalist, author, and street orator from whom Garvey got some of his political ideas. Ferris was a Yale- and Harvard-educated minister, author, and Black Nationalist. Bruce was a former slave and nationally syndicated journalist in the black press, who also founded the Negro Society for Historical Research in 1913. Harrison and Ferris in particular shared Garvey's feelings that black manhood needed to be restored.[29] Garvey also had ample help from black seamen in distributing the paper. Whereas Abbott had used black railroad porters, popular symbols of black masculine mobility during the Great Migration, to distribute his paper in the South, Garvey used black seamen to distribute his paper throughout the black diaspora. They too were symbols of black masculine mobility, as well as symbols of Garvey's black international imaginary, as literary scholar Michelle Ann Stephens notes.[30]

The paper's composition was unique compared with many contemporary black papers. When Garvey first arrived in the United States, the proud journalist thought that "the Negro press had no constructive policy." Denouncing the black press's sensationalism that highlighted crime, "the news published were all of the kind that reflected the worst of the race's character in murder, adultery, robbery, etc.," he said.[31] His *Negro World*, on the other hand, looked nothing like other popular and mass-oriented black papers. His was "A Newspaper Devoted to the Interests of the Negro Race without the Hope of Profit as a Business Investment." Amy Jacques, an eventual writer and editor for the paper, noted that he wanted to "present clean wholesome news."[32] Generally, the *Negro World* covered local chapter business and other news germane to the organizational affairs of the UNIA. It also functioned as Garvey's propaganda machine.[33] Indeed, unlike the mostly integrationist papers of his contemporaries, the *Negro World* was Black Nationalist. The text of Garvey's public speeches was typically published in the paper, usually starting on the front page, the page that most other black newspapers reserved for the most attention-grabbing headlines or pressing current events. Eventually, the paper featured pages in French and Spanish intended to appeal to readers throughout the non-English-speaking black world, further distinguishing it from other black publications.[34] Amy Jacques later wrote a page for women readers with editorials that concentrated "mostly on international subjects." She also organized news clippings for her husband to peruse in order to stay abreast of current events and to incorporate them into his writings and speeches. Occasionally, she advised Garvey on his editorials, though not always successfully. "Sometimes he sought my opinion before going to press," she remembered, "but he would not let me put my blue pencil through his copy where I found superfluity." Some of her suggestions commonly met his retort that "I am writing for the masses—people who have not been accustomed to serious reading matter—I must hammer in what I want to impress on their minds."[35]

In sum, the mass-driven *Negro World* was more committed to an expressly political purpose of issuing Garvey's propaganda than reporting everyday news or entertaining readers. Like other publishers, he was interested in selling papers, but his commercial interests in this regard centered more on building revenue for his political movement.[36] Still, the *Negro World* shared in sides of other black papers' sensationalism. Garvey's comments

"I am writing for the masses" and "I must hammer in what I want to impress on their minds" indicate his intent to use provocative and militant language, editorials, and headlines to try to attract the attention of readers and raise their consciousness. A disgruntled former Garveyite tried to incriminate him before colonial officials in part by citing this sensationalism. "So inciting and inflammable and purposely colored are the news and editorials in this paper," he charged, "that the authorities in several of the islands have been compelled to take energetic action to deny its admittance to those islands and prevent its circulation among the colored people thereof."[37] Indeed, the *Negro World's* militant sensationalism helps explain why many colonial administrations were swift to impose bans and penalties against it, including Rhodesia, Nigeria, Gambia, Costa Rica, and Cuba, to name just a few.[38] Colonial officials also blamed the paper for helping foment uprisings in Dahomey, British Honduras, Kenya, Trinidad, and Cuba.[39]

Many scholars credit Garvey's charismatic leadership and local and national organizers for galvanizing followers, but the newspaper was indispensable to building membership and sympathizers in far-flung areas of the United States and the world where Garvey and UNIA officials did not physically go. Rural black southerners, for instance, may not have been able to see Garvey speak in Harlem or participate in meetings, conventions, and UNIA parades there, but the newspaper brought him, his ideas, and the UNIA's activities close to home.[40] Amy Jacques insisted that "Garvey's front-page articles to the *Negro World* weekly were as forceful and foretelling as his speeches."[41] Readers in the South became as committed to Garveyism and its goals of Black Nationalism, black entrepreneurship, and race-first solidarity as any urban-dwelling member. In fact, the UNIA's membership was strongest not in urban centers but in the rural South, where members and admirers had no point of contact with the headquarters other than the newspaper.[42] Indeed, Rebecca Hall, a reader of the *Negro World* and a Jamaican immigrant working as a domestic in Key West, Florida, may have never seen Garvey. But when her employer, Mrs. Williams, told her to "throw away the darned paper, and never let me see you reading it again!," she answered, "Throw away this paper? You make me laugh, ma'am. . . . This paper is worth more to me than all the jobs you can give me. If I am to go I shall go with this paper, and if I am to stay I'll stay with it."[43] The *Negro World* first appeared with 3,000 copies in 1918; its circulation reached almost 50,000 six months later. Between 1920 and 1921, its circulation rose from 25,000 to 75,000. Garvey acknowledged the role of the paper in helping accelerate the organization's growth. "Being a journalist," he said proudly, "I edited the paper free of cost for the association. . . . By my writings and speeches we were able to build up a large organization."[44] As historian Mary G. Rolinson argues, the *Negro World* "provided both the spark that ignited the ideological inferno of Garveyism and the fuel that sustained it from week to week."[45] And as Abbott and DuBois had tried to do through their papers during the Great Migration, Garvey's *Negro World* became a base from which he launched his claims to racial leadership and attempted to build up black men.[46]

Garvey's messages in public speeches and the paper fit in very well with Harlem's radical politics and intellectual life.[47] Out-of-town papers such as the *Pittsburgh Courier, California Eagle*, and *Baltimore Afro-American* also supported Garvey. The *Courier*, for instance, published "UNIA News," a weekly column.[48] However, at least one newspaper found something negative to say about Garvey. The first mention of him in the *Defender* came in September 1918 and described his being sued by a former employee of the *Negro World*, or Garvey's "little sheet," as the *Defender* described it. The *Defender* followed up in November, reporting on another lawsuit brought against Garvey by another former employee. Abbott's paper again insulted Garvey's. To the paper with the largest black readership in the country, the *Negro World* was "a little two-page paper in Harlem."[49] Perhaps an attempt to belittle a journalistic competitor, these quips at Garvey would not be the *Defender*'s last.

By the 1920s, the circulation of the *Negro World* and the UNIA's remarkable business ventures elevated Garvey, rapidly making him a national leader. Garvey offered an agenda for race progress that prioritized black entrepreneurship. "If we . . . are to become a great national force," Garvey told a group in Baltimore, Maryland, "we must start business enterprises of our own."[50] The latter dimension of his agenda for race progress made a powerful imprint on race leadership at the time and would continue to over the next several decades. This especially appealed to New Negro sensibilities surrounding entrepreneurship and consumerism, in addition to intellectualism and activism.[51] The UNIA established auxiliary corporations: the African Communities League in July 1918, and what would become his most signal accomplishment, a steamship line, the Black Star Line (BSL) in June 1919.[52] Successful black enterprise, on the global scale that Garvey imagined for the UNIA, would do more than just guide the race at this time. It would free black people from economic dependence on whites and, in Garvey's view, earn their respect.[53] Never before had a black organization created, owned, financed, and managed a shipping line.[54] He repeatedly shared this point and story of the purchase of the UNIA's first ship, the *Yarmouth*, with the dollars of black people alone, in speech and print as a testament to his visionary leadership and the potential of black economic solidarity. A contemporary observer recalled that "the ship's launching was spectacular. Thousands were on hand, cheering and waving flags and dangerously jamming the pier." Many had "happily paid a half-dollar to go aboard and shake hands with the all-Negro crew." The UNIA's popularity soared in no small part due to the BSL. Eighty percent of UNIA divisions and chapters formed not long after the purchase of the ship.[55]

But UNIA business enterprises manifested Garvey's gendered conceptualizations of commerce and industry, often linking his promise of black entrepreneurship to the redemption of black manhood. As historian Martin Summers has shown, Garvey was deeply influenced by the Victorian model of the self-made man intent on mastering the marketplace, in addition to several other masculine models coming out of the Victorian era. Garvey paired these models with new ones emerging from changes brought on by World War I, the race riots, urbanization, and New Negro consciousness. To be sure, Garvey picked up on and echoed the prevailing definitions of national greatness established after World War I, particularly the emphasis on naval power, competition, and international trade. His emphasis on building black businesses also echoed the ideas of Booker T. Washington that racial uplift began with land ownership. Yet, rather than counseling the race to remain in the South and make their fortunes there, as Washington had once advised, Garvey departed here from the man whose autobiography inspired him. Drawing on "frontier manliness," as Summers notes, another popular model of manhood in nineteenth-century America, Garvey instead believed black people's land ownership should materialize in Africa. His romanticized African landscape would serve as the launching pad for a black empire—or Negro world. In fact, by 1920, Garvey would send a UNIA delegation to Liberia to begin solidifying plans for farm lands and black repatriation.[56] These ideas of national and imperial greatness shaped Garvey's intent to help black men cultivate proper black manhood. As he explained in the *Negro World*, the world was preparing for "great commercial warfare," an "age of survival of the fittest." Nations everywhere were putting their best men forward, and "the time has come when the Negro must take his stand as a man. If the white man is manly enough to put up a factory, the Negro ought to be manly enough to do the same thing." "The Negro would be less than [a] man" if black people did not compete and lead in this global commercial struggle.[57] To promote the UNIA, Garvey united notions of race, empire, enterprise, militaristic imagery, and masculinity.[58] Through the BSL, "the New Negro has risen in the might of his manhood and he has now determined within himself to . . . play his part as a man . . . now a full grown and wide-awake man."[59]

Garvey believed that the BSL was an opportunity for blacks to gain a commercial chance in a world that was becoming increasingly driven by industry, shaped by imperialism, and remade by working-class, racial, and manly assertions.[60] Accordingly, the BSL represented black people's chance at true manhood, Garvey argued, using a language of masculinity that many black male leaders and writers were increasingly mobilizing to express the aspirations of New Negroes.[61] The BSL would demonstrate to blacks and their oppressors that they too could be independent economic actors, like real men were thought to be, men capable of leading, more than just surviving, the new industrial age.[62] Some skeptics remained, however. In September 1919, the *Defender* again assessed Garvey's activities. "Our Race, it is true, is struggling hard here for justice, but the fiery little man who wants to start a black star line to Africa will find conditions almost bad in his own country, where he might better center his activities. . . . We can well dispense with the help of a man like Garvey."[63] Here, the *Defender* moved from belittling Garvey's "little" paper to deriding him as a "little" man. Editors of the paper decided to attack Garvey on a question of manhood in an attempt to undermine his growing influence.

Garvey argued that the UNIA's entrepreneurial program was the only comprehensive program for racial advancement, economic power, racial pride, and real manhood offered by a black organization. Moreover, the UNIA promised real womanhood for black women. Though Garvey sometimes broadly applied his appeals to manhood to the entire race, including black women by default, he still made particular overtures intended for black women. For example, Garvey delivered a speech in 1918 titled "The Burden of the Negro Woman."[64] Many of his appeals for building up the race and Africa incorporated black women as instrumental parts, but that involvement was always within strict gender roles.[65] He identified as a New Negro, but as historian Martin Summers has shown, Garvey was much like the middle-class men of his era, who were committed to bourgeois and Victorian ideals of masculinity and femininity. These ideals prescribed rigid gender roles for men and women that positioned men as leaders and public actors, and women as domestic helpmates, economic dependents, and political and public nonactors.[66] As a result, women's participation in the UNIA was constrained in many respects, though great in terms of membership. Historian Barbara Bair has shown that while UNIA rhetoric and organizational programs like the Black Cross Nurses elevated black women as "true women"—respectable, ladylike, feminine, and worthy of the economic and physical protection of black men—women's involvement and leadership in the organization was subordinated to the leadership and decision-making of men.

The organizational structure of the UNIA more often rendered women helpmates to men rather than equal partners.[67] In the imminent racial and commercial war of Garvey's imaginary, he predicted that "black men shall die . . . and black women shall succor our men."[68] Indeed, Garvey's masculine rhetoric helped undercut black women's participation in very real terms. Some black women circumvented the gendered restrictions imposed by the UNIA, and on one occasion even organized to protest them.[69] Prominent women leaders, such as Maymie De Mena, Henrietta Vinton Davis, Ethel Collins, and Amy Jacques, over time emerged to hold important roles as national organizers, executive leaders, and spokespersons for the UNIA. Yet they were exceptions to the rule.[70] Garvey appreciated the particular struggles that black women faced, even politicizing the rape of black women by white men as an issue of violence tantamount to the issue of lynching. But his vision of freedom meant that black women would fulfill their proper gender roles so that black men could fulfill theirs, both for the sake of the race.[71] Indeed, in the same breath, Garvey would write that Africa needed the "service of every Black man and woman" and also say that the UNIA represented "the New Negro manhood movement."[72] As historian Deborah Gray White has noted, black women were also motivated by postwar social changes and inspired by the New Negro era, but the rise of masculine-centered appeals in movements like Garvey's helped foreclose black female leadership in the postwar moment. The emergence of pro-masculine leadership, rhetoric, and racial representations in the New Negro era helped usher in the decline of black women–led uplift organizations, such as the National Association of Colored Women.[73]

However, some black women members and supporters identified with the organization's quest for black manhood. They saw it as inextricably intertwined with the achievement and protection of their womanhood.[74] Members of the Women's Auxiliary, who marched in the UNIA's first parade in 1920, wielded a banner that read "God Give Us Real Men."[75] A letter to Garvey from Susie Wilder, a supporter, read, "You are doing good work and I am so glad that you are having much success. . . . If all of us could see through your efforts, what it will do for us and ours, and every man and woman should stand up to their manhood and womanhood, what a great thing it would be."[76]

But Garvey and the UNIA's early successes played out against a backdrop of legal and financial problems and personal conflicts that began to concern other black leaders. Garvey's masculine rhetoric about black entrepreneurship and the promise of UNIA commercial ventures overshadowed his business incompetence and that of UNIA officers. Garvey, in particular, failed to maintain important records, neglected to pay certain federal taxes, and improperly used shareholder monies to pay off UNIA debts. In the spring of 1919, former employees of the BSL suspected him of misappropriating funds, and they contacted New York assistant district attorney Edwin Kilroe. Kilroe summoned Garvey on three occasions in June, and eventually suggested that Garvey incorporate the BSL so that he could protect himself. It was incorporated in Delaware on June 23, 1919.[77] But in July, two BSL officers, Edgar Grey and Richard Warner, filed affidavits against Garvey for misappropriation of funds. The "two Negro crooks," as Garvey described them, prompted a reorganization of BSL management, including the swift replacement of Grey and Warner.[78] In what became his characteristic bombastic style of oratory and writing, Garvey claimed in an August issue of the paper that Kilroe colluded with Grey and Warner because he wanted "to get Mr. Garvey out of the way." Kilroe sued for libel, and Garvey was found guilty and briefly jailed.[79] He later retracted his statements against Kilroe, Grey, and Warner, though libel suits by and against Garvey continued.[80] One black newspaper, the *New York World*, chided that Kilroe "torpedoed and sunk" the BSL. The paper may have intended the statement as metaphorical, but Garvey saw it as slander. He sued the paper for $100,000, though to no avail.[81] Increasingly, black newspapers were becoming organs for political battles that soon took on deeply gendered tones.

After the purchase of the UNIA's first ship, the *Yarmouth*, in September, Garvey traveled to Philadelphia, Pittsburgh, and Chicago to raise funds to pay off the new purchase. While in Chicago, Garvey found himself behind enemy lines, discovering that Abbott's opposition to him did not just exist on paper. Abbott fingered Garvey for breaking the Illinois "blue-sky laws," which were intended to protect the public from fraudulent sellers of securities. Abbott had hired a detective, who found out about the laws. The *Defender* celebrated the arrest, bragging that it would be "derelict if we failed to expose any scheme whereby the members of our race are made the victims of spurious investments." Garvey was fined and released. But with his arrest, the *Defender* declared on its front page that Garvey's ships had sunk, much like the *New York World* had at one point, and like the *New York World*, the *Defender* soon faced a libel suit. Garvey sued Abbott for $200,000. Abbott returned fire with fire, suing Garvey for libel. Garvey was eventually awarded a nominal six cents in the dispute, but was ordered to pay the *Defender* $5,000.[82]

On October 14, 1919, Garvey's troubles turned far more serious than rivalries with other publishers. In New York, George Tyler, a former member of the UNIA, shot Garvey four times. His .38-caliber revolver struck Garvey in the right leg and the right side of his head. Tyler claimed that Garvey owed him for a loan on a failed UNIA restaurant—another business that Garvey and UNIA officers in New York had mismanaged.[83] Garvey survived the life-threatening incident and turned his survival into an example of his manliness. Writing in the *Negro World*, he boasted that the would-be-assassin underestimated how much of a manly New Negro his target was. The "coward" attacked him while he was "unprepared." But Garvey could not be stopped because "the New Negro wants his liberty, and not even the powers of hell will stop him."[84] Increasingly, these internal UNIA problems became public fodder in the black press.

Garvey's financial and legal troubles led to more problems for him and his organization, which in turn inflamed criticism from black leaders. In many ways, critics were right to grow alarmed. Most Garvey scholars agree that he was an inexperienced businessman. At worst, he fatally mismanaged the BSL and prioritized the publicity and symbolism of the BSL over responsible day-to-day operations of the line. At the least, he grossly underestimated shipping costs, market forces, and the financial instability of the UNIA's working-class and working-poor members.[85] Ongoing mismanagement within the BSL compounded Garvey's travails. The *Yarmouth*, renamed the *Frederick Douglass*, had more costly repairs than financial rewards by 1920. The UNIA's other two ships later followed suit. One even capsized.[86] Complicating things further were some of the BSL's officers, who were more loyal to themselves than to the UNIA. For example, the BSL's highest official, Captain Joshua Cockburn, responsible for purchasing deals, inflated ship costs to Garvey so that he could pay himself the difference.[87] The financial troubles of the BSL exposed glaring defects in Garvey's leadership style. New York district attorney Edward Swann investigated BSL finances, while the BOI continued its investigation of Garvey.[88] But the scrutiny of Garvey began to spread beyond government authorities. When the BSL spiraled into sharp financial decline in 1921, black leaders appealed to the highly influential black public sphere to criticize Garvey and attempt to turn public opinion against him.[89]

Though the *Defender* had been taking swipes at Garvey for some time, DuBois was perhaps the first to publish his reservations about Garvey in an analytical manner. In July 1920, DuBois wrote Garvey, insisting that he wanted to publish for *Crisis* readers a "critical estimate" of the UNIA. He asked Garvey to answer a few questions about the organization's finances, membership, and properties.[90] Garvey did not reply.[91] Five months later, DuBois published in the *Crisis* his evaluation of Garvey anyway. DuBois challenged his business management skills. He praised Garvey for his aspirations toward black business ownership on the one hand but condemned him as a "stubborn, domineering leader of the mass" on the other. "When it comes to Mr. Garvey's industrial and commercial enterprises there is more ground for doubt and misgiving than in the matter of character," he wrote. For him, the BSL had too many red flags: the *Yarmouth* was "old and unseaworthy"; it was unclear whether the UNIA owned the other two ships; Garvey was an "inexperienced business man," whose employees were just as incompetent as he. Questioning Garvey's flamboyant style of leadership, DuBois wondered that if Garvey was really committed to racial advancement, "why then does he sneer at the work of the powerful group of his race in the United States where he finds asylum and sympathy?" DuBois took aim more at Garvey's methods and self-promotion than at his overall uplift program, urging him to be financially accountable to a public that he believed Garvey was duping.[92] In the early years of the *Crisis* DuBois had written that "no man [is] so important and no cause so triumphant that The Crisis will not attack them in the defense of right; but the attack will be on principle and not on personalities."[93] For a time, DuBois tried to keep his word.

But Garvey's leadership, however flawed according to DuBois, had actually attracted a following greater than any other black leader of the era, a point that Garvey harped on as critics emerged. He first responded to DuBois in a speech titled "W. E. B. DuBois and His Escapades."[94] In another response published in the *Baltimore Afro-American*, Garvey's sense of himself as an excellent journalist came through, suggesting that he was a better newspaperman than DuBois. Having established his journalistic career as a printer's apprentice and successfully published several papers in different counties, Garvey discussed the challenges DuBois faced in the early years of his journalistic career. "His literary ventures, the 'Moon' and the 'Horizon' [magazines], did not pan out well. . . . It was not until a few Boston and New York philanthropists took Dr. DuBois under their aegis and threw around him the prestige of their wealth and fame that he was able to make the Crisis and the NAACP go. And if these men should withdraw their support and prestige the Crisis might go the way of the 'Moon' and the 'Horizon.'" "Suppose," he said, "some over-inquisitive critic, before the NAACP was two years old, should demand an accounting and ask how much the philanthropists and Negro public were forced to contribute annually to keep the NAACP or the Crisis going, what would DuBois have said?"[95] Within the context of the growing relationship between black leadership and print media, DuBois's failed newspapers demonstrated the inefficacy of his leadership, at least for Garvey. DuBois, who had deployed gendered rhetoric to attack the leadership of Booker T. Washington at the turn of the century, now found the roles reversed as Garvey took shots at his masculinity.[96] "A brilliant student of sociology, a literary genius, a man of letters, Dr. DuBois could grace a chair in any university in the world, but when it comes to mingling with men and dealing with practical affairs, he sometimes strikes the wrong note." "History is not made by hypersensitive critics," Garvey continued, "but the men like Garvey, men of faith and vision, men of one idea . . . have been the makers of history and will be as long as men are men."[97] Yet Garvey did not just respond to DuBois with combative, emasculating words—he also filed a $100,000 libel suit. Garvey charged that DuBois misrepresented the *Yarmouth*, a steel vessel, as a "wooden" one. The case was settled out of court, and the *Crisis* retracted the statement in its next issue.[98]

Libel suits by and against Garvey reflected the intense ideological competition of the New Negro era, jockeying for leadership among rival black men, the spread of litigation in the urban environment, the outsized roles of newspapers, and the importance of the black public sphere. Given the growing climate of inflamed rhetoric against him, and his need to fundraise for the BSL, Garvey saw the suits as opportunities to fill UNIA coffers and/or settle outstanding debts.[99] But more importantly, the suits exemplified how the twentieth-century black press became the terrain on which black male leaders engaged in ideological combat. The black press magnified black male leaders' debates with one another, making their exchanges contentious down to every printed word. And libel suits became one weapon in these exchanges.[100] Garvey's lawsuits, even the threat of them, became a nuisance to members of the black press. For example, the *Norfolk Journal and Guide* later complained that the suits, and threats of suits and physical intimidation, frustrated black journalists' efforts to report on Garvey, even objectively. The *Journal and Guide* had tried, along with other papers, "to point out" to Garvey and his followers "the difference between news and editorial opinion but they look the same to a Garvey disciple." "We have decided to go on and print the news, when it is favorable to the Garvey movement, and when it is not." His supporters were "going to fume and fuss and slander all who do not agree with them anyhow. That has been not only our experience, but the experience of every Negro newspaper that has tried to publish both sides of the Garvey question." The paper encouraged other black papers not "to pander to the Garvey movement" for fear of intimidation. "No paper worth the name will encourage lawlessness, the suppression of free speech and free thinking."[101] In effect, initiating a suit also initiated a challenge to one's leadership, as well as a legal case. The suits illustrated how important a tool the black press was becoming to making and breaking racial leadership because the wrong printed word or phrase, literally, could damage to some extent the credibility of a leader if the suit was successful. Their printed ideological battles could easily become legal warfare that potentially jeopardized the financial stability that a leader needed to sustain their press, movement, and/or leadership. What was at stake in these suits was not just bragging rights over who got the last word and avoided embarrassment, but in part, whose paper, leadership, and visions were more credible before the black public.[102] In a gendered context, the winner of a suit emerged the better leader and the better man.

While DuBois questioned Garvey's business skills, A. Phillip Randolph and Chandler Owen took issue with Garvey's methods and plans for racial advancement. The two Socialists published the *Messenger*, and like DuBois, they tried to evaluate Garvey analytically. In their September 1921 issue, Randolph and Owen disagreed with Garvey over his remedy to European imperialism in Africa. To them, Garvey's plan to build an African empire failed to understand that oppression was not just racial, but also economic, and that capitalism, the source of imperialistic economic exploitation, was the real root of Africa's problems. They insisted that perhaps a boycott of imperial goods, rather than a war with imperial powers, would be more practical in helping to liberate Africa. Another critique repudiated Garvey's plan to start an all-black political party. Randolph and Owen reasoned that the party would be unsuccessful, for it could never become a majority party in the United States; that it wrongly prioritized racial interests over economic ones; and worse, that it could inspire its diametrical opposite—an all-white political party. To them, if there was any political party worth creating and blacks getting behind, it was a Socialist one. For a time, the *Negro World* bore some of the influence of radical Socialist Hubert Harrison, who wrote for the paper, but the *Messenger*'s Socialist publishers continued their criticism. In another article, Randolph tried to provide something of a theoretical explanation for Garveyism. It was "an upshot of the Great World War. It sprang forth amid the wild currents of national, racial and class hatreds and prejudices stirred and unleashed by the furious flames of battle." In other words, Garvey and the UNIA emerged as a result of the war and its role in weakening European imperialism. Garvey represented just one facet of countless oppressed people around the world now under the control of imperial powers since the scramble for Africa in the 1880s, and in reaction, had begun to agitate for their rights, economic and racial.[103] Being a product of these conditions, in Randolph's view, did not excuse the flaws in his philosophy, however. Garvey had fallen for "the doctrine of 'similarity.' . . . To the fallacy of 'white man first' Garveyism would counter with a similar fallacy of 'Negro first.'" For Randolph, Garvey's vision for a black version of everything white betrayed his failure to understand the actual workings of white supremacy and logic of imperialism.[104] By 1921, Randolph, who had introduced Garvey to his first Harlem audience in 1917, would become one of his most acerbic and constant critics.[105]

A litany of other Garvey detractors quickly emerged, solidifying a chorus of critics in the black press. To be sure, much of the criticism of Garvey started out generally principled and even-handed, usually questioning his bombastic leadership style and poor business management, without rejecting his goals of building black businesses, restoring black dignity, or uniting black peoples across the world against racial injustice and colonialism. But Garvey's ongoing financial and legal problems, genuine ideological differences with critics, and petty rivalries motivated critics.[106] It also disturbed the class sensibilities of some leaders that he was organizing the masses, whom those leaders deemed still in need of lessons in proper public deportment.[107] The UNIA held boisterous, costumed public parades during the organization's annual conventions, while Garvey struck the pose of the race's commanding leader during these demonstrations. Interestingly, Garvey and the *Negro World* often stressed to members that they be respectable and "behave decently, always and everywhere." The ideal of the self-made man, to which he in part subscribed, itself emphasized exhibiting restraint and self-control.[108] Garvey contradicted himself here, motivated by the need to construct an empowering public image for black people shared by many New Negro intellectuals, activists, writers, and artists, coupled with his need to influence the black public sphere to his vision for racial advancement. Garvey complicated his conceptions and performances of black manhood by embracing the "physical culture" and "virile" masculinity of New Negro identity that historian Davarian Baldwin has identified as a defining feature of the era.[109] Illustrating Garvey's ideological breadth and inconsistencies, and the often conflicting nature of gender ideologies, Garvey's leadership became highly demonstrative and performative. As one critic, James Weldon Johnson, admitted, Garvey had a "magnetic personality" that wielded a "torrential eloquence, and intuitive knowledge of crowd psychology. He swept the audience along with him."[110] The UNIA leader saw the spectacle of the parades and his bombastic rhetoric in public and print as a performance of the assertiveness and militancy of New Negro manhood. Still, critics took his carefully constructed public image as a display of an inflated personality, as if he was embodying the sensationalism that some observers of the black press decried. He was, they believed, an intemperate man, whose model of manhood was a perversion of New Negro masculinity—a flamboyant and dangerous machismo that would mislead the race.

The growing number of critics and their access to the black press made it possible for them to marshal black newspapers against Garvey, and in turn pushed him to use the *Negro World* to retaliate. As Garvey had used gendered terms centered on a vision of militant New Negro masculinity to popularize his leadership, he used emasculating rhetoric to attack critics. Garvey's critics came to include William Bridges, a New York street orator and publisher of the *Challenge Magazine*; Fred R. Moore of the *New York Age*; William Pickens, author and NAACP field director and former Garvey supporter; James Weldon Johnson, NAACP field secretary, who often wrote scathingly of Garvey in the *New York World* and *Baltimore Afro-American*; and Cyril Briggs, West Indian publisher of the *Crusader* and early Garvey supporter–turned–radical Socialist and anti-Garveyite. Briggs and Garvey had had a number of squabbles that at one time led to a court case. Briggs had successfully sued Garvey for libel, for calling him a white man.[111] Finally, *Defender* publisher Robert S. Abbott rounded out the chorus of critics.

Garvey's earliest opponent published the most influential black newspaper of the day and leveled its full force at Garvey in order to destroy his influence. Abbott's paper made a regular practice of publishing articles against Garvey. For the *Defender*, Garvey was "the president of an invisible empire," a "rabid agitator," and a "loud-mouthed bellower for race rights in this country, who himself is not even a citizen of the United States."[112] The paper gave frequent copy to news about Garvey's misfortunes, concentrating on his financial and legal troubles, discord within the UNIA, his rocky marital affairs with his first wife, and other black leaders' criticisms of him.[113] The *Defender* especially covered the libel suits between Abbott and Garvey. Abbott was a staunch integrationist and likely opposed Garvey's Black Nationalism and separatism. Further, Garvey's emphasis on redeeming Africa elevated visions of black land ownership that countered the *Defender*'s promotion of the urban, points that probably resonated with the mostly southern, rural-dwelling membership of the UNIA. It is also possible that the growing popularity and circulation of the *Negro World* bothered Abbott. Though they both valued black entrepreneurship, the model of the self-made man, and sensationalized discourse as a tool for self-promotion, Garvey reasoned that their rancor revolved around differences in publishing styles, as well as differences in ideology. "Abbott has always, through rivalry and jealousy, been opposed to me, and especially through my not being born in America and my criticism of his dangerous newspaper policy of always advising the race to lighten its black skin and straighten out its kinky hair," Garvey said, criticizing the *Defender*'s advertisements that he thought made the race ashamed of its blackness. "I am also hated by him because of my determination to dignify the term Negro against his policy of referring to the race only as 'race men' or 'race women.'"[114] Either way, Abbott seemed to have a visceral contempt for Garvey. Virtually any news that could embarrass him, smear his movement, and discredit his leadership obtained space in the *Defender*.

Much to the chagrin of Garvey, his opponents had immediate access to the press as publishers and writers, and their differences with him practically shut him out of any positive news coverage in any popular paper other than his own. Garvey's bombastic orations and flamboyant leadership style in part helped create the atmosphere in which his opponents responded to him so negatively. Yet his opposition to their leadership, and their battle for influence and control over the black public sphere, pushed Garvey to become even more caustic in his oratory and leadership style. Garvey and his detractors became resolute in utilizing black newspapers to bring the other down.

Two pivotal events in 1922 became the tipping point for many black leaders, effectively turning them against Garvey for good and accelerating his condemnation in the black press. The first was that Garvey was arrested on charges of mail fraud on January 12.[115] On February 16, Garvey and three UNIA officers, Vice President Orlando Thompson, Treasurer George Tobias, and Secretary Elie Garcia, were indicted. The indictment charged the organization with using the mails to solicit stock investments from UNIA supporters for a BSL that was failing financially and a phantom *Phyllis Wheatley.* It was the ship that the organization hoped to purchase but had not yet.[116] The charges emboldened Garvey's critics and confirmed for them that he was a charlatan, as they had long believed. Claude McKay, whose poem "If We Must Die" became a mantra for New Negroes, was also critical of Garvey. Garvey's "arrest by Federal authorities after five years of stupendous vaudeville is a fitting climax," McKay wrote snidely.[117]

The second event came on June 25, when Garvey accepted an invitation to meet from Edward Young Clarke, acting leader of the Ku Klux Klan (KKK). Clarke presided over a revitalized second-wave KKK that prioritized an aggressive and oftentimes violent fight for racial purity and segregation, among other things. When news of the two-hour meeting between Garvey and Clarke became public, Garvey's critics erupted in outrage.[118] What had been generally even-handed criticism of Garvey transmogrified into a cascade of very bitter ideological and personal attacks articulated in the press. To Garvey's detractors, the meeting exposed his model of leadership for what it really was: that of a dangerous ideologue, a maniacal profiteer of racial divisions, and therefore a threat to black Americans' hopes for integration and racial harmony in America. To them, no *real* race leader would dare meet on any terms whatsoever with the archenemy of black Americans. But Garvey, convinced of his resistant New Negro masculinity, played up the meeting in the *Negro World* as an example of manly leadership. "I have received copies of negro newspapers that have published me as joining hands with the Ku Klux Klan," he explained, but he claimed that he had met with Clarke in order to know more about the organization so that blacks could effectively confront them.[119] He contended that Clarke insisted that the United States was a white man's country and the KKK intended to keep it that way, confirming that separation was the only solution for racial advancement. Garvey thought he was doing a controversial but necessary thing that other black male leaders "have not the nerve" to do.[120]

Black leaders' outrage channeled into the "Garvey Must Go" campaign, the movement to oust him from the country. And with its participants embracing the assertiveness and militancy of New Negro identity, the campaign laid bare an all-out war in print between Garvey and his critics. The supposed crisis confronting a leaderless mass of black people had now turned into an actual crisis in black male leadership. The campaign was initiated a month after Garvey's meeting with Clarke by Randolph, Owen, and their Friends of Negro Freedom, a trade-unionist organization they founded in 1920 along with Carl Murphy of the *Baltimore Afro-American* and some

NAACP officials to oppose the UNIA.[121] The campaign strove to build a political and cultural atmosphere aimed at undermining his influence in America and abroad by hosting anti-Garvey meetings, encouraging federal investigations of UNIA business practices, encouraging his deportation, and denouncing him in various black newspapers.[122] Historian Theodore Kornweibel put it pointedly: "Organized opposition to this West Indian organizer and his followers reached its peak at the same time as did the Universal Negro Improvement Association, a peak of inflamed rhetoric, bitter charge and counterdenunciation." Historian Theodore Vincent called it "a bleak period in Afro-American history."[123] Randolph dubbed Garvey "the white Ku Klux Kleagle's Black Ku Klux Eagle" and the "Honorable Black Kluxer"—sarcastic snips at Garvey's imperial titles within the UNIA.[124] "What sort of newspaper is the *Negro World* anyway," Randolph asked in an attack on Garvey's paper, "which devotes its front page, the news page of every modern civilized, recognized newspaper in newspaperdom, to the varporings, imbecile puerilities and arrant nonsense of a consummate ignoramus?"[125] Garvey retaliated against the campaign by filing nine libel suits "against newspapers and Negro speakers . . . publishing or making slanderous statements concerning him." He also retaliated by waging his own campaign against them in the *Negro World*: "Some say[,] 'Garvey must go,' but we will see after a short while who must go."[126] Garvey succinctly captured this battle to break a rival black male leader.

Garvey prepared for war. He had been attacked once while he was "unprepared." This would not happen again. This war was a discursive and ideological battle, to be sure, in which the paper that had popularized Garvey's leadership increasingly became the forum for his public defense, deepening the competition with critics over whose message was going to gain sway over the black public sphere. Garvey may have indeed been an inexperienced businessman, but he was not an inexperienced journalist. Facing a political, legal, and media assault like never before, Garvey seemed to prepare in every way possible, including sharpening his printing arsenal. For instance, agent "800," an undercover BOI agent placed in the UNIA, reported to his superiors that on April 28, 1922, Garvey had purchased a printing plant at 2305 Seventh Avenue in New York. For the price of $12,000, Garvey was again poised to manage a printing establishment, as he had done as an ambitious eighteen-year-old. For a federal government interested in suppressing supposed subversives, including black papers they deemed radical, Garvey's latest purchase concerned the BOI greatly. "With this plant," 800 concluded, "he will be able to put out a vast amount of propaganda. He bought it as a commercial adventure but the fact is that it will be used more to print his own propaganda than for any other purpose."[127] The potential of the plant presented a problem for the BOI, as well as for critics. Garvey would be able to issue more propaganda and respond to opponents with even more frequency and efficiency.

Another way Garvey prepared for war was by couching his defense in the cultural politics of the New Negro era, asserting that the legal charges and criticisms of him represented an attack on New Negro manhood. Garvey unleashed a barrage of emasculating rhetoric to delegitimize critics, helping produce their most poisonous exchanges. Garvey marshaled the militant masculine rhetoric of the era that had become popular in the wake of black resistance to the Red Summer and ongoing violent attacks on black people. This rhetoric became increasingly deployed by black leaders, intellectuals, writers, and poets in staking claims to personhood, blackness, and racial leadership.[128] And many newspapermen mobilized this rhetoric too. For example, Roscoe Dunjee, publisher of the *Oklahoma City Black Dispatch*, declared following the riots, "Now the Negro is a man, a free man. I might say to make clearer my point that you have now with you a NEW NEGRO."[129] The *Kansas City Call* put it thusly: "The NEW NEGRO, unlike the old time Negro 'does not fear the face of day.'" Rioters "really fear[ed] the Negro is breaking his shell and beginning to bask in the sunlight of real manhood," stated the *Chicago Whip*. "The New Negro has arrived with stiffened backbone, dauntless manhood, defiant eye, steady hand and a will of iron," W. A. Domingo remarked in the *Messenger*.[130]

But as many blacks used this rhetoric to claim their value as human beings against racism, Garvey used it to claim the value of his leadership against critics. "The new Negro is here and he is not going to yield up without a fight," he declared to the black press.[131] The arrest was "but propaganda of certain European governments by which they will be able to dampen the spirit and ardor of the New Negro," Garvey said. "The new Negro likes a good fight," he continued; "they are going to get what they are looking for." "We came forward with a manhood program. It is so big they cannot understand it."[132] The "governments" prosecuting him were not acting alone, however: "behind it all is the Negro traitor . . . the Negro plotter; behind it all are those who have something to lose if the Universal Negro Improvement Association succeeds in its program." Critical black leaders had insulted his manhood, so he believed, because "I have no cause to rob anybody." "I was endowed with strength and ability always to do something for myself. . . . The man who steals, the man who defrauds another man, is the poor fellow who has lost confidence in himself." Garvey contended that he was too zealous a man to waver from his purpose in the face of a challenge, and that the members of his movement possessed the same kind of manly mettle. "I feel sure we must have made some real men . . . men who can face any crisis; men who can stand up anywhere and be ready to live and be ready to die." Under the banner of the UNIA, Garvey and his supporters were going to teach a "signal lesson" to those who had "no respect for the Negro and for Negro leadership."[133]

Garvey was deeply shaped by the gendered thinking of his era, and he wielded the *Negro World* to focus on attacking the manhood of his critics because he saw it as evidence of one's ability to lead. To be sure, he was well aware that the BOI was mounting a legal case against him, and he did not dismiss the federal government as one source of his troubles, for *they* were the ones actually prosecuting him—not his critics. In fact, his critics were not politically powerful enough to gain the support of either the U.S. government or colonial governments to the extent that Garvey imagined or argued. However, it did work to their benefit that the BOI and the Department of Justice were just as interested as they were in muting Garvey's influence. Still, Garvey chose to argue in public and in the *Negro World* that his critics were the chief conspirators in an "international plot to discredit" him.[134]

Arguing that black leaders were the impresarios of his legal troubles accomplished primarily two things for Garvey. First, blaming black leaders rather than the federal government helped him avoid exacerbating tensions with the BOI and the Justice Department. Second, by blaming critics, he tried to undermine their immense power in the black press to denounce him. Coverage of Garvey in major black papers had become overwhelmingly one sided and negative. As he put it, "a few organizations and a large number of Negro newspapers lined up against us who have been laying propaganda. . . . They have done everything. You have seen the big headlines about [the arrest]. The Chicago Defender had it in big headlines six inches deep in red. . . . They have manufactured all kinds of willful, malicious, wicked propaganda."[135] He complained too about his negative coverage in white papers. "Once upon a time you could not get [the white press] to mention anything about a Negro, excepting when he committed some hideous crime. . . . Now, this Universal Negro Improvement Association is causing them to spend hundreds of thousands of dollars annually to send cables and to relay messages around the world, to tell about the activities among negroes."[136]

Still, his focus remained the black press, and compared with contemporary black publishers, Garvey again thought himself the superior journalist. He even felt that his paper had helped spur other black publications to begin "publishing international news and writing intelligent editorials on pertinent subjects."[137] He took them to task for what he saw as their incompetency, rank sensationalism, profiteering, and denigrating advertisements that embarrassed the race. In fact, delegates at the UNIA's Third Annual International Convention in August 1922 devoted some of their sessions to discussing the merits of the black press. Delegates formed a committee on the future policy of the black press. Committee members recognized that the black press "can make or mar the entire race" and recommended that the association collaborate with members of the black press and help establish a "code of journalistic ethics" and an "Editor's Day . . . devoted to the discussion of matters affecting the Negro press and public."[138] For Garvey, black papers "delighted in carrying in bold print on their front pages the worst feature[s] of Negro life, advertising the evils and shortcomings of the race." He singled out Abbott's *Defender* as the leading culprit in this regard, pointing especially to the paper's advertisements of skin-bleaching products. The *Negro World* advertised beauty preparation products too but excluded ones of the skin-lightening variety.[139] Skin-bleaching products "destroyed the racial pride and self-respect of the race." Ultimately, black publishers promoted material "no matter how vile, or how discrediting to the race, so long as they were paid a dollar or five dollars or ten dollars." Early scholars of the black press noted this too. For example, Eugene Gordon, the black editor of the *Boston Post*, wrote a series around the mid-1920s that said black newspapers "resemble their more yellow contemporaries" in which "tales of murders, in all their gory details . . . [were] unnecessarily played up" along with "simple tales of marital lapses and dissatisfactions." Scholar Frederick G. Detweiler pointed to Abbott specifically. "The *Defender* often uses its red type to add prominence to news of crime."[140] As for Garvey's analysis, "We have a bunch of speculators," he concluded, "who call themselves journalists who do not know the first principles of journalism." Interestingly, Garvey seemed to appreciate the dialectical relationship between sensationalized crime reports and stories of racial uplift, even as he criticized other members of the black press on this measure. The *Negro World* sometimes printed crime stories that enabled its writers to make particular arguments about improving the race, racial purity, and Black Nationalism. Still, Garvey declared that the UNIA "had to establish a press," meaning the *Negro World*, because without it, he reasoned, "we have none."[141]

A month after the convention, Chandler Owen circulated a questionnaire to members of the black press, in addition to several prominent black businessmen, writers, and scholars. Twenty-five black men in total received the questionnaire "for the purpose of a symposium" in the *Messenger*, another effort of the "Garvey Must Go" campaign. It would publicize what individual black leaders in different lines of work thought of Garvey. Owen also intended to share with the men what he thought to be the criminal machinations of Garvey and his supporters to combat the "Garvey Must Go" campaign with intimidation. In a note preceding the questionnaire, Owen reported that members of the KKK had sent a severed human hand to Randolph in the mail, "directing him to cease his attacks in his *Messenger* Magazine and immediately become a paid-up member in the Garvey machine." There was no actual evidence connecting Garvey or his devotees to the eerie incident. Still, three questions followed this shocking bit of information: "Do you think Garvey's policy correct for the American Negro?," "Do you think Garvey should be deported as an alien creating unnecessary mischief?," and an open-ended "Remarks:." Respondents included historian Carter G. Woodson; Emmett J. Scott, now secretary-treasurer of Howard University; Kelly Miller, dean at Howard University; Carl Murphy of the *Baltimore Afro-American*; Joseph Bass of the *California Eagle*; DuBois; and Abbott. Most of them found Garvey's program to be problematic. Some flat out considered him "a dangerous character," though not all of them thought he should be deported. Abbott seemed too busy to provide a response himself. His assistant replied for him, stressing that "Abbott believes that Mr. Garvey's policy is not correct for the American Negro" and that Garvey should show his "sincerity" for the leadership of black Americans "by becoming a citizen of these United States." But Miller dissented, writing that Garvey had the right to share his ideas. He was "surprised" that the second question "should come from any Negro." "Freedom of speech is the bulwark of the weak; suppression is the weapon of the strong. . . . By no means should the oppressed become oppressor, nor the persecuted turn persecutor." The *Messenger* published the results of the questionnaire in December 1922.[142]

In general, black critics pegged Garvey a race traitor and dangerous leader in their papers. He countered by doing the same in his. His reputation in the black public sphere was sacred to him—it was critical to his fame, and now his vindication. His *Negro World* had in part launched him to national and international leadership, but now Garvey's *Negro World* faced a challenge from virtually every major black paper. Garvey was determined to clear his name and attack his critics in the *Negro World*, and his critics were determined to match that effort with equal force. For Garvey, their kind of leadership posed a threat to black freedom because it cowed before whites, did not build an ethic of self-reliance among black peoples, and failed to restore black manhood. Hence, the *Negro World* framed Garvey's leadership and the UNIA as the only pathways to a redeemed black manhood, and used emasculating rhetoric to explain attacks by critics and condemn their opposition. "For centuries we have been the underdogs of the world," he contended; "for centuries we have been regarded as less than men; but within the last few years a serious attempt was made by an organization known as the Universal Negro Improvement Association to lift the Negro from his ancient position as forced upon him by his so-called superior master to that of a man's place in the world. . . . Hence the international plot."[143]

Gendered language that Garvey had usually used to emasculate critics in years past grew venomous in order to vindicate himself and his vision, as well as win the support of those who believed in the redemption of black manhood. Some scholars have found that Garvey's tirades against the color line in America and across the globe grew increasingly conservative and less bombastic as his legal problems mounted, but his gendered rhetoric did not.[144] This is important to note for several reasons. First, his increased use of this rhetoric allowed him to continue calling out critics in a language that did not necessarily exacerbate the legal charges against him, or ongoing libel suits in which he was embroiled. Second, his increased use of this rhetoric demonstrates the extent to which he construed this conflict with critics as a personal attack on his masculinity, despite ideological differences with opponents. Finally, waging the ideological battle in gendered terms strove to strike a sympathetic public reaction. To a black public that embraced New Negro culture and politics, his gendered language of militancy and self-defense tried to appeal to the black masses' own beliefs in manhood.[145] Indeed, popular support for Garvey increased as black leaders came down on him harder, perhaps in part because of this robust masculinized defense.[146]

Believing that his critics were working together in a conspiracy to bring him down, Garvey thought it was a clear sign that they were not real men brave enough to confront him face-to-face. Here, Garvey again turned to the performative, "physical culture" and "virile" masculinity of New Negro identity to use pugilistic imagery to condemn his critics, references that invoked a sport viewed by many as the ultimate test of masculine prowess.[147] That Garvey and critics were increasingly exchanging verbal blows, back and forth with invective after invective, convinced him of this even more. "I am going to fight on with gloves or without gloves, hitting above the belt and below the belt," since he felt that they were not fighting fair.[148] "The Universal Negro Improvement Association likes a clean fight," Garvey insisted, "an open fight. . . . Why try to stab in the back . . . those who are behind the arrest[;] why wont you come out like men[?]"[149] "Only cowards fight in ambush. . . . This is a period of test," he declared. "Take the government away for one minute and let us go for them and in ten days we will crush them out of existence."[150] Some of his critics ridiculed his bodily dimensions as "portly," "fat," and "Lilliputian," perhaps suggesting that Garvey was physically unfit for the muscular demands of the sport he often referenced to confront critics.[151] Interestingly, Amy Jacques shared that Garvey usually "ate sparingly of lean meats because, he said, 'A full stomach slows up my thinking machine.'" In Garvey's estimation, he was simply "robust in his mind and his physical body."[152] He also asserted that his and the UNIA's politics were cut from the same cloth as the first black heavyweight boxing champion, Jack Johnson. For many blacks at the time, Johnson was the premier symbol of New Negro masculinity.[153] To Garvey, "the age of turning the right cheek if you are hit on the left is past. This is a Jack Johnson age, when the fittest will survive."[154] Unlike Johnson, who fought against real boxers, Garvey was engaged in an imagined physical fight with ideological opponents, whom he represented as "Old" Negroes, in direct contradistinction to his New Negro. Because they were too cowardly to come out in the open and fight him one-on-one, they were therefore bereft of the manhood necessary to lead the race effectively.

Randolph recognized Garvey's common pugilistic references, though comically. In the *Messenger*, he parodied an imaginary bout between Garvey and DuBois, using some of the actual words the two leaders had exchanged against one another at different times. "First round: Garvey leads, raining blows on DuBois' head: 'DuBois goes to Peace Conference to betray Negro peoples of the world. . . . Garvey lands staggering blow to jaw: 'DuBois is the agent of the National Association for the Advancement of *Certain* People.'" Though the fictitious fight initially seemed to be going in Garvey's favor, much to the dismay of "scrappy Weldon Johnson," sitting ringside and threatening to enter the fight in order to defend his NAACP colleague, DuBois ultimately leveled Garvey. However, the "decision is reserved on account of a charge by Kid Garvey that Battling DuBois struck foul blow below the belt, and that gloves were loaded."[155]

Though Garvey's allusions to physically fighting his critics were more hyperbole than actual invitations, Garvey *was* determined to take on all his opponents in a contest of masculinity within the *Negro World*. This would be the first of many more contests of masculinity within the black press. These contests constituted discursive matches between rival black men, who jockeyed for racial leadership, and were usually couched in highly gendered rhetoric as the men involved sought to displace their rival and their model of manhood. These contests usually did not involve women because the perceived intellectual, rhetorical, and manly demands of the contests could only be met by men, it was thought, beliefs that helped exclude black women's leadership at different times as the manly victor of the bout was thought to gain racial leadership. And Garvey embraced this. Calling out the organization of his former comrade Cyril Briggs, Garvey said, "That paper organization known as the African Blood Brotherhood" was "going to be dealt with."[156] After the "Garvey Must Go" campaign began, he emasculated Randolph and Owen as "those two boys who make up the Socialist Party." He attacked Pickens and Bagnall as servile men: "Whatsoever these Negroes do, they do it carrying out the commands of white men." Behind Randolph, Owen, Bagnall, and Pickens were white men from whom their organizations drew financial support, a glaring sign of dependence and therefore unmanliness in Garvey's view. To all of them, Garvey issued a manly "challenge": "Now I say, Pickens, Dubois, Weldon Johnson, Bagnall, Chandler Owen, Philip Randolph, come to Liberty Hall, state your case . . . if you are men—come across now."[157] Besides ideology, grades of manliness made another pivotal difference between him and rivals, Garvey asserted. He believed simply, "I am a man," and as such, it was impossible for "any other man to outdo me under the same circumstances."[158] Therefore, only his leadership was capable of giving to blacks the proper weapon to use in the fight for freedom: the "spirit of fearing no one," he claimed. "No longer should he [that is, any black man] act as a coward, or in a cringing way, exhibiting fear wherever he goes, but in a law-abiding, peaceful manner assert his manhood, and let the world know that he intends to fight for his rights and for his ideals. Then and then only will he be universally respected as a man, and treated with equality as such."[159] This idea that real manhood was an effective weapon in black people's fight for freedom would continue to reverberate for decades to come.

But for Garvey, there was no greater foe, and no greater symbol of the failure and unmanliness of black leadership, historically and otherwise, than DuBois and the NAACP.[160] As historian Martin Summers also notes, DuBois and the NAACP were Garvey's most constant targets.[161] "Among our bitterest critics and opponents are W. E. B. DuBois, James Weldon Johnson and their National Association for the Advancement of Colored People, yet, these persons have not the manhood to match the intelligence of their Association with that of the Universal Negro Improvement Association," Garvey charged.[162] DuBois represented to Garvey "a lazy dependent mulatto," his ultimate foil as a black man and black leader. DuBois had a mixed racial ancestry, a liberal racial agenda, and an elite education that he obtained in part at prestigious historically white universities. He had helped form an organization dedicated to racial advancement with the help of whites. And "in all his journalistic, personal and other business efforts he has failed," Garvey added.[163] All this made DuBois the consummate "old" Negro— servile, submissive, and only "appointed" by whites to lead the race.[164] The NAACP was out of step with the New Negro's racial politics, largely because it was run by whites and blacks who were detached from the sufferings of the black masses. The *Negro World* represented Garvey as the complete opposite of DuBois in terms of heritage, leadership, ideas, and authenticity as a black man. Accordingly, the UNIA was founded by blacks and was run by them to demand the freedom of black peoples and the independence of Africa. Garvey portrayed himself as heralding a sharp break with moribund and obsolete black male leadership, signaling the beginning of a more manly leadership supported by the black masses.[165] Garvey's penchant for referring to himself in the third person may speak to how he thought of himself in this regard, as if his public persona was indeed something greater than himself, his avatar even, as literary scholar Henry Louis Gates has suggested about New Negro cultural politics.[166] To Garvey, his leadership was the kind that the black masses needed and desired, and his and the UNIA's growing influence had come about precisely because the old guard had failed as race leaders and as men.[167] As this foil, Garvey returned to DuBois and the NAACP repeatedly to help explain what Garvey saw as the categorical failure of black leadership.[168]

Critics other than DuBois and the NAACP did not escape Garvey's attacks, to be sure, but with DuBois and the NAACP in particular, Garvey made facile, disparaging characterizations along a rigid binary of manly versus unmanly, strong versus weak. In addition to making blanket condemnations of black male leadership, Garvey often reduced very complex ideological differences with DuBois and other critics, and legitimate critiques of his flawed business management to this dichotomy of gendered terms. Garvey stressed not only the value of his own manhood but also masculinity as an appropriate unit of analysis in judging the efficacy of black leaders and their goals for racial progress.[169] To Garvey, even DuBois's clothing showed that DuBois was too effete to lead effectively. "Any man who believes that he can win a cause of human liberty sitting in a drawing room and wearing silk stockings and refusing to soil his shoes or his shirt or his collar is a misguided man. In order to lead you must be rough."[170] Here, DuBois was the reclusive, prim, and brooding intellectual, whereas Garvey was the active and demonstrative manly black leader, fearlessly engaging the outside world to labor strenuously for the black masses. In reality, Garvey and DuBois both dressed like men of their class and era. But in Garvey's mind, they dressed markedly differently, reflective of their levels of manliness. Garvey thought that he dressed like a man of the people, and during UNIA parades as the commanding imperial leader of his imagined independent African nation. Yet DuBois mocked Garvey's imperial regalia as the "dress rehearsal of a new comic opera."[171]

Garvey's attacks on DuBois and the NAACP also included attacks on DuBois's and the organization's sources of funding as further evidence of their unmanly leadership. Garvey contended that "programs that are put over by charity and philanthropy are circumscribed or limited. A program for liberty has never been put over by charity and by philanthropy but, on the contrary, by sacrifice." Black leaders dependent on the philanthropy of whites represented a prostrate leadership to Garvey, "going down on the knee and begging for help, so as to insure [sic] their luncheon and supper—a bread and butter leadership."[172] He advised readers of the *Negro World* to "beware of those Negro leaders who are too much in the company of the othe[r] fellow (whites). . . . Any Negro whom you see too much in the company of the othe[r] fellow is a dangerous Negro."[173] Garvey pushed his ridicule of the interracial leadership of the NAACP as a sign of weakness as far as it would go, even invoking imagery of taboo interracial sex within the NAACP: "Anything that is black, to him, is ugly. . . . It is no wonder that DuBois seeks the company of white people. . . . He likes to dance with white people, and dine with them, and sometimes sleep with them." This was a cardinal sin before Garvey's emphasis on racial separation and racial purity, as well as one for whites who had lynched black men under the same idea.[174] Garvey's bitter gendered rhetoric against DuBois strove to belittle the foremost black intellectual and civil rights leader of the day precisely because he was arguably the foremost contemporary black male leader, as well as a leading black male publisher, social positions that Garvey wanted for himself, but thought only "manly" men deserved.[175] Garvey's emphasis on manly leadership as necessary to racial advancement helped reinforce the conflation between black leadership and rigorous masculinity that would become a hallmark of Black Nationalism in the 1960s.

The *Negro World*'s emasculating rhetoric against various black leaders was visible for all to read. The resistance of Garvey and his critics to one another, and their assertiveness and fierce tactics of self-defense, demonstrated, at least discursively, the militancy that represented New Negro manhood. Their verbal sparring revealed their investment in ensuring that black people had the "right" kind of black male leadership with the "right" vision and public image, points that would continue to be crucial to the black freedom struggle. But the acrimony between Garvey and critics again went beyond print. It was *Crusader* publisher Cyril Briggs who assisted the BOI in bringing charges against Garvey in the first place. William J. Burns, a BOI agent, had been working to build a case against Garvey for some time. It was a case that the BOI almost did not have until agent 800 found that Briggs, disgruntled with Garvey, had been pressing the post office department to prosecute Garvey for using the mails to promote a UNIA-owned ship that it did not really own. Still, it took fifteen months for the case to go to trial because of a lack of judges.[176]

Throughout the course of this battle for control over the black public sphere, the torrent of criticism had appreciable effects on Garvey's standing among blacks, even dividing many of his followers into opposing camps. As noted earlier, the negative position of some prominent blacks could be seen in the *Messenger*'s publication of the symposium on the "Garvey question."[177] But the *Defender*'s criticism of Garvey, for example, won him the support of papers like the *Chicago Whip*, one of the *Defender*'s local competitors. It seems that as rivalries went in Harlem, competing papers in the same cities elsewhere only stiffened existing competitions over Garvey.[178] The battle revealed Garvey's true devotees, who only cleaved to the UNIA and strengthened their support for him as critics' attacks confirmed their beliefs that he was their persecuted leader, possibly seeing attacks on him as attacks on their manhood too. In addition to issuing offensives from the *Negro World*, Garvey went on speaking tours across the country to shore up public support, especially as members of the "Garvey Must Go" campaign conducted speaking tours too. An intelligence officer trailed Garvey on one of these tours through Los Angeles, San Francisco, and Oakland, California, in June 1922. The officer reported to federal officials, "The negroes seem to have a childish faith in him. This faith in Garvey makes for strength. He has many followers among the educated negroes as well as the ill[it]erate." British colonial officials worried that Garvey planned to make a "speaking tour of the world" that would target some of their colonies in order to combat the "misrepresentation" of the UNIA.[179] Garvey redoubled his media-based efforts to counter critics by starting another paper in 1922, the *Negro Daily Times*. The publication was short lived, however.[180] Some followers in New York, Philadelphia, Cleveland, Pittsburgh, Toronto, Chicago, and Cincinnati were so committed to the vision of their besieged leader that they defended him against critics using violence. Even DuBois had been "threatened with death by men declaring themselves his followers," he stated.[181] But there were also followers who reversed course. Garvey lost Hubert Harrison, one of his respected editors, who resigned in November 1921.[182] Garvey also lost the support of Joseph and Charlotta Bass, publishers of the *California Eagle*. The criticism, and later the federal charges, compounded existing fissures within the UNIA. Some UNIA chapters began to fracture by 1922. Some followers not only apostatized but also came to challenge Garvey's leadership and organization outright. For example, Reverend James Eason, the American leader of the UNIA who had had rancorous disagreements with Garvey for some time, founded a rival organization, the Negro Improvement Alliance, after being expelled from the UNIA in August 1922. In February 1923, the next leg of Garvey's public relations effort to combat critics, as well as improve his image before whites, appeared. It was the first volume of a collection of his essays organized and edited by Amy Jacques titled *The Philosophies and Opinions of Marcus Garvey*.[183] When Garvey's trial was approaching, the prosecution solicited some of his defectors to testify against him. Eason was going to be one of them until on January 1, 1923, alleged loyal Garveyites shot him before he could. He died three days later. Ostensibly, some of the faithful were willing to kill for Garvey.[184]

The continued delay in Garvey's trial, black leaders' outrage over his meeting with the leader of the KKK, and Eason's murder prompted Owen and eight others, including Abbott, Pickens, and Bagnall, to write U.S. attorney general Harry Daugherty on January 15, 1923. They urged Daugherty to make haste in prosecuting Garvey, while disclosing some of their class sensibilities, as well as the role of their media-based rivalry in shaping their hostilities toward Garvey's movement. They argued that the UNIA's membership comprised "the most primitive and ignorant element of West Indian and American Negroes," a mélange of "ministers without churches, physicians without patients, lawyers without clients and publishers without readers."[185] It is striking that members of the black press, who had themselves been the targets of government surveillance and repression a few years earlier, now encouraged federal officials to investigate a black publisher. And the BOI seemed to appreciate this. In the weeks following the Daugherty letter, agent William J. Burns received a letter stating that black leaders' problem with Garvey "reduces itself to a cannibalistic scheme of one rival getting rid of the other by annihilation or otherwise."[186] Next, Carl Murphy of the *Baltimore Afro-American* authored an editorial pressing Daugherty to explain the delay.[187] Garvey published the letter to Daugherty in the *Negro World* to expose the "enemies of their own race."[188] Interestingly, DuBois, the leader whom Garvey considered his greatest foe and wrongly blamed as the main source of his troubles, refused to participate in this effort to take him down. While Garvey was certainly "a thoroughly impractical visionary," DuBois said, he thought critics focused on the wrong things about Garvey, such as his character. DuBois insisted at the time that Garvey should not be deported.[189] But leaders of the "Garvey Must Go" campaign certainly thought so. Many of them had criticized him for his flamboyant public displays without giving serious consideration to their part in contributing to this newspaper-based crisis in black male leadership that pointed up an unflattering public spectacle perhaps no less flamboyant on their end.

On May 18, 1923, Garvey's trial finally began. A few days earlier, he attempted to have the judge, Julian W. Mack, replaced for reasons in part having to do with the opposition Garvey faced from the black press. Garvey's petition to the court argued that Mack was a member of the NAACP and reader of the *Crisis*, which, under the editorship of one of his opponents, had denounced him. It was Garvey's "honest belief" that Mack "would be unconsciously swayed to the side of the Government against this petitioner . . . for, as a reader of the 'Crisis,' it is fair to assume that your Honor has read the bitter and unfavorable criticisms of the petitioner and his work." Mack's very subscription to the paper had "assisted in the circulation of matter adverse" to Garvey. Garvey could not therefore have "a fair and impartial trial," he reasoned.[190] Mack had in fact made contributions to the NAACP, but affirmed that this would have no bearing on his role in the case. Garvey's motion was denied.[191] Still, he affirmed to readers of the *Negro*

World that "Garvey goes to court like a man," seeing the case less as a trial and more as a showdown and a test of masculinity. "Don't be afraid about Garvey; Garvey knew the consequences and, like a man, he is going to face it. . . . For the first time probably in the history of the Negro you will see a real Negro fight, a real battle for racial liberation."[192] Indeed, Garvey transformed the proceedings into a final display of his performativity, bombastic oratory, flamboyant style of leadership, and New Negro masculinity. The drama unfolded beginning the second day of the trial, when Garvey retired his lawyer, Cornelius McDougal, and decided to represent himself.[193] Garvey explained that when Edgar Grey, Richard Warner, and Edwin Kilroe, the men with whom Garvey had his first legal skirmishes, were called to testify, he decided to take over. He "desired to give himself the fullest opportunity to prove his innocence . . . on his own account."[194] If this indeed was going to be the manly showdown that he imagined, then he needed to demonstrate his combat skills and fight for himself.

Perhaps knowing that his comments would be published in his *Negro World*, and that other black papers would be reporting on the trial too, Garvey decided to use his defense to appeal to the influential black public sphere and vindicate himself before the New Negro masses, as much as the judge and jury.[195] His closing argument made this appeal especially clear. In what the *Negro World* called "GARVEY'S BRILLIANT SPEECH," he denied the credibility of the charges and the testimony of the witnesses. In fact, Garvey impugned the character of the witnesses. Grey was a "scoundrel"; Warner was a "rubber-stamp man without any character"; Kilroe was a "man of vengeance" who "desires to get even with Garvey."[196] When the prosecution presented *Negro World* articles as evidence against him, an embattled Garvey responded, "Garvey admits writing some of the articles in the Negro World. Garvey denies some of those articles." He explained that "at times Garvey would be away and his articles would not get to New York in time and someone would write [the] articles and stick Garvey's name [on] them. I knew the phraseology was not mine, but the district attorney seized upon it as [a] valuable bit of evidence."[197] Here, the seasoned journalist denied, to some extent, contributing to his own paper. He was the victim of his own busy work uplifting the race, and as a result, was sometimes taken advantage of by subordinates. But Garvey reaffirmed the vision of the UNIA. "Study the race question and you will find that the program of the Universal Negro Improvement Association and the Black Star Line is the solution of the problem which confronts us, not only in the country, but throughout the world." He finally insisted, "I ask for no mercy.

If you say I am guilty, I go to my God as I feel, a clear conscience and clean soul." "The district attorney will tell you it is Garvey, Garvey, Garvey. Garvey is the master mind, Garvey is the genius; Garvey is but a man."[198]

Garvey was confident in this performance, almost nonchalant about the case, fearless even, at least as he argued before New Negroes with language intended to appeal to their gendered sensibilities. "Garvey has just started to fight," reported the *Negro World*. "Garvey has not given his first exhibition of his fighting prowess yet." He had "no fear about going to jail." "There is no verdict that would disappoint me. . . . If they were to give any other verdict than guilty, Marcus Garvey will be very much disappointed." In the face of the impending verdict, Garvey only brimmed with New Negro manhood, and so did the UNIA, he proclaimed. "Those of you who have been observing events for the last four or five weeks with keen eyes and keen perceptions will come to no other conclusion than that—through the effort to silence Marcus Garvey—there is a mad desire, there is a great plan to permanently lay the Negro low. . . . But the world is sadly mistaken. . . . 400,000,000 Negroes are determined to [be a] man to take a place in the world and hold that place." "We want you to understand that this is the age of men, not of p[y]gmies, not of serfs and peons and dogs, but men, and we who make up the membership of the Universal Negro Improvement Association reflect the new manhood of the Negro."[199]

Some black newspapers remained unconvinced. They were sure that Garvey had succumbed to the trappings of his own flamboyance. Roy Wilkins, managing editor of the *St. Paul Appeal*, quipped, "Imagine if you can the kind of impression created by a pudgy black man striding back and forth across the courtroom pulling his moustache majestically, twirling a gold monocle, dramatically bellowing out ridiculous questions with every move and syllable showing more plainly his inordinate vanity."[200] For the *Kansas City Call*, the trial was the "sensation of New York City." This was not necessarily a positive evaluation, however. "The irregularity of his examination of witnesses, his attire, his shortness of temper, all were the cause of remarks from the bench, and for humorous stories in the daily press," which weakened Garvey's defense. "In short," the *Call* reported, "the defense put up by Marcus Garvey for himself was frail in that it was poorly executed. . . . Instead of trying to prove he was innocent of fraud, he seemingly was taking this opportunity for exploitation of the U. N. I. A."[201]

On June 21, 1923, the jury was ready to render its verdict. According to the *Call*, the judge advised the jury, "If Garvey has been foolish, you can't convict him for being a fool." Meanwhile, Garvey "sat at the counsel table or walked up and down, mopping his face with his handkerchief and fanning himself intermittently."[202] The verdict came down: guilty on one count. Garvey was sentenced to the maximum five years. His codefendants were acquitted.[203] Garvey "immediately burst into a storm of rage," reportedly shouting to the judge that he was "satisfied to go before the world" to "let them say whether I am innocent or not." A "crowd of sobbing s[y]mpathizers" watched as eighteen U.S. marshals escorted him away.[204]

It appeared that critical black leaders had won the war against Garvey. The black press weighed in, sardonically. "The man who acts as his own lawyer has a fool for a client. Perhaps Garvey knew little or nothing of this very true saying," the *Pittsburgh Courier* concluded. "At least he has no criticism of his 'lawyer,' nor can he say he was not given the widest opportunity to 'put in' his case. . . . If Garvey conducted his business as he did his trial, there is little wonder that it failed."[205] DuBois thought that it was Garvey's flamboyant leadership that had doomed him, remarking that he "is, without a doubt, the most dangerous enemy of the Negro race in America and in the world." "He is either a lunatic or a traitor," he continued. "No Negro in America ever had a fairer and more patient trial than Marcus Garvey. He convicted himself by his own admissions, his swaggering monkey-shines in the court room with monocle and long tailed coat and his insults to the judge and prosecuting attorney." Remembering how "everybody, including the writer, who has dared to make the slightest criticism of Garvey has been intimidated by threats and threatened with libel suits," DuBois determined that "this open ally of the Ku Klux Klan should be locked up or sent home."[206] The *Defender, Amsterdam News*, and *Messenger* echoed many of these points.[207] Some patrons of the black press also thought Garvey's critics had won the fight, though in a "cowardly way." Ida May Reynolds, a *Crisis* reader, was not necessarily a supporter of Garvey, she told DuBois in a private letter, but nonetheless felt that the "methods" used to undermine him were "uncalled for" and "unmanly." She blamed DuBois for the letters Garvey's opponents wrote to state authorities and scolded him, saying that he should have done more to help Garvey rather than "trying to wreck" the UNIA. DuBois did not actively participate in the "Garvey Must Go" campaign, to be sure, but the charge that he had helped destroy Garvey followed him well into the 1950s, testifying to the wide impact of this media-based crisis in black male leadership and the unflattering public spectacle it pointed up.[208] By September 1923, a reporter for the *Baltimore Afro-American* observed activities at Garvey's printing plant, or the lack thereof. The "linotype and stereotyping machinery purchased to print the UNIA publications," the reporter stated, were "idle and covered with canvas." The reporter was told that the *Negro World* was going to be printed elsewhere as the machinery was closed to creditors.[209] Garvey's quest to display his manliness perhaps blinded him to the legal realities he faced.

On the other hand, the trial and conviction may have helped him complete that quest, at least in achieving something of the manly martyrdom New Negro manhood demanded of black men when necessary. Garvey scholars have argued that representing himself was a costly move. Though a mesmerizing orator, Garvey was no lawyer. These scholars maintain that in choosing to represent himself, he helped sabotage his own case.[210] Yet within Garvey's gendered understanding of achievement, representing himself demonstrated a signal point about manly black leadership and New Negro manhood. In defending himself against critics in the *Negro World*, Garvey waxed poetic about being an independent, manly black man, who could fight for himself on his own. Representing himself in court followed naturally from this. He had told crowds years earlier that "a man who cannot stand by his convictions and die by his convictions is a coward." For Garvey, the trial demanded this very language and demonstration. Because of his gendered thinking, and his belief that blacks around the world suffered in part because they lacked manhood, it is likely that Garvey saw the need to represent himself not only because he felt that his own manhood was under assault but also as a way to display the militant, New Negro manhood he envisioned the race achieving.[211] Garvey embraced the image of New Negro self-defense, as well as another component of New Negro manhood: black resistance even if it meant self-sacrifice. The masculine rhetoric used by many black male leaders at this time had elevated calls for courageous self-sacrifice and martyrdom in the face of racial challenges. Thus, Garvey seized on the trial as an opportunity to embrace a martyrdom that he thought would help secure his place in history as a persecuted leader, who had willingly accepted his fate for the sake of the race and a much greater cause.[212] Through this final manly act, Garvey demonstrated an important sign of racial solidarity, racial pride, and black manhood that he hoped would inspire "a greater and more dangerous Marcus Garvey," or future generations of Race Men, who would carry on his work.[213] Self-sacrifice and martyrdom would remain a hallmark of manly, black male leadership for decades to come.

Garvey's quest to restore black manhood, and demonstrate his own, elevated him as the most exciting figure of the era, though it also elevated him as the one black leader the black press mobilized against. Garvey rose to prominence during the growth of New Negro consciousness, the proliferation of the black press, and expansion of the black public sphere, all of which worked to his advantage and disadvantage. As Henry Louis Gates has argued, black leaders, artists, writers, and thinkers celebrated blackness for the first time during the era and engaged in a discursive enterprise of representing and re-presenting blackness in ways that separated the negative models of blackness from the positive.[214] This was a process in which black publications became deeply involved as their publishers criticized one another in order to expel certain ideas and masculine models from black Americans' broader goals of racial advancement.[215] Shortly after his conviction, the *Baltimore Afro-American* lamented that Garvey's followers were now "a group without leadership in the world." "If Garvey does not lead the group who will?" it asked.[216] But this statement by the paper elided the part black newspapers, even the *Afro-American*, had played in helping answer this question. It was the black press that helped propel Garvey, and when this helped make him a household name as a subject of intense interest and controversy, it became the vehicle for his rapid undoing. Scholars have acknowledged how Garvey's business deficiencies and federal repression might have doomed his movement anyway, but it should not be underestimated how oppositional black newspapers also helped sound the movement's death knell. Before he faced trial and imprisonment in court, rival newspapermen were determined to convict him before the black public sphere's court of public opinion. Members of the black press construed Garvey as a threat to black Americans that warranted their wielding of black newspapers to advocate for the proper vision for racial advancement as they saw it, and thus decide who should lead the race and on what terms. The episode helped solidify black papers as the terrain on which black men worked out ideological battles, demonstrate the influence of the black press in making and breaking black male leadership, and show the utility of gendered rhetoric in shaping both.[217]

Yet Garvey felt that he emerged the ultimate victor in the war of words to see which black male leader would be made or broken first. For him, the trial and its outcome were "a matter of history," an epochal episode for the ages that did not spell defeat, despite his sentencing.[218] The outcome of the trial was but a ruse. In "The Negro's Greatest Enemy," an essay he published three months after his conviction, Garvey explained the lengths to which he thought his "Negro rivals" had gone to try to defeat him. But he was "not made to be whipped." Perhaps this was the case in part due to his parents. His father was "unafraid of consequences" and refused to "yield even to superior forces if he believed he was right." His mother was "ever ready to bestow charity upon her enemy."[219] His father had failed in life at some point, but his son had not because the son had seemingly taken the best qualities of the two. This enabled Garvey to claim ideological and moral victory in the face of apparent losses. These losses, he argued, were only parts of his contribution to racial advancement, the evidence of which would bear out in time to show his manly self-sacrifice. His belief that he was an experienced journalist of the highest caliber helped assure him of this victory even more. In addition to his Black Nationalism, he showed how emasculating rhetoric could be used to wage and settle intraracial conflicts, a rhetorical strategy that would be used by black male leaders and activists in later decades. His equation of interracialism and integration with femininity or weak manhood would also reverberate widely after his demise. Indeed, as a longtime journalist only "doomed" to become a race leader, Garvey appreciated the influence leaders and their press could have in shaping ideas immediately, and over time. Thus, it was he, not his enemies, that had won, he argued, because "the tiger is already loose," he declared in the *Negro World*.[220] It was his masculinized way of saying that despite imprisonment, it was already too late to contain his influence and ideas.

3 The Fraternity

Robert S. Abbott, John Sengstacke, and a New Order in Black (Male) Journalism

· ·

By the late 1920s, some members of the black press worked to make up for the Garvey affair. In August 1927, William Pickens, for instance, who had been one of the signatories to the Daugherty letter, advocated for Garvey's release.[1] Even Garvey's earliest opponent, Robert S. Abbott, was among them.[2] Yet while Garvey, the leader with imperial dreams of building an independent African nation, was deported to Jamaica in 1927, Abbott's publishing empire, the Robert S. Abbott Publishing Company, was expanding.[3] Promotional pamphlets for the *Defender* boasted that it had acquired a new printing press worth "$100,000." Its "net paid circulation exceeds that of any other twenty racial weekly publications combined," it added. The cost of "building equipment, $375,000; indebtedness, none . . . and the man still behind the gun is the same Robert Sengstacke Abbott."[4] In October 1930, he launched *Abbott's Monthly*, a literary and arts magazine dedicated to showcasing the work of black writers and artists. Nearly 50,000 copies were initially sold with circulation eventually reaching 100,000.[5] The *Defender* remained his signal venture, however, with circulation soaring upward of 200,000 a week, representatives claimed. Abbott was reportedly making an annual salary of $104,000.[6] In March 1929, the *Opportunity* magazine prepared to praise the publisher and his paper. "Just imagine yourself in the hub of Negro activity in Chicago—you are standing in the heart of the great, teeming Negro metropolis. Turn to the west and walk a few blocks, to the south, to the north or east, and you will encompass the territory in which the Negro lives and thrives. In other words, you are standing in the home office of *The Chicago Defender*," it stated. The magazine even insisted, "*The Chicago Defender* IS Robert Sengstacke Abbott. If you know one, you know the other."[7] The *Opportunity*'s comments spoke to the impressive levels of success and influence that Abbott had achieved now. Its compliments also suggested that the *Defender* and Abbott were synonymous, even extensions of each other, forming one body, one spirit, one man.

Abbott likely appreciated this conflation. By the end of the decade, he had outstripped much of his competition and achieved levels of commercial success unseen by many black publishers. In fact, he was about to close out the 1920s having been part of a cadre of black business leaders in Chicago that had helped make the city's Black Belt a hub of national black enterprises.[8] And the *Defender*'s headquarters symbolized his business leadership to him and others.[9] "Step into the *Defender* office," the *Opportunity* continued, "at any time between nine o'clock in the morning and six in the evening, and you will more than likely run into Mr. Abbott. Is he a busy man? Yes, with the weight of the world upon his shoulders—why shouldn't he be busy? With a plant representing the largest investment of any Negro enterprise in Chicago—with hundreds of persons, white and black, depending on him for sustenance, why shouldn't he be busy?"[10] The *Defender* emphasized these points about his success, the headquarters, and significance of both to the race especially when the paper celebrated some of its anniversaries. But for as much as the headquarters revealed about Abbott's success before the public, it also hid from public view much of what it took Abbott to produce the "World's Greatest Weekly," particularly during the next decade. If Abbott and the paper were one and the same, as the *Opportunity* suggested, then to venture inside the plant was to venture inside the man, his mind, his body—it was to glimpse the inner workings of the paper and the inner workings of its founder. Inside both the *Defender* organization and Abbott's mind emerged deep concerns over the future of his paper, concerns that reflected widespread anxieties about men's manhood in the wake of the Great Depression—a national economic crisis.

The economic, political, and cultural upheavals that the Depression unleashed helped expose much of what went into the production of the *Defender*. This chapter examines how this production was tied to the production of Race Men as Abbott worked to groom his nephew, John Sengstacke, to take over the paper. Scholars of the black press usually regard the *Defender* as one of the greatest black newspapers of its day, if not the standard bearer for the modern black press.[11] Yet this chapter returns to Abbott and the *Defender* to examine both at a time when the paper's supposed greatness was imperiled by the Depression, and the gendered ways in which Abbott and Sengstacke decided to confront these struggles. The Depression hit black Americans hard, much harder than it hit other Americans. The exigencies of the moment reshaped New Negro politics into working-class politics. Interestingly, Garvey's idea that black commercial power supported by strong black men on a national and global stage would win white people's respect and redeem the manhood of the race retained wide appeal among black people in the 1930s.[12] In urban America, once a symbol of enormous opportunity for African Americans, black unemployment exceeded white unemployment by 30 to 60 percent. Black farm tenants and wage laborers were among the most impoverished farm workers in the country.[13] Black social institutions and businesses, including the black press, suffered too. Some black businesses were able to stay afloat because of the "Don't Buy Where You Can't Work" campaign. The boycott called for black people to make a conscious effort to patronize black-owned businesses.[14] But a national consensus formed among contemporary essayists, foreign observers, psychiatrists, and scholars that the Depression had sent men's masculinity spiraling into a crisis.[15] Massive unemployment undermined men's gender role as family breadwinner, and many Americans considered gainful employment critical to achieving and maintaining proper manhood. For African Americans, this crisis was particularly acute. That joblessness was more widespread among black Americans compounded long-standing challenges to their capacity for manhood and womanhood. While the black press helped contribute to the popular view that manhood was imperiled, it did so in terms of black men, focusing on suggesting ways to restore their manhood by addressing the economic and racial issues they faced. Scholarship on black manhood tends to stop short of or look past the 1930s, neglecting a crucial period of changes in conceptions of black masculinity.[16] One leading conception at this time included what this chapter calls the underutilized black male worker, an image constructed by black leaders, activists, and newspapers, working to address the plight of black men whose manhood was destroyed by joblessness and Jim Crow segregation.[17]

This construct, which asserted a masculine right to economic participation and production in the life of the country, gained wide traction as national attention focused on male joblessness throughout the decade, and black economic nationalism, class and labor consciousness, and Communist and labor organizing exploded in response to it. Redeeming underutilized black male workers took center stage for many black leaders, activists, and newspapers, oftentimes subsuming discussions about jobless black women. Again, the press accentuated the struggles of black men as pivotal to black people's quest for inclusion and full citizenship rights.[18] The *Defender* joined other black newspapers in this discussion. Yet these crises in economic stability and masculinity hit very close to home for Abbott. Letters exchanged privately between Abbott and Sengstacke showed that inside Abbott's mind were concerns over how to prevent these crises from taking root inside the institution he had worked so hard to build. This chapter's exploration into the mind of two black publishers at this time illuminates a side of black newspapers that scholars of the black press have largely been unable to examine due to a paucity of sources from black male publishers. As a result, scholarship on the black press has paid greater attention to what their papers printed, sometimes unable to access a vantage point that reveals developments behind what was printed, that is, the business and personal decisions that shaped the production of black newspapers and the companies that published them.[19] This examination illuminates how gender ideologies, particularly ideas of black manhood, shaped the production of black papers from the outside in and the inside out.

When economic challenges brought on by the Depression began to threaten the future of his publishing empire, Abbott decided to "make man," as some contemporaries put it. In other words, Abbott decided to meet these challenges by engaging in processes of institution-building *and* man-building, two inseparable efforts in which he worked to transfer to his nephew the leadership of the paper, along with the masculine identity he had cultivated as a black publisher. Abbott first publicly articulated aspects of this identity at the paper's twenty-fifth anniversary. He explained how shepherding the *Defender* marked a pivotal juncture in his experience as a man. For him, founding the paper represented a seminal act that, over time, had led him to not only a very accomplished stage of his life but also a stage of manhood that adult men were thought to enjoy when they helped build an important institution that also helped them make their mark on the world.[20] This story of professional and masculine success helped Abbott instantiate his image as a Race Man before the public, while elevating the black male newspaper publisher as a model of black business leadership, racial leadership, institution-building, and black manhood. The story shared the subjectivity of a black male publisher, revealing a perspective that other black newspapermen may have also shared. At different times, the *Defender* organization hired young boys to sell the paper in Chicago, and even provided some of them with mentoring opportunities. Since 1923, the *Defender*'s Bud Billiken page, a section for children readers, demonstrated Abbott's interest in entertaining and educating future generations of Race Men and Race Women to embrace stories of racial uplift like his own.[21] Now, Abbott worked to groom Sengstacke, a future Race Man, to succeed him by transferring his manly image of the black male publisher, and the sense of manhood he derived from it, to Sengstacke. Abbott hoped that Sengstacke might maintain the *Defender* as he had, take it to new heights, and be a "man" like him. Many black leaders, activists, and newspapers argued that redeeming black men at this crucial time would help redeem the race, and Abbott similarly thought saving his nephew would save the *Defender*. For Abbott, institution-building and man-building became one and the same. Sengstacke, who was inspired by his uncle, embraced this process intended to make him a "man." Yet he also became inspired by the racial politics of the Depression era, particularly the ideas and organizing efforts of black labor activists. These ideas and efforts he also embraced. Thus, Sengstacke charted his own path toward a manhood that, while not a complete break with Abbott's model of masculinity, improved on its limits by updating it, and expanding the role black male publishers could play in shaping racial advancement. Sengstacke fused together his uncle's ideals and that of activists, an ideological union that led him to found a media institution of his own.

Black people were among the first to feel the initial signs of the economic crisis, a fact that the *Defender* pointed out in gendered terms.[22] As early as two months after the stock market crashed, the *Defender* reversed its position of a little over a decade earlier that black southerners should move north. The urban had failed now, and it advised black workers to remain where they were so that they could "hold [their] jobs" no matter how "unsatisfactory." "One thing is certain," the *Defender* affirmed: "the man who has a job will be better off than the man who has to find one because jobs are scarce and times are not improving."[23] Discussions about job security in general and black male joblessness in particular would now become a fixture in the black press. The *Defender* developed a column exclusively dedicated to counseling readers on how to survive the economic crisis. "What Is Your Plan for Economic Security?," written by Frazier T. Lane, declared in one issue that "the most appalling tragedy of the depression is the present waste of man-power and likewise manhood." He encouraged readers to do their best to remain thrifty.[24] One poem in the *Defender*, "Job Wanted: Male," spoke to the underutilized black male worker, who represented a "waste of man-power." The poem described a nomadic, self-loathing man concerned about the welfare of his family. He regarded public relief to be an insult to his manhood because work was his "just birthright." He was strong, healthy, and willing to work, but his strength was sapped by staggering rates of unemployment "eating up [his] manhood."[25] Some readers agreed with this image. Fred Almond of Philadelphia put forward a list of eight things that would help the race "show signs of manhood." In the midst of the Depression, he insisted that when financial resources were unavailable, the solution was to "up and fight your fight like a man, [and] take what is yours by united force dedicated to the worthy cause of economic uplift." He advised black people to cultivate strong leadership and pool resources to build black businesses and that every member of the race contribute a dollar to an economic improvement program he called the "Economic Forward March."[26] For the *Defender* and many readers of the black press, the Depression signaled a far more devastating prospect for black men because it exacerbated the already tenuous social and economic position they held in American society as men.

But discussions of economic hardship and black male unemployment hardly made it into the May 3, 1930, edition of the *Defender*. Instead, the issue was devoted to celebrating Abbott and the *Defender's* economic success as the paper marked a milestone of twenty-five years of operation. Writers mustered every bit of fanfare to celebrate. With detailed images of Abbott, staff members, and the paper's state-of-the-art operation equipment, writers took readers inside the *Defender*. In a "glance into the Defender files," the paper reviewed its leading news stories over the years, many campaigns against racial oppression in Chicago and the nation, and how "it has figured not as a pacifist, but as a live, militant institution—an organization standing in the forefront of battle."[27] It congratulated itself for having "never wavered from the straight path it was hewing for the complete emancipation of its people," a "vision" with "men willing to fight—to die, if need be—for the principles which they consider essential to real manhood."[28] With all its success, writers called the *Defender* the "spokesman" of black Americans. The paper asserted for Abbott the role that many black men desired to have in order to speak for the race, even crediting itself with having inspired the founding of other "militant, fearless" black newspapers. The celebration lionized Abbott as an exemplar of black male individual uplift, business and racial leadership, and institution-building. Abbott was the "moving spirit" of the *Defender*, who went from being the "one-man newspaper" of 1908 to the "one-man force" now, building the *Defender* from nothing, except from his sheer will and determination to serve the race.[29] And his service was to "a living cause! What better excuse has an institution for living? What greater justification is there for a man or thing remaining alive?" "She [the *Defender*] Has Carried the Beacon—Calling Men to Higher Hopes and a Greater Understanding," the paper said as writers feminized it perhaps in order to project Abbott's manly control of or paternal care for the *Defender*.[30] Abbott and the paper together represented the "emblem of what a black man and a black institution can accomplish in the face of the most disheartening adversities."[31]

In "A Recapitulation of 25 Years Work, Editor Robt. S. Abbott's Story of Early Struggles and Success of the World's Greatest Weekly," the "Twentieth Century Moses" recalled his influential part in the Great Migration. Abbott seemed to put his many accomplishments modestly, however. "It is not unseemly that I, as founder, owner, and editor, should be gratified in the success [the *Defender*] has attained, in the good it has done and in the purpose it has served." Abbott explained how he got his start in the field and recounted his early struggles. Some of these struggles showed him the "shortcomings of the various newspapers published by our group," helping him realize "that a paper properly managed, giving to the people the information which they desired, would pay." Thus, he "determined to open up a new field of journalism," though many people discouraged him and even tried to "destroy both me and the Defender." "This history of business institutions owned and operated by our group shows us that they begin to decline in less than twenty years. . . . The Chicago Defender, beginning in its infancy, with its editor and publisher borrowing a quarter from his landlady, has stood the test of twenty five years with an enormous investment in machinery and equipment," he affirmed. "At the end of 25 years, I rejoice in the consolation and satisfaction which follows a successful pursuit in the task undertaken and the principles espoused." He and the paper remained engaged, as they had been from the outset, he argued, in "helping to usher in the glad era of an enlightened civilization and the universal acknowledgement of the brotherhood of man."[32]

Abbott credited his stepfather, John Herman Henry Sengstacke, with instilling in him the purpose of publishing. This part of his success story invoked powerful images of a father transmitting knowledge to his son, a hallmark of masculinity thought to be important to cultivating proper manhood, and the production and reproduction of Race Men.[33] Sengstacke published the *Woodville Times*, and it was his professional connections with local publishers that gave Abbott his start as a young reporter.[34] "I do not hesitate to say that it was from my stepfather that I received . . . my basic training for the work that has kept me busy through the years," Abbott recalled. He came to regard Sengstacke as his adopted father, gaining from him "everything required by a boy." His stepfather having groomed him in the art of publishing, Abbott regretted the passing of Sengstacke in 1904, before Sengstacke had the opportunity to see his adopted son found the

Defender in 1905. Abbott said that it was after his stepfather's funeral that he decided to create the *Defender*, for it was "the vision of my father constantly before my eyes—a beacon showing me the way—that I launched upon the project of which I dreamed so long." From his stepfather he received "one bit of advice": "that to be a newspaperman one must study not only his own needs, but the needs of those about him."[35] "A good newspaper was one of the best instruments of service and one of the strongest weapons ever to be used in defense of a race which was deprived of its citizenship rights," his stepfather told him. This advice was "sacred" to Abbott, and he "endeavored to give expression to my love for him, my Race and humanity through the columns of the *Defender*."[36]

Abbott's relationship with his stepfather was deeply important to him and his sense of professional and masculine success, and the relationship he had come to build with the *Defender*'s headquarters was too. The celebration highlighted the plant. Purchased in 1921, it was perhaps the most conspicuous evidence of the *Defender*'s commercial and spatial growth over the years. Through the headquarters, a former synagogue, valued at a million dollars and one of the largest black businesses in the city, Abbott contributed to the Chicago landscape and the growing black metropolis.[37] When Abbott migrated to Chicago, he envisioned it as the place where he would succeed. The plant was part of the proof that he had done just that.[38] Historian Michael Kimmel has shown that during the early twentieth century, office work came to be popularly viewed as feminine for men, stripping them of their independence, individuality, and interaction with the outside world.[39] This was not so for Abbott. The headquarters housed the many offices and pieces of technology that were the lifeblood of the *Defender*, as detailed photographs of both in the anniversary edition revealed. Throughout the years, the plant attracted throngs of visitors and tourists. Women reportedly dressed up to visit it.[40] In particular, the plant was "seventy-five by one hundred twenty-five feet, two stories high, located at 3435 Indiana Ave., with every facility used in the operation of a modern newspaper. . . . The Defender employs one hundred and ten people, fifteen of whom are women, the others members of both races."[41] The headquarters contained his pride and joy: the goss straightline sextupile rotary press, a top-of-the-line printing press. The press, which was capable of printing "72,000 papers per hour" and valued at "$100,000," was "another reason why the *Defender* is the World's Greatest Weekly."[42]

The headquarters was the most state-of-the-art black publishing plant in the country, and Abbott's journey to owning it was a "fairy tale."[43] He had gone from having a "folding card table and kitchen chair (borrowed)" for office equipment in the fledgling years of his career, all located in the "portion of a back room in a State St. flat" in which he boarded, to operating a national commercial press from his own plant. The paper also expressed this journey in gendered terms of fathering and raising a child. The "baby *Defender*" was "born" at 3159 State Street in the home of Henrietta P. Lee, the "Mother of the Defender." Abbott boarded in Lee's home, where he printed the first 300 issues that launched the *Defender*. She was also the woman from whom he borrowed twenty-five cents to start the newspaper. He used it to buy some tablet paper and pay a printer.[44] The "lusty youngster" tried to make a move to 2935 State Street but returned to 3159 State Street until the newspaper grew "big enough" to move to the present headquarters at 3435 Indiana Avenue.[45] Abbott, "the man in whose brain [the *Defender*] was conceived," brought the paper "to life at a time when the Race needed it most."[46] Accordingly, Abbott "gave birth" to the *Defender* and then nurtured it to maturity like a model father. He was successful as both a publisher and a Race Man, who had accomplished the seminal things that Race Men were thought to do: he had "birthed" and "fathered" a powerful black social institution through the *Defender*.[47]

Abbott's story of success, the quintessential narrative of a self-made man, articulated his personal odyssey to manhood through newspaper publishing.[48] The story also helped define the relationship between media and masculinity, elevating black male publishers as a model of black manhood among many others. Its fundamental tenets of individual uplift, dogged determination against the odds, and the search for a proper gender identity likely resonated with many readers. Other black male publishers likely related to Abbott's success story, especially those who had worked just as diligently over the years to move their papers forward. Some publishers had also been one-man operations early in their careers. But few of them could claim the pioneering role that Abbott held, a fact that helped him instantiate his image as a trailblazing Race Man before the public.[49] *Defender* writers elevated his particular experience as a one-man operation in dramatic ways, employing some of the sensationalism for which the paper had become known. His and the paper's emphasis on having been a "one-man newspaper" spoke to his early hardships in the field, as well as his desires to be the leading, if not single, publisher or "one-man" who dominated a highly competitive black newspaper market. Further, it suggested his oneness with the paper—the two rhetorically and symbolically forming one body, one spirit, one man. Dr. Jasper Tappan Phillips, a reader, wrote Abbott personally to commend him. "The thirtieth anniversary Edition of the Chicago Defender was delivered to me today. The subject matter and mechanical make-up reflect credit upon your paper which through the years has stood for 'a square deal' for our group in all walks of life." "You have watched your paper grow from a little acorn to a mighty oak," Phillips wrote, agreeing that the *Defender* was a great living institution dedicated to serving the race, "and people far and remote rejoice with you in this celebration. I convey to you my personal congratulations. May you and the Chicago Defender live long and continue . . . to fearlessly champion the cause of 'The Man Farthest Down.'"[50]

The twenty-fifth anniversary edition glorified the *Defender* as one of the greatest black institutions of the day, but the celebration betrayed the financial challenges emerging within Abbott's publishing empire. The organization began to feel the ravages of the Depression as early as 1931. According to financial records, the company operated at a deficit of $66,383.14 during the 1932 fiscal year. In fact, between 1931 and 1932, Abbott had transferred "various sums of [money]" from his personal account to the company's commercial account to help balance the books.[51] Abbott wrote his nephew in October 1933 to share with him some of the *Defender*'s business difficulties. "I am hitting the ground in spots as my dirigible is trying to rise. I am being bled on every hand in finances."[52] To cope, one thing that Abbott did was lay off some workers. One of these workers was "the highest paid woman worker I had and had been so for years, now that the business is about on the rocks we just had to trim everything." Abbott had even sacrificed his own salary for the last "3½" years. His friend of many years, personal attorney, and general counsel to the company, Nathan K. McGill, had gone unpaid for two years. McGill was one of Abbott's most trusted employees, for Abbott had looked to him at one point to "help me carry the responsibility which had for so many years been borne by me alone," even turning the management of the paper "over to him."[53] Abbott advised Sengstacke to "hold on to every penny" because "things are desperate."[54]

That he was helping finance his nephew's education did not ease matters. At this time, Sengstacke attended Abbott's alma mater, Hampton Institute. Abbott was also supporting other family members financially, including Sengstacke's siblings as they pursued their educations. To be sure, Abbott's stepfather had helped Abbott cover his expenses when he was going through college, and thus Abbott might have felt that such was part of the role of the family patriarch.[55] But it was a position that was both rewarding and taxing. He complained to Sengstacke that the family too often acted "as if I were a millionaire."[56] Around 1934, *Abbott's Monthly* began failing. Eneil F. Simpson, the business manager, proposed a "vigorous editorial campaign" focused on black "re-employment," suggesting also a change to the magazine's "present makeup" to highlight "stories of a 'racketeer and sensational' type that would appeal to the lower masses and be of an understandable nature." Despite the organization's efforts to save the publication, using their tried-and-true methods of sensationalism, *Abbott's Monthly* folded.[57] By 1935, circulation of the *Defender* would reportedly drop to 70,000.[58] Making matters worse was Abbott's health, which began to decline around 1930 due to Bright's disease, a condition affecting the kidneys.[59] The anniversary celebration had represented him and the paper as inseparable. Interestingly, the decline of the *Defender* paralleled the decline of Abbott's health.

Other black papers faced similar financial straits. Whereas the black press expanded following World War I, it contracted now due to the economic downturn. The *Negro World*, for example, ceased publication in the summer of 1933. The *Chicago Whip*, the *Defender*'s local competition, failed.[60] Many small-town papers folded. Popular papers scaled back their staffs, reduced the number of pages in each edition, or cut multiple editions altogether, all while they experienced rapidly declining readerships no longer able to pay subscriptions.[61] Other papers, like the *New York Amsterdam News*, increased a few cents in cost to help recover plummeting revenues, though its circulation continued to drop as debts only mounted.[62] W. E. B. DuBois, who once beamed with pride that the *Crisis* was self-supporting, lamented that it could not continue this way by 1933. "The mass of Negroes, even the intelligent and educated, progressively being thrown out of work, did not have money for food, much less for magazines," he remembered. The NAACP now had to share the periodical's operating costs.[63]

For many black leaders, the deteriorating economic conditions required a reevaluation of longtime strategies for racial advancement. For example, in August 1933, Joel Spingarn, chairman of the National Association for the Advancement of Colored People (NAACP), hosted the Second Amenia Conference. Finding that the "primary problem is economic," the conference brought together several black intellectuals to "make a critical appraisal of the Negro's existing situation in American society and to consider underlying principles for future action." Conferees argued that improving black people's economic standing required a new labor movement that could build an alliance between black and white labor.[64]

Beginning in January 1934 on through the summer of that year, DuBois took this effort to reevaluate the strategies for black economic uplift a step further. The *Crisis* editor criticized the NAACP's prioritization of the fight for civil rights over economic rights, a point that became a concern of his as early as 1930.[65] He published several editorials proposing a "voluntary determined cooperative effort" requiring blacks to "segregate ourselves," to "herd together," and to develop an "economic nation within a nation."[66] To NAACP leaders, DuBois's call for black economic self-reliance to the point of separation, tones somewhat reminiscent of Garvey, compromised the organization's goals of integration. For Walter White, executive secretary of the NAACP, segregation in any way had always meant "inferior accommodations and a distinctly inferior position in the national and communal life." DuBois's plan meant "spiritual atrophy for the group segregated," White contended, and "it is because of this that the N. A. A. C. P. has resolutely fought such segregation."[67] Some members of the black press supported White. The *Defender*, for example, charged DuBois with being a "quitter," who had "hung up his armor and capitulated to the enemies of his cause." With the NAACP now sharing in the magazine's costs, DuBois knew it meant them having "a right to a larger voice in its conduct and policy." He had always required absolute control in the editing of his papers.[68] But he remained determined to "seek through my editorship of the *Crisis* slowly but certainly to change the ideology of the NAACP and of the Negro race into a racial program for economic salvation along the paths of peace and organization."[69] By May 1934 the differences between DuBois and NAACP leaders became so sharp that the cofounder of the NAACP and *Crisis* editor of twenty-four years resigned from the organization.[70] "The span of my life from 1910 to 1934 is chiefly the story of the *Crisis* under my editorship," he wrote. "This was not an easy decision," he remembered; "to give up the *Crisis* was like giving up a child." Like Abbott, DuBois felt that he had fathered and nurtured his publication and was "unwilling at this late date to be limited in the expression of my honest opinions."[71]

Indeed, anxieties over the status of unemployed black people marshaled the voices of various segments of black America, including the black press, to offer different solutions. But while conveying their concerns in terms that addressed the economic dislocation of the race as a whole, leaders and the press spotlighted the particular plight of black men.[72] Some writers reasoned that the Depression was "a test of manhood and a real man is the better for having been so tested."[73] Historian and social critic Carter G. Woodson, for example, maintained that "poverty teaches manhood, teaches a man what to fight for. . . . For the Negro then, the door of opportunity is wide open."[74] But a manly fight to overcome poverty was difficult when the breadline was perhaps the most visible display of the economic assault on manhood. It exposed men as wards of the public dole rather than as strong contributors to society, exacerbating the perceived crisis in masculinity. Like other men, black men may have felt, as one *Defender* reader, Reverend J. C. Austin, insisted, that public relief reduced men "to the level of tramps, paupers, common beggars. Strong men find their joy now with a loaf of bread under their arms. . . . This system cannot make man. We want work!" The emasculating implications of the breadline, among other effects of the Depression, meant that "our purpose" should be what was "declared from the heart of God, 'let us make man'" by giving them work; "the making of man," Austin affirmed, was the "greatest thing, the essential thing."[75]

Many considered the breadline a public humiliation, a glaring sign of emasculation that prompted the *Defender* to call it a form of "slavery." The "free man" did not accept the "lovely coercion of charity and sustains himself in the emancipated powers of his being."[76] For a people not far removed from the actual experience of slavery, the term conjured memories of powerlessness and defenselessness, and in gendered terms suggested submission and emasculation. Many activists called for public works rather than public aid—partly because it promised to help repair the dignity and self-esteem of unemployed men. For example, officials of the Urban League commented in the *Defender* that public works "gives unemployed workers a chance to earn a living again instead of being on relief at the mercy of what amounts to public charity."[77] But reflecting the views of some that black men were not taking enough initiative to find work on their own, the *Atlanta Daily World* suggested that black men turn to newspaper publishing. By working for the black press or even creating one's own paper to report on present conditions, a man could "uncover that rich vein of talent that is going to waste and harness his efforts in the line of manly achievement . . . [and through] . . . the winged power of the press, lift himself to the level of economic and industrial independence."[78] Indeed, Abbott had himself demonstrated the potential publishing had in providing a pathway to manhood and financial success, though the *Atlanta Daily World* neglected the extent to which publishers of existing black papers were struggling to stay afloat.

Black women faced a set of economic problems too, that, like black men, reflected their gendered experiences in the job market and society more broadly. Drawing on President Franklin D. Roosevelt's promise of a New Deal, the highly regarded educator and activist Nannie Helen Burroughs proposed a "New Deal" of her own for young black women. Burroughs had devoted much of her career to advocating for black women, and her New Deal would train them in "womanhood." She asserted that "the economic plight of the Negro woman is tragic. During this depression she is bearing the economic burden of the race almost alone. She has the longest hours and she gets the lowest pay."[79] Like black men, many black women struggled to keep their jobs or find work. Domestic work, the most common job for black women at the time, enabled some black women to use their meager earnings to help supplement the otherwise low or sporadic income of their male partners, if not completely support the household in general.[80] Journalist Marvel Cooke and future civil rights activist Ella Baker lamented the struggles of domestics in what they called "the Bronx Slave Market." Published in the *Crisis* in November 1935, the article examined "our economic battlefront," one of exploited black women so eager to find work that they waited on street corners to hire themselves out as day laborers.[81] If black men's form of "slavery" was the breadline, then this was black women's, argued Cooke and Baker. Desperate times pushed some women into the "informal economy" of prostitution in order to survive, a development that the black press decried for the supposed moral ruin it caused women and the race. "The Negro race can't climb anywhere upon the shoulders of prostitutes," the *Pittsburgh Courier* declared.[82]

Many black women organized against their particular economic and gendered crises by deploying their buying power as a weapon, an effort that developed into the National Housewives League movement. Founded in 1930 in Detroit and spreading to other cities, the movement offered a class consciousness and activism for black women that fused the female uplift ideology of the black women's club movement with calls for black economic nationalism. Their efforts also countered many black male leaders' use of masculine rhetoric to promote black economic nationalism as discussions of unemployment among black men eclipsed discussions of the same problem among black women.[83] Employment was the right of men, the archetypal worker and chief source of economic security in families and communities, from which women benefited by default, so it was thought.[84]

Some black men and women contributed to the effort to reclaim black manhood as a part of a need to reclaim black womanhood.[85] Rebecca Stiles-

Taylor, a well-known women's organizer and leader in the National Association of Colored Women, asserted that black women had "to inject manhood into her men," meaning they had to do their part too to help build up black men during this crisis.[86] One woman writer for the *Defender* would insist that "A Woman's Creed" was having a positive self-image and appearance, raising children, and believing "in the men of my race—their strength, their endurance, their valor, their manhood. . . . Firmly I believe that I am my sister's keeper—likewise my brother's. . . . If I believe not these principles I am not worthy to be called a woman. . . . I shall bring shame upon the sex of which I am a part." For Nannie Helen Burroughs, "Negro men are entirely too idle." Connecting work to masculinity, she wrote that "men cannot be made under [these] conditions"; "the manhood of the race is going to waste." To Burroughs, it was a woman's duty to help. "There are women," she insisted, "who can do a great deal to turn the race around." "Our social problems are staggering, but it is up to us to solve them," she affirmed, elevating black female leadership, perhaps appealing particularly to black women organizers of the period. Here, black women's leadership was also supposed to make redeeming black manhood a priority. "I am inclined to believe that if the women had more voice in our efforts we would be better off," Carter G. Woodson asserted. "Our women are so much better than our men. . . . Women are more faithful to our people." "They do more for the elevation of the unfortunate element of our men," he continued, using some emasculating rhetoric to inspire black men to be "men" and find work.[87]

The focus on restoring men to work for the sake of preserving proper gender roles influenced the black press, as well as federal policies. In an April 7, 1932, radio address, for example, President Roosevelt used a phrase that justified federal efforts to put the nation on the path to economic recovery, a phrase that would gain immense traction in this gendered discourse on joblessness: "the forgotten man at the bottom of the economic pyramid."[88] The phrase invoked the image of the suffering male worker, whose redeemed masculinity was thought to be critical to restoring national strength. And some black newspapers held up black men as the "forgotten man."[89] Though the Roosevelt administration intended the New Deal to be a transformative economic and social program that incorporated all Americans, concerns about rescuing men in particular from the emasculating effects of unemployment influenced the administration's plans for economic recovery.[90] Historians Bryant Simon and Jason Smith have shown that many New Deal programs reflected this. The Civilian Conservation Corps, for instance, reportedly Roosevelt's favorite program, was considered a project to rebuild men, as much as it was supposed to rebuild the environment.[91] Many New Deal programs provided employment in public works and construction, sectors that tended to exclude women from the job pool.[92] Given their disproportionate presence on relief rolls, black men may have especially looked to the New Deal to alleviate their particular plight.[93] Like many black Americans, one *Defender* writer thought that the New Deal would give jobs to unemployed blacks, putting them and other Americans back on "the road of self-sustaining manhood and womanhood."[94] Though the New Deal would bear mixed results for black people because many programs were rife with racial discrimination, one *Defender* article praised the administration at least for its efforts to return men to work.[95] "It is refreshing to know that the federal government has reached a definite decision with respect to the dole system. Nothing has so undermined the unemployed," "their manhood and their morals." "The President's decision to at once remove the relief rolls is a step in the right direction," the paper argued.[96]

As anxieties over economic security and manhood suffused popular discourse, national policy, and many of the columns of the black press, they also suffused parts of Abbott's mind. Amid increasing talk of building black and white labor alliances, and rebuilding the strength of the nation's economy and the manhood of its male workforce, Abbott rebuilt his declining *Defender* by building up his nephew. When Abbott wrote Sengstacke to apprise him of the company's business affairs in October 1933, it was because as early as October 1931, Abbott had begun grooming Sengstacke to take over the paper. Sengstacke was born in 1912 in Savannah, Georgia. The son of Abbott's half-brother and one of seven children, Sengstacke was named for his grandfather, the first family publisher, who founded and published the *Woodville Times*. Sengstacke's father, Herman Alexander Sengstacke, took over his father's paper, and renamed it the *West End Post*. Publishing was in Sengstacke's blood, so to speak, and yet he remembered that for a time he "wasn't too keen on it."[97] Still, Sengstacke worked with his father on the paper, a foundation that Abbott wanted Sengstacke to continue building on. "I remember Mr. Abbott coming down to Savannah to see my mother," he said, "and telling us he wanted me to go to Hampton Institute, where he went to school. He wanted me to learn the fine points of printing and do my college work there, for which, he said, he would pay." After some time at junior colleges, Sengstacke enrolled in his uncle's alma mater in 1930. But rather than studying printing, as Abbott had, he majored in business administration. Given his work on his father's paper, he felt that there was no need to pursue printing because he already "knew that well enough."[98]

Sengstacke's grooming involved Abbott teaching his nephew what he thought were fundamentals in business, institution-building, and proper manhood. Many adult men of Abbott's generation, black and white, thought that manhood was something young men grew into as they aged, a natural process on one hand, but a cultivated one on the other that required proper training from an elder man.[99] Abbott and Sengstacke corresponded over the course of Sengstacke's matriculation at Hampton. Examining their exchange from Abbott's side is especially telling. Abbott did not have any children, and he looked to his nephew to carry on his work. The twenty-fifth anniversary celebration showed how Abbott's ideas of a black manhood premised on ideals of the self-made man helped make him successful. His exchange with Sengstacke revealed this even more, as well as his effort to encourage Sengstacke to adopt this same masculine identity to ensure his success and that of the paper's. Popular discourses around "making men" at this time influenced Abbott as he worked to make Sengtsacke a publisher and Race Man in his own likeness. On October 8, 1931, he instructed Sengstacke to

> study hard. . . . Be a real man and push yourself to the front[.] [Always] remember that you are a "front" man and not a man to be in the back ranks. You must take up where I left off and make a name for the family and for me, please hold up my honor and let those fools see that the Sengstackes and Abbotts are go getters. . . . I want you to make your own fortune like I did and have a lovely family home like I have . . . [and] . . . have lots of money in the bank. . . . Remember that I have chosen you to head up the family.[100]

In essence, Abbott was telling Sengstacke to begin cultivating some of the fundamental qualities of his own model of manhood: the self-made man. But his choosing Sengstacke to take over what Abbott had himself created essentially negated self-made manhood, by definition, or at least it seemed. Here, Abbott was beginning to create for Sengstacke perhaps a new category in his concept of the self-made man that spoke to the exigencies of the Depression era, as well as the malleability of manhood. Abbott was carving out a space for what was going to be Sengstacke's inheritance of the *Defender*, and, therefore, Abbott's manly model of black newspaper ownership. It was a transfer of manhood by which Sengstacke would become self-made, if not by virtue of his uncle having already achieved that ideal then by fulfilling his uncle's expectations to take the paper to new heights.

Sengstacke was nearing his nineteenth birthday, and being a "real man," charged with eventually leading the family, seemed secondary to his foremost concerns at the time. "I am glad you are in your office and doing fine," Sengstacke wrote on January 31, 1932. By 1931, Abbott was bedridden due to his illness.[101] For Sengstacke, Abbott's return to the office, the special masculine space that represented for him a part of his successful ownership of the paper, signaled an improvement in his health. Sengstacke's other concerns included his summer plans. "Uncle, please see what you can do to get me a job next summer if you are not planning for me to go to summer school. I really want to work and make some money this summer." Sengstacke's request showed the beginnings of his initiative, which Abbott likely appreciated. Sengstacke was also trying to apply this same initiative toward his academic performance. "I am an average student, I know," but "trying hard not to 'flunk,'" he assured Abbott.[102] On March 21, 1932, an excited Sengstacke thanked his uncle for finding him work for the summer at the *Defender*, his "first 'real' job."[103] In April 1932, Sengstacke began typing his letters to Abbott, which were previously handwritten. It seems that Abbott instructed him to do this, perhaps in order for him to hone the skill even as they corresponded privately.[104] Sengstacke would eventually work several summers at the *Defender*, where he practiced his typing skills, among other things. "When I arrived that first summer," he recalled, "Mr. Abbott [thought] I should have what he called the 'finishing touches' in the printing industry. So he arranged for me to go to the Chicago School of Printing, which was operated by the International Typographical Union [ITU]. We had only one Negro in our pressroom at that time, and he was Mr. Abbott's cousin. He would just clean up trash for the foreman; they wouldn't teach him anything. There weren't any Negroes in the ITU, and because of my uncle, I was the first Negro the ITU permitted to go to its school. I learned a lot there—about color work, job printing, and what not."[105]

Sengstacke returned to Hampton in the fall. On October 6, 1933, Abbott notified him of a tuition bill, and some matters concerning their family. The bill was for $331.67, and Abbott advised Sengstacke to be "mighty careful in your spending because this is a trying time for me." But the family patriarch was more worried that, "honestly, it looks to me as if the family is going backward in every way. Sometimes I think the family has fully collapsed. . . . I hope that everything goes well for you and that you will come out of school with flying colors and with the expectation of trying to help me back on my feet. I need you."[106] For Abbott, what the Depression had wrought appeared bleak for the nation, his family, his paper, and the future of self-made men. The future of the paper, the family, and Abbott's legacy were in the hands of Sengstacke, a point that Abbott made especially clear on October 13, 1933. "I am pulling hard for you in my business," he wrote. "I hope you will do everything that you can to see that your Defender doesn't hit the bottom. . . . It is up to you to go over the top and lay the foundation for our family. Your father failed and I am trying to put you on the right track. I am so anxious to do this."[107] In no equivocal terms, Abbott handpicked Sengstacke to be his heir over other men in the family, including the family's other publisher, Sengstacke's own father. Over the summer of 1933, Sengstacke took classes in business administration at Ohio State University to continue preparing for the task ahead.[108]

When Sengstacke was nearing graduation in the spring of 1934, Abbott was more adamant about his future in the company. Much of the letter is worth quoting at length:

I do hope that you will listen to the things that I try to tell you from time to time. Of course, I don't mean that you shouldn't have any initiative. I want you to have that and plenty of it because in this business if you are going to keep ahead of the other fellow, you must have initiative and guts to push forward. . . . These requisites every business man should have no matter what business he is in, and yet, it is seldom found in Colored organizations: that is, loyalty to the man from whom you are drawing your pay; a thorough knowledge of your work that you hire yourself out to do; trustworthiness in a businesslike way in order that you can talk about it with the ease and familiarity that a baby talks to its mother about something to eat. . . . When an order is given by the boss to the department head, that order is sacred in the confidence of the man to whom it was given and should be treated as a sacred trust and not talked all over the streets and to everybody in the firm. As a rule, that is what's done in Negro organizations. . . . Time is another important factor. So much time is wasted in Colored organizations. Employees stand around for five, ten and fifteen minutes, just talking and waiting until the foreman arrives. . . . The White man can give them orders and they will respect his confidence and do as they are told without a complaint but there are so few of our people who will be that loyal to a firm giving them a decent living—much more than the White man would ever think of giving a Negro. . . . I tell you these things so that you can see the great obstacles the average colored business man has to deal with. . . . Above all, I would like to stress that you be thoroughly acquainted with the business that you will have to do. . . . In the newspaper field it is particularly important that you be familiar with advertising . . . and yet our people think that it requires no additional training.[109]

Abbott shared some of his ideas about what made the model black businessman and worker, and he encouraged Sengstacke to adopt this. He also advised Sengstacke not to drink, for "the man who wants to make a place for himself will never do so much by such procedures." He cited the white industrial magnates, John D. Rockefeller, Henry Ford, and John Pierpont Morgan, as examples of great businessmen, who, according to Abbott, did not let heavy drinking compromise their business acumen. His anxieties about the future of his business, his family, and Sengstacke embracing the proper manhood shaped this letter in ways that made Abbott appear to be unburdening himself. But Abbott assured his nephew, "I tell you these things so that you can see the great obstacles the average colored business man has to deal with."[110] The *Defender*'s financial decline and Abbott's illness both made him even more anxious to prepare Sengstacke to be "a well-rounded business man."[111] Abbott thought that Sengstacke's embrace of his ideals would help ensure his success, the family's security, and the *Defender*'s continued leadership in black journalism.

"I am happy to know that you are coming out and to know that we will be able to give you a place in the company," Abbott wrote closer to the time of Sengstacke's graduation. "I trust that you will learn everything possible in order that you may be able to enter into this field and be of service in every way to the institution, to safeguard its interests and help keep your grandfather's name alive," Abbott wrote. He also enclosed "a check that you may get yourself together so you will look presentable for the occasion."[112] A few weeks later, Sengstacke replied: "Well, you told me not to come back to Chicago unless I brought my diploma with me. . . . Look for me soon with diploma in hand . . . ready to hand over to you for inspection."[113] Completing Hampton did not mean his training was over, however—it was to continue under Abbott at the *Defender*. And Abbott would expect his nephew to become so committed to the publication that years later he reportedly told Sengstacke's wife that she would have to be secondary to the paper.[114]

As Abbott had learned the art of newspaper publishing from his stepfather, along with the role publishing could play in building Race Men and black manhood, so too was Sengstacke to learn this from his uncle. Abbott had insisted on publishing as a pathway to black manhood and wanted Sengstacke to join their family tradition, which seemed for Abbott to be an imagined, exclusive fraternity of family publishers. But this "fraternity" based on the family's media men may have been too exclusive for Sengstacke's emerging ideologies. Though the Depression era's impact on the nation, Abbott's family and paper, and opportunities for self-made men appeared bleak to Abbott, things looked a bit more promising to the youthful Sengstacke. He saw enormous political, cultural, and economic potential in the organizing of the era and changes in strategies of racial advancement. Over time, he came to embrace the lessons that Abbott tried to impart, while updating some of the fundamentals of those lessons in ways that reflected Depression-era organizing and his generation's new style of racial mobilization.

Sengstacke came of age ideologically in the midst of massive labor and Communist organizing, and more aggressive approaches to black protest. Communists had been organizing in the United States since the end of World War I but made unsuccessful attempts in the 1920s to rally blacks to their cause. Many black people distrusted them at the time for their radicalism and lack of public commitment to racial justice, despite the Communist International's announcement of the "Black Belt Thesis" in 1928.[115] But by the close of the 1930s, black people would see Communists as an ally, a vehicle for racial mobilization, and a voice of worker and civil rights advocacy.[116] Many other working-class Americans embraced them too throughout the decade. The Depression and surging joblessness, the New Deal's National Industrial Recovery Act and Wagner Act, which supported union organizing and collective bargaining, and the rise of militant unions like the Congress of Industrial Organizations (CIO) created a moment ripe for Communists to promote working-class radicalism. Communists generated a cultural, social, and political turn to the left in the 1930s that produced a radical culture that elevated, as historian Michael Denning has argued, the "laboring" and "proletarianization" of American mass culture. In many respects, the Communist Party's emphasis on the heroic and militant worker dovetailed with the black press's emphasis on redeeming the manhood of underutilized black male workers. This radical worker culture came to be known as the "Popular Front" and produced a vocabulary in which "labor and its synonyms" shaped the rhetoric, cultural productions, and social democratic culture of the period.[117]

For many black leaders, Communist influences, federal support for unionized workers, the rise of radical unions, increasing interracial organizing, and the radical culture that resulted helped provide activists with the language and backing to argue and organize for racial justice. The rhetoric and ideology of black self-determination accelerated especially as Communists and union organizing helped influence and mobilize black workers to be more militant in their demands for economic mobility and security.[118] Not only were militancy, worker solidarity, and aggressive organizing en vogue, but the state, through the New Deal, seemed to be more amenable to them. These developments penetrated the black press. Employees for the *Amsterdam News*, for instance, unionized, and after management discharged three workers, employees went on strike for the "cause of labor."[119]

Black intellectuals, civil rights activists, and white allies mobilized in 1935 to contribute to this growing radical, worker-oriented social milieu and to form an organization that would fuse worker rights, civil rights, and aggressive black activism. They gathered at Howard University to discuss "the position of the negro in our national economic crisis." The meeting sparked the founding of the National Negro Congress (NNC) in 1936, a broad network of labor-based organizers and interracial alliances of liberals and radicals that became, as historian Erik S. Gellman has put it, the "black vanguard of the Popular Front." The NNC organized people to boycott, strike, march, and engage in other militant forms of activism that challenged worker abuses and Jim Crow. Such activism not only helped pressure employers and the federal government for change but also heralded changes in strategies for racial advancement. As Gellman argues, their militant tactics used "the streets as spaces of negotiation, breaking from other black leaders who met privately with welfare capitalists they hoped to persuade." Under the leadership of veteran labor leader, organizer, and publisher A. Phillip Randolph, the NNC worked to create racial unity and black worker consciousness and activism that would ultimately generate a labor-based civil rights movement. The organization's motto, "Death Blow to Jim Crow," invoked an aggressive, if not violent, image of a manly attack on white supremacy.[120] Indeed, activists expressed much of the rhetoric that followed this new culture of radical labor organizing in rhetorics of masculinity, men's rights, brotherhood, and manly agitation. In fact, Randolph called the NNC and its efforts a "march toward the true status of men."[121]

Sengstacke came to be influenced and eventually moved to action by many of these developments. In fact, his thinking in this regard began taking shape as early as his time at Hampton. One of his class papers, for example, recognized "How I Depend on Others," arguing that a "civilized man" was unable to succeed in life "unless assisted by others." The class paper emphasized the "dependence of the individual upon others, (and vice versa)," a point that reflected the exigencies of the Depression era and his relationship with Abbott, but also differed with some aspects of the independent "'front' man" that Abbott had encouraged Sengstacke to be. By the late 1930s, he would use the language of labor organizers to say that whites and blacks depended on one another. "There are several race organizations that will not admit the whole race. . . . There are white organizations in our community [that] will not admit negroes. Where are we? Each on the other side of the fence, when both should be on the same side . . . in a well organized community. . . . Lets form a <u>United Front,</u> forgetting petty jealousies" (Sengstacke's emphasis). And citing his uncle's influence, he stated, "It has been the firm stand of the Defender for 32 years that our race should unite with other races for unified action."[122] Here, Sengstacke was attempting to fuse the ideas he had learned from Abbott in advancing the race through the work of self-made men with labor activists' ideas of self-determination. Indeed, if Abbott could create new gendered categories for his nephew, then so could Sengstacke for himself. In many ways, he was exhibiting more initiative. Abbott had encouraged Sengstacke to "make your own fortune," "have a lovely family home like I have," and "have lots of money in the bank," and to emulate John D. Rockefeller, Henry Ford, and John Pierpont Morgan. Sengstacke found such ownership appealing, and these legendary captains of industry and their work inspiring, but he would eventually begin thinking of how to organize black men of a similar ilk to do more for the race than only serve as examples of individual uplift.[123] Though this conception of organizing remained middle-class based, he would work to open up opportunities for black newspapermen as a particular class of black entrepreneurs to assert more of a role in this moment of racial organizing. And such organizing, as he would come to imagine it, would also bolster their businesses. The work of individual capitalists was inspiring, but activists who were increasingly exerting influence over both the marketplace and political arena were too. As Communist ideology and worker consciousness and activism grew in popularity, Abbott's model of manhood premised on exclusive ownership and individual financial success in the marketplace might have appeared more and more out of touch with contemporary racial politics. Sengstacke was beginning to update the self-made man. Given these dramatic changes in the black freedom struggle, this model of manhood, as it pertained to black male publishers particularly, needed to be updated so that they could not only keep pace with their readers but also be more useful to them, or one day find themselves irrelevant and underutilized.[124]

W. E. B. DuBois, who had participated in the founding of the NNC, noticed these increasingly outdated class sensibilities and generational and ideological shifts as early as at the time of his departure from the NAACP and *Crisis*. He too saw the pressing need to modify them. "The Association seemed to me not only unwilling to move toward the left in its program but even stepped decidedly toward the right," he remembered. "What astonished me most was that this economic reaction was voiced even more by the colored members of the Board of Directors than the white. . . . The younger and more prosperous Negro professional men, merchants, and investors were clinging to the older ideas of property, ownership and profits even more firmly than the whites. The liberal white world saw change that was coming" but "the upper class colored world did not anticipate nor understand it."[125]

For now, Sengstacke was one less underutilized black male worker as the next phase of his grooming involved his employment with the company. First, he took classes at Northwestern University. In one course, "Industrial Management," he did not do well, and his fears of flunking materialized. He received a failing grade.[126] But with or without a successful performance in the classes, the training he would receive at the *Defender* seemed sufficient to prepare him. He began work in September 1934 at a salary of $15 a week in the bookkeeping department. "I didn't know anything about the editorial side," he remembered, "but I did know something about the business and mechanical working of the Defender." He told his uncle, "You run the editorial department, and I'll run the business. That's my deal."[127] He advanced quickly through the ranks of the organization, though not without some apparent challenges. At twenty-six years of age, he succeeded Nathan K. McGill, who had been with the company since around 1925. McGill was fired in 1934 over issues concerning missing sums of money and checks he had improperly signed without Abbott's knowledge. Sengstacke discovered these discrepancies while working in the bookkeeping department.[128]

As Sengstacke advanced, *Defender* offices were again important to providing a certain masculine space conducive to a productive work ethic, especially for Abbott's presumptive successor. Having a decent office was important to understanding both his business and his manly role in the future of the paper. For example, Eneil F. Simpson circulated a memorandum in October 1934 intended to "eliminate any conflicts in authority by the appointment of John H. Sengstacke as Office Manager." He recommended

> the following plan of operation be adopted: 1. The Office Manager
> take the office formerly held by the writer. This will lend more dignity
> to the organization as a whole and make it possible for both him
> and myself to render a larger degree of service to this organization
> by being in private offices. 2. That in order for the Office Manager
> to become thoroughly acquainted with all phases of the business, he
> be assigned definite duties with the understanding that on all
> important matters he will be called into consultation. . . . By
> starting the office manager out on a definite mission such as above,
> his progress will be materially faster than the present set-up.[129]

In a "Notice to All Departments," the founder himself weighed in to solidify Sengstacke's quick integration into the organization. "I have after careful consideration appointed my nephew John Sengstacke, office manager," Abbott stated. "I shall appreciate your cooperation and sympathy in making him a success in this capacity. He is not a spy or a so called stool pigeon but an office manager with duties and responsibilities to perform. . . . Those of you who have been loyal to me I'm asking that same loyalty for him."[130]

By January 1935, Sengstacke was a voting member of the board of directors and nominated to be the vice president and treasurer.[131] Yet not only did Abbott and higher-ups work to integrate him properly into the business; they also made efforts to introduce him officially to the reading public. In 1938, Sengstacke became a part of the *Defender*'s thirty-third anniversary celebration as readers were again invited inside the *Defender*. *The Inside Story of the Chicago Defender*, a promotional pamphlet, commemorated the anniversary. It featured several images of personnel and the plant, including Abbott in "his executive office from which he directs the affairs of his great institution." The pamphlet reiterated Abbott's success story from the one-man newspaper: "Number of newsboys in Chicago selling to their own customers—one"; "Number of employees on staff (editors, reporters, etc.)—one." Now, the one newsboy had grown to 653. "One" employee was now 115. "The man power and capital still behind the gun is the same Robert Sengstacke Abbott, but an institution with over a half million dollars worth of assets. Indebtedness, NONE." The pamphlet emphasized the plant's valuable pieces of technology as symbols of the paper's greatness. The plant's equipment remained a "mighty combination of machinery and man power."[132]

Then there was Sengstacke's public introduction. "Still in his twenties, [Sengstacke] is establishing himself as an executive by handling with dignity and competence, the business and financial affairs of THE CHICAGO DEFENDER and the ROBERT S. ABBOTT PUBLISHING COMPANY, INC." In one section, uncle and nephew were pictured together with Sengstacke standing over Abbott, who was seated at a desk. "Here we see Hon. Robert S. Abbott, President, and John H. Sengstacke, Vice-President and Treasurer of THE ROBERT S. ABBOTT PUBLISHING COMPANY," the pamphlet stated, "together going over plans for the remodeling of the Defender plant. Since that time over $35,000 has been spent on the plant, machinery and new office equipment. Today, the CHICAGO DEFENDER has the largest and most complete plant of any Race newspaper in the world."[133] This family portrait symbolized the bonds between uncle and nephew, mentor and mentee, creator and successor. The image poignantly captured the foundation and future of the company, while gesturing toward continued manly institution-building and greater technological growth for the *Defender.*

The pamphlet intended to show "many readers who have never seen anything but the finished product . . . what it takes to bring the Defender to their doors."[134] Yet again, another anniversary celebration did not display all of what it took to produce the paper. Hidden from public view was the company's ongoing financial challenges, problems that Sengstacke would now have to help resolve. By the mid- to late 1930s, Abbott had been "taken off" some of his official business "because of illness."[135] As early as June 1936, an audit reported that the company was $146,728.80 in the "red." While "[Abbott] has long been regarded as one of the wealthiest and most influential men of his race in Chicago," the audit found that "he is understood to have sustained some financial reverses in recent years." His "circulation and income declined" and "the machinery valuation being higher, due to recent investments in linotype machines . . . but the company continues to owe heavily on its principal."[136]

By July 1938, financial troubles only mounted. It was then that the Internal Revenue Service (IRS) said the company owed $2,896.83 in taxes for the years 1936–38. "We have failed to file heretofore," Sengstacke responded, "because of our inability to make the required payment. However, we are endeavoring to secure additional capital which should enable us to handle this obligation within thirty days."[137] On August 11, 1938, the IRS responded, giving the company a deadline of August 22, 1938, to satisfy the debt.[138] Seng-stacke seemingly scrounged to find the money to meet the debt and others. "Due to unforeseen circumstances, the payroll will not be ready until Mon-day, September 12, 1938. Your cooperation will be appreciated," he ex-plained to employees.[139] Another memorandum informed employees of a "slight reduction in salaries. This position was taken in order not to cause undue suffering to any one individual by letting out or by complete elimi-nation of any one department." The "10%" reduction was "necessitated by an emergency which is temporary. . . . I wish to assure you that as soon as this emergency is over, and pressing outstanding obligations are retired, we will go back to our regular salary schedule."[140] In May 1939, Nathan K. McGill, Abbott's onetime friend and personal attorney that Sengstacke replaced, sued the company. McGill wanted back pay due him for the years 1933 and 1934, the years he went unpaid as the company fought to survive the Depression.[141]

Competition from other papers cut into some of the *Defender*'s profits and compounded financial problems. One memorandum described the compe-tition between the *Courier* and *Defender* as a "battle," though representa-tives thought the *Defender* was beginning to gain ground. There remained a "fight" with the *Amsterdam News*, however. Sengstacke suggested to one representative that writers focus more on covering "state news" and "cut down on the amount of news in other sections of the country." Sengstacke thought this might be the "best way to increase circulation throughout the country."[142] Another representative even took a tour through cities east of Chicago to gauge the competition. By traveling through Indiana, Ohio, Pennsylvania, and New York, the representative was able to determine which papers sold the most, where, and for how much.[143]

By February 1940, Sengstacke seemed to have also risen in the ranks among family, for they had begun to look to him for support, much as they had Abbott. For example, W. B. Abbott, likely a cousin, wrote Sengstacke, seeking a position in the company. Congratulating him on his "rapid ad-vancement," Abbott stated that he was "desperately in need of a job. I am seeking a job with the Defender through you, as you are the only one to place me." He suggested that he could help the paper to "re-gain the Circu-lation that the Defender once enjoyed," signing off with "Remember me kindly to R. S. and [I] trust his health is much improved."[144] Though this underutilized black male worker promised to help increase the *Defender*'s sales, Sengstacke did not help.[145] "It was kind of you to write me and I want you to know that I appreciate the interest you feel for the Defender,"

Sengstacke responded a few days later. "I wish that it was possible to place you here in some capacity now, but at present there are absolutely no openings." Sengstacke's uncle had helped him find work at the *Defender* despite the organization's financial challenges and layoffs at that time. Sengstacke might have sympathized with this family member, but he balked. "Please be assured that I shall keep you in mind. . . . I shall convey your regards to R. S. and the family," Sengstacke said in closing.[146]

As Sengstacke grappled with these challenges, the *Defender*'s strained finances and circulation drops took root inside his mind. A besieged Sengstacke began reaching out to other members of the black press some time in 1939, motivated to help get the business affairs of the black press organized. On January 6, 1940, Claude Barnett received a letter from Sengstacke, seeking "co-operation on the part of our newspapers and other publications."[147] Barnett was the founder of the Associated Negro Press (ANP), who had gotten his start in journalism as an employee for the *Defender* in 1918. His ANP was the leading black newswire service of the day. Since its founding in 1919, he had become a successful institution-builder too. In January 1936, he had even offered to purchase or lease the *Defender* from Abbott during its financial slump.[148] Sengstacke contacted Barnett to share his desire to form an organization intended to help black newspapers become better organized and therefore become stronger businesses and racial institutions. The National Negro Press Association, founded in 1909, was originally designed to do this. But for Sengstacke and many of his contemporaries, the moribund organization had failed.[149] Sengstacke explained to Barnett that "the Negro newspaper is recognized as the mouthpiece through which the entire race speaks," and though it "has weathered the storm of the depression, as well as, if not better than, any commercial enterprise manned and controlled by our race," he charged that "we seem to be the most disorganized body in the entire set-up of Negro business."[150]

Sengstacke echoed Abbott's sentiments in 1934 that black businesses seemed disorganized. But he could also attest to this personally, having experienced it firsthand at the *Defender*. In fact, he may have felt that business management was not necessarily his uncle's strong suit, a personal limit of Abbott's, despite his incredible success. For example, Abbott shared during the twenty-fifth anniversary celebration that at one point, "people within my employ" had attempted to destroy him and the *Defender*.[151] Issues with Nathan K. McGill illustrated this. Enoch P. Waters, a *Defender* editor who joined the staff in 1935, commented that in the five years he knew Abbott, he found the publisher not to be an "astute businessman."

"He was naively trusting of others who took advantage of his simple faith. He was not only overcharged by his suppliers, misled by his advisors, but also robbed by some of his most trusted employees." Ironically, these claims resembled issues that Abbott had once played up in news coverage against Garvey in order to highlight Garvey's poor business management and therefore questionable leadership. In fact, Waters concluded that Abbott "made money, but couldn't manage it." In general, Waters felt that the "founders of black newspapers were crusaders unprepared to assume the financial responsibilities associated with a publishing enterprise. In their determination to correct what they perceived to be an intolerable social justice, they chose to ignore the practical realities of their ventures."[152] Yet Sengstacke's suggestion to form an organization that might change the face of the entire black press launched him on his own path as an institution-builder, as his uncle had encouraged him to do years ago. This would enable him to make his mark as a trailblazing businessman and Race Man in his own right. But Sengstacke's conception of better organizing the black press had to do with its potential as a racial institution to help mobilize black people as much as its capacity as a business institution. Its potential to do this was perhaps even greater now amid Depression-era organizing and militant masculine rhetoric. "If you feel, as many publishers do, that the time has arrived for us to come together and discuss matters for our mutual benefit and interest," Sengstacke wrote, "let us have your opinion and suggestions."[153]

The NNC and black labor organizers heralded a new tide of racial mobilizations, and Sengstacke envisioned something similar for black newspapers. The black press was the one black institution best equipped to promote collective, mass organizing, Sengstacke reasoned. And in addition to promoting racial organizing, the black press could also model it as a united body of newspapermen. "The struggle of the Negro masses to attain democratic parity with the whites on those basic principles that give meaning to American citizenship," Sengstacke would explain years later, "would be advanced to fruitful ends were the Negro press, which controls a considerable body of public opinion, willing to consolidate its energy, unify its aims, and concentrate on a practical strategy for a sustained frontal attack on the issues, institutions, and personalities which are blocking the progress of the race."[154] Fusing Abbott's ideals with that of labor activists, Sengstacke sought to update and organize the "self-made men" of the black press. Organizing in this way could help black newspapers exert influence over the marketplace to buttress the economic position of the black press, while also exerting influence over the black public sphere to mobilize blacks to pressure employers and the federal government for change. Though this approach to racial organizing remained middle-class based, it was what black publishers could do with their papers that made Sengstacke's vision of the black press democratic and egalitarian, so he believed. The language Sengstacke used to propose organizing black newspapermen is significant, revealing his gendered thinking in conceptualizing the group. He pitched the organization to Barnett and other black newspapermen as a "fraternity for the common good and welfare of all," to be like the "clubs and fraternities" of the "masses whom we lead and serve."[155]

On one hand, Communist's and labor organizers' ideas and ideals of brotherhood helped construct a vocabulary of masculinist terms that many activists used to articulate demands for rights, and mobilize for them.[156] Sengstacke's ideas and language here reflected this. This fraternity was Sengstacke's attempt to build a new coalition out of the black press, too long a disparate body of numerous small-town and big-city publications that stretched across the country, covering news for different locales and populations, oftentimes with overlapping but competing spheres of influence. Despite differences in location, ownership, ideology, business models, budgets, plant technology, and circulation, all of them seemed invested in a common goal of advancing the race. And it was on this point that Sengstacke imagined that members of the black press could cut past their obvious differences and unite, at least editorially and professionally, if not entirely as an institution. Though their competitions had helped build a vibrant black public sphere, the competition had at times compromised the capacity of black papers to help foster and exemplify racial unity, so Sengstacke thought. This competition exposed another limit of Abbott's and of the publishers of his generation. Their competition represented "petty warfare when black publishers were hurling brickbats and slinging mud at one another," Sengstacke said years later. "My Uncle, Robert S. Abbott, publisher of the Chicago Defender didn't speak to Vann, publisher of the Pittsburgh Courier, Vann wouldn't speak to Murphy, publisher of Afro-American and Murphy wouldn't [speak] to C. B. Powell, publisher of Amsterdam News. Incredible as this may sound, it was the trend and social ethics of the day."[157] Soliciting Barnett's help may have further illustrated Sengstacke's goal of replacing the ethic of competition with a fraternity forged through brotherhood because he was Abbott's old enemy, reportedly.[158] Since its inception, the modern black press had encouraged readers to unite in action. Sengstacke determined that it was time now to do the same for black publishers.

On another hand, in framing the new organization as a "fraternity," Sengstacke tapped into a long history of black male organizing, socializing, and solidarity that had preceded Depression-era organizing by decades. Indeed, fraternal life had been important to black men of Abbott's generation and remained such to succeeding ones.[159] Abbott was a member of Kappa Alpha Psi Fraternity, a Greek-letter black fraternity, and reportedly received at one point one of their highest honors.[160] Abbott had emphasized to Sengstacke that a proper sense of masculinity was important to shaping professional black men and had also encouraged Sengstacke to value his imagined exclusive fraternity of family publishers. And Sengstacke appreciated this from his uncle. Over the course of his lifetime, Sengstacke became a member of several fraternal orders, such as the Masons, Elks, and Royal Order of Snakes.[161] Sengstacke applied and extended to the black press these histories of black fraternal life, and his own fraternal experiences, knowing that the pursuit of proper black manhood and bonds among like-minded men were powerful points around which black men had tended to come together for some time already. Organizing under such a gendered framework was familiar to other newspapermen, who, like Sengstacke, were also members of fraternities. Some fraternities had also published papers of their own.[162] A fraternity for black newspapermen underscored the gendered implications of the label "newspaperman," further solidified the relationship between media and masculinity, and might therefore appeal to the largely male workforce that constituted the black press. Indeed, Sengstacke wanted the group to address the "foremost problems . . . that we as newspaper men must necessarily be concerned with."[163] His conception of a fraternity for black newspapermen broadened contemporary conceptions of brotherhood to hinge on the fusing of two seemingly unconnected expressions of brotherhood: that which was expressed by working-class labor activists, and that which had long been practiced organizationally by middle-class, professional black men.[164] Here, like his uncle, he was engaging in man-building, a process to which male newspaper owners and workers could relate.

But Sengstacke's masculine framing of the organization failed to account for newspaperwomen, at least in gendered terms. Many black newspaperwomen's writing, columns, reporting, and work as clerical staff were just as vital to the influence and success of the black press as those of their male counterparts. In fact, as the era's labor and black activism inspired men like Sengstacke, it also inspired black women, who were among the era's most strident organizers. The National Housewives League movement demonstrated this, along with the National Council of Negro Women (NCNW). Founded in 1935, a year before the NNC, its leader, Mary McLeod Bethune, a nationally known educator and longtime advocate for black women, wanted the NCNW to organize black women activists already involved in a number of other women's groups across the country into an "organization of organizations." She also wanted them to collaborate with interracial and progressive labor movements. Bethune was tapped in 1935 to lead the Negro Division of the National Youth Administration in President Roosevelt's administration, which aided her work for the NCNW.[165] And, as historian Deborah Gray White notes, the NCNW's "most steadfast affiliates were the sororities," especially members of Alpha Kappa Alpha and Delta Sigma Theta, black Greek-letter sororities. These groups had wide cultural and social currency in black communities. Indeed, many considered black sorority women symbols of black middle-class and female uplift, models of proper black womanhood, and purveyors of a "sisterhood." The organization also published the *Aframerican Woman's Journal*. Whether as labor activists or sorority members, black women were just as active in organizing as black men were, often simultaneously.[166] And in addition to their broader activism, some black women worked to resist the masculine rhetoric of the era because of the ways it helped subordinate their particular economic, social, racial, and gender struggles to those of men at this time.[167]

Sengstacke's explicitly masculine frame in organizing black publishers revealed the ways he had come to conceive of newspaper ownership and production as a masculine project. Black newspaperwomen came to join Sengstacke's effort, to be sure, drawing on long-standing and new developments in black women's organizing at this moment while also demonstrating their commitment to strengthening the black press. Still, he figured black media as a fundamentally male domain, ideas that reflected Abbott's influence, black men's numerical, editorial, and managerial domination of the black press, prevailing gender ideologies and rhetoric that emphasized a relationship between masculinity and labor, and popular anxieties over restoring proper manhood. This exposed one of Sengstacke's limits. His seeing the world of media as a manly space was a view that many other newspapermen shared, black and white, owing to some of the sexism that some black and white women journalists faced within the industry.[168] Yet ensuring proper black manhood was a powerful point around which many black communities had organized, including some black women.[169] Perhaps some women could thus relate to Sengstacke's framing. Carl Murphy, publisher of the Baltimore *Afro-American*, was a member of Alpha Phi Alpha, a black

Greek-letter fraternity; his wife, Vashti (Turley) Murphy, was one of the original founders of Delta Sigma Theta.[170] Even Bethune at one time embraced the masculine rhetorics of many male organizers. For example, her acceptance speech for the NAACP's Spingarn Award in 1935 was titled "Breaking the Bars to Brotherhood." "Equality of opportunity is necessary to brotherhood," she said. "Let us as workers under this banner make free men spread truth about economic adjustment; truth about moral obligation; truth about segregation; truth about citizenship."[171] Perhaps women who decided to join Sengstacke would embrace his "fraternity" as an opportunity for inserting themselves into some kind of leadership role in the black press that helped carve out a new category in gender ideologies that might reflect black women's worker consciousness and organizing efforts, and help to make specific changes for black newspaperwomen.[172]

Invoking the language of labor activists, Sengstacke called for a "Solid Front on National Issues Affecting the Race" to convene the first National Conference of Negro Publishers in Chicago. On February 29, 1940, at the Wabash Avenue YMCA, twenty-eight publishers, editors, and executives from "New York to Nebraska," representing twenty-one papers, accepted his call. Two newspaperwomen, Fannie McConell, a stenographer, and Marian Downer, the manager of the *Courier*'s Chicago office, attended. The rest were men.[173] In many ways, Sengstacke was but a neophyte in the midst of some of these veteran black journalists and publishers, though many of them had learned how to make their papers influential and profitable from the *Defender*.[174] Some of the conferees thought he was attempting to regain the prominence the *Defender* had enjoyed in the 1920s.[175] But Sengstacke explained that their meeting was intended for "harmonizing our energies in a common purpose for the benefit of Negro journalism."[176] Their agenda items included addressing "policies that will be of benefit to Negroes and Negro newspapers," issues with editorial policies and advertising, and "building our business."[177] Perhaps they would succeed where the National Negro Press Association had failed to remain active because the new group was organizing like a fraternity. Set to proceed from February 29 to March 2, something unexpected interrupted the first day of the conference. That morning, attendees learned that Abbott had died.

They adjourned, but not before honoring his memory. Calling him "the dean of Negro publishers," attendees lauded Abbott for revolutionizing black publishing. Indeed, many of them likely agreed that Abbott's example of race journalism and newspaper ownership had set the standard that many of them followed.[178] "We bow our heads in deep sympathy . . . and . . . find solace only in the fact that the institution he founded for the service of the people and humanity will continue to inspire, fight and build in the spirit, and with the courage and wisdom of Robert S. Abbott."[179] When the conference resumed later that afternoon, they discussed, for example, strengthening their businesses by gaining better control of national advertising and news-gathering resources, and compiling facts "on issues affecting the general welfare of the race."[180] Their work eventually led to the formation of the Negro Newspaper Publishers Association (NNPA). Members elected Sengstacke the first president, and the new organization helped launch what historian Bill V. Mullen has termed a black "cultural front."[181] Chester Franklin, publisher of the *Kansas City Call* and newly elected western vice president of the NNPA, commented, "This is the greatest gathering of Negro Publishers I have ever seen." Sengstacke hoped that the conference would put the black press "on the road to perfect understanding and solidarity among the Negro publishers."[182] Other observers remarked that the meeting marked "a new order in Negro journalism."[183] Indeed, at once, the NNPA signaled the founding of a business organization, racial organization, and black fraternity. Abbott's death symbolized the passing of one era as a new order dawned under the leadership of his nephew. For Sengstacke, the moment must have been quite poignant. He lost his uncle on the same day that he was trying to apply some of what Abbott had taught him: to have "plenty" of "initiative."

In the ensuing weeks, the *Defender* heaped praises upon Abbott. He was a "titan," a "hero," a "bridge-builder," and a "martyr to the cause that Black Men Shall Survive."[184] Longtime *Defender* writer Lucius C. Harper wrote that Abbott "educated his race to demand their rights as men." The "Toussaint L'Ouverture of journalism," Abbott "was a man of one idea, which is all that the brain of any man of action can ever hold." "LUCKY ARE THE sons of black men when such martyrs and faithful servants to a race as Robert S. Abbott are born upon the earth."[185] David Ward Howe, another writer, declared that "perhaps more than any other man, Robert S. Abbott was responsible for the [Great] migration."[186] Writer Clarence Muse even suggested that someone make a movie about Abbott. He was "a man who started with nothing and with only a SUPER-NATURAL belief in HIMSELF and his people, created an institution that will live long." "See if you can visualize ACROSS the marquee—this week—'WORLD'S GREATEST WEEKLY' and THE MAN."[187] The highlight of these tributes, however, was an eleven-article installment titled "Quest for Equality." Running from March 16, 1940, until May 25 of that year, the series was Abbott's autobiography that he penned sometime before his death. A large part of Abbott's success as a publisher was due to his adept skill in promoting sensationalized human-interest news stories. Sengstacke had likely learned this skill under Abbott's tutelage. The promotion of such stories would not change in Abbott's absence, especially since this story was about him. What better way to demonstrate the continued strength of the institution during this crucial period of transition than celebrating the life of the man who created it? The autobiography educated readers about his life, as well as served as a promotional tool for the paper. Statements of "To be continued" or "Continued Next Week" followed the end of all but the last article, informing readers that they could keep reading the series—pending their purchase, of course.[188] Though it is not exactly clear when he wrote it, Abbott's was a story of successful individual uplift in service to the race. Readers had been familiar with the story since the twenty-fifth anniversary celebration, but the posthumous publication of the autobiography made the narrative more illuminating, and put the *Defender*'s image of him as an ideal model of black manhood in greater relief. Literary scholar David L. Dudley has observed that black men's life narratives have tended to center on a "quest for freedom," the tale of an isolated black man trying to make his way in the world and establish a path for other black men to follow. Abbott's was a "Quest for Equality."[189]

Sengstacke praised his uncle and mentor too and promised to carry on his work. Many twentieth-century black newspapers had died along with their founders, but Abbott's grooming of Sengstacke prevented this for the *Defender*.[190] In fact, throughout his career, Sengstacke would continue to cite Abbott as his muse, while framing himself as the steward of Abbott's legacy. In this way, the *Defender* remained the material manifestation of Abbott's ideas and body, as he and his paper remained inseparable even in death. A trustee of Abbott's estate shared in the *Defender* that "[Abbott] appointed John Sengstacke to manage the Defender and guided him through many months—this training must be utilized and I am glad that Mr. Sengstacke will continue at the helm of the publishing company. I predict a continued upswing under Mr. Sengstacke's direction." Sengstacke was named the chief executive officer. "I pledge every reader and the staff of the *Defender*," he said, "my best thoughts and efforts for the progress of the institution. Mr. Abbott was and is my ideal—during the years I have been associated with him he has continually stimulated my heart and brain for the forward surge of the *Defender*."[191] Over the years, the paper had become a part of Sengstacke's inner workings, just as it had been for his uncle. Abbott's memory and legacy would be added to this.[192] Close friends of

Sengstacke's family wrote letters offering their condolences. The *Defender* published several letters that were written by prominent individuals, such as the governor of Illinois, the mayor of Chicago, and major black leaders. One of the letters spoke to Sengstacke directly. The letter repeated elements of Abbott's success story, recognized the role of masculinity in shaping his publishing, and acknowledged his part in helping make a generation of men, including Sengstacke. "Possessing little capital, and training," Dr. Richard Winston and Attorney Henry J. Richardson Jr. of Indiana wrote, "he blazed the ways as the father of Negro newspapers in America. . . . He was truly a lover of humanity, an uncompromising fighter for his Race, a maker of men whose ideals embodied true Americanism. It is indeed fortunate that he trained young capable men as you . . . and others to carry on his ideals and business. . . . We are sure that many of your fine characteristics and qualities can be attributed to his sincere guidance and teaching."[193]

Indeed, Sengstacke had accepted the transfer of the mantle of newspaper ownership from his uncle, while giving birth to a media institution of his own. It would take some time, however, for some members of the *Defender* family to fully embrace their new leader. For example, the more senior Lucius C. Harper, who had been with the *Defender* since the Migration era and helped Abbott create the Bud Billiken page, continued to treat Sengstacke like a child.[194] At one point, Abbott's widow from his second marriage, Edna R. Abbott, contested Sengstacke's leadership over legal matters related to her late husband's estate.[195] Still, Sengstacke had become in many ways his own man, updating the self-made man, and organizing the black press accordingly. Shortly after the founding meeting for the NNPA, other black newspapermen began to share the gendered implications of his goals in forging a cooperative effort among black newspapermen. For example, D. Arnett Murphy, the advertising manager of the *Afro-American* and eastern vice president for the NNPA, wrote Sengstacke on May 27, 1940, "It is very gratifying to feel that our efforts toward better cooperation among the members of the newspaper fraternity are meeting with some degree of success and I feel sure that you are in a large measure responsible for initiating this movement."[196] Within a few years, Sengstacke's vision of an economically strong and united black press backed by the NNPA materialized as many major black newspapers came together to protest segregation in defense industries and the armed forces through what became known as the "Double V" campaign. Many of them also collaborated to protest lily-white major league baseball, which resulted in Jackie Robinson becoming the first black player to integrate the majors. Their influential editorial campaigns on these fronts focused on racial equality and winning opportunities for underutilized black men. Sometime in the mid-1940s, the group helped issue a twenty-one-point statement to President Roosevelt, their agenda for racial advancement during and following the war that encouraged the government to do more to protect the civil rights of black people. By 1943, Sengstacke envisioned the black press, March on Washington movement, NNC, NAACP, Urban League, and other black activist groups all uniting in a "solid unit" to pressure the government on racial justice.[197] Long ago, Abbott told him that "all the Negro wanted was to be a man and a good American citizen," to "be a man and have the fullness of American citizenship." The NNPA lasted longer than any of its organizational predecessors.[198]

Sengstacke's founding of the NNPA and the rising militancy of the black press in the 1940s reflected an upsurge of militant organizing among blacks that grew out of the exigencies of the Depression era. For Sengstacke, this organizing had also grown out of issues within the *Defender* organization, however.[199] The Depression era unleashed unprecedented economic, social, and political change in America. The economic crisis, emergence of a social democratic state, and labor organizing imbued the American working class with a new agency and impetus for political and cultural assertion.[200] The era was thought to have also unleashed a crisis in masculinity that helped produce a new and increasingly masculinized class politics in the country as policy leaders and activists tried to confront both crises, which they saw as intertwined.[201] The black press constructed the image of underutilized black men to argue for restoring them to work and manhood. But these discourses penetrated the institutional foundations of the *Defender* in special ways. Many Americans, black and white, linked the fate of the nation to the fate of men, and likewise, Abbott linked the fate of his publishing empire to Sengstacke. Throughout the 1930s, Abbott groomed him in his own professional and gender ideals, a process that resulted in Sengstacke taking over the paper, and doing a bit more. His uncle had been a pioneer black male publisher, and drawing inspiration from both Abbott's model of manhood and Depression-era labor and racial organizing, Sengstacke updated the model of the self-made man, and made his own contribution to the field of black journalism by founding a media institution that helped elevate the black press to new levels of influence in the black public sphere.

Defender representatives wanted to use Sengstacke's new public image as a trailblazing Race Man, institution-builder, and successor to Abbott's historic publishing empire to their advantage. Sengstacke had become a "'front'" man, though on his own terms. Still, he maintained parts of what he had learned from his uncle, how to lead and present a proper public image, though things may have been different inside the *Defender*, behind the walls of the institution. Indeed, he and three *Defender* representatives prepared sometime in the 1940s to restore the paper to its erstwhile lead. Sengstacke was genuinely committed to the goal of uniting the black press, but he was also careful to maintain a degree of discretion in his pursuit of other goals that might affect the fraternity of black newspapermen he was trying to build. They met at Sengstacke's home and the home of Metz Lochard, one of the paper's editors, to discuss "the splendid opportunity now confronting the Defender in becoming the most influential organization in the national picture if proper coordination is achieved." Among several strategies they devised in order to restore the *Defender* to being "the strongest publication in the Negro field," the confidential memorandum stated, Sengstacke's new public image was key. "The technique to be used in building prestige for the paper was discussed. It was agreed that Mr. Sengstacke, as president of the organization, must be a symbol of its power," much like Abbott was. "This organization could never be a major factor in shaping the destiny of Negroes unless the techniques of big-time business were adopted. That Mr. Sengstacke must be a symbolism of this strength, just like Ford [and] Morgan are symbols of organizations that they head." These men represented some of the masculine models of business ownership that Abbott had long wanted Sengstacke to adopt. With his uncle's influence still shaping the organization's business decisions, their actions seemed to pay off within just a few years. In 1945, *Black Metropolis*, the landmark encyclopedic study of black life in Chicago by black sociologists St. Claire Drake and Horace Cayton, evaluated the *Defender* positively as the "most widely known" black paper in Chicago. The scholars repeated elements of Abbott's success story encapsulated in the paper's twenty-fifth anniversary celebration and reported that "the *Defender* is a stable business enterprise." Yet, having begun implementing Sengstacke's symbolic image based on his updated self-made man, Drake and Cayton distinguished Sengstacke from his uncle. The "present publisher is somewhat more responsive to the wider currents of general American liberal and progressive thought than was Editor Abbott." Only one thing seemed not to have changed much, however. "The paper itself remains an ardent 'Race Paper.'"[202]

4 A Challenge to Our Manhood

Robert F. Williams, the Civil Rights Movement, and the
Decline of the Mainstream Black Press

. . . .

For a time, Robert F. Williams seemed to be an unlikely publisher. He joined the army in 1945, serving during the years in which the black press experienced its greatest levels of organization, popularity, and influence. By the end of the war, black newspapers had led their most successful editorial campaigns. The black press broke free of the Depression, along with the national economy, and began expanding again with circulation jumping 43 percent from 1,276,600 to 1,808,060.[1] More papers joined the roster of the Negro Newspaper Publishers Association (NNPA). In 1944, the organization released the "Credo for the Negro Press," written by P. B. Young Jr., son of the founder of the *Norfolk Journal and Guide.* "I Shall Be a Crusader . . . I Shall Be an Advocate . . . I Shall Be a Herald . . . I Shall Be a Mirror and a Record," the "Credo" declared.[2] What was becoming a "golden age" of influence for black newspapers led Swedish sociologist Gunnar Myrdal to praise the black press in his 1944 study *An American Dilemma.* The landmark work on black life in America counted 210 black newspapers and upward of 129 magazines. In an extraordinary finding, Myrdal determined that virtually every black person was exposed to the press on a regular basis on some level, by reading it directly, hearing it read aloud, or simply discussing it in social circles. He found the black press's influence to be so pervasive that he asserted that "the importance of the Negro press for the formation of Negro opinion, for the functioning of all other Negro institutions, for Negro leadership and concerted action generally, is enormous." "The Negro press causes, on the one hand," he continued, "an intense realization on the part of the Negroes of American ideals. On the other hand, it makes them realize to how small a degree white Americans live up to them."[3] Two polls taken by members of the black press showed that over 90 percent of readers supported its militancy. According to one *Defender* poll in 1945, 81 percent of the black public relied on the stance of the press to determine their opinions on important issues. The *Defender* insisted that 97 percent of those polled felt that many of black people's gains in equal rights had been largely due to the relentless advocacy of the press.[4] On other fronts, the press was also growing. For example, Louis Lautier of the *Atlanta Daily World* and Alice Dunnigan of the Associated Negro Press became the first black reporters to be accredited to the congressional press galleries in 1947. In 1955, Lautier would integrate the National Press Club and Dunnigan did the same for the Women's National Press Club. Even white businesses were beginning to take greater advantage of the advertising markets the expanding black press offered.[5]

By midcentury, the mainstream black press seemed ascendant. At the peak of their cultural and political power, the black press of the postwar years became staffed with more writers and national and foreign correspondents, improved printing facilities, and increased access to national white advertisers. As a result, the press was able to intensify its part in covering the struggle for racial justice and in helping to direct it.[6] For example, Chicago entrepreneur John H. Johnson followed up the success of his first magazine, *Ebony* (1945), with the founding of three more: *Tan* in 1950, *Jet* in 1951, and *Hue* in 1953. *Ebony* was popular among middle-class black readers for its grand lifestyle approach and omission of political content. *Jet* was intended to maintain a better pulse on current affairs and black freedom struggles.[7] In 1951, John Sengstacke launched the *Tri-State Defender* in Memphis, Tennessee.[8] Four years later, the *Defender* celebrated its fiftieth anniversary, and in conjunction with the occasion, Sengstacke published a book-length biography of Abbott. Again telling Abbott's success story during a milestone anniversary, the biography was titled *The Lonely Warrior*, a new expression of one of his old monikers, the "one-man force."[9] In 1956, Sengstacke announced that the weekly *Defender* was going to become a daily in order to report news as soon as it unfolded. The *Courier* led this golden age, however, having outstripped other papers by leading the black press's most effective editorial campaigns in the 1940s, the Double V campaign and the desegregation of lily-white baseball.[10] The *Courier* construed the half-century as an occasion to celebrate "Fifty Years of Progress" for black people in a number of arenas, including music, business, politics, education, the arts, and the press. It praised the new preeminence of black newspapers and their historic service as a "Flaming Sword in Fight for Race Progress" whose "Unifying Role Brought Negroes Closer Together." The *Courier* anticipated greater things being on the horizon for the black press, promising that it would "continue to grow in power and influence until it no longer serves any need," a time that "still seems to be rather distant."[11]

If its first five decades were any indication of the future, then the next five would also be a triumph.

Within a few years, the expansion of the black press even extended to Monroe, North Carolina, where Williams launched a newsletter, the *Crusader Weekly Newsletter*. This chapter examines Williams and his newsletter, particularly closely examining the challenge they presented to strategies for racial advancement, the mainstream black press, and changing ideas of black leadership and black manhood. In fact, Williams represented a new kind of black male publisher with a new kind of black publication. Indeed, Williams was not like many of the middle-class black newspapermen that had long typified the mainstream black press. He was working class and a black veteran, who returned home in October 1955 to Monroe. But he returned around a time of tremendous strides in the burgeoning southern civil rights struggle, on one hand, and a violent white backlash against civil rights activists that marked a crisis, on the other. On May 17, 1954, the NAACP's long strategy of waging litigious warfare against segregation culminated in its most decisive court victory, *Brown v. the Board of Education*. The Supreme Court's unanimous decision declared segregated public schools unconstitutional and struck a blow to state-sanctioned racism. The *Cleveland Call and Post* declared it an "important milestone," but warned there would be a backlash "calculated to arouse the Negro people to anger and revolt. . . . The stakes are the highest this generation has ever played for."[12] The paper was right. A backlash of racial violence exploded in the South in reaction to *Brown*. As legal scholar Michael Klarman has argued, the decision "crystalized resistance to racial change." Segregationists were determined to intimidate black people, black activism, and public support for black civil rights, often through violence.[13] One of the most egregious examples of this violence was the lynching of Emmett Till in August 1955. After a seemingly improper interaction with a white woman, the fourteen-year-old Till was thrown into an inviolable southern world of race, gender, and violence in which scores of black men had been lynched for even the smallest perceived untoward action before a white woman. Till's killers mutilated his face beyond recognition. At the insistence of his mother, Mamie Till, the wrenching image of his corpse inside the open casket was plastered across the cover of *Jet*.[14] One incensed reader looked to the black press for guidance in the wake of the murder. "We must be instructed through your newspaper," he stated to the *Defender*, "to fight the white man in the South with bullets. . . . The white man in the South is bad, and we must be bad also to survive. . . .

It is up to our leaders through our newspapers to advise us on these things." Till's lynching and the acquittal of his murderers by an all-white jury signaled a flagrant miscarriage of justice that outraged black America and revealed the brutality of a backlash that only worsened throughout the decade. Another reader simply thundered: "Negroes in every state . . . should declare war on the state of Mississippi."[15]

Williams knew something about war, having served in the Korean War. Trained to confront enemies directly, Williams was prepared to fight back as civil rights activism increasingly put black lives and bodies at heightened risk during this crisis. This chapter considers the "war" Williams and other activists saw emerging in the South after *Brown*, the response of the black press to how activists decided to fight this war, and what the discourses and images the fight produced would mean for ideas of black manhood and the black press.[16] Williams's fighting back took a number of different but related forms, however. The backlash intimidated and curtailed some black activism, but motivated activists like Williams to become even more resolute in arguing for black civil rights and asserting the right of self-defense. Like many black veterans of America's wars, Williams returned home frustrated with having served in the name of democracy only to come back to a country where Jim Crow segregation prevailed alongside the violent resurgence of white supremacy. And like other black veterans, a citizen-soldier frame of mind shaped Williams's outlook on the civil rights struggle. This mentality influenced veterans, black and white, to be committed to the ideals and lessons they had learned as servicemen, even in civilian life. Yet this line of thinking worked differently for black veterans, as scholars have shown. For them, the exigencies of the freedom struggle convinced many black veterans that they were still at war, fighting literally and figuratively for their lives and rights.[17]

But Williams's soldier-citizen mentality led him to fight back using essentially three approaches. First, he joined and led his local chapter of the NAACP. Next, he called for the use of self-defense and organized local activists to deploy armed resistance to racial violence. Scholars have especially noted the first two approaches, but less examined is how Williams turned to newspaper publishing in the third approach.[18] That his *Crusader* barely reached the size or circulation of the publications this book has thus far considered is part of what made his paper even more distinct. The *Crusader* helped him champion black self-defense couched within strident calls to black manhood that challenged not only the NAACP and other members of the civil rights establishment but also the black press. Both the NAACP and black press had achieved a level of popular authority in the black public sphere and shared a public image as historic institutions, especially since both emerged together out of the same contexts. Williams believed that self-defense helped black men redeem their manhood, an essential component, in his view, in the literal fight for racial advancement. All three approaches were intertwined for Williams, resulting in his publishing of a black periodical that was not the product of a historic, commercial publishing enterprise with a large personnel and cutting-edge technology capable of printing thousands of issues at a time, as it was for many mainstream black papers like the *Defender*. Nor did Williams inherit his publication through a transfer of gendered ideas from a seasoned black male publisher, as Sengstacke had. Rather, the newsletter was a grassroots paper shaped by his soldier-citizen mentality, working-class resources, militant activism, and militant constructions of black manhood. His activism, gendered ideologies, use of self-defense, and publishing helped invigorate Monroe activists with new approaches to social change. The Jim Crow South had long hampered the ability of southern black newspapers to be as militant as black papers in the urban North, which, according to Myrdal, were "less afraid." But shaped by his military experiences, activism, beliefs in self-defense and redeeming black manhood, and commitment to using both rhetoric and action to influence the black public sphere, this was not the case for Williams's southern-based paper. The northern black press had set the precedent for media-led black militancy, bolstered by northern black protest organizations. But while somewhat safely situated away from the racial violence of the South, it seemed to challenge southern black papers to be as vocal and militant as they were about protesting racial injustice. Williams's *Crusader* became one of the few southern-based black papers to accept this challenge, though Williams also came to issue a challenge of his own to the civil rights establishment and black press.[19]

Like mainstream black newspapers, Williams used the press to help advance the race as both the mainstream black press and Williams circulated their papers amid a crisis—the racial backlash. It was a moment in which the wrong printed word could bring harm to the freedom struggle, important black institutions, and activists themselves. The mainstream black press and Williams's grassroots paper confronted these challenges differently, however. Here, Williams solidified his departure from the mainstream black press. Black newspapers celebrated the sacrifices and contributions of black soldiers during and after the world wars. Since the Red Summer, many black publications had promoted a militant vision of black manhood that centered on the image of black men defending themselves and their rights, and that of the race, even if it meant self-sacrifice. Marcus Garvey's model of manly black leadership had, in a way, ultimately embraced this. Williams, a veteran, embodied parts of this vision as he advocated and practiced self-defense. But having been a trained soldier, Williams found a shortcoming in this model: if black men practiced self-defense effectively when necessary, they would not have to accept self-sacrifice. Thus, Williams rejected the idea that black men should willingly sacrifice themselves to defend the race, for proper and immediate self-defense would prevent this. Yet the rise of Martin Luther King Jr. and his promotion of nonviolent protest would offer an alternative vision of militant manly black leadership that rejected black self-defense entirely to promote manly self-sacrifice in ways that promised to restore black men to a deeper black manhood.

Williams's stance in favor of black self-defense as a strategy for racial advancement sparked a debate in the black press over the utility of black armed resistance versus nonviolence, a discourse that came to be carried out in gendered terms by activists and black newspapers alike as many of them couched the debate in martial metaphors that spoke to the perceived war facing activists at this time. Given its history of promoting militant ideas and ideals of black manhood, the black press should have agreed with Williams, even as he refined the meaning of black self-defense. But Williams's battle cries for black self-defense came at a precarious political time in the United States, when it was difficult for black activists to promote civil rights, especially in the ways he emphasized. Constrained by the violent white backlash, McCarthyism and Communist hysteria, and the NAACP's focus on pursuing racial justice through legalism and the courts, the black press broke with its own history and endorsed King's new model of militant black manhood that jettisoned self-defense for nonviolence. Black newspapers helped nonviolent proponents present their case to the public that the strategy required black men to summon the most "masculine" elements of masculinity: courage and self-restraint in order to confront Jim Crow. This move on the part of the press helped advocates of nonviolence promote the strategy against a long-standing history of black self-defense. The black press elevated nonviolence over self-defense as the ideal strategy for the freedom struggle, and through this, promoted the courageous nonviolent activist, or "strong man," as King came to call him, as the new model of black masculinity. King would become the black male leader best embodying this new model. But given the war that activists seemed to be fighting, both Williams and King called into question what militancy was for activists and the black press at this time, and which weapon was best to win the fight: rhetoric, guns, or the nonviolent black male body.

For Williams, militancy was not only defending oneself and one's rights through armed resistance, as scholars have shown, but also maximizing a toolbox of militant options that included organizing black men, the use of highly masculinized and gendered language and performances, an aggressive style of black leadership and protest to be deployed at different times in different situations, and a commitment to rhetoric and action.[20] These were points that the black press had long appreciated and promoted. Like Sengstacke, Williams sought to organize like-minded black men to his vision. But as a publisher, Williams emphasized print *and* practice, what he thought would move the black press and readers beyond martial metaphors on paper to actual black armed resistance, restoring black men to the manhood black people and their papers had long argued for, he thought. This chapter's close reading of the black press's reaction to Williams reveals how it helped answer the question of which weapon was best, a response that tested its long-standing reputation as a militant institution. Black newspapers came to reject the image of the war-ripened black veteran, which they had celebrated in previous decades. Ultimately, the stance black newspapers adopted regarding Williams reversed its militant heritage, a historic change that, among other things, helped usher in the decline of the mainstream black press.

When Williams returned home, he was perhaps a new man. For some time, he had been chasing sporadic employment in Detroit; Woodbridge, New Jersey; and Los Angeles. But in Detroit in particular, Williams became familiar with the extent to which other parts of the United States were not unlike the South in terms of racial conditions and racial violence.[21] He joined the Marines in 1954, following his time in the army, and served for eighteen months. His years as a serviceman were especially formative. They conditioned him to defend himself, trained him to view self-defense as a necessity under life-threatening battleground conditions, and further acquainted him with America's liberal creed and principles of democracy, its constitutionalism, and its promises of citizenship rights. Williams affirmed that "the Army indoctrination instilled in us what a virtue it was to fight for democracy and that we were fighting for democracy and upholding the Constitution."[22] Indeed, he felt that his service to the country meant that he was due his rights as an American citizen, and black Americans, whom he had served to defend along with every other American, were by extension due theirs too.

Williams's experiences as a serviceman imbued him with a strict interpretation of the U.S. Constitution, the law, and rights, which included the right to bear arms.[23] These experiences also moved him to see racial violence in Monroe as yet another war he would have to fight. In Monroe, where black people's demands for equal rights were increasingly met with violence, black people's right to defend themselves was a matter of life or death. According to Williams, racial violence in Monroe was "our way of life."[24] The KKK and mobs of whites perpetrated violence, and both were protected by state agencies and local authorities unwilling to do anything to stop them. While these conditions were common throughout the United States, Monroe was the southeastern regional headquarters of the KKK.[25] Whites' acts and threats of violence, and economic reprisals in Monroe, had intimidated black residents, and paralyzed activism, a familiar scenario for other struggling NAACP chapters in the rural South.[26] When Williams joined, the local chapter was practically defunct, a total of six members about to disband. In fact, members elected Williams chapter president just before five of them withdrew, leaving only one other member, Albert Perry, who became vice president.[27]

But Williams rescued the beleaguered chapter by in part applying some of the insights he had gained from military service. He revived it by adopting aggressive modes of self-defense and organizing black men to form an armed guard to patrol Monroe's black community on a daily basis. Started in 1957 under Williams's leadership, the patrol was composed of about twenty volunteers, many of whom were veterans trained for combat. Their cache of weapons consisted of rifles and handguns.[28] The armed guard helped in recruiting new NAACP members, especially black residents long intimidated to join the organization because of white violence.[29] Williams drew on experiences he gained as a union organizer in Detroit, and he, Perry, and another veteran began recruiting new members at pool halls, beauty parlors, street corners, and farms.[30] Within four years, the chapter, a rather unique group of working-class black people, veterans, and liberal whites, had 121 members, the largest the group had ever been. The jump in membership showed the success of Williams and Perry's targeting of working-class blacks, as well as black residents' new confidence that an armed guard would protect them from violent segregationists.[31] In Williams's view, encouraging black people to defend themselves through arms helped empower them with the self-confidence to assume leadership roles within their community more generally. As historian Marcellus Barksdale has argued, Williams's approach to organizing residents helped build an "indigenous movement" in Monroe that helped members respond to the needs and exigencies of Monroe's black community specifically.[32] Like Ella Baker, Septima Clark, Myles Horton, and some other civil rights activists across the South, Williams was invested in helping make ordinary, local people into local leaders, through what historian Charles Payne has called the "organizing tradition."[33] Williams's belief that self-defense worked to cultivate the leadership potential of ordinary people was most visible in his insistence that self-defense was really "armed self-reliance," a view that in part invoked long-standing ideas of racial uplift through self-help.[34] Williams's approach was beginning to show that black communities in the South could also organize in militant ways, much like black protest in the urban North had for decades, efforts that had helped make the urban North a crucible of organized black political struggle. In fact, Williams had participated in some of this organizing during his stints in the urban North.[35] And his NAACP chapter would gain "the reputation of being the most militant branch of the NAACP," he remembered.[36]

Indeed, the role of the armed guard was pivotal. In October 1957, for example, it came to the aid of the chapter's vice president. Reacting to the resurgence of black activism in Monroe and the chapter's protest against the city' segregated swimming pool, a KKK motorcade and two police cars made an attempt on Perry's life. Williams and the armed guard successfully repelled them by firing at the attackers until they fled.[37] The incident was reported in the *Baltimore Afro-American, Norfolk Journal and Guide,* and *Jet.* In fact, *Jet* carried photographs of the armed guard.[38] Williams and the black men he had helped organize had shown what effective black self-defense could do.

While black activists in Monroe deployed self-defense with great results in their community, Martin Luther King Jr. and the Montgomery bus boycott demonstrated that nonviolent protest was just as effective in their particular community, however. On December 5, 1955, the Montgomery Improvement Association (MIA) launched a protest against segregated busing in the city, although as historian Danielle McGuire has shown, the boycott was motivated as much by black women's demands for dignity and struggles against sexual violence as it was by a desire to end segregation. The activists, particularly members of the Women's Political Council (WPC), rolled out 52,500 flyers from a mimeograph machine that encouraged people to join the effort. They also circulated a newsletter during the protest, which was edited by Jo Ann Robinson, the president of the WPC.[39] Ethel Payne of the *Defender* helped bring national attention to the boycott as her reporting dominated the paper's front page. She left her post in Washington, D.C., as Washington bureau chief for the paper in order to cover the protest for three months. Weeks before the story of the Montgomery activists broke in other papers, she announced that "A NEW TYPE OF LEADER is emerging in the South." "He is neither an NAACP worker, nor a CIO political action field director. Instead, the gladiator going into battle," she wrote in martial tones, "wears a reverse collar, a flowing robe, and carries a Bible in hand. This new, vocal, fearless, and forthright Moses who is leading the people out of the wilderness into the Promised Land is the Negro preacher."[40]

King, a young, little-known Baptist preacher, led the 381-day protest that resulted in a Supreme Court decision on November 13, 1956, declaring the city's segregated bus line unconstitutional. The success of the boycott was a cause célèbre in the black press. Headlines trumpeted its success as a "Huge Blow to Bias," that "Bus Segregation Loses."[41] The *Los Angeles Sentinel* praised King for being a "New Kind of Negro Leader" too. To the "curious . . . [who] . . . still wonder: What kind of magic did Rev. King use? What kind of man is he? From whence cometh his powers?" The paper answered that King "was a Messiah," who had "wrought a miracle."[42] The *Courier* featured a piece on King's "Life Story," offering an explanation for his remarkable leadership. He was "marked for leadership," as Benjamin Mays, the well-known educator, activist, president of Morehouse College, and mentor to King, reported. "Add to that a heritage of leadership and religion and there is the man who looms as the Number 1 candidate for THE leader Negroes have waited for the last quarter of a century," the paper continued. *Time* magazine stated that "the scholarly Negro Baptist minister in little more than a year has risen from nowhere to become one of the nation's re-markable leaders of men." "His leadership extends beyond a single battle," *Time* continued in a martial metaphor, due to King's "spiritual force."[43] The press was helping construct an image of King as a new brand of manly black leadership.

Yet at the beginning of the boycott, King was not fully committed to non-violence, at least not privately. Like many other participants and leaders of the protest, he was skeptical of nonviolence as an all-encompassing philos-ophy and strategy. "I had not the slightest idea," he remembered, "that I would later become involved in a crisis in which nonviolent resistance would be applicable."[44] After segregationists bombed his home on January 30, 1956, King had armed men guard his home at night. King and Reverend Ralph David Abernathy, the pastor of First Baptist Church and one of the organizers of the MIA, began carrying sidearms following the incident.[45]

Subsequently, two workers from the New York–based pacifist organization the Fellowship of Reconciliation, Bayard Rustin, a Quaker and veteran civil rights organizer, and Reverend Glenn Smiley, a white Methodist minister, both mentored the young King, teaching him to embrace nonviolence not just as a protest tactic but also as a philosophy and a way of life. "We have discovered a new and powerful weapon—nonviolent resistance," King wrote in martial terms not long after the successful boycott. "Through forced separation from our African culture, through slavery, poverty, and deprivation, many black men lost self-respect," he continued now in gendered tones. Over time, "Negroes lost faith in themselves and came to believe that perhaps they really were what they had been told they were—something less than men," but *"we Negroes have replaced self-pity with self-respect and self-depreciation with dignity"* (King's emphasis). Indeed, King traded his sidearm for what he later called "Christian weapons." In 1958, King wrote that nonviolence "is ultimately the way of the strong man," terms that came to strike the image of a brave, nonviolent soldier.[46] For the rest of his life he advocated nonviolence, working to convert skeptics in and outside the movement to its power. The mainstream black press would come to play an instrumental part in this effort.[47]

King's and activists' use of nonviolent protest was intended to display the moral force of movement participants against the brutality of their attackers, as well as their middle-class respectability to a conservative postwar American audience. Activists were considered "outside agitators," "trouble makers," and "communists" in many white papers, especially southern ones, such as the *Montgomery Advertiser* and the *New Orleans Times-Picayune*.[48] Movement leaders hoped that the respectability of nonviolence would counter stereotypes of black people as aggressive and volatile; appeal to the cultural values of postwar America that stressed restraint, order, and propriety; and underscore the violence of segregationists. This strategy, movement leaders hoped, would win mainstream (white) support for the civil rights cause. King became philosophically committed to nonviolence, deploying it as a spiritual and tactical strategy of resistance. But King and activists also deployed it highly aware of the publicity that nonviolent protest would receive in the black and white press, intending to use the strategy as a tool of both protest and respectability. They were careful to deploy tactics that cast them as demonstrating proper public behavior and decorum, cornerstone values of middle-class respectability in 1950s America. Montgomery activists deployed the respectability of the era, even in protest, as a powerful political and cultural weapon that could be used to gain certain leverage against the acts and public image of violent segregationists.[49] Headlines in some major papers picked up on this, and showed the effectiveness of the two-pronged assault that nonviolence offered. The *New York Times* declared, "Non-Violence Held Aid to Integration." The *Washington Post and Times* described it as "Exemplary Race Relations." "Non-Violence Plan Wins White Friends," announced the *Courier*.[50] The success of the boycott and the nonviolent approach catapulted King within the black and white press as a national figure of interest.[51] At the time of the Montgomery triumph, Williams praised the protest as the "patriots of passive revolution."[52] The two men's activism demonstrated the part of some southern black communities in joining the long-standing protest efforts of black activists in the urban North.

But Williams's stance on self-defense contradicted the rhetoric and strategies of civil rights leaders like King and would soon put him at loggerheads with the NAACP's national policy and leadership at a difficult time for the organization. On one hand, the NAACP was enjoying new prestige after its victory in *Brown*. With the success of *Brown* and several other Supreme Court victories in favor of integration, the NAACP became even more committed to a gradual strategy of legally achieved desegregation. On the other hand, it was facing violent resistance to school integration. In fact, the members and chapters of the NAACP were some of the most common targets of violence because of their conspicuous part in waging legal warfare against Jim Crow. As the oldest and most influential civil rights organization, the NAACP had weathered similar racial and political storms before. But this backlash was especially virulent, particularly for members and chapters in the South, where they were physically assaulted, economically intimidated, and politically attacked. Many segregationists accused the organization of being Communist controlled, which was intended to taint the black freedom struggle as un-American and unpatriotic. This opened the NAACP up to a barrage of McCarthy-era hysteria and hostile anti-Communist sentiment.[53]

Further, some states in the South had the Internal Revenue Service (IRS) investigate the tax status of the organization. Six states made it harder for the NAACP to bring suits against segregation by implementing criminal penalties for "stirring up litigation." Five states in the South required the NAACP to register and provide membership lists—a way for segregationists to identify activists by name. The association was banned in Alabama for almost a decade for violating a court order to submit its lists. Texas and Arkansas also banned the NAACP for a period of time. As a consequence of many of these political attacks, NAACP membership rolls rapidly declined.[54] Some activists curtailed their work or pursued other means of racial advocacy that might reduce racial antagonism. Continuous reports of racial violence inundated the national office, and the organization pursued litigation against the violence. Still, the NAACP's de facto national policy promoted nonviolent protest as the ideal strategy for members and chapters.[55] And Williams was a chapter president. While he wholeheartedly believed in the integrationist fight of the NAACP, Williams, as contemporary observer and cultural critic Harold Cruse noted, "differed not in aims but in tactics."[56]

Williams's and the NAACP's differences in tactics came to a head in May 1959 when the verdict for the trial of a white man who attempted to rape a black woman was announced. The man was acquitted. Overwhelmed with anger at the court's unwillingness to punish sexual violence against black women, Williams exclaimed to members of the local press, "This demonstration today shows that the Negro in the South cannot expect justice in the courts. He must convict his attackers on the spot. He must meet violence with violence, lynching with lynching."[57] Local coverage turned national when the statement was reprinted across the country. Headlines in the *New York Times*, for example, blared, "N. A. A. C. P. Leader Urges Violence." NAACP officials moved swiftly into damage control to prevent any harm to the organization's reputation and public image, or as Roy Wilkins, executive secretary of the NAACP and editor of the *Crisis*, worried, the "position and the effective functioning of the Association."[58] Wilkins knew all too well the influence of the press, being the editor of the *Crisis* and a longtime newspaperman himself. His career in journalism began in his teenage years, first when he edited his high school yearbook. In college, he edited and reported for the school paper, the University of Minnesota's *Minnesota Daily*. From college, he went to the *St. Paul Appeal* as managing editor in 1922, then an editorship at the *Kansas City Call* in the 1930s, and finally the *Crisis* not long after W. E. B. DuBois vacated his post in 1934. He had faced controversy during his journalistic career and had even helped stir some up. Wilkins had followed the lead of some of Marcus Garvey's opponents by wryly commenting on his trial, for example. Though Wilkins considered Williams a "hot-tempered man," Wilkins privately shared his sentiments. "I could understand his hard feelings," he remembered, but "I couldn't condone what he said"; he could not support "one of the N. A. A. C. P.'s own presidents to advocate the rope."[59]

The day following Williams's strong statements, Wilkins censured him by telegram and suspended him as branch president for six months.[60]

Attempting to diffuse the controversy, Wilkins told the press that "[black people] see Negroes lynched or sentenced to death for the same crimes for which white defendants are given suspended sentences or set free. They are no longer willing to accept this double-standard of justice." Still, Wilkins maintained that "the N. A. A. C. P. does not and has never in its history advocated the use of violence."[61] Williams had violated NAACP policy, as well as the valuable image of middle-class respectability that the NAACP and the Montgomery boycott had worked to cultivate for political and cultural leverage against segregationists. That Williams was working class made his advocacy of self-defense even more threatening to the strategic framework of carefully constructed public images for the movement. Williams also jeopardized the effort of nonviolent strategists to debunk stereotypes of black men as aggressive and violent.[62] Much to Wilkins's relief, members of the white press, even those in the South, commended him for disciplining Williams. The *Winston-Salem Journal Sunday and Sentinel*, for example, commented, "Law-abiding citizens of both races can applaud the prompt action of NAACP leaders in disassociating themselves from Mr. Williams's alarming statements." Still, some of the discursive damage had been done, at least in the black press.[63]

Black newspapers across the country weighed in, underscoring their role in shaping black freedom struggles, the nature of black leadership, and strategies for racial advancement. One *Defender* article identified Williams as the "Violence Advocate."[64] Another *Defender* report shared that Congressmen Adam Clayton Powell of New York and Robert Nix of Pennsylvania, both of whom were vocal advocates of black civil rights, condemned Williams's comments. Powell called the statement "shocking," while Nix found it "foolish and uncalled for."[65] For Robert Spivack of the *Defender*, it was "easy enough to understand Mr. Williams' strong feelings on the subject. . . . It's also understandable that Roy Wilkins of NAACP headquarters would promptly suspend the outspoken gentleman and repudiate the use of force to achieve equal rights." Nonetheless, in light of Williams's words, Spivack thought "we ought to reexamine the situation on civil rights all over the country, and ask ourselves: Are we making progress?"[66] But longtime black women's advocate Nannie Helen Burroughs put it frankly in the *Courier*: "We Must Fight Back but . . . with What and How?" In her view, Williams had given "reckless advice, without counting the cost . . . [which] makes about as much sense as telling the Negroes of the south to commit suicide." Williams was setting a "death trap," she continued, based on a position that was "unintelligent" and would only embolden "ignorant whites of the south with a first-hand excuse for using any weapons at their command in so-called self-defense." The proper way to fight back, she affirmed, was with Christian values of patience, forethought, and waiting on God, certainly a supportive reference to the model of resistance that King had demonstrated in Montgomery.[67]

But other members of the press offered some support for Williams. Louis Lautier charged Wilkins with "engaging in semantics." "Williams merely implied that colored people should defend themselves if and when violence is directed at them," Lautier asserted, even suggesting that "instead of hearing charges against Mr. Williams, [the NAACP] should hear charges against Mr. Wilkins for abuse of authority."[68] Daisy Bates, the head of the Arkansas State Conference of branches for the NAACP, commented too. Bates published the *Arkansas State Press*, along with her husband, L. C. Bates, who had worked for some time for the *Kansas City Call*. Together they "decided to lease the newspaper plant of a struggling church paper and invest our savings" to found the paper in 1941. Though they sometimes struggled to operate it on their shoestring budget, they saw themselves as crusaders, not unlike Williams, and remained convinced that "a newspaper was needed to carry on the fight for Negro rights as nothing else can. If we could get advertisers to support a crusading paper, all well and good. If not—well, that was part of the gamble." Bates was the manager, editor, and writer for the paper.[69] The sixteen-page sheet reached 20,000 in circulation by 1957, and made her one of the few black women who owned and operated a black newspaper during the twentieth century.[70] She was better known, however, for her role in the 1957 Little Rock crisis, when Arkansas governor Orville Faubus attempted to stop the integration of Little Rock Central High School by nine black students.[71] At the time of the ordeal, the *Arkansas State Press* advised, "Somebody has to display intelligence, and why not let it be the Negro. We are appealing to you to be calm, but in no way are we remotely suggesting that you 'Turn The Other Cheek.' . . . Under no circumstances should we weaken from our objective." At the time, Bates saw nonviolence as a sign of weakness. She had once stated publicly that she too armed herself and seemed to understand why Williams made the statement. "At times it is pretty hard to suppress certain feelings, when all around you, you see only hate."[72]

Executive editor of the *Courier* Percival L. Prattis reaffirmed an ambivalent position he took regarding nonviolence in 1957.[73] It was then that Prattis questioned King and his strategy, writing that "nonviolence was a diversionary tactic. It is not sound strategy. It will not solve our problem."

Prattis argued, "I differ seriously with this young Montgomery leader."[74] Prattis wrote five articles contesting the practice of nonviolence and challenging King, who was becoming popular and respected among many black people for his leadership and eloquent outspokenness on civil rights. Throughout the series, Prattis maintained that while he respected King and his efforts, most black people were ill-prepared for the demands of nonviolence, unwilling to sacrifice their own safety and lives. Prattis insisted that black people should instead be prepared to "put his fist in somebody's face if he is going to win respect."[75] But now Prattis admitted that Williams's statement had raised the stakes and signaled a glaring contradiction for the NAACP. "The NAACP simply cannot afford to have anybody in its ranks who talks about using violence. That would destroy the effectiveness of the organization," he affirmed. Yet he added sarcastically that Williams was justified. "Williams was giving voice to what is in the dark brother's mind. He is not going to submit passively to rape and lynching. Some day his patience will wear out. But of course you should not talk out loud about such probabilities."[76] For New York City councilman Earl Brown, a columnist for the *New York Amsterdam News*, too much credit was being given to King's "cheek turning" for the Montgomery victory. He contended that it was not the nonviolent strategy that forced the hand of the bus line but the boycott's "bankrupting [of] the local transit company." Citing the recent brutal lynching of Mack Charles Parker, a black man accused of kidnapping and raping a pregnant white woman, as an example of the need for self-defense, Brown affirmed that "the sooner [that] Negroes carry their economic warfare a step further and employ bullets in self-defense the sooner they will gain the respect and security they must have in order to exist as free men in the South."[77]

During Wilkins's conversations with Williams, Williams was defiant, and told Wilkins that despite the censure, he "didn't intend to be silent."[78] Williams could not have been more sincere. Determined to access a range of militant options and defend himself even discursively, he joined the debate within the press when, as he recalled, "the first issue of *The Crusader* came off the mimeograph machine June 26, 1959." The *Crusader* was his grassroots publication that he and his wife, Mabel, their friends, and volunteers began distributing in Monroe. It disseminated Williams's ideas and helped build support for the local movement, especially during this controversy.[79] Williams shared the integrationist goals of the NAACP, but he also felt that the New York–based national office did not know the depths of the violent conditions on the ground in Monroe as well as he did, conditions that resembled a battleground for black activists.[80] Williams's efforts to make the chapter more responsive to its own community needs over the directives of the parent body included publishing the *Crusader* to address his community's particular struggles. In one way, he was trying to "counteract Roy Wilkins and the *Crisis*," he later explained. In another way, the paper resulted from the trial about which he commented. It made him "more convinced than ever that one of our greatest and most immediate needs was better communication within the race. The real Afro-American struggle was merely a disjointed network of pockets of resistance and the shameful thing about it was that Negroes were relying upon the white man's inaccurate reports as their sources of information about these isolated struggles." He then "concentrated all of my efforts into developing a newsletter that would in accurate and no uncertain terms inform both Negroes and whites of Afro-American liberation struggles taking place in the United States and about the particular struggle we were constantly fighting in Monroe." He hoped that the *Crusader* would help inspire and organize activists in Monroe, and have the same effect across the country. Perhaps his embrace of Second Amendment rights and stringent interpretation of the U.S. Constitution also gave him an equally fervent appreciation for the First Amendment.[81]

However, Mabel Williams contended that the paper was not founded as a response to the NAACP's censure of Williams, because as early as the summer of 1958, they had plans to start a paper.[82] Still, as had been the case for black men vying for positions of leadership and influence in preceding decades, Williams turned to publishing a paper. "I started appealing to readers everywhere to protest to the U. S. government, to the U. S. Justice Department; to protest the fact that the 14th Amendment did not exist in Monroe."[83] His desire to couple the NAACP's integrationist fight with a physical one, where needed, on behalf of terrorized black residents in Monroe shaped the tone of the paper. The front page of the first issue reiterated his controversial statements and endorsed self-defense and its potential in helping restore black manhood while also criticizing the strategy of nonviolence. "Big cars, fine clothes, big houses and college degrees [won't] make a Negro respected being called a MAN," Williams declared. "Unless a man has some measure of pride, he is not worthy of the dignity to be called MAN. . . . A true man will protect his women, children and home. . . . The Negro is never going to be respected in this nation as a man until he shows a willingness to defend himself and his women."[84]

Williams differed in many crucial respects from the conventional black publisher who had long typified the mainstream black press.[85] Unlike

Robert S. Abbott, W. E. B. DuBois, Marcus Garvey, and John Sengstacke, Williams's model of masculinity was not cut from the era of Victorian-influenced erudition and entrepreneurship, New Negro militancy, or Depression-era labor organizing. He also did not experience a transfer of manhood from an elder black man, who was also a seasoned black male publisher, as Sengstacke had. Williams's transfer of manhood instead came through two other forms. First, Williams's masculinity derived from a model of black manhood long important to black people: the war-ripened black soldier. Williams was like many other black men of preceding and current generations who found their masculinity through soldiering, but he wanted to communicate the gendered and racial implications of that experience in the medium through which Abbott, DuBois, Garvey, Sengstacke, and others had found theirs—newspaper publishing. In fact, he shared with these men, and mainstream black papers more broadly, a manly vision for racial advancement. The second form was drawn from many southern black people's long-standing efforts to defend themselves against racial violence. Both forms convinced Williams to reject notions of self-sacrifice as critical components of black manhood, and broadcast these points to the black public sphere through a publishing praxis of print *and* practice. Williams named the paper the *Crusader,* honoring Cyril Briggs's paper of the same name from the 1920s. Williams probably learned of Briggs while living in Harlem for a stint. The paper's name also invoked the historic role of black newspapers, which was captured by the first tenet of the NNPA's "Credo for the Negro Press." But whereas many black publishers of major papers had been middle class and relied on state-of-the-art facilities to produce their papers, Williams was working class, struggling for funds, peeling his four-page press off a hand-operated mimeograph machine. He did not inherit a publishing empire like Sengstacke. His newspaper staff and team of correspondents comprised his wife and friends. With Williams as editor, his wife as circulation manager and cartoonist, and friends as columnists, they and volunteers pushed the paper door-to-door for ten cents. Eventually, they mailed it to readers across the country.[86]

Like Abbott, who initially lacked certain financial and publishing resources in the beginning of his career, Williams found a way to carve out a share of the black public sphere using what tools he could afford. The mimeograph machine was a piece of technology that would be used by many a dissident, including the Montgomery activists. The machine, as historian John McMillan has shown, helped make newspaper production more accessible, democratic, grassroots-oriented, and militant by the 1960s.[87] The

Crusader staff educated themselves on how to use the machine. Finally, the paper's name reflected Williams's particular work as an activist. The name invoked images of a soldier with a missionary-like zeal for self-defensive action that also suggested that action should accompany a paper's rhetoric, helping construct a potent discourse through print *and* practice. Williams hoped that the black public would embrace both. Here, the differences between him and his mainstream contemporaries deepened. Historically, mainstream black publishers had advised readers to do the critical activist work that Williams was doing, as they constructed and reflected discourses in which important issues and ideas were envisaged and mobilized, especially during real and perceived times of racial crisis. This often transformed into successful editorial campaigns that influenced black public opinion, policy makers, and political, economic, and social institutions. Crusading editorially against racial injustice had usually been the form activism took for most members of the black press. But for Williams, the activist and publisher, there was little distance between literal and figurative militancy, print and practice. Williams's militancy included using armed resistance, as well as resistant rhetoric couched in gendered terms articulated through public statements and his press. The *Crusader* circulated in Monroe and neighboring towns, and later among at least a thousand national subscribers.[88]

Williams's publishing technology, small paper, and small staff probably would have precluded his membership in the NNPA, though the activism of working-class people during the Depression had helped inspire Sengstacke to form the group. Membership in the NNPA was "restricted to 'independent, secular newspapers sold to the general reading public.'"[89] Still, similar to Sengstacke, Williams worked to organize like-minded black men, although to be civil rights activists in the full sense of the word.[90] Indeed, Williams had strong editorial differences with members of the mainstream black press, in addition to class differences with its publishers. But Williams's conception of print and practice could perhaps help black newspapers to exert even more influence on the black public sphere. Williams and his paper exemplified a burgeoning grassroots black press being published by movement activists rather than prominent, enterprising black publishers. This would help signal the beginning of major changes for the mainstream black press and later the emergence of the radical black press.

Williams coupled the newsletter with practice, his activism in Monroe, using both to promote an explicitly gendered advancement strategy that elevated a black manhood rooted in self-defense. He challenged both the civil rights establishment and the mainstream black press along these lines. Williams reflected popular ideas about the prerogatives of manhood and argued that using self-defense helped restore black men's confidence in themselves as men, thereby helping redeem their manhood before whites and black women. For Williams, blacks showed that they were the "sissy race of all mankind" when they failed, or were too afraid, to physically resist racial injustice and defend themselves. Violent attacks on black people, especially sexual violence against black women, were a "challenge to our manhood, especially to veterans, who had been trained to fight." Protecting black women from physical assault and sexual violence had long been a matter of concern for black men and women. Indeed, since its founding in 1946, members of the WPC had been organizing to draw attention to physical assault and sexual violence against black women and to resist them.[91] Williams, like many men of his era, believed that men had the patriarchal right and obligation to protect women from harm, especially harm from other men.[92] Williams's frequent battle cries to manhood within the *Crusader* strove to encourage Monroe black men, as well as black male readers elsewhere, to confront head on the racially violent conditions that ravaged black communities everywhere in the country.[93] Williams would write years later that he believed that "a man cannot have human dignity if he allows himself to be abused . . . [and] to allow his wife and children to be attacked." "When a man learns to use arms he gets more self-confidence," he said, emphasizing effective black self-defense.[94] One *Crusader* reader in New York said that the paper was "a giant step in the right direction."[95] Another reader in San Francisco thanked Williams for his "'controversial' statement," for "saying what so many of us are thinking. . . . It is a relief to see someone saying the militant things that need to be said."[96]

Williams had indeed articulated what many black people felt and desired and in some cases were doing for themselves, for Williams was not alone as an activist in the civil rights struggle who rejected notions of self-sacrifice and employed armed resistance. For example, Hartman Turnbow and Fannie Lou Hamer, activists in Mississippi, and Reverend Fred Shuttlesworth, a close associate of King's and cofounder of the Southern Christian Leadership Conference (SCLC), did also.[97] Turnbow and Hamer lived in Mississippi, a bastion of white violence in the South, where Emmett Till was killed and activists Medgar Evers, James Chaney, Andrew Goodman, and Michael Schwerner would be killed in the 1960s. According to historian Simon Wendt, armed self-defense helped Turnbow, Hamer, and other activists protect themselves, their families, and their efforts to advance the freedom struggle. And, as historian Akinyele Omowale Umoja has argued, their use of armed resistance ran the gamut of weapons, including "fists, feet, stones, bricks, blades, and gasoline firebombs," in addition to guns, exemplifying the range of militant options to which Williams also appealed.[98] Despite the rigid lines of demarcation that movement leaders would draw between nonviolence and self-defense, these activists on the ground embraced more flexible or fluid approaches, deploying either tactic when necessary.[99] Williams's promotion of black self-defense in the midst of the violent backlash elevated this long-standing history of black southerners' attempts to defend themselves against racial violence.[100]

At the NAACP's national convention in New York City in July 1959, the organization marked its fiftieth anniversary and planned to stage a public representation of its commitment to nonviolent social change. Williams's suspension was one of the issues up for review. He planned on explaining himself and clarifying his earlier statements, especially since he believed that his statements had been taken out of context by the press. "These court decisions," the *Atlanta Daily World* reported that Williams meant to say, "open the way to violence. I do not mean that Negroes should go out and attempt to get revenge for mistreatment or injustice. But . . . Negroes have to defend themselves on the spot whenever attacked by whites." The *Courier* reported that Williams, the "NAACP Maverick," planned "an all-out fight on the issue of whether Negroes should protect themselves against racial violence."[101] At the convention, Williams insisted: "I have not advocated lynch law. I have only advanced self-defense. A Negro woman, who was pregnant, was beaten by a white man because she would not submit to his advances. Yes, and I could go on to cite many more cases of violence inflicted by these Negro haters." Again, Williams emphasized that his own manhood, and by implication the manhood of the race, was at stake. "No matter what you do to me," he declared, "I will believe in self-defense. I believe we men should stand up as men and protect our women and children. I am a man, and I will walk upright as a man should. I WILL NOT CRAWL."[102] It was another provocative statement from Williams, and yet another public battle cry, though it was also his effort to maintain the particular manly public image he was cultivating through the *Crusader*. Yet the "most electrifying moment," according to the black press, was not Williams's jeremiad; it was when the convention voted unanimously to uphold his suspension, even as it affirmed the right of individual members to defend themselves against unlawful violence.[103] Members of the white press reported on the convention too. "NAACP Convention Approves Suspension of Carolina

Leader," ran a headline in the *Washington Post and Times Herald*, the article featuring quotes from convention attendees denouncing Williams, including King's own instructive words. "It is the strong man," King said, "who can resist evil without violence. . . . Nonviolence calls for love, but it is not a weak and sentimental love; it is a strong love that organizes itself into positive social action."[104] King's nonviolent "strong man" struck the image of a soldier-like figure, juxtaposed against Williams's now suspect image as the war-ripened veteran.

Williams's statement before the convention only exacerbated tensions between him and the NAACP's leadership. In fact, the statement solidified his estrangement from the national office and icons of the civil rights establishment. Jackie Robinson, the first black baseball player to desegregate lily-white baseball, condemned him.[105] Robinson was a premier example of nonviolent integration for many black people, activists, and members of the black press who had helped pressure baseball to desegregate. Daisy Bates vehemently denounced Williams before the convention for jeopardizing the goals of the movement, though her paper had reported objectively on him at the beginning of the controversy.[106] Wilkins had personally requested that she be there. So that Bates would agree to leverage the full force of her public image as the heroine of the Little Rock crisis against Williams, Wilkins offered to financially support her and her family for a few months to help them recover from the economic reprisals whites had imposed on them for their activism. Some of the economic intimidation she and her family faced had come against her *Arkansas State Press*. Her presence and rebuke helped ensure Williams's suspension.[107]

Following the convention, the *Crusader* did some damage control for Williams's public image. Williams's friend and *Crusader* writer Ethel Azalea Johnson, writing under the pen name Asa Lee, reminded readers that Williams was compelled to insist upon meeting "violence with violence" because the "smug, triumphant, expressions on the faces of whites [in the courtroom] served to infuriate every ounce of manhood in him. . . . The virtue of Negro women and Negro rights must be defended as all rights of other races are defended."[108] Members of the Monroe Branch telegraphed Wilkins, asking that Williams "be continued in his post," since he had merely "reflected community views."[109] Indeed, community support for Williams demonstrated how much his ideas on self-defense and its relationship to manhood resonated among activists in Monroe. But Williams took the suspension in stride as "only a matter of policy." "The Union County branch has won the Respect of the Entire World," he declared to *Crusader* readers, advising them to "JOIN THE NAACP." "[Let's] rededicate ourselves to the cause of first class citizenship."[110]

The *Crusader*'s damage control also included shoring up support for Williams's ideas, political outlook, and brand of militancy. Despite his support for the integrationist goals of the NAACP, the *Crusader* gave voice to emerging currents of Black Nationalism, including coverage of revolutionary struggles against colonialism, the failures of American democracy, and, of course, advocacy of black armed resistance. Williams began to see black Americans' freedom struggles in terms of an anti-colonial one, not unlike those raging across Africa, Asia, and South America. Since the 1930s and through World War II, the mainstream black press had seen the racial struggle in America in these terms also, particularly linking the struggles of Africans with black Americans into a global struggle against white supremacy, colonialism, and racial oppression. Mainstream black newspapers' emphasis on these links was interrupted by Cold War pressures to rearticulate the civil rights struggle in an Americanist paradigm, shorn of internationalist solidarities and leftist sympathies.[111]

But Williams revived an international outlook, and especially stressed that some anti-colonial struggles were using armed resistance to gain national independence. DuBois had long emphasized this outlook too in his activism and writing. In fact, in February 1959, DuBois accepted an invitation from the Chinese Peace Committee to visit Mao Tse-tung's China. By the early 1960s, he would expatriate to an independent Ghana and become a citizen. Similarly, Williams would visit Fidel Castro's Cuba in June 1960.[112] For now, though, he followed international developments and revolutionary struggles abroad, applying the insights he gleaned to the racial situation in Monroe, the country, his conception of black armed resistance, and his belief that the manhood of black men needed to be redeemed. "History proves that physical resistance to brutality, oppression and tyranny is the most powerful weapon in the arsenal of liberation. . . . The white supremacist is overjoyed at the thought that the Negro is willing to be killed in a cringing, submissive manner," he wrote in the *Crusader*, wryly pointing to the emasculating effects of self-sacrifice as he saw it. Whites were less inclined to attack blacks willing to defend themselves, and more apt to respect them, he reasoned. "If the Negro musters enough courage to fight back against his violent oppressors in America, the day will be hastened when we will be free and respected."[113] In the *Crusader*, Williams relished in making provocative statements about black self-defense. Not unlike the mainstream black press, Williams sensationalized his columns in order to build interest in his position, and, most importantly, a political consciousness among readers that centered on the logic of self-defense, its constitutionality, potential for redeeming black manhood, and importance to ensuring the success of the movement against violent segregationists. Williams understood the political import of the black press's history of militant journalism and capitalized on it for the *Crusader*. He sensationalized the criticism he faced as well, also in gendered terms intended to emasculate critics, utilizing highly gendered language as another militant option. Because his publication was "too outspoken," he declared, "some of our local professional Negroes are squealing like probed pigs." "We have a certain class of white men's lackey always ready to admit that the white man's oppression of the Black man is wrong, but that we should not [let] him know how we feel." He called these people "poor semi-men and women." To conclude his gendered attack on critics, he wrote that the *Crusader* "sympathizes with those spineless Negroes who are afraid to be in the same town with a voice that speaks unequivocally for the rights of men."[114]

Much like the ways in which King philosophized on nonviolence in public, Williams philosophized on self-defense in the *Crusader*, theorizing ideas that asserted a deep relationship between manhood and self-defense. Both black and white men of Williams's era assented to this view. In fact, segregationists often justified their use of violence against black activists in terms of defending white manhood and white womanhood.[115] Williams believed that the links between self-defense and manhood were so powerful that the use of self-defense should be undertaken by men only, a point that many men of the time likely supported, reflecting gender relations within the movement and society more generally. Women were instrumental to helping Williams build his local movement, to be sure. Many of them worked as volunteers, prepared food, handled phones, and wrote for and/or distributed the paper.[116] But some of their service was shaped by perceptions of proper gender roles held by Williams and his male associates. For example, though Williams trained his wife to use guns, Williams and the other men refused to let women participate in the armed guard.[117] Historian Tim Tyson has argued that Williams's resolve to defend women did not hinge on "an abstract rhetorical commitment to black patriarchy" as much as a sense of a "deep and daily responsibility" to women. Indeed, as historian Peter Ling has suggested, Williams's advocacy of self-defense endorsed a "more masculinist defense of dependents; of women and children."[118] Still, his gendered subjectivity, shaped by the exigencies of racial conditions in Monroe that posed, in his view, a "challenge to our manhood," motivated Williams to see self-defense and black armed resistance exclusively as a male prerogative. Women were not supposed to protect others, even themselves, but were to be protected by men. Men, on the other hand, were supposed to protect themselves and women above all, for the man who was able to protect himself but not a woman was not a man at all; a man too afraid to protect both himself and a woman was even worse.[119]

Gender relations shaped nonviolent activists too, as well as the movement in general, a fact that would become especially apparent by the mid-1960s and eventually help divide certain civil rights activists and organizations. Indeed, Williams and King shared common ground in their maintenance of traditional patriarchal gender roles within their movements. As many scholars of the civil rights era have shown, gender ideologies often determined who led, in what capacity they led, the style of their leadership, and who had a legitimate voice in setting the agenda for movement struggles. Gender ideologies that elevated male leadership and control while designating women as workers and organizers in the movement reflected and revealed patriarchal relations and gender roles in broader society. This was especially the case in postwar America, which stressed a return to men's and women's "traditional" roles.[120] To be sure, because of their ecclesiastical backgrounds, King and his ministerial comrades were used to imposing a hierarchy in their work with others that elevated them to positions of authority— shepherds of the flock, so to speak.

But that same hierarchy tended to elevate male leadership, in particular, and served to shape gender relations within the movement in chauvinistic ways. For example, veteran activists Ella Baker and Septima Clark tried to challenge the chauvinism of the male-dominated leadership in the SCLC, as well as their monopoly over setting the organization's agenda to the exclusion of other members. Activists founded SCLC in 1957 to forward the momentum of the Montgomery boycott after its success, and King served as president. Here, King, like Williams, strove to especially organize like-minded black men and elevate their leadership in confronting racial injustice. "We were a militant organization which believed that the most powerful weapon available is non-violence," Coretta Scott King, Martin's wife, recalled. "Martin and his colleagues spearheaded the drive for direct confrontations between the just black cause and the white power structure." Even with nonviolence, "Martin also did his best to prevent that confrontation from becoming a blood bath," she insisted.[121] But Baker, in particular, struggled to prevail against the organization's male leadership, resulting in her departure from SCLC in 1961. She went on to become deeply influential in helping mentor black student activists through the Student Nonviolent Coordinating Committee (SNCC).[122]

Williams and the *Crusader*'s framing of black self-defense and black armed resistance in deeply masculine terms, coupled with gender divisions of labor within the movement, helped put the debate over self-defense and nonviolence into gendered terms that provided activists and the press different means of promoting one or the other approach. As historian Christopher B. Strain has argued, activists and the media oversimplified both approaches by reducing them to a rigid binary that pitted one against the other at the expense of understanding the benefits each approach offered the movement. The gendering of the debate compounded this oversimplification. Williams, in particular, underestimated the confrontational nature of nonviolent resistance that required activists to put their bodies, their gendered bodies, as historian Peter Ling has pointed out, on the line.[123] Williams and King did not escape the trappings of this rigid dichotomy, and, in fact, both exacerbated the differences in order to promote their approach, often using the other as an example of the limits of the other's strategy.[124]

Recalling an earlier debate over tactics between Marcus Garvey and his critics, this binary of violence versus nonviolence was also portrayed as manly versus unmanly resistance. Williams continually emphasized this point in the *Crusader* and statements to the press as he criticized nonviolence. An article he published against nonviolence in *Liberation Magazine* in September 1959 in part exemplified this. The article was titled "Is Violence Necessary to Combat Injustice? For the Positive: Williams Says 'We Must Fight Back.'" Williams began the essay by stating that he "was an enlisted man in the United States Marine Corps." Here, he authenticated and justified his aggressive tactics as a former serviceman, while also making a brief claim to a respectability that might appeal to middle-class readers. He "returned to civilian life" after the *Brown* decision, he continued, to face "acts of violence and words and deeds of hate." "The Southern brute respects only force," he affirmed, insisting that "nonviolence is a very potent weapon when the opponent is civilized, but nonviolence is no repellent for a sadist." A group of "cringing, begging," nonviolent black ministers in Monroe pleaded before the city officials to stop the attacks of the KKK. But not until the emergence of a group of "Negroes who showed a willingness to fight," who had not "been infected by turn-the-other-cheek-ism," did the officials comply. Williams maintained his belief that "Negroes must be willing to defend themselves, their women, their children and their homes. . . . Men who violently and swiftly rise to oppose tyranny are virtuous examples to emulate. I have been taught by my government to fight. Nowhere in the annals of history does the record show a people delivered from bondage by patience alone."[125]

Indeed, Williams's gendered line of thinking and rhetoric also shaped his attempts to counter critics of black self-defense.[126] As Marcus Garvey and his *Negro World* had attempted to do to W. E. B. DuBois, the *Crusader* deployed emasculating rhetoric to delegitimize the leadership and strategies of his critics. The paper lambasted King through coded language that portrayed him as an unmanly, cowardly lackey of white liberals so afraid to alienate their support that he willingly sacrificed the bodies, lives, and manhood of black men. "We are not yearning to die even in the cause of self-defense, and we certainly are not going to willingly die wagging doggie tails as we tag along behind our white masters singing pious hymns," one *Crusader* caption read, rejecting self-sacrifice.[127] Writing as Asa Lee, and showing that some black women participated in the construction of this physically resistant black manhood, Ethel Azalea Johnson wrote that "the Negro needs dedicated leaders. Not men who will swallow their courage and bury their manhood for material things."[128] In terms that hearkened to the emasculating effects of slavery, Lee asserted that "non-violence is only an excuse for continuing the conditions that have made the Negro a second-class citizen. . . . Once again the Negro finds himself on a slave block. This time he is being sold by non-violence."[129] Some of Williams's supporters did not see the dichotomy between him and King as clearly, however. One *Crusader* reader commented that he was "one hundred percent in accord with Dr. Martin Luther King and Mrs. Daisy Bates appeal for love and nonviolence . . . [but] . . . I pray that real leaders like Mr. Williams will not become discouraged and give up the sincere fight for justice in such a realistic manner, for when a man realizes that you are not a coward and will fight back, he will take a second thought before he threatens you."[130]

Williams's strong rhetoric, in addition to the importance and social relevance of the gendered binary in popular culture, prompted proponents of nonviolence to increasingly present their strategy as a moral *and* manly approach. The black press began doing the same as early as 1957, as it gave more and more favorable coverage to King. Over time, some papers would go from presenting King as a miracle-working preacher or debating the merits and practicality of nonviolence to stressing the "strength" that nonviolence demanded, much like King did. This framed the discourse in gendered terms that particularly adopted King's soldier-like image of the nonviolent "strong man," especially as men like Williams continued to influence segments of the public. For example, when the *Los Angeles Sentinel* identified King as a "New Kind of Negro Leader" in 1957, the paper reported him saying that "non-violence is our testing point. The strong man is the man who can stand up for his rights and not fight back."[131] By 1959, the *Atlanta Daily World*'s coverage of the Southwide Institute on Non-Violent Resistance in July reported the words of Ralph David Abernathy, the vice president of the SCLC: that "the opponents to Negro freedom would not be lulled into thinking that the new attitude of non-violent retaliation . . . is a sign of weakness . . . [but] . . . Gandhi proved the power and strength of non-violence."[132] Coverage of the same event by the *Defender* reported, "Non-Violence Shows Strength, Not Weakness"—that, as attendees had argued, "the non-violent philosophy is not a manifestation of weakness but of 'dynamic spiritual strength.'"[133]

Much of the mainstream black press joined movement leaders trying to use positive publicity to gain momentum and white allies for the freedom struggle. In giving positive coverage to King's argument that nonviolence represented a "dynamic spiritual strength," the black press helped the non-violent leader promote the strategy and helped promote King in particular as the harbinger of a new kind of manly leadership and resistance. Using militant language and images, the black press had long argued for black self-defense. The *Defender*, the *Crisis*, and the *Negro World* advised blacks to assert the manly right of self-defense in confronting racial violence after World War I, for example. During World War II, the *Courier* especially celebrated defiant black soldiers, who resisted racism in the armed forces, and promoted their right to fight as part of its Double V campaign. The *Courier* praised the exploits of valiant and defiant black soldiers like Doris "Dorie" Miller, who fought bravely during the attack on Pearl Harbor in 1941, coverage that helped make the Double V campaign perhaps the most popular and influential editorial crusade the black press ever waged.[134] Over time, black newspapers' aggressive editorializing against racial injustice and black defenselessness helped the press cultivate quite a reputation for militancy that readers, scholars, and federal officials recognized. Scholars and observers had commonly highlighted this since some of the first studies done on the black press. Some even commented that its protest ethic was problematic because it made black newspapers myopic and partisan, invested "to an irrational extent with the colored man's grievances against the white man," as one critic put it.[135] Many other observers appreciated this, however, and usually described the black press in terms of martial metaphors that likened the words of publishers, editors, and writers to weapons.

For example, Myrdal called the black press a "fighting press." Black journalist Enoch P. Waters admired one paper's "editorial guns." Black journalist and writer Roi Ottley called the black press a "weapon of protest and propaganda." The black sociologist E. Franklin Frazier wrote in his 1949 study *The Negro in the United States*, "The Negro reporter is a fighting partisan. The people who read his newspaper . . . expect him to put up a good fight for them. They don't like him tame. They want him to have an arsenal well-stocked with atomic adjectives and nouns." He continued that "they expect him to invent similes and metaphors that lay open the foe's weaknesses and to employ cutting irony, sarcasm and ridicule to confound and embarrass our opponents. The Negro reader is often a spectator at a fight. The reporter is attacking the reader's enemy and the reader has a vicarious relish for a fight well fought."[136] These metaphors had helped inspire and mobilize readers at different times. In this way, editors and writers for black newspapers remained discursively armed—until now. The success of the Montgomery boycott, the positive national and international attention King was helping to bring the freedom struggle, and the moral and respectable implications of nonviolent resistance helped make the black press a convert to nonviolence against its own history of promoting a self-defensive black militancy. Federal repression of the press's militancy after World War II, and the precarious position black newspapermen and women faced in aggressively criticizing Jim Crow during the Cold War, also influenced press support for King against men like Williams.[137] Indeed, these things forced members of the black press to join some activists in curtailing their discursive militancy or face governmental suppression. In either case, as King preached nonviolence, he received a great deal of aid from the press. Black newspapers increasingly endorsed nonviolence, and what fighting they could do at this point they did in very strategic ways in print, on the side of King's model of resistance. Against these growing limits in the militancy of black newspapermen and newspaperwomen, Williams emerged as one of the few truly militant black male publishers, committed as he was to print and practice.

It helped black newspapers that supporting King did not mean abandoning the powerful image of the resistant black man that they had long elevated, for King's promotion of nonviolence offered a new model of militant black masculinity that took ideas of black manhood to deeper, spiritual levels. King's nonviolent model stressed, as historian Peter Ling has put it, the "capacity of the masculine body to endure" and hold a moral high ground over the enemies of racial justice by demonstrating extraordinary self-discipline, self-restraint, and manliness to courageously resist one's adversaries directly without becoming physically combative in return.[138] The black press had commonly stressed over time an ethic of self-sacrifice as an important component to proper black manhood. In addition to drawing on his studies on Mohandas Gandhi's nonviolent activism and mentorship from Bayard Rustin, King may have also found support for his ideas from this discourse within the black press. In many ways, his model formed the next iteration of black newspapers' discourse on self-sacrifice, perhaps its ultimate expression for some. As early as 1957, King explained the transformative masculine power of nonviolence as he saw it in "Nonviolence and Racial Justice," an article he published in the *Christian Century*, a liberal Protestant magazine. King wanted the article published in this forum especially because the *Christian Century* had been favorable in its coverage of the Montgomery boycott. Its "sympathetic treatment" was of "inestimable value," King said, pointing to his intent to capitalize on good publicity for nonviolent protest.[139] Sharing his take on nonviolence in theological terms couched in stark gendered language, King stated firmly: "This is not a method for cowards; it *does* resist. The nonviolent resister is just as strongly opposed to the evil against which he protests as is the person who uses violence" (King's emphasis). For him, nonviolence helped free blacks from a long history of racial injustice that forced them to have a "subservient attitude" and "patiently submit to insult, injustice and exploitation." "Passive or nonaggressive in the sense that he is not physically aggressive toward his opponent," King distinguished nonviolence as an active form of resistance, for the nonviolent activist's "mind and emotions are always active. . . . [Nonviolence] is passive physically but strongly active spiritually; it is nonaggressive physically but dynamically aggressive spiritually." Because "it avoids not only external physical violence but also internal violence of spirit," nonviolence offered a path to redemption through "agape," the highest form of love that "means understanding, redeeming good will for all men . . . the love of God working in the lives of men." Conscious of the positive public implications of the strategy, King encouraged activists to "wage the struggle with dignity and discipline," while he conceded that nonviolence "challenges all people struggling for justice and freedom." Despite this challenge, nonviolence remained the best approach because it was "on the side of justice" and "the method that seeks to redeem," a point of extreme import to the ongoing dual quest to gain racial justice and redeem black manhood.[140] King would expand these points throughout his public career as they remained a mainstay of his continued elaboration of the nonviolent philosophy.

King's framework reinvigorated manly self-sacrifice. The nonviolent strategy did not depart from the long-standing history of black resistance to white violence, but rather transformed it into a militancy that was non-violent, a nonviolent militancy that put black men and the black male body at the center of dramatic confrontations with segregationists in order to dismantle Jim Crow. Along these lines, there was no need for weapons in the sense that Williams argued because the black male body, the vessel from which this indomitable spiritual might was ignited and released, *was* the weapon. That nonviolent protest required activists to put their bodies at heightened risk was to miss the point. Williams would contend that the "average Afro-American is not a pacifist. He's not a pacifist and he has never been a pacifist and he's not made of the type of material that would make a good pacifist."[141] Because of such beliefs held by Williams and others, King argued that it was possible for blacks to come to be made of that "type of material," for the black male body at heightened risk experienced a heightened sense of spiritual awareness and manly mettle. Nonviolent masculinity seemed to be the ultimate manhood because it called on black men to be more manly than ever in resisting white violence by rejecting the corporal power of physicality, aggression, revenge, and violence for a more powerful mental and spiritual strength.[142] Additionally, it engaged the prospects of a martyrdom that had become a hallmark quality of manly black leadership since the 1919 race riots. Through nonviolent black masculinity, black men also countered the long-standing stereotypical image of black men as naturally violent. The masculine and redemptive implications of nonviolence remained important to King's thinking and preaching about the tactic for much of his public career, emphasizing those implications especially as gendered calls for black self-defense increased.

Perhaps most importantly for King's nonviolent model of black manhood, nonviolence helped black men trade a limited and limiting path to masculinity derived from the physical or a gun for a powerful, everlasting one emanating from the spirit. In 1958, King's memoir on the boycott, *Stride toward Freedom: The Montgomery Story*, appeared and elevated the role of black men in the struggle. King stated that the "native sons" of the South were "best" to lead it out of its racial crises.[143] He argued in his second book, *The Measure of a Man*, a rather interesting title for a tract published in 1959 in the midst of the gendered debate over nonviolence, that "man is a being of spirit"; that while he was also a sinner, he was made in the image of God and was therefore "different from lower animals. He is not guided merely by instinct. He has the ability to choose between alternatives, so he can choose the good or the evil, the high or the low."[144] King's arguments reflected his tendency to frame nonviolence in deeply philosophical and theological questions and themes that were oftentimes lofty and sermonic, but probably resonated with the black and white churchgoing public of postwar America.[145]

But King seemed to avoid this religious framing when he decided to challenge Williams, a fellow "native son" of the South, opting to be clear and direct. In the same year as the release of *The Measure of a Man*, King published a rebuttal to Williams in *Liberation Magazine* a month after Williams's article appeared in the same forum. As had been the case in previous decades, black leaders turned to the press to air their ideological differences. Williams had characterized a group of local ministers as "cringing, begging," and unwilling to fight. But this minister decided to take Williams on. Reflecting on their domestic life, Coretta insisted that King was "sure of his manhood. . . . He was a real man in every respect."[146] King's article argued that "pure nonviolence . . . requires extraordinary discipline and courage" and insisted that Williams "would have us believe that there is no collective and practical alternative. . . . There is more power in socially organized masses on the march than there is in guns in the hands of a few desperate men. Our enemies would prefer to deal with a small armed group rather than with a huge, unarmed resolute mass of people."[147] King characterized Williams as an advocate of violence, promoting it "as a tool of advancement," rather than as the advocate of black self-defense that he really was, symptomatic of the nonviolent-violent dichotomy to which many members of the movement and press had come to follow. The black press, which had long endorsed a physical black resistance, continued to do so, but in this new form modeled on King and nonviolent militancy. Giving in to violence by becoming violent was the new weakness—confronting violence by embracing nonviolence was the new strength, as King insisted. By 1960, he would write that the strategy gave nonviolent activists "new self-respect; it calls up resources of strength and courage that they did not know they had."[148] Indeed, many black male civil rights activists felt they had discovered this strength and couched nonviolence in martial terms that helped emphasize the manliness of the strategy, playing up the image of the soldier-like nonviolent strong man that King was promoting. For example, activist Wyatt Tee Walker described nonviolent activists as a "nonviolent army." James M.

Lawson Jr., another activist, went further, calling for the actual training of a "nonviolent corps" to lead a "nonviolent revolution." For him, this struggle would help produce a new generation of Race Men through "the womb of revolution," which "involves the whole man in his whole existence."[149]

As the ideological differences between Williams and King showed, the debate over the proper strategy for racial advancement and its leadership involved another contest of masculinity, the winner of which the black press would again help determine. Through Williams and King, the black press presented two competing models of black masculinity. Williams represented a familiar model, one that black newspapers had long promoted, that of the black man courageous enough to resist racial violence and defend himself, black women, and the race. Williams also represented the war-ripened black veteran, an image that the black press had usually celebrated. King, however, represented a new model that took that long-standing vision and transformed it into a morally superior man who used a spiritual fortitude to defend himself, black women, and the race. It is a wonder why, especially in the midst of these debates, King, an author, thinker, and activist, did not start his own paper, as many black men vying for public influence and racial leadership long had. Indeed, as early as 1957, he was looking for ways to broaden his movement, admitting that "there was a problem of getting this method [nonviolence] over because it didn't make sense to most of the people in the beginning." Coretta was also invested in helping her husband and the movement gain a positive public image. It was during the boycott that she found she could not "depend on the mainstream [white] press" to do this, concerned with "the ways they mangled the truth" regarding King.[150] Having his own paper could have helped him solve these problems early on. Perhaps he and Coretta could have formed a publishing team like Daisy and L. C. Bates. Yet, his increasingly demanding schedule probably discouraged him from founding a newspaper. Coretta remembered that during the boycott he was "too busy racing around, preaching, and being at the forefront to record his efforts." Indeed, *Jet* magazine called him the "Man on the Go."[151] Also, King was at this time based in the South, which might have hampered his ability to do so if he had tried, doomed ultimately to face the same challenges as the Bateses, for example. But perhaps because he was receiving such favorable coverage from northern black papers and eventually some mainstream white papers that together offered him widespread access, he did not have to found his own paper.

The press's elevation of King and his brand of militancy was partly driven by political necessity, however. As historian Jeff Woods has noted, "the ultimate success of the civil rights movement depended in large part on public opinion. Changing minds about the condition of blacks under segregation meant reaching the ears of those with the moral conscience to listen. At the same time, it meant defending the movement against damaging publicity."[152] The militancy of activists like Williams had become a political liability for movement leaders and their intent to use respectable images of black men and activists to their advantage in order to gain white support. Leading an aggressive editorial crusade, as the black press had usually done to influence the black public sphere, seemed at this time to be a political liability too. Many mainstream northern black papers instead increasingly documented the struggle over editorializing about it, a conservative move that still had the effect of giving a lot of coverage to the movement, and helped elevate King.[153] Yet the press's promotion of King was also due to the potential his new model had to elevate black male leadership, strategies of resistance, and racial advancement to a greater level of manliness that might destroy not only Jim Crow but also long-standing beliefs that black men were not real men brave enough to confront white supremacy head on. These contests of masculinity in the press, and the implications they raised for the movement and the redemption of black manhood, helped obscure and displace black women's leadership in the movement. Historian Danielle McGuire has shown that while black women's anti-rape activism helped spark and sustain the Montgomery bus boycott, men assumed leadership of the protest. Black male activists displaced, for example, Jo Ann Robinson, a chief organizer of the boycott, though she had helped organize black women through the WPC many years before Williams and King started organizing black men. "The men took it over," Robinson reflected.[154] To appeal to ideas of respectability, black male activists held up Rosa Parks, a militant activist who had been organizing for civil rights and anti-rape issues for some time before the boycott, as "a saintly symbol," historian Danielle McGuire notes. Though women's organizing fueled the protest's momentum, King was framed as the leader largely responsible for galvanizing the black community in Montgomery. The press played an instrumental role in this framing, as well as in framing the movement as a male-led, male-defined struggle among men.[155]

When young activists initiated the sit-in movement, introducing mass direct action and mass civil disobedience, the black press for the most part did not see it as the challenge to the gradualism of older nonviolent activists that younger activists intended, but interpreted it as the expansion of King's nonviolent philosophy. On February 1, 1960, four black college students at the historically black North Carolina Agricultural and Technical College initiated a sit-in at a Woolworth counter in Greensboro, North Carolina, that ignited the sit-in movement among young black activists. The event barely made front-page news, however. The *Courier*, for example, started covering the sit-ins on February 13 with reports appearing on page four. The paper reported one of the activists as saying, "Many of our adults have been complacent and fearful and it is time for someone to wake up and change the situation and we decided to start here," challenging the courage older activists had emphasized in the "strong man" model as not being brave enough. By March, reports on the sit-ins filled the *Courier*. Yet, still missing the young activists' crucial point in pushing the older establishment to adopt a more confrontational approach, the *Courier* pointed to King as the leading example for the students to follow. The paper gave them some advice, couched in the terms of respectability and proper public decorum that adult nonviolent activists had been using:

Don't strike back or curse back if abused

Don't laugh out

Don't hold conversations with floor workers

Don't leave your seats until your leader has given you instructions to do so

Don't block entrances to the stores and aisles

Show yourself friendly and courteous at all times

Sit straight and always face the counter

Report all serious incidents to your leader

Refer all information to your leader in a polite manner

Remember the teachings of Jesus Christ, Mohandes K. Gandhi and Martin Luther King, Jr.

Remember love and non-violence and may God bless each of you[156]

King would give them some advice too, emphasizing the spiritual strength that nonviolence required. "The tactics of nonviolence without the spirit of nonviolence," he admonished, "may become a new kind of violence."[157] In April 1960, student activists met at the historically black Shaw University under the guidance of seasoned activist and former SCLC organizer Ella Baker and founded SNCC to support the student nonviolent movement, using more militant nonviolent direct action. Young activists intended their approach to challenge not only Jim Crow segregation in public accommodations but also what they saw as the older leadership's slowing momentum, growing gradualism, and overwhelming control over the civil rights agenda.[158] Coverage of the young insurgents helped further elevate non-violence in the black press, but the challenge they issued to older leadership did not register in most black newspapers. It was instead subsumed under the press's increasingly King-centered interpretation of the movement.

Yet the more confrontational nature of the sit-ins perhaps did more to help black men redeem their manhood than did King's approach, at least for some activists. For example, Franklin McCain, one of the four students who conducted the sit-in on February 1, 1960, commented, "I probably felt better on that day than I've ever felt in my life. Seems like a lot of feelings of guilt or what-have-you suddenly left me, and I felt as though I had gained my manhood, so to speak, and not only gained it, but had developed quite a lot of respect for it. Not Franklin McCain only as an individual, but I felt as though the manhood of a number of other black persons had been restored and had gotten some respect from just that one day."[159]

Still, the new activism of black youth encouraged black newspapers to promote nonviolence as the new militancy and ideal strategy for black protest and racial advancement and frame King as the ideal type of masculine leader in the fight. Following the sit-ins, the *Defender* commented that "two things became abundantly clear": that the movement for civil rights was "no fad" and that "thousands of participants in The Movement had captured the spirit of non-violent resistance. . . . They called forth unknown strength."[160] The *New York Amsterdam News* remarked that the "young American teenagers . . . have boldly stepped forth as protagonists of democracy. Their courage and amazing restraint have inspired millions and given a new dignity to the cause of freedom." Invoking the image of King's nonviolent "strong man," the *Amsterdam News* argued that they represented a "new, non-violent brand of freedom fighter," inspired by "the one man who, more than any other, symbolizes the new spirit now sweeping the South—the Rev. Dr. Martin Luther King, Jr." "It is his doctrine of non-violence which has inspired and guided the students," the paper argued. It also insisted that "the defense of Martin Luther King, spiritual leader of the student sit-in movement . . . is an integral part of the total struggle for freedom in the South." Celebrating the "creative daring of the students and the quiet heroism of Dr. King," the paper urged readers to provide moral and monetary support for the growing movement and its expanding forms of nonviolent resistance, appealing especially to prominent blacks for financial contributions. Its long roster of black notables included Nat King Cole, Harry Belafonte, Diahann Carroll, Dorothy Dandridge, Ossie Davis and Ruby Dee, Mordecai Johnson, Sammy Davis Jr., and Jackie Robinson.[161] As they had always done, black newspapermen and newspaperwomen used the black press to build support among black readers for racial struggle, this time mobilizing black political action to support the nonviolent black freedom movement over black self-defense. Given King's growing stature in the press and admiration by many, including some student activists, black newspapers framed them as King's mentees, despite the young freedom fighters' intention to keep their movement student-led and free from the influence of more established civil rights organizations like the SCLC and the NAACP.[162]

Unlike many southern black papers, Williams's paper commended the young activists and the sit-in movement. The *Atlanta Daily World*, for example, chided, "There is no need for any group to take matters into their own hands in misguided attempts to gain civil rights. . . . Such attempts merely create ill-will and set up situations that endanger the lives and property of everyone. . . . The answer is to be found at the conference table, [at the] ballot box, and in the courts of law; to do otherwise is unsound, dangerous, and impractical." Percy Greene, editor of the *Jackson Advocate*, Mississippi's leading black paper, reported, "SITDOWN PROTEST DARKENS U. S. RACE PICTURE." Greene and his paper's location in Mississippi positioned them in a bastion of racial violence, though Greene was also deeply conservative and tended to criticize civil rights activists as agitators.[163] But Williams hailed the young activists as "militant and courageous voices of the oppressed." He also used their new strategy as an opportunity to scold black people, especially black men who were too afraid and unmanly to take part in the struggle and the new strategy of direct action. Williams expressed his frustrations in the *Crusader* through a poem titled "Egos and Heroes":

You say you're a shot
Who excels
Well tell me Mack, how come you aint in one of them jails?
You say you came up
Through heartbreak and strife,
That you're a big man
Who made a mark in life.
In spite of all you say or do
Mack there's something
That just don't ring true.
You say you've got a yacht
And a degree,

But Mack, how come you aint free?
Man I don't think
You're no big ta do,
I know students bigger than you—
You may be an actor in your expensive car
But Mack you sho aint no star.
Man you call yourself heavy,
But you're a fool
You'd carry more weight
On a lunch counter stool.
Man you aint no shot
Of noble feat—
You're too damn scared
To sit down and eat.
Boy you aint nothing
In Jim Crow land
With a tail that wags
More like a dog than a man—
Man o' man
You're an educated fool
To do you're struggling
On a bar room stool—
So long Mack, cant buy your tale
I'm on my way to help fill the jail.[164]

Mainstream black papers based in the urban North celebrated the students too, but framed them as the triumph of nonviolent direct action over self-defense. Events surrounding the protests of the Freedom Riders in Monroe in August 1961 confirmed that triumph even more for many black newspapers, solidifying the press's rejection of Williams and black armed resistance. Led by James Farmer, the president of the Congress of Racial Equality, the 1961 Freedom Rides were nonviolent protests that involved black and white activists riding interstate buses through the South to challenge segregation. Determined to make their way through the South, the campaigners encountered violent resistance from whites in South Carolina, Alabama, and Mississippi. Invited by Williams to Monroe, the young activists were determined to prove the power of nonviolence, while he was eager to demonstrate his support for them.[165] Williams intended to practice nonviolence in support of the protest and encouraged members of his local movement to do the same. But knowing the violent resistance of local whites that transformed Monroe into battleground conditions, he also "saw it as an opportunity to show that what King and them were preaching was bullshit."[166] Tensions mounted throughout the week of the protest. Many activists were arrested and threatened with violence by whites. Rising hostilities, ongoing harassment by whites and police, and continued arrests finally bubbled over into violence. And Williams, the armed guard, and Monroe blacks reacted, organizing quickly to defend themselves and the activists.[167]

Williams's use of self-defense again threw him into the national spotlight. The events that followed indicated to movement leaders and the press the futility, foolhardiness, and danger of black self-defense at this time.[168] The *Defender*, for example, presented the protest positively before the violence erupted. "'Freedom Riders' staged a mass demonstration . . . led by Robert F. Williams . . . against North Carolina segregationists," it commented.[169] But when violence broke out, the *Defender* emphasized in a report five days later how Williams had a controversial history of promoting black self-defense. "'Passive' Resistance Plan Explodes," the paper declared, in what was "billed as a test of passive resistance, but it followed blunt talk of violence." "Local Negro leader Robert Williams, who sponsored the demonstrations, is known as an advocate of 'meeting force with force.' He was expelled from the National Association for the Advancement of Colored People in 1959 for his extreme views." Preparing to protect activists because local police seemed reluctant to do so, Williams said, according to the *Defender*, that he and others "were stockpiling small arms for use in self-defense."[170] Another *Defender* article stoked anti-Communist feeling by emphasizing Williams's relationship to Fidel Castro. "Officers with shotguns and tear gas guns raided the headquarters of Robert Williams, bearded admirer of Cuban premier Fidel Castro."[171] Williams's defensive actions this time put him in the crosshairs of local authorities and the FBI. During the melee that followed the protest, Williams took a white couple into his home in order to protect them from Monroe blacks and the armed guard, who were ready to spring into defensive action. The white couple entered the black community to insult the activists and rile them up, a move that was about to turn disastrous for them until Williams intervened. But local authorities slapped him with spurious charges of kidnapping. To avoid arrest, and possibly murder at the hands of police, Williams fled Monroe for New York, then Canada, and finally Cuba.[172]

Black civil rights leaders long critical of Williams simply reasoned that his appeals to self-defense had finally caught up with him—the inevitable result of armed black resistance as a strategy, they thought.[173] One *Courier* article shared with an air of intended irony, "Fiery Robert F. Williams, whose advocacy of giving violence for violence to white racists projected him into national prominence two years ago, was being hunted by FBI agents following his indictment by a Union County grand jury on kidnap charges."[174] The *New York Amsterdam News* quoted the FBI: "He has previously been diagnosed as schizophrenic and has advocated and threatened violence. Williams should be considered armed and dangerous."[175] Their part here in helping construct an image of Williams as a deranged, mentally unstable black man showed how far the black press had moved from arguing a logic to black men's self-defense. The image of the war-ripened black veteran and defiant black soldiers, who were celebrated during and after the world wars, was now overwhelmingly rejected. "Monroe Integrationist Asks Asylum in Cuba," the *Defender* reported, though, as two other papers, the *Militant* and *National Guardian*, had done, the *Defender* also published Williams's explanation of the events that led to the charges.[176] From Cuba, ensconced in the aftermath of a successful revolution brought about by armed struggle, Williams continued writing and publishing the *Crusader*, now as a monthly. He would later call himself, "Publisher in Exile." For years, his paper had discussed links between black freedom struggles in America and anti-colonial struggles abroad. In continuing his activism from Cuba, he reaffirmed that at least for him, there was little distance between print and practice.[177]

For the black press, their condemnation of Williams appeared even more fitting given that as a black publisher he seemed to be jeopardizing the goals of racial advancement that many mainstream black newspapers were now mobilizing behind, goals based at this time on the civil rights struggle through nonviolent resistance modeled by King. It had not been uncommon for black publishers and editors throughout the black press and/or within a single paper to have differences of opinion, but many major black papers were again uniting under a uniform editorial policy, as the press had done against the segregated army and lily-white baseball. Thus, Williams, the publisher, had broken ranks. Other members of the black press would too, and came under scrutiny for being out of lockstep with black newspapers' support for the movement, especially among northern black papers. For instance, George S. Schuyler, a black conservative, satirist, longtime writer for many black periodicals, and associate editor for the *Courier*, was critical of King and the nonviolent struggle. In 1957, he wrote in his column "Views and Reviews" that "the Montgomery bus boycott might have been a noble experiment but now that it has been 'won' . . . so what? Montgomery

Negroes could have owned the bus company without doing all that walking if they had used their heads instead of their feet and their tonsils." But by 1962, he and other critical staff members were warned by the *Courier*'s management to tone down their criticism of King. A memo from William G. Nunn of the *Courier* told him, "We here feel that King is doing a tremendous job. He's a symbol of a new kind of thinking among Negroes." "Right or wrong, his courage and singleness of purpose is continually putting the white South on the defensive," Nunn continued; the "*Courier* should go all-out in its support of the man and his actions." Schuyler's criticism, among other things, continued unabated, and by 1964, the *Courier* let him go.[178]

For Williams, it was the black press that was breaking ranks by lowering its "editorial guns" and sacrificing its historic role. From exile, Williams continued to criticize the failures of American democracy and some of the leadership and strategies of the freedom struggle. He also criticized the black press. Convinced of the crucial links between print and practice, Williams construed its overwhelming endorsement of nonviolence and its advocates at the expense of black self-defense as a stark sign that the black press had lost its militancy, perhaps its own "manhood" in his mind, a matter that he lamented.[179] "To varying degrees," Williams wrote sometime around 1962, "most of the Black press has supported the Negro struggle for human rights in the racist USA." But he charged that it had now gone from being unapologetically militant to doling out "light slaps on the wrist," becoming more and more "timid." The *Atlanta Daily World, Defender, Baltimore Afro-American, Courier, Amsterdam News, Norfolk Journal and Guide,* and John H. Johnson's magazines were among a slate of popular black publications that he called out as "a graphic example of the timid line carried by some of the so-called 'responsible' and 'respectable' Negro press." They "display cautious traits, bordering on dual policy, based on the militancy towards the denunciation of social injustice, while at the same time displaying loyalty towards the system that produces it. . . . By failing to support the Afro-American struggle for human rights a Negro publication may keep some white advertisers but it will lose some of its readers," a process by which the black press was forced to "prostitute its independence for financial advantages," Williams asserted in stern gendered terms. He warned that the "rising new militancy on the part of black Americans is creating a grave crisis for the established Negro press" that could portend its "destruction": "It is only logical to assume that violence, coupled with the fact that the Afro-American masses are becoming more revolutionary, that the Black press as a whole will be forced to take on a more militant stance . . . [and] . . . will have to side unequivocally with the struggling masses or lose support."[180]

What black militancy was or should have been was clear to Williams, though it was also clear to King, changing but more and more clear to many mainstream black papers. Williams remained convinced that the mainstream black press was becoming anything but militant. His belief in this regard was partly influenced by E. Franklin Frazier's 1957 seminal polemic, *Black Bourgeoisie*, which Williams cited in his critique. Rather than seeming to praise the black press as he had in his 1949 study, Frazier now presented a withering appraisal of black publications. Possibly because so many members of the black press and civil rights establishment viewed Williams's ideas as extreme, Williams turned to Frazier's observations to help legitimize his claims. Frazier, a reputable and respected scholar, offered a scathing evaluation of black middle-class life and values and argued that the black press was the "chief medium of communication which creates and perpetuates the world of make-believe for the black bourgeoisie." The editorial content of the black press, founded as an "organ of the 'Negro protest,'" had emphasized the values and goals of the black bourgeoisie since the press's inception, and in Frazier's view, had "little relation to the world of reality."[181] Early critics of the black press charged that by highlighting crime and/or promoting racial justice, and sensationalizing both, black newspapers actually did little to help improve black people's public image. Now Williams and Frazier argued something similar, if not far worse: the black press had lost touch with the masses, constructing worlds of fantasy and functioning primarily as a tool of black middle-class visions for racial advancement. Black newspapers' "society page is a consolation prize for a victimized class society whose ethnic heritage bars it from the mainstream of a racist caste system," Williams contended, arguing that society news increasingly consumed more space in mainstream black publications than the black freedom struggle.[182] That he was a grassroots publisher with working-class resources marshaling his paper against the middle-class civil rights establishment and middle-class black newspaper publishers and writers, who had strongly endorsed leaders like King, likely shaped Williams's support for Frazier's views. Perhaps John Sengstacke's fears that mainstream black publishers would one day find themselves irrelevant and underutilized in the midst of sharp changes in the black freedom struggle were beginning to materialize.

To be sure, what Williams identified as a "grave crisis" for the black press was more complex than changes in editorial stances on the black freedom struggle, though this remained a significant contributing factor along with its endorsement of the nonviolent model of black male leadership and masculinity. The shift from decades of militant racial advocacy to a conservative policy of simply reporting news was driven by a number of factors black newspapers could not control.[183] Circulation numbers for many major newspapers began to drop as early as 1950 and accelerated over time because of these factors, leading ultimately to sharp changes in the relevance and influence of certain major black publications that would become clear by the end of the decade.[184] First, the editorial policies and content of many black newspapers became less militant because many publishers tried to avoid exacerbating the racial backlash, facing accusations that the movement was Communist inspired, and experiencing federal pressure to conform to Cold War politics. Second, the press joined black leaders and activists trying to use positive publicity in the press to gain momentum and white allies for the movement. Many black newspapermen and newspaperwomen downplayed militant rhetoric, avoiding coverage and editorials that might alienate critical white support.[185] Still, many white advertisers began to bolt from the black press when it escalated its coverage of the movement. This was a third factor as some publishers were forced to choose allegiances to advertising revenue over reporting closely on the movement. L. C. and Daisy Bates's *Arkansas State Press* was one such casualty of this dilemma. When they chose to support the movement, opponents pressured black advertisers, which the Bateses deliberately chose to use over white advertisers, to withdraw their support. Opponents also pressured the black owner of the building that housed their paper to terminate their lease. The paper's circulation of 20,000 in 1957 dropped to 5,000 by 1959.[186] After facing death threats and attacks on their home for their activism in deed and print, the Bateses shut the paper down on October 20, 1959, just months after Daisy had denounced Williams for his activism.[187]

Fourth, the movement and other racial matters began to increasingly attract the interest of white mainstream papers and their readers as the struggle progressed. As early as 1950, a meeting of the Mississippi Press Association, for example, encouraged Mississippi journalists to do a better job of covering racial issues fairly, even in gendered terms. Co-publisher of the *Chronicle Star* of Pascagoula, Mississippi, remarked, "Mississippi will not abandon its 48th place in the United States until it starts treating the Negro as a man. . . . We can raise the Negro, if we treat him as a man in the papers. . . . Tagging him 'colored' is not only bad journalism, but it is an injustice to a man who needs justice."[188] Following the *Brown* decision in 1954 and the lynching of Emmett Till in 1955, white coverage of racial matters increased greatly, though the quality of the coverage was oftentimes lacking.[189] Still, white reporters were increasingly giving the movement front-page coverage in the white press, and for the first time ever, some white papers were beginning to feature decent, true-to-life news about black America.[190]

White papers and readers' interest in the movement had the positive effect of publicizing the struggle to whites, but the negative effect of generating a competition over sales and the siphoning off of black readers. For the first time, black newspapers had to compete directly with the white press for black readers. Making matters worse, white publishers began hiring black reporters to intensify coverage of the movement. Black reporters, it was thought, were more suited than white ones to go into black communities for stories. This siphoning off of black reporters created a "brain drain" of talent on the black press.[191] These developments drove some black publishers to begin to cover the movement without weighing in editorially as it had always done through advocacy journalism. Some publishers flat out refused to endorse the efforts of civil rights activists altogether, however. C. A. Scott, publisher of the *Atlanta Daily World*, for example, cautioned, "We have everything to lose [by getting mad] and nothing to gain." "What we want is goodwill. The less friction we create today, the less we will have to undo tomorrow."[192] The *Atlanta Daily World* exemplified the continued reticence of some southern black newspapers and illustrated how markedly different the southern-based *Crusader* was at this time.

Noticing the militant turn that the movement was beginning to take, especially with the rise of black radicalism in the urban North, an optimistic Williams argued that "the vacuum is being filled by organizational publications. A myriad of mimeographed publications are appearing in many communities," using the same technology that made the *Crusader* possible. Some observers derogatorily called these papers the "extremist sheets."[193] As an activist and publisher, Williams was at once on the cusp of dramatic changes in the movement and in the black press. He hoped that the press would "regain its independence" and remained confident that the emerging militant turn signaled the day in which "a captive Negro press is forced to serve as an agent of apology for US racism and imperialism, is drawing to a close."[194] While exiled, Williams published *Negroes with Guns* in 1962, a memoir that reaffirmed his stance on self-defense as a deterrent and tool of empowerment for black people's sense of confidence and black men's sense of manhood. He wrote, "I do not advocate violence for its own sake, or for the sake of reprisals against whites. Nor am I against the passive resistance advocated by the Reverend Martin Luther King and others. My only difference with Dr. King is that I believe in flexibility in the freedom struggle. This means that I believe in non-violent tactics where feasible. . . . But where there is break-down of the law, the individual citizen has a right to protect his person, his family, his home and his property." "When an oppressed people show a willingness to defend themselves," he charged, "the enemy, who is a moral weakling and coward is more willing to grant concessions and work for a respectable compromise." His belief in "flexibility" pointed to his conception of a militancy based on the freedom to access a range of self-defensive options that included organizing black men, and using armed resistance, radical rhetoric, highly masculinized and gendered language and performances, and an aggressive style of black leadership and protest. Any of these options could be deployed when necessary. "We must create a black militancy," he bluntly stated. To the civil rights establishment and supportive white liberals, who were focused on "good public relations," he asserted, "We're not interested in a good press. We're interested in becoming free."[195]

Williams's use of self-defense and promotion of armed black resistance in the *Crusader* set him on a collision course with the local KKK, local authorities, the civil rights establishment, eventually the FBI, and the mainstream black press. "What has happened and continues to happen in Monroe, N. C., illustrates an old truth," he wrote in *Negroes with Guns*, "that words used in common by all men do not always have a meaning common to all men. Men have engaged in life-or-death struggles because of differences of meaning in a commonly held word." The particular word Williams was referencing here was "freedom," though his broader point also extends to militancy.[196] Williams's militancy and embrace of self-defense embodied the models of black masculinity that black newspapers had long constructed and promoted. But with the rise of the modern civil rights movement, the new styles of black leadership and protest that the movement offered, and the virulent racial backlash that followed it, the black press jettisoned the old models for new ones. For the black press, the vision of masculinity that Williams embodied and promoted had become a political liability and a danger for movement leaders and activists. Shaped by precarious political and social developments on the ground that could suddenly accelerate the movement or cripple it, the black press reversed its long-standing militancy in defending the race and forcefully demanding racial justice in order to promote a more pragmatic racial advocacy in the vein of nonviolent struggle. Here, the press helped nonviolent proponents argue against the long history of black self-defense, and, in particular, helped elevate King and his nonviolent militancy as the new ideal vision of black masculinity and manly black leadership.

With a mimeograph machine, Williams claimed some space in the black public sphere and countered with his own press what he saw as mainstream black newspapers' overwhelming support for the nonviolent model of black male leadership and masculinity. Through the *Crusader*, as well as provocative statements to black and white newspapers, Williams did what black men vying for a position of leadership and influence had long done—he used the press to raise a critical voice, as well as elevate his particular vision for black masculinity and racial advancement. He and the *Crusader*'s counter-discourse touched off a debate over self-defense and nonviolence that played out in the press and showed the role of black newspapers in helping decide the matter but also helped show the limits of media-led black militancy at this time. The mainstream black press resisted the forms of black militancy promoted by men like Williams, prioritizing documenting the freedom struggle over waging another militant editorial campaign as it had always done.[197] Even Roy Wilkins, who had denounced Williams's militancy, lamented this tremendous change in the mainstream black press: "The minute [black newspapers] stop being crusaders and become chroniclers, they're done."[198] Williams would have agreed. He remained confident that at some point there would be more black people on the side of self-defense and his vision of black militancy than not, as if a greater black militancy was dormant, only waiting for the right conditions to explode. "When it is no longer some distant Negro who's no more than a statistic, no more than an article in a newspaper; when it is no longer their neighbors, but it means them and it becomes a matter of personal salvation, then will their attitude change."[199]

5 Walk the Way of Free Men

Malcolm X, Displaying the Original Man, and Troubling the Black Press as the Voice of the Race

· ·

Brother Frank 8X Lopez sold *Muhammad Speaks* on the streets of New York. The paper was the official news organ of the Nation of Islam (NOI), a faith-based black separatist organization led by Elijah Muhammad. Lopez was a member, as well as one of its leading salesmen for the paper.[1] *Muhammad Speaks* was one of the "organizational publications" that convinced Robert F. Williams that a greater black militancy was on the horizon for the black press and freedom struggle. In fact, he called it one of the "most vocal" black papers of its day.[2] Williams had confidence in *Muhammad Speaks* for good reason: he was friends with its founder, Malcolm X. The two met in 1958 and came to share a commitment to black self-defense, the redemption of black manhood, and eventually print and practice.[3] And Malcolm was as unlikely a newspaperman as Williams was, if not more. Born Malcolm Little in Omaha, Nebraska, in 1925, his father was an outspoken Baptist preacher and Garveyite, who was thought to have been killed by white vigilantes when Malcolm was six years old. Malcolm's mother struggled to hold their family together after his death and was later committed to a mental institution. Malcolm, their seventh child, was sent to foster care for a time. He fell into a life of crime by his midteens and was incarcerated for larceny and breaking and entering at twenty-one years old. He converted to the NOI in prison, and, paroled in 1952, he quickly became one of Muhammad's leading ministers. By the late 1950s, he was Muhammad's national spokesman.[4] In terms of black people's freedom struggles, Williams had pushed for complete integration. Malcolm instead promoted Muhammad's vision for racial advancement, a message previously widely unknown until it was brought to the attention of the mass public on July 10, 1959, with the airing of "The Hate That Hate Produced." This televised documentary introduced Malcolm, Muhammad, men like Lopez, and the NOI to America.[5] The documentary ignited a firestorm of controversy around the NOI, but prompted Malcolm to respond by founding *Muhammad Speaks* in May 1960. The paper served as the organization's propaganda organ, while marking the beginning of a robust media campaign in which Malcolm and men like Lopez were crucial. *Muhammad Speaks* helped counter critics of the NOI, attract interest and followers, and promote Muhammad's vision for racial advancement before an increasingly militant black public. That vision was predicated on "Separation or Death."[6] This pithy but heady declaration reflected Muhammad's eschatological beliefs, Black Nationalism, and demand for a separate black state.[7] And Muhammad, NOI leaders, and *Muhammad Speaks* directed this message especially at black men. "I'm after you the black man. . . . You are the man that is asleep," Muhammad asserted in the paper. "The time is long past for the black man to start doing some serious thinking about what he must do to become wholly free."[8]

This chapter examines the role of *Muhammad Speaks* in promoting Muhammad's agenda for racial advancement, as well as serving as the fulcrum of a robust media campaign through which the NOI displayed living examples of redeemed black men before the public. Like many men of his generation, Muhammad was concerned about the production of proper Race Men, and his paper, like that of many other black newspapermen throughout the twentieth century, reflected this. Yet the paper departed from its predecessors and contemporaries along these lines in significant ways that heralded a break with mainstream black papers and the rise of the radical black press. Other black papers had long constructed ideas, ideals, and images of black manhood by gendering their coverage of pivotal moments in the black freedom struggle to be moments for black men to stand up and be men. *Muhammad Speaks* did this too, but went further, displaying this message on its pages, as well as on the bodies of the Nation's men. In this way, an increasingly militant black reading public could read both the paper and the men and find a dialogic relationship between the two in which one reinforced the other. Nation men exemplified Muhammad's "Original Man," his model of proper black manhood that he and the paper constructed as an imitable figure and masculine identity that black men should adopt by embracing his ideologies. For Muhammad, the race was facing a crisis "that points to self-help or oblivion," as the paper put it.[9] While many mainstream black papers continued to promote integration, *Muhammad Speaks* argued that black people's ideas of racial advancement had turned too long on being part of a society that was categorically incapable of giving black people their rights, respect as human beings, and real manhood and womanhood.

Much of the proof of this crisis was in the urban. Whereas the black press of the early twentieth century had helped promote the urban as a promised land for black people during the Great Migration, *Muhammad Speaks* condemned it. For the NOI, the urban had failed black people and black men in particular. Years before some policy makers, black leaders, and black activists argued that America's urban centers were decaying and failing black people, especially black men, the paper promoted Muhammad's plans for an urban renewal that promised to renew black people's communities, job opportunities, and gendered selves.[10] To be sure, many black people, leaders, and newspapers had long argued that the urban had definite shortcomings, making these points especially during the Red Summer and the Great Depression. *Muhammad Speaks* continued this, but in a sensationalized fashion that reflected and shaped the black militancy of its moment, and distinguished the paper and the organization it represented before the black public sphere. Black people living in cities like Watts, Chicago, Detroit, Newark, and Harlem in the 1960s, cities that would explode in urban rebellions by the mid- to late 1960s, would have agreed that the urban had failed them. For many of them, the urban was a cauldron of intractable racial tensions, police brutality, deplorable housing conditions, soaring poverty, and abysmal economic opportunities.[11] *Muhammad Speaks* spoke to them and these conditions directly. What was the *Defender*'s discursive bifurcation of the country into a manly North and unmanly South would be erased by *Muhammad Speaks*. Under Muhammad, the paper argued that the entire country was an indivisible, monolithic landmass of white supremacy and black subservience, a vast wasteland stripping the race of its full potential, and black men of proper manhood.[12] If there was to be any division that established real lines of demarcation, it should be in black people's complete separation from the "wilderness," "Hell," "Lion's Den," and "modern Babylonian Captivity" that was America, terms that reflected Muhammad's eschatological religious beliefs.[13] That black people were languishing in these conditions was part of what convinced Muhammad that the separation of black people from America was necessary for true racial advancement.[14] The *Defender* had applied the racial and gender identity of the Race Man to black men living in the urban of the Great Migration era. Muhammad applied the "Original Man" for black men, who decided to reject the trappings of the urban and to embrace his plans for racial progress.

The NOI advocated complete separation and an independent black state in tones reminiscent of Marcus Garvey, but until it materialized, the Nation argued what it could do for the race through *Muhammad Speaks* and its men. Scholars have succeeded in examining the polarizing political, economic, cultural, and theological dimensions of the NOI. The group's paper remains underanalyzed, however. Even less considered has been the critical role it played in helping the Nation signal to the public its goals of redeeming black men.[15] As much as the conditions of the urban North of the early twentieth century helped produce the modern black press, the conditions of the urban North in the 1960s helped give rise to the radical black press. Many mainstream black papers continued providing positive coverage of the civil rights movement. But in the face of intransigent racism and a growing segment of black people, who were becoming more frustrated with the pace of the black freedom struggle and its tactics of resistance, some activists began to shift to a new black militancy.[16] And much of the black reading public shifted too. Upward of 217 radical black publications emerged throughout the decade, including *Freedomways*, *Black America*, and *Liberator Magazine*.[17] Despite the proliferation of radical black papers at this time and the large readerships they acquired, black press scholarship has rarely considered them, though scholars of Black Power have tended to recognize their importance.[18] If black press scholarship defines the black press as black-owned media that largely served black markets, addressed black people's issues, promoted activism on those issues, and represented a "fighting press," then radical black newspapers must be seen as a vital part of black press history.[19] In fact, *Muhammad Speaks* quickly led in circulation among its radical contemporaries, in addition to eclipsing the lead of many longtime major black publications, showing that the most popular black newspapers among black readers were not always liberal and integrationist.[20] While reflecting growing black discontent over the failures of urban life, Muhammad, the paper, and NOI men showed the black public how the Nation could still make the urban a productive space. One way the NOI did this was through its robust media campaign, which went far beyond the typical editorial campaign the mainstream black press had long used to appeal to the black public. The NOI's campaign transformed decaying inner-city streets into a vibrant public stage that displayed what the NOI model of black manhood had already done for its male members, and could therefore do for other black men.

Yet inner-city streets were but one of several public stages that Nation men seized on to display the NOI's brand of black manhood, as Malcolm helped show, but perhaps to a fault. Malcolm argued for a time that Muhammad's agenda for racial advancement provided the only real means for black people to become truly free, and many NOI men shared stories in the paper about Muhammad's power to free them. Malcolm, on the other hand, came to use other media platforms, particularly television, to tell his story. Muhammad "rescued me when I was a convict," joining, as Malcolm put it, Muhammad's legion of "convict-converts," or products of the Nation's successful prison ministry.[21] That many of the NOI's male members were ex-prisoners made their appeals to a real freedom for black men even more striking. Many of them were determined to signal to other black men the imperative of being free, or spiritually, mentally, physically, and culturally liberated, they thought.[22] Malcolm was especially determined to do this. Though his story is well known to scholars, the broader and critical role media played in shaping his rise and end remains submerged in most analyses.[23] Further, many scholars and admirers tend to cast Malcolm as a teacher-like figure, a prophetic evangelist or consciousness-raising public intellectual.[24] But it must be acknowledged that Malcolm was also a publisher. Moreover, the teacher-like Malcolm was also a student, an autodidact, to be sure, as scholar Jed B. Tucker has pointed out. Efforts Malcolm took to teach himself vocabulary and debate skills in prison dovetailed with mentoring he received from Muhammad.[25] But Malcolm also worked to teach himself how to promote Muhammad amid rapid changes in the black freedom struggle and media landscape of the 1960s. Television would become especially useful to Malcolm in elevating Muhammad and displaying the NOI's brand of black manhood through one of the most visible platforms of his day, which was granting more access to black commentators on racial issues than it ever had. But Malcolm's effort in this regard presented an inherent conflict in the context of the long-standing relationship between black newspapers and black men's leadership, and the place of that relationship now during these dramatic changes in media. Indeed, Malcolm founded *Muhammad Speaks* to help Muhammad assert a "voice" that would enable him to speak for the race against competing voices from other black leaders. But Muhammad's and Malcolm's grappling with this conflict exposed both the mainstay and the limits of black newspapers as the voice of the race. Within the history of the modern black press, this conflict was unprecedented, marking the one time in which a black newspaper completely turned against its own founder. Eventually, the conflict helped launch Malcolm on a personal odyssey to a new model of black manhood and manly vision for racial advancement as the NOI's media campaign became a very serious business that could emphasize renewing life to black men or taking it away.

In the late 1950s, Malcolm was the NOI's national representative and its burgeoning publisher, who helped the NOI establish a bold media presence. In addition to organizing mosques for the Nation across the country, Malcolm worked to improve the NOI's public image and reach. Indeed, in the

1940s and early 1950s, the NOI appeared from time to time in white and black newspapers for being a strange cult of men often convicted of draft-dodging during World War II and the Korean War.[26] Working to combat this negative public perception, Malcolm first looked to mainstream black papers for a forum. After trying to "woo" black publishers, as one black journalist stated, Malcolm succeeded in helping the Nation land some space in three popular black publications.[27] In 1956, "Mr. Muhammad Speaks," a column by Muhammad, appeared in the *Pittsburgh Courier*. Malcolm's column "God's Angry Men" appeared in 1957 in the *Los Angeles Herald Dispatch* and the *Amsterdam News*.[28] And with "Messenger Muhammad writing in the Courier, his followers began circulating the paper in every village, town, and city where the so-called Negro lived," NOI leaders stated. Mobilizing its men to sell papers, they "would sell 10,000 New York Amsterdam News newspapers after they got off work in an hour," NOI leaders claimed; "Mr. Muhammad's followers sold many Ebony subscriptions for Johnson publications."[29]

Muhammad's *Courier* column likely represented to Muhammad his return to a career in journalism dashed initially in the 1930s. He was born Elijah Poole in 1897 in Sandersville, Georgia, the seventh son of a Baptist preacher. By the 1920s, Poole had joined thousands of black southern migrants heading to Detroit during the Great Migration in search of better opportunities, as well as a chance at real manhood and womanhood. His quest for these things stretched into the Depression era, however, as steady, well-paying work continued to be a challenge for him in taking care of himself, his wife, and then four children. But in 1931, Poole encountered the teachings of W. D. Fard, a charismatic itinerant preacher. Fard mixed variants of Christianity and Islam, Marcus Garvey's Black Nationalism, racial uplift ideology, and black mysticism articulated by the likes of Noble Drew Ali, another preacher.[30] Fard promoted this confederation of ideas to economically depressed black people in Detroit under what he called the Nation of Islam. Poole became one of his most devout followers. Fard eventually handpicked him to be his chief minister, changing Poole's surname to "Karriem" and finally to "Muhammad." But internal divisions disrupted the group, and, after seeing Fard one last time in mid-1934, Muhammad relocated to Chicago in September 1934 and moved the group's headquarters there. An organizational paper, the *Final Call to Islam*, soon followed. A newcomer to Chicago, seeking to build his influence and the Nation, Muhammad joined many black men before him, who used black newspapers to spread their message. And Muhammad attempted this in the same city that had witnessed the unprecedented rise of Robert S. Abbott's *Defender* and Claude Barnett's Associated Negro Press, as well as John H. Johnson's publications by the 1940s. And, like Abbott, his initial journalistic venture was short-lived, a casualty of the Depression and readers unable to pay subscriptions. Other NOI publications that followed also failed.[31]

For Malcolm, his and Muhammad's columns represented only the embryonic stages of a more mature, influential media presence the burgeoning newspaperman hoped to build for the then "relatively small Nation." In prison Malcolm had cultivated an affinity for the printed and spoken word.[32] He read the dictionary and the likes of Socrates, Schopenhauer, Kant, and Nietzsche, as well as W. E. B. DuBois and J. A. Rogers, both black intellectuals and influential black journalists.[33] Malcolm also enrolled in debate classes offered to inmates. His "word-base broadened," he remembered, and later he marshaled it on behalf of Muhammad for a time.[34] Some black newspapers' coverage of the NOI somewhat improved as Muhammad's and Malcolm's columns circulated. For example, in February 1958, the *Defender* carried a three-part series on the group. Muhammad's "persuasive oratory and patient teaching" had led to twenty-five temples nationwide, an organization of "well-dressed" members, working toward "a future of a black man supreme after the battle of Armageddon."[35] However, Malcolm felt his and Muhammad's columns were still "very limited efforts to employ the power of print." His father used to sell Garvey's *Negro World*, which helped Garvey build the largest mass black movement in America.[36] Malcolm "kept wanting to start, somehow, our own newspaper, that would be filled with Nation of Islam news." While visiting Los Angeles to organize a temple in 1957, he made a stop by the offices of the *Herald Dispatch* and was able to "observe how a newspaper was put together." He prided himself on being a fast learner. "Quick 'picking up'" was a survival tactic he once honed during his days as a criminal.[37]

His chance to publish came not too long after the airing of the "Hate That Hate Produced." In spring 1959, Louis Lomax, a black journalist, contacted Malcolm to ask if the Nation would be interested in being the feature for a television documentary. Lomax was collaborating with Mike Wallace, a white journalist, to put the feature together. Lomax began his career with the *Afro-American*, but his inroads into the white press signified the transition some black journalists were beginning to make from black newspapers to the white press at this time. Wallace signified the new interest that some members of the white press were beginning to take in covering racial issues. Together, Lomax and Wallace's documentary represented the rise of news documentaries and coverage from certain television networks on social issues, an interest that would explode in the 1960s as the civil rights movement progressed.[38] Many black male leaders had historically relied on black print media to raise public consciousness to their goals. The Nation was becoming known to some readers of the black press, even the FBI, but the opportunity to take advantage of television through Lomax's offer seemed ideal.[39] Television emerged in the 1930s but became a cultural force in American life by the 1950s. Ninety-two percent of American households would own at least one television set by the early 1960s.[40] The chance for access to a broader public through television could help expand Muhammad's reach. "Every Muslim happily anticipated," Malcolm recalled, "that now through the white man's powerful communications media, our brainwashed black brothers and sisters across the United States, and devils, too, were going to see, hear, and read Mr. Muhammad's teachings."[41] Malcolm was wrong.

Aired on New York's WNTA-TV, the series presented a "kaleidoscope of 'shocker' images," Malcolm chagrined. "Instead of a one-shot, single-night broadcast, the customary fate of most documentaries, we cut the report into five separate pieces and featured it . . . every night for a week," Wallace beamed, speaking to the novelty of the new documentary format. "Then, at the end of the week we patched the pieces together" into a one-hour documentary. He considered it one of his "most explosive pieces": "The title sounds like tabloid hype, but the story more than lived up to its billing." "It was pure hatred." For Malcolm, "the newspapers' ink wasn't dry before the big national weekly news magazines started: 'Hate-teachers' . . . 'violence-seekers.'"[42] What was beginning to be some positive news coverage for the group quickly eroded as the documentary touched off an avalanche of negative publicity from such major publications as *Time* magazine, *U.S. News and World Report*, and the *New York Times*. Malcolm tried to respond in press interviews, but struggled to prevail against the one-sided coverage. "I don't care what points I made. . . . It practically never got printed the way I said it," he recalled bitterly. "I was learning under fire how the press, when it wants to, can twist, and slant." Malcolm was beginning to add the changing media landscape to his studies. Still, "my bitterness was less against the white press than it was against those Negro 'leaders' who kept attacking us."[43] Negative reactions also came from the mainstream black press.[44] Just months after black newspapers debated the tactics of Robert F. Williams, Muhammad was cast as the "Shrewd Cult Leader" of "a 'grass roots'-style cult with a 'black supremacy' and 'hate the white man' philosophy," the *Defender* reported, for example. Muhammad's NOI offered "followers a line of fiery 'black manhood'" and was "belatedly under scrutiny by the FBI and police authorities." The *Courier* reacted more sharply, however. The paper terminated Muhammad's column just weeks after the documentary aired, despite the column's apparent popularity.[45]

Criticism only mounted, though Muhammad initially cautioned Malcolm and other ministers against counterattacking black critics, lest they fall for the "white man's tricks" of dividing the race. But as the attacks went unabated, he gave Malcolm permission to begin "returning fire with fire," which included founding a paper. *Messenger Magazine* was one of Malcolm's first tries in the spring of 1959. It failed, but was followed by *Muhammad Speaks*.[46] "The white man's press, radio, television, and other media," Malcolm reflected, "thrust the Muslims into international prominence," inadvertently accelerating the NOI's media presence into a robust media campaign by the early 1960s.[47] Initially published as a monthly, the paper also brought to fruition Malcolm's dream of publishing a paper for the NOI. In the beginning, he edited the paper, served as one of its main writers, and published it out of his basement.[48] Writers for *Muhammad Speaks* capitalized on this attention and marketed the organ as a dramatically new kind of black newspaper.

It partly explained its break with the mainstream black press by taking jabs at the *Courier*. "The weekly newspaper would be out of business today had not Mr. Muhammad and his many followers across the nation come to its rescue," NOI leaders claimed, pointing to drops in circulation that many mainstream black papers were experiencing by this time as they retreated from protest journalism.[49] That the NOI's men had helped sell some of these publications was part of what shocked Nation leaders about their rejection by the black press. But "now comes the time to put forth the effort we have given others to our own!"[50] An even greater jab included the name Malcolm gave the new paper. *Muhammad Speaks* curiously resembled the name of Muhammad's *Courier* column. Malcolm likely used the paper's name to try to lure loyal readers of the *Courier* column to the new publication.[51] But the name also reflected Malcolm's intent to promote the voice of his leader against the voices of other black leaders offering solutions to racial oppression. As Mike Wallace remembered, "there were so many leaders, there were so many black voices" at the time, "one vying with the other for attention."[52] Interestingly, Muhammad was not "eloquent," having a "sluggish tongue," according to Malcolm. But Muhammad was the "Messenger," as NOI members called him, emphasizing what they saw as the prophetic role of his voice. And "whatever he uttered had an impact on me that trained orators did not begin to have," Malcolm affirmed. The paper's name thus foregrounded the powerful potential of that voice. The name also invoked the "voice," or influence, that many black male leaders had long asserted in speaking for the race. It was the "paper that speaks out for you. . . . Muhammad Speaks!"[53]

Focused on spreading Muhammad's message, meeting the tastes of a changing black reading public, and influencing the course of the black freedom struggle, the Nation mobilized the Fruit of Islam (FOI) to sell the paper. The FOI was a cadre of elite, disciplined male members trained in martial arts and responsible for protecting the Nation and individual members from attack. They also modeled the NOI's austere lifestyle and brand of manhood before members and the public.[54] "A man reaches real stature in the movement when he becomes a member of The Fruit of Islam," Louis E. Lomax found in his 1963 study on the Nation. Among their regiment of duties, selling the paper on "ghetto sidewalks," as Malcolm put it, became a top priority. Lomax observed that members "lead an exacting, regimented life. . . . Brothers can be seen on the streets every day selling Muslim newspapers."[55] Whereas Robert S. Abbott had black railroad porters at one point and Marcus Garvey had black seamen to help distribute their papers, Muhammad had the FOI, "The Greatest Brotherhood in the World," as *Muhammad Speaks* announced.[56] They served this crucial role in the NOI's media campaign, making them virtually synonymous with the paper before the public.

Subscription campaigns solidified this relationship. "The building of a mass subscription base," launched as early as July 1962 by Herbert Muhammad, one of Elijah Muhammad's sons and director of the subscription department, was "necessary to guarantee that the teachings and messages of the Honorable Elijah Muhammad go uninterrupted into the thousands of houses which otherwise could not be reached on a regular basis," Herbert said.[57] Operating "mainly on person to person sales," salesmen became some of the most conspicuous extensions of the Nation and usually among the first to acquaint the public with the NOI and its program by making "new inroads into areas which never before had Muhammad Speaks subscriptions."[58] In 1962, a reader could purchase twelve issues for $1.80 or twenty-four issues for $3.60. "Blizzard, nor flooding rain, nor blazing 100 degree heat nor 20 below icy cold" could stop the NOI's disciplined salesmen, *Muhammad Speaks* argued.[59] The paper sometimes recognized "outstanding" salesmen, who sold impressive numbers of copies. Some of them received trophies and awards, including a "Japanese-made camera," and were later offered all-expense-paid vacations, or the choice between a "Chevrolet or a Ford automobile." Eventually, one representative for the paper received an award from the Negro Newspaper Publishers Association "in recognition of the journalistic contributions MUHAMMAD SPEAKS is making in the cause of freedom."[60] But these prizes paled in comparison to the greatest reward: "the knowledge that they are agents for a top-flight newspaper," which, through the "voice" of Muhammad, was "shaking oppressed people out of their slumber of complacency" into "the Honorable Elijah Muhammad's bold program for true emancipation."[61]

Dispatching the FOI to the streets of urban centers to sell *Muhammad Speaks* helped its writers make the point that it represented a drastic break with mainstream black newspapers. This break clearly signified the rise of the radical black press. Abbott used to hire young boys to sell his paper in Chicago. The NOI mostly deployed adult men, reflecting the paper's promise to be "Dedicated to Freedom, Justice and Equality for the Black Man." Readers were going to get "ACCURATE REPORTS OF CONDITION OF SO-CALLE[D] NEGRO," as well as "THE TRUTH ABOUT THE ORIGINAL MAN. You will be given knowledge of just 'who' is the original man! You will be given the true identity of the 'colored man.'"[62] One writer later identified other major differences between *Muhammad Speaks* and mainstream black papers, denouncing certain sides of their sensationalism:

> The paper is put together and produced primarily for the enlightenment and benefit of our own Asiatic people. . . . It is by no means a Negro publication; its material content (inclusive of advertising) sharply differs from that of all publications owned or nominally controlled by Afro-Americans. As a matter of policy, MUHAMMAD SPEAKS does not print gory stories of carnage and sex orgies. It carries no announcements of so-called "beauty" contests and dances. Nor does it print pictures of nude or semi-nude women or promise vulgar immodest fashions . . . and will never accept ads featuring [cigarettes] and intoxicating beverages as well as pork and pork products.[63]

Initially, the paper sold for ten cents, though it was "Worth More!"[64] Further distinguishing the paper, readers' purchase of *Muhammad Speaks* was a real financial investment in the race, writers argued, which would fund the eventual building of Nation-owned structures, such as a "hospital. . . . It is building a library . . . a school."[65] These institutions would help renew the landscape and opportunities of the urban. Soon writers claimed that "this paper is in such great demand that each issue is practically sold out before it goes to press."[66] Though clearly an exaggeration, the paper may have had a point. By June 1962, NOI leaders claimed 310,000 in circulation and upward of 1.25 million readers collectively, supplanting the *Courier*'s circulation of 300,000. *Muhammad Speaks*' numbers only continued to climb throughout the decade, eventually reaching as much as 500,000 copies a week. Ultimately, the publication became the NOI's most lucrative business enterprise.[67]

Part of the paper's rapid rise in popularity was due to its explicit, racially militant appeals to the race, especially to black men, precisely at a time when many mainstream black papers were struggling to hold on to readers who wanted coverage framed in these terms. Intended for a mass audience, but particularly for an increasingly militant black public, the paper's rhetoric, images, and news coverage showed readers that the paper did in fact herald a new kind of black newspaper. In addition to international news on liberation struggles in Africa and Asia, pieces by adroit black writers like Richard Durham, and even some coverage of Robert F. Williams's activism abroad, much of the paper's content revolved around Muhammad's teachings.[68] Writers often drew this content from the speeches he gave at public rallies.[69] The rallies became the second leg of the Nation's media campaign. Here, the public could hear Muhammad actually speak. NOI leaders admitted members of the black press, and later the white press, to the rallies so that they could provide coverage of Muhammad and the Nation.[70] The rallies reportedly attracted thousands. The speeches were highly publicized in the paper, and though Muhammad had given public speeches in the late 1950s, the paper was critical in publishing the speeches verbatim in whole or as excerpts.[71] Like Garvey's *Negro World*, the paper reached readers who could not attend Muhammad's public speeches in different cities across the country, providing coverage of virtually every word. "Twenty million so-called Negroes should not be begging the white man to do for them what they can and must do for themselves," Muhammad charged before a crowd of 16,000 in Washington, D.C. "The white race have never believed in God—not the God of freedom, justice and equality."[72] The reported number of attendees testified to the interest of a black public that was becoming more militant, and Muhammad couched his words in caustic racial appeals intended to strike at the heart of their changing sensibilities. Indeed, *Muhammad Speaks* and the NOI benefited from these shifts, while at the same time influencing them.[73]

Despite attracting such large crowds, Muhammad seemed to find some aspects of his public role uncomfortable. Through a private letter, Malcolm learned that he was "not a man who loves to pose for pictures," nor was he "craving for publicity," believing "the message he is delivering from God is sufficient for publicity." Instead, Muhammad's letter emphasized the importance of his printed words in *Muhammad Speaks* and other papers. Indeed, as he stated in a memorandum to NOI leaders, Muhammad regarded the paper to be more important than any public speech the organization made, for the paper "will do more to convert behind the door a hundred of our people to our one from the Speaker's Stand!" He prioritized the publication, telling NOI men, "The papers are little ministers rolled up in your hands."[74]

Muhammad's caustic language reflected his Black Nationalist and religious beliefs, though the language also reflected black journalists' longstanding efforts to use sensationalized rhetoric and imagery to attract public attention to crucial racial issues.[75] Black civil rights leaders critical of the NOI recognized the appeal they were having before an increasingly militant black public, even as the Nation mobilized rhetoric that repudiated and emasculated many of the leaders of the civil rights movement.[76] "If the Negro does not receive freedom within a certain period of time, will he turn to Communism or some other movement similar to the Muslim movement," *Muhammad Speaks* reported Martin Luther King Jr. saying, following a report by the *Amsterdam News*.[77] Daisy Bates warned that "a large portion of the Negro masses is losing faith in American democracy. . . . This is demonstrated by the growing influence on the American Negro of the Nationalist organizations that have sprung up during recent years," pointing to the "Black Muslims" specifically. Roy Wilkins affirmed that black people opposed "any group, white or black, political or religious, that preaches hatred among men." Still, he said that the NOI "have gained a following only because America has been so slow in granting equal opportunities and has permitted the abuse and persecution of Negro citizens." By July 1961, the cover of *Jet* featured Muhammad's name and visage along with that of Wilkins, King, and James Farmer as the magazine queried, "WHO SPEAKS FOR THE NEGRO?"[78]

Muhammad Speaks insisted that "Mr. Elijah Muhammad is not [a] man who teaches hate," posturing to downplay its sensationalism. "Sometimes his frank and unrestrained revelations of conditions under which his people suffer in America, may give the impression of a hate campaign," but "he only admits to telling the truth. The truth is sometimes stranger than fiction and often shocks the sensibilities of those who are guilty of wrong doing," the paper argued.[79] Muhammad's bombastic rhetoric helped distinguish his voice from other black leaders. "The voice of Mr. Muhammad is being heard by progressive thinking young men and women of his race and they are rallying to his call."[80] As historian Michael A. Gomez has noted, estimates of NOI membership in the early 1960s ranged from as low as 20,000 to as high as 250,000, while the number of sympathizers influenced by their robust media campaign was even harder to count.[81] *Muhammad Speaks* and NOI leaders portrayed Muhammad as the "boldest" and "most powerful" black man in America, though the paper's photographs of him showed that he was not a man of imposing physical stature.[82] Malcolm called Muhammad, who was five and a half feet tall and less than 150 pounds, a "little, gentle, sweet man!"[83] Still, as religious scholar C. Eric Lincoln wrote in one of the seminal studies on the Nation, *The Black Muslims in America* (1961), Muhammad's incendiary rhetoric made the "little" man appear to be "the most fearless Black man in America."[84]

And many readers enjoyed Muhammad's "fearless" talk in the paper. "It is without a doubt that this great newspaper . . . is an outstanding achievement in the field of black journalism. It is what the black public needs. It is a moral upliftment in black pride. It is a forthright edition of Basic Truth," said one reader. "My husband and I were greatly influenced by your talks to the so-called Negroes," one admirer wrote after reading only one edition. "We were so inspired by reading the many truths . . . [that] . . . my entire family went to the Muhammad mosque. . . . You speak the Truth, hiding nothing from the white man either and we believe that your teachings are the only teachings that will help us to help ourselves." She wanted to "receive everyone [*sic*] of 'Muhammad Speaks' newspapers as I do not want to miss any of them since reading just the one paper has started me thinking differently for my family and myself."[85] The paper's charged language in part demonstrated the racial and economic independence that the NOI argued black people should have, a point about funding that Marcus Garvey had also raised. Because the NOI produced the paper through NOI-owned facilities and mostly relied on member-owned businesses for advertising, unlike some mainstream black papers that relied on white advertisers, the organization had the autonomy to print what it wanted.[86]

Muhammad's fearlessness suggested to many sympathizers just how free a black man he was, and therefore how free he and the Nation could make other black men by redeeming them through his concept of the Original Man. Muhammad publically articulated this concept as early as in his 1957 publication *The Supreme Wisdom*, but it was also publicized in the paper to inform the black masses that they were the authentic man from whom all other men derived.[87] Accordingly, God created black people. They were the origin of humankind, the first man and only authentically real man on earth, who had erected the first great civilizations. All other men were grafted versions of black men, though white men in particular came from a botched experiment in the manipulation of black men's genes by an evil scientist named Yacub. As a result, white men were a lesser, defective, and evil form of the Original Man. Here, white men, who had long represented in the popular imagination and popular discourse the standard of manhood, were not men at all.[88] As the paper put it, black people were "the first inhabitants of the earth as we know it today," and white people were "only cave dwellers," living in "bestial savagery." "The white race represents the children of the devil and the black race represents the children of God," *Muhammad Speaks* writer Tynetta Deanar asserted. "Because the white man is the opposite of the original man, he represents the weaker part of human creation."[89] Muhammad's creation story countered racist pseudoscientific theories against black humanity influential especially in the early twentieth century with some of his own. Muhammad's creation myth was just as patently racist, to be sure, but it should be seen as a mythologized analogue to black men's long-standing efforts to "make men." Muhammad's story about God specially making black men was intended to empower black men with an extraordinary sense of self-value. Because they were this Original Man, NOI leaders and the paper commonly referred to black people as the "so-called Negro," suggesting that this long-standing racial nomenclature was a misnomer.[90] For a brief period, the paper ran a cartoon series titled *Lazz*, their derivative of "Lazarus," the man Jesus resurrected from the dead. The series illustrated the misadventures of a black man living without the knowledge of his original nature and the guidance of Muhammad's teachings.[91]

The Original Man not only formed the central character of Muhammad's creation story; it also formed an imitable figure and identity his men and other black men were supposed to adopt. For Muhammad, this model of black manhood revolved around self-help and black men's entrepreneurship, qualities that he thought would infuse their minds, spirits, and physical bodies with a power capable of building an economically independent black nation, gendered and economic ideas of racial advancement that hearkened to Booker T. Washington and Marcus Garvey. In fact, some members of the Nation felt that Muhammad was whom Garvey predicted when Garvey suggested that "A messenger will follow me!"[92] Deteriorating urban conditions had helped impede black men's ability to embrace their identity as the Original Man and all its advantages, ranging from self-knowledge to self-employment. Whereas the *Defender* published stories of black people who had succeeded in the urban of the early twentieth century, *Muhammad Speaks* shared stories of trenchant black urban struggle. Other contemporary black papers would carry similar reports, but scarcely in the fashion that *Muhammad Speaks* did, as it used sensationalized rhetoric that especially pointed to the plight of black men. Because of "the Shameful Economic condition of the so-called American Negro," the paper stated, "the black man has grown so indolent, lazy and indifferent to his dependence-on-the white man's philosophy for what he eats, for his shelter, for his protection."[93] "You can go into any of the urban areas or industrial cities; and you see thousands of so-called Negroes walking the streets, idle. . . . Our people are filling the employment agencies, compensation lines and relief lines seeking means of support from the white man," the paper railed.[94] For *Muhammad Speaks*, public housing was a "'Prison without Bars,'" "the prison houses of North America," "High Rent Tombs!"[95] "We are trapped in a building, prisoners of the white man," Malcolm said in a public speech, pulling from the Nation's staple of prison metaphors to which he and many male members could relate personally.[96] *Muhammad Speaks* rejected governmental plans for urban renewal, charging, "Urban Renewals Are Tomorrow's Slums" and questioning whether "Slum Removal" was really a guise for "Negro Removal."[97] Muhammad demanded a plan for black urban economic rehabilitation that would make black people owners of businesses and property. To Muhammad, black men once built the first and greatest civilizations on earth. In line with this supposed tradition, he and the NOI hoped to help black men build the next.

Muhammad Speaks published Muhammad's solutions to the failures of the urban, intended to restore black economic opportunities and black men to their rightful place as men before their families, communities, and the public. As early as 1961, the paper argued that in order "to attain economic solvency, Negroes must own factories and plants of their own to make shoes, clothes, farm implements, [and] machinery," goals that were "within reach" if "the black man stops investing his money in expensive cars, high living, whiskey, needless pleasure trips, and various sinful pursuits." The paper urged readers, "Help Us to Buy Farm Land to Raise Food to Feed the Poor of Our People."[98] "We cannot depend on the white man to provide jobs, homes, clothes and food for us forever," the paper maintained, "especially when we are the last hired and the first fired."[99] *Muhammad Speaks* frequently featured vivid illustrations of rehabilitated urban spaces sometimes juxtaposed with pastoral images of industrialized agricultural production, all productive imagined spaces that NOI leaders hoped would eventually actually emerge under Muhammad's plan.[100] But whether or not these building blocks of their nation materialized as an actual geographically defined space, the NOI laid claim to ghettos that were becoming powder kegs of black discontent. "The Honorable Elijah Muhammad is absolutely cleaning up our society and is making it a fit place in which to live," *Muhammad Speaks* added. The Nation demanded a separate black state, but Nation-owned businesses dotted the landscape of many urban centers across the country.[101] In fact, the group's membership was greatest among working-class black people living in inner cities like Harlem, Boston, Newark, Philadelphia, Detroit, Chicago, and Los Angeles.[102] Indeed, *Muhammad Speaks* often asserted, "We Must Have Some Land!" while declaring at the same time, "We Must Control Our Neighborhoods!" Muhammad enumerated a ten-point agenda for racial advancement, "What the Muslims Want, What the Muslims Believe," which emphasized these goals, among others.[103]

Muhammad Speaks salesmen symbolized the black economic independence, self-employment, and renewed black manhood Muhammad and the paper promised black people. Much of his overwhelmingly male membership, mostly between the ages of seventeen and thirty-five, had been recruited from poor, working-class inhabitants of the urban.[104] NOI leaders argued that by selling *Muhammad Speaks* they could make a "comfortable living," supporting themselves and their families. The salesmen also symbolized the ways in which Muhammad's teachings were cleaning up the urban, a "cleanliness both internal and external."[105] Because of salesmen's growing public presence, their having a proper public image was paramount in order to physically show their being redeemed black men, whose conversions emanated from within to radiate outwardly. Because salesmen were usually the public's first point of contact with the Nation, potential customers and recruits could read the paper *and* their bodies.[106] This "body language," so to speak, a "public transcript," required only a "glance" for readers to grasp, Abdul Basit Naeem asserted. Naeem was an author, newspaper publisher, Pakistani Muslim living in New York, and writer for *Muhammad Speaks*. In a "glance," the public could see that Muhammad's members "are no longer what they used to be (deaf, dumb, and blind)," he said.[107] "Look at any follower of the Honorable Elijah Muhammad," Charlene Whitcomb, a woman member, added, "and you'll see a black man in America—a proud, dignified black man who walks erect, looks straight ahead and fears no one."[108]

Therefore, NOI leaders expected salesmen, as well as members of the movement in general, to look "clean," that is, to be presentable in their physical appearance and attire in order to project what the NOI could do in redeeming black men.[109] The paper's advertisements of Nation businesses helped signal the point. "To be successful . . . look successful by keeping your clothes neat," Temple No. 2 Cleaners advised. Temple No. 2 Clothing Store got patrons "Dressed for Leadership." "Meet Success Halfway . . . by Keeping Well Groomed," Temple No. 2 Barber Shop insisted.[110] As early as Muhammad's forays with the *Courier*, salesmen had donned the look, usually a dark suit and neck-tie. A point of pride for the NOI, "it became a common sight to see the young clean-cut Muslim men during the week selling the Negro newspapers," claiming what "clean-cut and courteous familiar figures they became in the community."[111] For Lorenzo X Williams, the look was a measurement of his personal growth. "A young Muslim brother sold me a newspaper," and after "reading the all-enlightening words of the Messenger of Allah . . . I too had become one of Mr. Muhammad's devoted followers." He once "had only one suit," but under Muhammad, "I now own a business and my wife and I both have cars, have a bank account and can change suits at will."[112] Serious-looking men selling a serious paper, they were quite the positive public spectacle. One observer in the 1960s "enjoyed watching these handsome, strong, well-dressed men darting in and out of traffic to sell their materials." This observer, who was then a young boy, recalled, "The image impressed me greatly." He later became a member of the NOI. King and civil rights activists had also used respectable clothing to show the dignity of their cause. The same worked for the NOI. As Gertrude Samuels of the *New York Times* would observe about the Nation in 1963, "their code emphasizing race pride and individual decorum, is helping to shatter the Negro stereotype of shiftlessness and lawlessness and has undeniable appeal."[113]

NOI men mobilized the look in public to great effect, as did Malcolm, who was helping the Nation grow its public presence through other means, namely, television. By the early 1960s, some television networks had extended their news formats from fifteen-minute segments to thirty-minute ones. Internally, some networks were still developing their use of television, working to improve lighting, formatting, sound, content, and presentation styles, for example, even as they started airing programs that featured news and discussions dealing with civil rights activism.[114] Though usually aired in select markets or during less peak viewing hours, the shows were still significant in expanding many stations' content. They provided viewers opportunities to engage real-world issues, especially topics concerning black people against the typical network lineup of western and detective dramas, fantasy shows, and animated series in which black characters were few and far between.[115] As civil rights activism and currents of black radicalism mounted, so did televised coverage of the black freedom struggle, though not without some challenges for both activists and networks.[116] Malcolm was swept up in these developments that offered black leaders, activists, and commentators new and greater points of access to the broader public sphere. Invitations for Malcolm to comment, interview, or speak poured in from newspapers, colleges, radio stations, and discussion-based television shows from around the country, and later from around the world.[117] Given the successful circulation of the paper on inner-city streets, perhaps he could work to circulate the NOI message and image through these other means, especially, television.

As he learned how to navigate these opportunities and media, Malcolm tried to develop a presentation style and mien, an effort in which his look and eloquence were crucial to projecting to broader audiences the NOI's brand of black masculinity. Malcolm had internalized Muhammad's ideas of black manhood that came to emphasize cleanliness and a disciplined black male body. And interviewers read this on Malcolm. For example, in an interview on *The World at Ten*, PBS newsman Joe Durso recalled that Malcolm was dressed in "a pinstripe suit—and he looked for all the world like a businessman or a person who might make news behind the scenes but not like somebody who was out front and visible and fiery."[118] Malcolm had come a long way from wearing zoot suits topped off with a conk, which were popular styles of dress and coiffure among black working-class youth in the 1940s that Malcolm sported when he was engaged in criminal activities.[119] Through suits sewn by Muslim women, bearing the material evidence of Muhammad's influence, "he and his friends were immaculately dressed, with no outward sign of their belonging to either a separate sect or the ministry," black psychologist Kenneth B. Clark remembered after interviewing Malcolm in 1963 for a television show.[120] Malcolm applied the NOI look, as well as what he had learned about mass media since his botched interviews following "The Hate That Hate Produced." His style of speaking and self-presentation had improved. Durso thought Malcolm was "low-key" but "very forthright." "He didn't make fiery speeches; he responded to questions and he made his points compellingly, in a dialogue. . . . He was more cerebral than physical. He reasoned. He was almost like a college professor."[121] For Clark, he was "a tall, handsome man," with "a dominant personality" and "disciplined power," who was "conscious of the impression of power which he seeks to convey," speaking "with the vocabulary and the tone of a college-educated person." Impressed that he "has been interviewed on radio, television, and by newspapermen probably more than any other Negro leader during the past two years," Clark continued, "he shows the effects of these interminable interviews by a professional calm, and what appears to be an ability to turn on the proper amount of emotion, resentment, and indignation, as needed." "One certainly does not get the impression of spontaneity. On the contrary, one has the feeling that Minister Malcolm has anticipated every question and is prepared with the appropriate answer, an answer which is consistent with the general position of the Black Muslim movement, as defined by the Honorable Elijah Muhammad."[122]

As Malcolm gained more and more access to television, he began to turn from black newspapers, the long-standing means through which black men vocalized themselves publicly. He was learning to adapt to rapid changes in mass media, becoming, as biographer Peter Goldman put it, "the first of the media revolutionaries."[123] Malcolm's children and wife, Betty, would watch him on television, though she contended that his public image betrayed who he was in private, someone more "tender."[124] Indeed, like other black male publishers, Malcolm carefully crafted a manly public image, one intended to display NOI manhood. His public image and oratory helped attract members of the press, including Alex Haley, a black reporter. Haley was another example of the talented black journalist who had made inroads into the white press. Haley had previously interviewed Malcolm for *Reader's Digest*, the *Saturday Evening Post*, and *Playboy* magazine.[125] In early 1963, Haley wanted to write a book on the Nation framed around Malcolm's electrifying public persona. With Muhammad's permission, he and Malcolm began work on the book. Malcolm wanted to dedicate it to Muhammad, who "cleaned me up, and stood me on my feet, and made me the man that I am today."[126]

Indeed, Malcolm's clean look spoke to the profound internal cleansing he underwent under Muhammad's guidance. "My own transformation was the best example I knew of Mr. Muhammad's power to reform black men's lives." This was a point he often shared in interviews. Malcolm had emerged from the same streets the NOI sought to save. During his youth, he hustled in Boston and Harlem, trying to survive the "poverty-ridden ghetto" by supporting himself first with sporadic work but ultimately choosing hustling, numbers-running, and selling drugs as his preferred line of employment. Malcolm smoked and drank, living and thinking like an "animal" inside the "ghetto jungle." "I was a true hustler," he claimed.[127] But it was as Malcolm "X," the name that marked his conversion to the NOI and embrace of a new self-consciousness and manhood, that he looked back on his "'before' life" regrettably.[128] He was grateful that Muhammad's program for reforming black men had rescued him and "virtually raised me from the dead." This profound transition convinced him, like other members of the Nation, that Muhammad had the power to provide effective solutions to black people in general and black men in particular. Muhammad mentored him while he was in prison and then directly for many months, training him "in his home, as if I [were] his son." In fact, it was at "Mr. Muhammad's table, I found my tongue," he said. "I could *feel* Mr. Muhammad's *power*" (Malcolm's emphasis), Malcolm said glowingly, a power that enabled Muhammad to erase people's past failures, renew them, and "resurrect the black man." Muhammad "made me," Malcolm affirmed simply.[129] And, as Betty recounted, Muhammad provided a "father image" for Malcolm, who lost his own father at six years old. Both men were the seventh child born to their families and the sons of Baptist preachers.[130] As Robert S. Abbott and John Sengstacke showed, elder black men's teaching of masculine models to young black men was thought to be crucial to their proper development as men. For Malcolm and many NOI members, Muhammad embodied the Original Man, and they based their ideas and performances of proper black manhood on him and what he dictated. Muhammad was increasingly ill, which compromised his speaking schedule, and this probably motivated him even more to elevate his spellbinding national spokesman to represent him in his stead.[131]

Malcolm was quick to testify to Muhammad's powerful influence before audiences across multiple mass media. And Muhammad generally approved of this, even advising Malcolm on how to present, stressing that he not "go too much into details on the political side," and later, that he pace himself. "It is not nice of you to not to give way or refrain from talking when [other panelists] put forth their talk."[132] With Muhammad's encouragement, Malcolm worked mass media, insisting, "As long as the little red light glowed 'on the air,' I tried to represent Elijah Muhammad and the Nation of Islam to the utmost." Indeed, he routinely prefaced his statements with "The Honorable Elijah Muhammad teaches us" and would then launch into a "beguiling," "all but hypnotic" authoritative discourse, as Louis E. Lomax described it. "Anyone who has ever heard me on radio or television programs knows that my technique is non-stop," Malcolm remarked, "until what I want to get said is said. I was developing the technique then." His confidence was growing as he learned to work mass media.[133]

Muhammad confirmed Malcolm's success in this regard through private letters to Malcolm and in public through *Muhammad Speaks*. Muhammad offered his "sincere thanks for all your striving and for all you have done in the cause of Islam for our Nation, my family and myself. . . . I am truly thankful to Allah for you," he wrote to Malcolm. "No one could have better followers than you."[134] In the paper, Malcolm was Muhammad's "brilliant orator" and "fiery leader," whose "eloquence as a speaker surpasses, say many critics." Malcolm "tied" one television host up in "knots" in "the Triumph of Elijah Muhammad's Teachings Presented by Malcolm X," the paper gloated. Malcolm "has that 'extra' ammunition found in the Truth as taught by Messenger Muhammad."[135] "I thank him for all the good he was saying of me," the paper reported Muhammad stating.[136] Malcolm claimed that Muhammad once told him, "I want you to become well known." "If you are well known, it will make *me* better known" (Malcolm's emphasis). According to Lomax, Malcolm said that "it is my mouth working, but the voice is his."[137]

But sometimes there was still much for Malcolm to learn in handling media, some of which he learned the hard way. For instance, he learned that his invitations to speak always had to be cleared first with Muhammad. This move was among the first of Muhammad's many attempts to control Malcolm's media presence, even as Muhammad encouraged that presence. After failing to clear a scheduled televised appearance in Canada in September 1962, the Nation leader scolded him. "Be careful of making yourself available to radio, T. V., or newspaper conferences, colleges, and universities without first consulting me." "To keep you and me not in conflict with each other on what we say to the public . . . give your leader just what you have in mind to say." On another occasion, Malcolm failed to get Muhammad's approval for his talking points before an interview. But he assured Muhammad that though the show had already been taped, "I hope when you hear it, it wont be too displeasing to you," especially since his performance had "caused the dead to show greater interest."[138] Confident, Malcolm believed that he was helping the NOI reach a wider audience.

Through the paper, other NOI men joined Malcolm in testifying to undergoing a powerful internal cleansing under Muhammad. In "What Islam Has Done for Me," a section added to the paper in August 1963, *Muhammad Speaks* brought in the voices of many NOI men from across the country to explain their conversion experiences. Many of them, including ministers and rank-and-file members, couched their stories in religious terms of being "resurrected" and "free," which they also linked to gendered terms of a redeemed manhood.[139] Edward 4X reported, "I'm a Better Man Because of Islam," testifying to the "Messenger's program . . . that regardless of what you did yesterday, if you come in here and act like a man today, all of that is forgotten." "Islam made a civilized man of me," another man said. "Lying, stealing, smoking reefers, drinking large quantities of alcohol and occasionally shooting dope, were mere sport to me. . . . I was thoroughly corrupt in my mind and body." But "the Messenger's teachings have made me a dedicated Muslim man" and "will uplift the downtrodden black man here in this man-made hell called America." "He has taught us how to be clean within and without; the importance of doing for self," another member added; "he is raising the dead to life."[140] Reminiscent of underutilized black men of the Depression era, these men's past failures exemplified the failures of the urban but now represented the success of Muhammad's plans for urban renewal in their own lives. The paper showed that his teachings could erase black men's checkered pasts, clean the men up, redeem them where they had fallen short, and guide them to a new life of meaning and manhood. "Mr. Muhammad's formula" for redeeming black men, the paper explained, centered on "giving the black man a belief in himself, by creating pride and dignity within him, by giving him a knowledge of his past and future potentials and by giving him meaningful activity."[141]

Other black leaders voiced plans for racial advancement, to be sure. In fact, later in the same month that "What Islam Has Done for Me" appeared, civil rights leaders mobilized tens of thousands of people to demonstrate in the nation's capital for the March on Washington for Jobs and Freedom. Organizers and speakers made an economic appeal arguably more influential than that of Muhammad and the NOI, one that differed from the Nation by linking economic rights to civil rights and seeking governmental support over self-help. Days before the march, Roy Wilkins and Martin Luther King Jr. went on *Meet the Press*, a discussion-based television show about politics, to promote the demonstration. And it was at the march that King's voice reverberated powerfully as he delivered his most resounding oration, what came to be known as the "I Have a Dream" speech.[142] But "What Islam Has Done for Me" helped the NOI argue that despite other leaders' voices and plans, only Muhammad could do what black men really needed. Indeed, *Muhammad Speaks* constructed ideas and ideals of a proper black manhood through the stories of the men it featured. Unlike black newspapers in the past, which had also constructed ideas and ideals of black manhood in part by citing exceptional cases of black men as exemplars of proper Race Men, Muhammad did it on paper *and* in real life through the men his teachings had redeemed. Translating this long, print-based discourse on redeeming black manhood into a demonstrably live one, the public could read messages that testified to Muhammad's power on two different but interrelated texts. Muhammad had produced legions of living embodiments of his teachings, the evidence of which required only a glance to see how renewed they had become.

And Muhammad's program "makes men out of boys," as well as "women out of girls." In the paper, women members attested to being radically transformed just as much as their male counterparts. *Muhammad Speaks* insisted that the "so-called Negro woman must return to femininity," and indeed, many women members felt they had.[143] "Before I became a follower of the Honorable Elijah Muhammad," Sister Marilyn A. X remembered, "my life was nothing. All the vices the white man had, I had. I would swear, smoke, drink, fornicate and do everything that was unclean and indecent." But "Allah has blessed me and I have become a clean, respectable, decent, upright woman."[144] For Sister Jean X. Reynolds, "[Islam] taught me I am an Original Blackwoman, Queen of the Universe and Mother of civilization. . . . Allah has given me a clean slate to begin life anew."[145] Sister Gertrude Bogans's confidence and renewal came in a different way. She was most impressed by what a minister "said about how the Muslim men were taught to respect the women; that Muslim men did not stay out all times of night or drink or commit acts of adultery or fornication, but were taught how to put their money to good use." She deeply appreciated the difference Muhammad was making for many women members' romantic lives in "teaching our men how to treat them." "We know that we were not used to this kind of treatment before. The Messenger is teaching our men how to act and think. What other leader is teaching this? None!"[146] One woman put it simply: Islam "gives [women] pride in womanhood."[147] And women members had an important look too, intending to be public examples of NOI womanhood in the same ways that male members modeled NOI manhood.[148] The *Los Angeles Times* once reported that women donned "ankle-length, flowing dresses and white or pastel-colored scarves." According to *Muhammad Speaks*, the Nation's women would "dress modestly" in a "silk head covering" with "simple accessories" and not much makeup. As the internationally known black writer James Baldwin put it, Muhammad had succeeded in investing "both the male and female with a pride and a serenity that hang about them like an unfailing light."[149]

However, it was NOI men, from salesmen to Malcolm, that the NOI ritually put on display before the public, prioritizing their redemption among the first steps in racial advancement, points that the paper reflected. To be sure, the rigid notions of gender and gender roles that Muhammad and

Nation leaders prescribed to women within the movement precluded most women's activity in public space, let alone the streets where the papers were sold. Many scholars have illuminated the Nation's "hypermasculine" ideas of black manhood that emphasized patriarchal authority, male leadership, the redemption of black manhood, and women's coerced and voluntary submission to male control. And Malcolm promoted many of these ideas in public statements about black women, praising them as beautiful and worthy of black men's protection, on one hand, while using some of his biting rhetoric to cast them as naturally weak and manipulative, on the other. As literary scholar Farah Jasmine Griffin has argued, Malcolm embraced these beliefs, gender ideologies that tended to undercut black women's agency, before, during, and after his membership in the NOI.[150] Though *Muhammad Speaks* occasionally recognized "salesladies," or women who sold papers, Muhammad's delineation of men's and women's different natures, leadership roles, and separate spheres of work clearly made men his preferred sales force.[151] Women, on the other hand, were "man's field to produce his nation," gendered language that spoke to Muhammad's plans of nation-building in part by developing Nation-owned farm lands.[152] "Women's Features," or sections of the paper dedicated to women readers, helped advise them on matters thought to pertain to their specifically gendered concerns, issues regarding the home, children, and cooking. Here, women were crucial to helping their families maintain the "clean" lifestyle that Muhammad dictated, which included members' eating habits, clothing, and physical appearance, among other things.[153]

For Muhammad, the practice of nation-building was primarily a manly exercise in which men were supposed to exert leadership and control. Muhammad wanted to build a "United Front of Black Men," a goal he had promoted publicly since the late 1950s. That his membership was predominantly male spoke to this. Asserting that "we need leaders at every level to challenge the lies of the white man," Muhammad intended this united front to "take the offensive and carry the fight for justice and freedom to the enemy." "Every level" included inner-city streets and, at least for Malcolm, television screens. The world in general but America in particular was spinning out of control, teetering at the precipice of cataclysm because of unprecedented changes, according to Muhammad and the paper. The NOI leader and *Muhammad Speaks* constantly cited certain "signs" of America's instability and impending collapse, including what they identified as white men's manipulation of atomic energy, severe weather conditions, the space race, automation, moral depravity, birth control, excessive makeup on women, and popular dances like the twist.[154] NOI men exemplified the discipline and order that Muhammad thought needed to be imposed on the world at this time. Muhammad hoped that the Nation's real efforts to build a united front of black men, in part by mobilizing and publicly displaying the men it reformed, would ultimately create the means by which "every Black man in America [will] be reunited with his own."[155] As for women, Muhammad reasoned that if he succeeded in building this front, then black women's particular redemption would naturally result, benefiting by default from black men's restoration to what was thought to be their proper social and economic positions as men.[156]

Salesmen appreciated the import of representing Muhammad's public front of black men, a valuable display that seemed to match Malcolm's presence on television, meeting his techniques in handling the media by crafting techniques of their own. Salesmen recognized that they were living promotional tools for the Nation.[157] "Being in the public eye . . . makes a brother a living witness to the greatness of the Honorable Elijah Muhammad," a salesman commented. Brother Leonard 4X was "one of the Messenger's most successful distributors" perhaps because he had embraced his father's legacy, who used to organize for Marcus Garvey.[158] For Walter 3X Kemp, "SELLING MUHAMMAD SPEAKS is the greatest thing that has ever happened to me. . . . It has made me stand up and walk straight."[159]A woman member reported, "My husband is putting into practice that which Messenger Muhammad teaches (selling *Muhammad Speaks* Newspapers and striving to put into practice the other phases of righteousness). . . . Through my husband, the head of the Family, the children and grandchildren see the work of the Hon. Elijah Muhammad."[160] Yet Brother Frank 8X Lopez's sales pitch made him one of the NOI's most dynamic salesmen. "The paper is sacred," he declared. "When we are holding the paper we must be careful how we react to people, because we are holding the words of Almighty God, who is represented by the Honorable Elijah Muhammad. The clothes we wear, the smile on our faces, consideration, justice are all a part of our sales technique. . . . We are successful when we approach people as though Allah Himself would approach them." Lopez's impressive sales strategy was "a winning philosophy about selling Muhammad Speaks."[161] Positioned against the backdrop of urban decay, salesmen used their renewed bodies to help point up the stark contrast between their being and looking clean vis-à-vis the streets in which they operated. Seizing on the streets as their public stage, salesmen struck a powerful image for those reading their redeemed bodies amid public debates about the decline of inner cities and some ghetto-dwellers' actual struggles for better living conditions.[162]

And if Muhammad could build up black men, then he could certainly build up a nation of better prospects for black people, the paper argued. In July 1964, *Muhammad Speaks* published Muhammad's consolidated plan for urban renewal, the "Three-Year Economic Program for Black America." This solution to the failures of the urban hinged on encouraging black people to save their money, reform themselves morally, and be "clean." "Spend only when necessary and according to their income," Muhammad advised, "save just 5 cents a day . . . 25 cents a week, $1 a month." A portion of the money readers saved was to be sent to the NOI's Chicago headquarters to support the eventual construction of an NOI-owned national savings bank. Readers could "also aid us by subscribing to the MUHAMMAD SPEAKS newspaper."[163] Yet being clean and well dressed was critical to the plan. Muhammad proposed establishing a "Committee of Cleanliness" to "teach and force our people to be clean" by compelling "our people to clean their bodies as well as their houses." In many ways, Muhammad was reiterating similar calls for personal and domestic care that black elites issued to the race following Reconstruction, believing that doing so projected racial progress.[164] "If they only have one suit of clothing, they should wash it and press it each night. . . . You must shave yourselves and look like men. And our women should clean up." Cleanliness would "get our people into the spirit of self-respect," helping make black people the "equal of other civilized nations of the earth," and therefore earning the respect of the world. He advised readers to "cut our extravagances" and "sacrifice for three years; confine ourselves to not more than three dress-suits of clothing a year, never exceeding $65 in cost."[165] Their savings would then "help fight unemployment, abominable housing, hunger and the nakedness of the 22 million black people here in America."[166]

Muhammad's plan for urban renewal had glaring limits. The plan noticeably emphasized self-help over the structural issues that some proponents of government-sponsored urban renewal hoped to address.[167] The plan's emphasis on personal and racial redemption reflected the social, political, and economic conservatism at the core of Muhammad's teachings, which betrayed his radical rhetoric to emphasize using moral reform and respectability politics as a strategy in advancing black people. Like Martin Luther King Jr. and other segments of America, the NOI was influenced by postwar conservatism, religious and otherwise. Along with King, Muhammad appealed to a religiously minded black public, though he couched those appeals within a black Nationalist framework. And both men believed that the disciplined black male body could serve as a moral weapon in the service of racial uplift. But unlike King, who was now increasingly making economic arguments and leading demonstrations that sought governmental support in addressing black poverty, Muhammad rooted his programs for black progress in ideas of racial advancement through self-help, business development, and agrarian mastery.[168] Though Muhammad was no policy expert or formal urban planner, the commercial success of many NOI-owned businesses demonstrated that the NOI had some level of expertise in combating urban decay, at least for members.[169] Writers for the paper would later argue that Muhammad's plans were "better" than social and economic programs under the War on Poverty that President Lyndon B. Johnson championed through the Economic Opportunity Act of 1964. As the paper insisted, only Muhammad's plan offered the "Real War against Poverty."[170] The NOI argued through *Muhammad Speaks* that not only was the government solely committed to ensuring white supremacy, it and the United States were destined to be destroyed by God. "Follow me and live," he declared, but he warned, "Reject me and die." Muhammad's vision for racial advancement turned on his eschatological framing of the world in rigid, irreconcilable binaries of free and slave, separation and integration, man and woman, manly and unmanly, life and death.[171]

Limits in Muhammad's agenda for racial advancement paralleled many limits in the NOI's media campaign. The campaign had become a very serious business that, at the least, required a lot of time and energy on the part of the men so central to it, and at the most, could endanger their personal freedom and safety.[172] For some salesmen, the clean-cut look did not always work. Rodnell P. Collins, the nephew of Malcolm X, recounted that he "tried to imitate [Malcolm's] style when selling papers in Boston." But his "looking squeaky clean" did not impress the "stuck-up, bourgeois, status-quo Negroes" there. "I mistakenly thought they would be impressed by the sight of a young brother trying to make a few dollars legitimately. They were not," Collins stated, pointing to some of the class conflicts that hampered the NOI's image before black middle-class publics.[173] *Muhammad Speaks* had insisted that selling the paper enabled diligent salesmen to be self-employed, exemplifying Muhammad's promise to provide economic independence to black men.[174] But, as historian Bruce Perry has pointed out, salesmen had to purchase a certain number of copies themselves, anywhere from 200 to 300 copies at a cost of eleven cents per copy. Salesmen did this though purchasing costs continued to rise over time, even as many of them and their families were working class. As early as 1962, Malcolm complained about this to Muhammad, while arguing that the Nation was in some ways losing more money than it was making on the paper. "Men in New York City have a take-home-pay that averages only $55 per week. The living costs are high, they are budgeted right down to their last penny," he wrote, "and after paying rent, food, etc and donating to the Temple they don't have anything to buy papers with."[175]

And still, salesmen and the mosques they represented had to satisfy quotas, while growing profits from the paper went to the headquarters in Chicago. Salesmen who failed to meet their quota could face disciplinary action by other FOI, measures that sometimes included corporal punishment.[176] NOI leaders in Chicago placed these burdens on salesmen even as the headquarters sometimes failed to meet its responsibility in sending papers to paid subscribers, as W. G. Lyons Sr., a reader, complained to Malcolm. Lyons's letters to the headquarters about the matter "went unanswered," and he found the situation "quite distressing." He asked Malcolm to "use your influence" to "see that the good brothers in [Chicago] carry out their duties as required. . . . I want my paper and I want it each month as stated."[177] Further, in some cases, salesmen sabotaged other salesmen, even by using violence. Sister Willa Ruth X was one of Muhammad's "salesladies," but she wrote Muhammad, pleading for him to intervene on her behalf against a salesman. The salesman had harassed her and her family, driven away her customers, "over one hundred regular customers," to be sure, and even struck her. The captains of her mosque had even refused to give papers to her for her to sell, though the salesman who was sabotaging her "is freely supplied with papers which he never tries to sell." Having previously written Muhammad to share this information, but to no avail, she was struggling to prevail against the NOI's hierarchy of leadership, rigid patriarchy and gender proscriptions, and some of the violence that shaped the organization, as much as she was struggling to simply sell the paper.[178]

Subscription campaigns only put increased demands on salesmen to satisfy quotas. One salesman was grateful to his customers "for their cooperation in making it possible for me to sell one thousand copies of Muhammad Speaks." Malcolm occasionally helped some salesmen by buying copies himself.[179] But police compounded these challenges for salesmen. Displaying NOI masculinity on the inner-city streets that had become their public stages exposed them to the kinds of problems with police that would help spark urban rebellions by the mid- to late 1960s.[180] As religious scholar Edward E.

Curtis has suggested, members had a host of daily ritualized activities that made their bodies into "a locus of social protest."[181] Police read this on salesmen. According to one apparent police memorandum, some identified the FOI as "well trained," "highly disciplined" men, "'clean-cut'" and "well dressed" but "extremely dangerous," a "type of fanatic," who "will kill any police officer" and was "willing to die for their cause."[182] As subscription campaigns increased the presence of salesmen in public space, wielding their printed instruments of black consciousness and manhood, police reacted.[183] Some arrests resulted from police provocation and harassment, reflecting a long-standing history of surveillance against the black press by state authorities since the Migration era. Over the years, Malcolm had planned rallies and protests in New York to address police brutality against members and black people, even writing appeals to President Kennedy, demanding federal intervention. In January 1963, Malcolm demanded that the New York district attorney investigate the "brutal manhandling" of two salesmen who were selling the paper in Times Square on Christmas Day.[184] But police also arrested some salesmen for aggressively hawking the paper to the point of harassing pedestrians. Some of these salesmen may have turned aggressive in order to meet their quota and avoid discipline by fellow FOI. Increasing police harassment of salesmen eventually led NOI leaders to demand "freedom of this press." They swore to resist any impediments "designed to prevent the sales or distribution of MUHAMMAD SPEAKS to block the verbal voice of the Messenger of Allah," affirming that the paper was "not designed for 'white people' in the first place," though they also capitulated, stating that "After MUHAMMAD SPEAKS is put into the hands of salesmen, it is no longer the responsibility of their publishers as to what manner or means these independent salesmen may utilize their product."[185]

When Los Angeles police shot and killed Ronald X Stokes on April 27, 1962, in a maelstrom that wounded at least seven other Muslims, the importance and seriousness of the media campaign to the Nation was further revealed, even at the expense of the lives of NOI members.[186] Malcolm was often dispatched to handle situations with police. But in this particular case, Malcolm wanted to retaliate violently with an army of NOI men. Muhammad stopped him.[187] Muhammad responded to the slaying by calling for a "United Black Front," and pointing to the centrality of the paper and the media campaign. Fearing that members may begin targeting police in retaliation, he advised the Nation to "hold fast to Islam"; "we are not going out into the street now to begin war with the devil. . . . No, we are going to let the world know he is the devil: we are going to sell newspapers."[188] Another subscription drive followed in July 1962. The drive would help bring "more assurance of readership," "more free time for FOI sales force," and "less police harassment in areas where sales of *Muhammad Speaks* is illegally opposed," according to Raymond Sherrieff, captain of the FOI and Muhammad's son-in-law. Sales of *Muhammad Speaks* reportedly totaled 400,000 copies in July. The paper then shifted from a monthly publication to a biweekly.[189]

Stokes's murder and Muhammad's inert response to it deeply disturbed Malcolm, and by 1964, it was even clearer to him just how serious the campaign was in other ways. By now, the campaign had greatly expanded, stretching across different spaces and media from the street to rallies in major cities to radio to television to recorded albums of Muhammad's speeches.[190] The campaign even included recorded music, a song by Louis X, the minister of Boston's Temple and one of Malcolm's protégés. The song was titled "White Man's Heaven Is a Black Man's Hell."[191] Malcolm's role in the campaign consumed a lot of his time and energy, much like salesmen. But he noticed that as early as 1962, his coverage in the paper was contracting as the campaign was expanding. Around this time, NOI leaders shifted his management and editing of the paper to Herbert Muhammad in Chicago.[192] According to Louis E. Lomax, management of the paper was moved from Malcolm in order to free him from the responsibilities of the paper so that he could concentrate on being "ambassador-at-large." But some, like Betty, sensed it was because of his widespread publicity that certain jealous ministers seized control of the paper.[193] Still, in using television as another, if not better, avenue of publicity for the NOI, Malcolm may not have necessarily needed the Nation's publication to perform his job as spokesman at the time.[194]

But one meeting with the press severely compromised him. On December 1, 1963, Malcolm commented on the assassination of President John F. Kennedy, who was killed a week earlier. Malcolm's caustic comments that Kennedy's slaying was a case of the "chickens coming home to roost," his way of saying that America's violent practices around the world had returned to U.S. soil, violated an order issued by Muhammad for ministers not to speak on the matter. NOI leaders rushed to damage control and Muhammad silenced Malcolm for ninety days. "Minister Malcolm did not speak on behalf of the honorable Elijah Muhammad, the nation of Islam, or any of Mr. Muhammad's followers. . . . We with the world are very shocked at the assassination of our President," leaders reported in the *Defender*, as well as in other media outlets.[195] Members of the press still descended on the

Nation, however.[196] Malcolm's comments were a display of the NOI's militant and fearless black manhood, his "technique" in handling the press, and the sensationalism that had come to characterize the rhetoric of NOI leaders. It was not, however, a display of NOI men's discipline in obeying Muhammad.[197]

Malcolm's silencing was significant for several reasons concerning the history of black newspapers and its long-standing relationship to black male leadership and the black public sphere. Examining this important moment within this context alongside the rapidly changing media landscape of the 1960s reveals another complicated side to the internal developments that eventually led to Malcolm's exit from the Nation. Newspapers had been black men's long-standing vehicle for leadership and vocalization, especially men of Muhammad's generation, through which they asserted a "voice." They hoped this voice would gain enough influence in the black public sphere that they could then speak for the race. Malcolm's being Muhammad's spokesman raised an inherent contradiction here, especially as Malcolm utilized other media to represent Muhammad. Comments Malcolm once shared with Louis E. Lomax bore this out. "There is no difference between the Messenger and me," he said. "I am his slave, his servant, his son. He is the leader, the only spokesman for the Black Muslims."[198]

That Malcolm was part of a generation of black male leaders that could now access television and other media to a greater extent, in addition to newspapers, exacerbated this contradiction. Significant generational and ideological shifts were again shaping the black press and the men behind it, as it had during the Depression era. Martin Luther King Jr. and James Farmer, for example, were also doing a number of television interviews or getting televised news coverage that allowed them to broadcast their fight to a wide audience. In fact, their coverage increased as some networks came to prefer their message to that of the NOI.[199] Some writers for *Muhammad Speaks* were attuned to these developments, but the NOI considered these civil rights leaders and their messages antithetical to the Nation's cause.[200] For NOI leaders, Malcolm seemed to be participating in this, and, most importantly, appeared to be utilizing television to the extent that he was getting too much press, or gaining a public image that increasingly overshadowed Muhammad's. Malcolm swore that "in every radio or television appearance, in every interview, I always made it crystal clear that I was Mr. Muhammad's *representative*" (Malcolm's emphasis). Malcolm imagined that he was locked in a contentious battle with "white newspaper, radio, and television reporters," who were "trying to trick me" and were "determined to defeat Mr. Muhammad's teachings." But Nation leaders charged him with self-promotion, signaling the kind of visibility that television increasingly provided Malcolm beyond the newspaper page, and, as a result, a "voice" virtually unto himself. It probably did not help that television was the leading form of mass media at the time and, by 1963, was increasingly transforming many readerships into viewerships as the majority of Americans reported using television as their chief news source.[201] Muhammad's and Malcolm's differences with one another straddled these dramatic changes in mass media even as the two straddled dramatic changes in the black freedom struggle.

Muhammad kept a rigorous radio schedule, but warned against too much television, a symptom of rapid changes that probably disturbed his conservative sensibilities. Indulging in more pseudoscience, he insisted that "scientists now warn you against gazing into TV sets for any long length of time, because this can produce cancer in the body." "This is certainly true of children, who prop themselves in front of TV sets and gaze for hours at close range." He urged the public to "stop using things which destroy your health," like television, he argued, and instead to embrace his economic program. One *Muhammad Speaks* article contended that television was part of "subtle propaganda that sneaks into our homes at night . . . into our conscious and subconscious minds . . . a combination of propaganda and entertainment so beautifully disguised and so masterfully presented, that we fall helpless under its spell."[202] Malcolm had been increasingly considering ways the NOI could strengthen its active involvement in the black freedom struggle. Perhaps this included increasing the NOI's television presence to match that of civil rights leaders and activists, among other things. Indeed, as the civil rights movement pressed forward with greater strides and greater publicity, Malcolm was ruminating both on how the NOI could become more active and on how their "militantly disciplined Muslims" could be involved, mobilized, and displayed to a greater extent for "all the world to see, and respect, and discuss." Being another way for the NOI to display its renewed men on one of the largest public stages of the time, perhaps it would eventually lead to saturating the black public sphere with living images of proper black manhood both on television and on the street.[203]

Malcolm had also been contemplating the limits of Muhammad's "voice," particularly the Nation's "tough talk," that is, its penchant for radical rhetoric without much corresponding radical action, however radical its voice may have been. Black people's growing militancy could eventually expose this voice as mere sensationalism. In many ways, Malcolm was moving toward Robert F. Williams's stance on print and practice. "I felt the very real potentiality that," Malcolm worried, "considering the mercurial moods of the black masses, this labeling of Muslims as 'talk only' could see us, powerful as we were, one day suddenly separated from the Negroes' front-line struggle."[204] Muhammad's conservative Three-Year Economic Plan pointed to this, concerned more with black people's cleanliness and morality than with helping directly correct their endemic structural, economic, political, and social problems. Perhaps Malcolm was starting to see that Muhammad's brand of black masculinity made black men so disciplined and clean that it rendered their bodies inert beyond moving about in public space to sell newspapers. The NOI model of black manhood was therefore detached from a real active and physical engagement with the black freedom struggle, reflecting Muhammad's policies against involving the Nation in civil rights demonstrations. This approach essentially fixed black men's bodies in decaying urban space at the same time that Muhammad talked about liberating them from it. Like photographs frozen in the columns of a newspaper page, the Nation's display of black manhood made black men's bodies virtually "still" vis-à-vis the "activism" of civil rights demonstrators, a quiescence that ultimately helped to maintain the "stillness" black people were expected to exhibit in not physically or directly challenging the white power structure, as historian Stephen A. Berrey has argued. Along these lines, Malcolm saw Nation men's renewed bodies heading toward a state of physical, political, and social atrophy. For him, it was becoming more and more the case that a proper manly vision for racial advancement required sustained and vigorous action on the part of black men. "Elijah is willing to sit and wait, [but] I'm not," he would later say, highlighting the NOI's stillness. The Nation was "dragging its feet."[205]

Malcolm began to sense that *he* was coming to represent an "image of leadership" to an emerging generation of young black radicals. Indeed, his ideas and rhetoric were beginning to have a strong influence on some student-centered civil rights groups, such as the Student Nonviolent Coordinating Committee and the Congress of Racial Equality, much to the chagrin of many established civil rights leaders. Some young activists had even begun quoting him in their public statements. He claimed that even a white reporter told him that "the whites need your voice worse than the Negroes."[206] Louis E. Lomax sensed some of this too. "Whereas Elijah Muhammad is the maximum leader of the movement, Malcolm X is the man who will have to save the Black Muslims from becoming just another sect or cult," he wrote. He reasoned that none of the other NOI leaders could "capture the mind and imagination of TV viewers as Malcolm X has done. . . . They cannot cause the nation's press to beat a path to Muhammad's door, as Malcolm has done."[207] Given the voice that Malcolm seemed to be developing, his silencing was Muhammad's attempt to discipline him, and at the same time again control his media presence. Indeed, the silencing was really the culmination of efforts to control Malcolm's media access that had been in motion since Nation leaders moved *Muhammad Speaks* away from him and to Chicago. The silencing denied Malcolm access to mass media that would have enabled him to continue asserting a voice on television that was beginning to rival Muhammad's own in speaking for the race in print. The silencing "was the most quick and thorough publicity job that I had ever seen the Chicago officials initiate," Malcolm said.[208]

Malcolm waited for Muhammad to reinstate him. Muhammad suspended him indefinitely. On March 8, 1964, Malcolm announced to the press his departure from the Nation.[209] His developing ideological changes and suspension notwithstanding, Malcolm was motivated to leave because he had discovered that Muhammad had fathered children outside his marriage, and, along with members of Muhammad's family and some NOI leaders, was reaping enormous profits from Nation businesses. All of this constituted extreme violations of the clean, moral, and modest lifestyle Muhammad demanded of members.[210] Within a week of the split, Malcolm, the publisher, planned to start a new publication, the *Flaming Crescent*. "We believe in the power of the press," he declared. He knew that now there was no way for him to access *Muhammad Speaks*, even though "I am the founder of the paper."[211] Whereas W. E. B. DuBois resigned from the *Crisis*, Malcolm was expelled from *Muhammad Speaks*. Muhammad's clarion calls for a "United Front of Black Men" took on even deeper meaning now in the midst of their very public schism.[212] In fact, through a number of television interviews, including one with Mike Wallace, Malcolm put Muhammad on full public display—in terms of his improprieties and failed manhood, that is. Muhammad was "confronted with a crisis in his own personal and moral life," Malcolm charged in one interview, "and he did not stand up as a man."[213] NOI leaders exploded. Using *Muhammad Speaks*, they directed the full force of the Nation's robust media campaign at Malcolm.

Malcolm felt that the Nation's rhetoric and men should be better mobilized, but now NOI leaders mobilized both against him in the paper. Targeting him was the next leg of the media campaign in order to redeem Muhammad's public image and combat Malcolm by demonizing his. Again, a black newspaper worked to break a rival black male leader. But, in an unprecedented move, this time that black newspaper did so by completely turning against its own founder. The paper distinguished Malcolm as the most dangerous of all Muhammad's critics, having been redeemed by him, welcomed into his inner circle, extended the honor of speaking on his behalf, and embraced like one of his own sons. Malcolm's name and image appeared in the paper more often now than when he was spokesman, though in excoriated and caricatured forms.[214] One of the most obvious signs of this next phase of the campaign came through "What Islam Has Done for Me." Members' positive testimonies about their conversions, the Nation, and Muhammad increasingly praised the Messenger against Malcolm. On March 27, 1964, just weeks after Malcolm's exit, *Muhammad Speaks* featured a slate of thirty-two "dedicated ministers," some of whom Malcolm had trained himself, contrasting them against the NOI's famous defector. Some of them took the contrast further by publishing attacks on him in the paper over the next several months. Some identified Malcolm in coded language as "the most outspoken [of] opponents." Others plainly identified him by name.[215]

In either case, Malcolm was the "Biggest Hypocrite," as well as a problematic, would-be black male leader, who had manipulated different media to attempt to replace Muhammad as the ideal black male leader.[216] Scholars have noted Malcolm's personal and ideological differences with Muhammad, as well as the aspersions NOI leaders heaped on him, but have missed many of the implications those attacks registered about changes in mass media at this time, NOI leaders' struggles to grapple with some of these rapid changes, and the competition those media presented to Muhammad's voice in speaking for the race through *Muhammad Speaks*. Louis X argued that Muhammad had "lifted him from obscurity and placed him in a position of national prominence," but Malcolm had now become an "international hobo." Malcolm "began to fill the newspapers with stories to the effect that there was a 'split' in the ranks of the Muslims, and that such information came from 'inside sources,'" Louis said in another article. "They did come from 'inside sources'—from the typewriters of Minister Malcolm himself."[217] Another said that Malcolm "loves worldly praises; he likes to see his picture in the newspapers, over the radio and television."[218] Jeremiah X and Joseph X decided to contest the stories Malcolm had told the press about his "'before' life," an attempt to paint him as a liar. "It has been common belief that Malcolm Little was a former big-time operator that had gone to jail for having been a 'pimp' in Harlem." But "with the skill of master surgeons," both men "strip the popular image of Malcolm of all its deceptive outer veneer to expose the 'real' man as a small-time 'operator.'"[219] Even Malcolm's brother, Philbert X, who had introduced him to the Nation, denounced him. "My brother Malcolm will do anything and say anything to gain mention and his picture in news coverage."[220] The attacks only continued to ferment over time, and play out very publicly and caustically in *Muhammad Speaks*, "the youngest and greatest of the major black newspapers in America founded by the Honorable Elijah Muhammad." In other words, in the spirit of Muhammad's power to erase black men's pasts, writers erased Malcolm as the founder of the paper, making a profound point about this battle over different media, among other things. "We used to have a monthly newspaper, then a bi-weekly and now a weekly," a member remarked. "You know who is responsible for that?—that's right—Muhammad."[221]

Striving to make their attacks even more effective, members gendered their condemnations of Malcolm. Malcolm was not the only well-known NOI man on television, to be sure. Muhammad Ali, the heavyweight boxing champion of the world, was in fact more famous than Malcolm. One outstanding salesman even received ringside tickets to one of Ali's fights as a reward for impressive sales.[222] But Malcolm's alleged uncritical embrace of publicity seemed intended to replace Muhammad as the face and the leader of the Nation and as the voice of the race. The working friendships Malcolm had in fact built with some members of the black and white press over the years, including Louis E. Lomax, Mike Wallace, and Alex Haley, among others, only helped exacerbate this perspective.[223] These gendered attacks are critical to note for understanding the ways in which this episode played out in the terms black male leaders had historically used to stake their claim to leadership and argue for the merits of their programs against real or perceived rival black male leaders. Here, NOI leaders and writers for the paper elevated Muhammad's manhood over that of Malcolm's, rhetorically emasculating Malcolm on different levels. First, they framed Malcolm outside of proper NOI masculinity and his status as an Original Man. Characterizing him as having reverted in his morals and manhood to the base levels of his "'before' life," Malcolm had "jumped off of the springboard of intelligence and honor into the chasm of shame, regret, despair and hatred."[224] Malcolm was a "misguided brother" who could not "control his emotions," having deserted the discipline of NOI men, according to Charles 19X Harris.[225] In the second frame, Malcolm was the adopted son, who had betrayed his adopted father. Minister Isaiah Karriem praised Muhammad's generosity in having taken Malcolm "out of the garbage can and nursed as he would a baby until he didn't want for anything."[226] For John Shabazz, Malcolm destroyed a relationship that once represented the strongest bonds between the two men. "YOU, Malcolm, were treated like a SON by the Messenger," Shabazz said. "He did more for you than your real parents ever could. . . . You reminded Mike Wallace that when you were a Muslim you spoke for Messenger Muhammad, but now you are speaking for yourself."[227]

Next, the paper projected Malcolm as overcome by jealousy of Muhammad's position as the leader of the Nation and voice of the race. Minister James X thought that "the effort of the press to cite Malcolm as a 'leader' is disgusting." Again, placing Malcolm outside of NOI masculinity and Original status, James X stripped Malcolm of his "X." "Negroes never have experienced such a traitor, or double crosser, as Malcolm Little. I believe that name 'Little' is what he is trying to outrun."[228] "Messenger Elijah Muhammad exalted Malcolm over the rest of his ministers" but "Malcolm wants to be the No. 1 man (the Messenger of Allah)," he charged.[229] "Do not follow those self-made leaders who are seeking only the praise of the people," Muhammad himself added. They "have no good in mind for you and will lead you back into becoming more of a slave than ever."[230] According to Muhammad, Malcolm's leadership and model of black manhood would return black men to the state of unmanliness and submissiveness that slavery had long represented in gendered terms. Robert S. Abbott had embraced the masculine model of the self-made man, and, in some ways, Muhammad had promoted the ideas fundamental to that model by emphasizing self-help, financial independence, and business ownership for black men. But Malcolm's turning self-made in this case was a problematic notion because, to Muhammad, no black man could achieve real, race-worthy leadership by himself. For Muhammad, only he had the power to make real men. Malcolm would have agreed years ago, but in the midst of this heated war of words, he was beginning a personal odyssey to a new model of black manhood.

Finally, the battery of gendered attacks against Malcolm in *Muhammad Speaks* came down to a contest of masculinity wherein Malcolm was no match for Muhammad's manly power. Malcolm came to have complicated personal, ideological, and religious differences with Muhammad, to be sure. The urban rebellions of 1964 could have been a moment for the NOI to show greater racial leadership and involvement directly in the black freedom struggle, especially since the urban was a focal point of Muhammad's program. This was a point that could have begun to satisfy Malcolm's desire for the Nation to take more action, or at least to help mute his criticism in this regard.[231] But NOI leaders avoided engaging Malcolm on these issues, deciding instead to appeal to the rigid gendered binaries of manly and unmanly poles present within Muhammad's eschatological beliefs in order to spurn Malcolm's leadership. A public rally that Muhammad gave in Harlem, the headquarters for Malcolm's Muslim Mosque Inc. and the Organization of Afro-American Unity (OAAU), the new organizations he started after his departure, revealed the manly differences in their leadership. The rally figured an imagined showdown between the manhood of the two, likening Muhammad to a commanding general in their escalating war of words. "When Messenger Muhammad entered New York on June 28, 1964," he "showed the wisdom and strategy of a general leading a victorious brave, and fearless army against the cowardly hypocritical dog (Malcolm). Malcolm thought that he had mastered—or could with his oration—New York against the wisdom and cleverness of Muhammad. But he and his followers were so openly defeated and put to a flight by Muhammad's intelligent and well-disciplined F. O. I. members (with their coolness, display of obedience to and love for their leader made them the envy of most organizations in America) that Malcolm changed his mind."[232]

The supposed face-off took place in the same city that Marcus Garvey imagined a showdown with his critics. The episode displayed the Nation's disciplined men alongside Muhammad's manly power, while exposing Malcolm to be "like a silly general without an army," according to *Muhammad Speaks*.[233] NOI leaders hoped that Malcolm, with his leadership excoriated and manhood reduced in the paper to that of an ungrateful child, covetous of his father figure's deserved position of leadership, would fail to attract followers. Perhaps framing him this way would discourage black men interested in achieving a proper black manhood. Indeed, Malcolm was struggling to attract large numbers to his new organizations.[234] Some readers of the paper recognized this contest of masculinity, couching the two men's differences in terms of their manliness and, like sides of Garvey's conflict, their physical size. "Although I am not a present follower of the Honorable Elijah Muhammad," Herbert Ancin of San Francisco, California, said, "I disagree with those who are trying to smear and libel him so that few will listen. Mr. Muhammad has struck us here as a man among men, a giant of a man and such giants are rare indeed." In reality, Muhammad was shorter than Malcolm, who was six feet three inches tall, 170 pounds. But Ancin, a reader of *Muhammad Speaks* for many years, felt that Muhammad would "win out clear and above board in his present dispute within his own family—evidenced by the newspaper—and from such small-time defectors as Malcolm X."[235]

The vitriol spewing at Malcolm in *Muhammad Speaks* was visible for all to read. But NOI leaders' appeals to the side of Muhammad's eschatology that turned on life and death also helped make their condemnations of Malcolm particularly grim, and the media campaign yet even more serious.[236] The front page of the April 10, 1964, edition of *Muhammad Speaks* blared, "Walk the Way of Free Men!" but told readers to "obey" the Messenger. Ostensibly, black men's freedom entailed strict obedience to Muhammad, in addition to them gaining mental, spiritual, and physical liberation. And a provocative cartoon inside the same issue intimated what could happen if one was disobedient. It showed Malcolm's severed head tumbling down a road that "Judas," Brutus," and "Benedict Arnold" had traveled. The head cried out, "I split because no man wants to be number 2 man in nothing"; "the officials at headquarters fear my public image!"[237] One member reminded readers that "it is the Honorable Elijah Muhammad who is responsible for our not being alcoholics anymore. . . . It is he who stopped us from being niggardly," but warned that "filthy talk about our leader . . . will bring about grave consequences." Declaring that Malcolm "had gotten popularity, and then became jealous of his teacher and his teacher's place," Louis X made one of the direst forecasts, identifying Malcolm by name. "Only those who wish to be led to hell, or to their doom will follow Malcolm. The die is set, and Malcolm shall not escape, especially after such evil, foolish talk about his benefactor." "Such a man as Malcolm is worthy of death," Malcolm's former protégé declared.[238] The NOI's robust media campaign used to emphasize renewing life to black men. But as Malcolm and Muhammad battled over which black male leader was going to speak for the race, the campaign turned to elevating the power to take life away from those who apostatized from Muhammad.

Again resembling parts of Garvey's battles with his critics, the competition between two black male leaders *and* newspapermen for the greater share of the black public sphere came down to deadly threats. Papers, such as the *Defender*, reported the threats. Malcolm told the *Amsterdam News*, "My death has been ordered." He felt that "any death-talk for me could have been approved of—if not actually initiated—by only one man."[239] Malcolm claimed that he was not afraid, however, invoking the fearlessness valued by the NOI. Malcolm had long sensed that he would die prematurely, given his "'before' life" as well as his own father's violent death.[240] His mien might have indicated this fearlessness. "He appeared calm," photographer Gordon Parks remembered in a meeting with Malcolm in his last days. "Somewhat resplendent with his goatee and astrakhan hat," as Parks recalled, Malcolm's well-preened, sartorial look was still intact, reflecting the internal cleansing he was then undergoing, another profound personal transformation. Ideologically and spiritually, Malcolm felt now that he "must wear two hats," as he put it in a letter to a colleague, that of "a Muslim religious leader and an Afro-American freedom fighter."[241] Malcolm was "glad to be free" finally, telling Parks that "it's a time for martyrs now" as he embraced the prospects of a martyrdom that had become a hallmark quality of manly black leadership. Yet Malcolm was also facing the reality of the NOI's death threats, given that two assassination attempts were made on his life in January 1965. His confidence that he still had his "technique" in making strategic use of different media perhaps made him even more fearless. The NOI's malicious media campaign was plainly visible, but "I had one asset," Malcolm reasoned, "an international image." Indeed, one of Muhammad's sons, Wallace, who, like Malcolm, was beginning to shift away from the NOI, shared in a private letter to Malcolm that his father "fears the attention given you by news medias." Malcolm "knew that if I said something newsworthy, people would read or hear of it, maybe around the world."[242]

Garvey had retaliated against his critics in part with libel suits. Malcolm instead defended himself in this war of words with the Nation through press interviews and public speeches. "If he [Elijah Muhammad] is the leader of the Muslims and the leader of our people, then lead us against our enemies, don't lead us against each other," he stated at the founding rally of his OAAU in June 1964.[243] That month, NOI men showed up to sit in the audience of one of his public debates. Soon, Malcolm would reach out to contacts in the international Muslim world for help in combating the NOI's powerful media campaign. "If the Muslim religious officials in that part of the world . . . expect me to be the one to expose [Muhammad] and to project the right image of Islam, then they should realize also what I am up against."[244] In December 1964, *Muhammad Speaks* announced that Muhammad would be making two television appearances to promote his teachings, though he had previously decried the mass medium.[245] The paper opened the New Year, advertising a "Night with the F. O. I.," set for January 12, 1965, at the Audubon Ballroom in New York. At the price of $6.50 for couples or $3.75 for singles, the public could see the many talents of the "disciplined and militant men who follow The Honorable Elijah Muhammad." Again, the Nation planned to put its men on public display.[246] Yet *Muhammad Speaks* also announced that the New Year would be a "crucial year." "It is a year in which the most out-spoken opponents of the Honorable Elijah Muhammad will slink into ignoble silence."[247]

Several weeks later, on February 21, 1965, assassins took Malcolm's life as he delivered a speech about brotherhood to the OAAU.[248] Three NOI men were eventually convicted of the murder. Scholars have long wrestled with whether the assassins acted alone or whether NOI leaders ordered the hit, or whether there was collusion among NOI leaders, New York police, the FBI, and the Central Intelligence Agency.[249] Additionally, though, scholars must account for how the NOI's media campaign may have helped inflame members and influence their actions. Some members of the press reasoned that Malcolm had lived by the sword and therefore died by it.[250] More sympathetic observers thought that Malcolm's death signified his being a definitive black leader.[251] The *Herald Dispatch*, the paper that used to print Malcolm's column, elevated him to a position of racial leadership long desired by many black male leaders. He "was the most promising and effective leader of American Negroes in this century." Though dead, "there are a thousand other Malcolms. They will rise!" the paper said, assuring his part in reproducing Race Men.[252] For Shirley Graham DuBois, the widow of W. E. B. DuBois, "Afro-American newspapers separated themselves from the powerful ruling white press" finally. "Only the Afro-American press gave the full text of the eulogy delivered by Ossie Davis," in which Davis declared that "Malcolm was our manhood . . . our living Black manhood."[253]

There was not much comment in *Muhammad Speaks* from NOI leaders, though one of the paper's writers, Abdul Basit Naeem, had a lot to say.[254] In several articles, including a four-part series that he wrote, Naeem seemed to regret Malcolm's fatal demise, but affirmed that Muhammad had no role in Malcolm's death, contending that Malcolm's end was "Decreed by God, Not the Messenger." Malcolm's fall involved his "fondness for publicity," a "major weakness" that led him to speaking in the "first person." It was "entirely too late . . . to realize or correct his many mistakes," mistakes that started with Malcolm's misplaced belief that Mike Wallace's 1959 documentary would help the Nation, he argued. But "the once virile, extremely articulate and eloquent Malcolm" was "silenced finally and eternally by his Maker." Naeem shifted culpability from NOI leaders to Malcolm himself. "The past is dead. . . . It is the future to which we should now look forward," he added, suggesting several things members could do to move on. He recommended reading Muhammad's writings, listening to him on the radio, and selling *Muhammad Speaks*, prioritizing the particular media the NOI found most acceptable.[255] Muhammad's comments on the matter came indirectly through the publication of *Message to the Black Man in America*, however. Released in October 1965, the virtual exegesis on the NOI's religious and social beliefs was compiled from many *Muhammad Speaks* editorials. The volume included sections on the Original Man, the Nation's economic plans, and "Hypocrites, Disbelievers and Obedience."[256]

The book Malcolm had been working on with Alex Haley was published just days after Muhammad's book, titled *The Autobiography of Malcolm X*.[257] In June 1964, Haley wrote Malcolm, telling him that the book "will give you a greater voice as a single man than the entire nation of Islam ever had collectively."[258] And through it, from beyond the grave, Malcolm spoke. In this story of his redemption and personal odyssey to his own model of black manhood, he explained in detail many of the stories he had shared in press interviews, his changing ideologies and ideas of racial advancement, and his side of his and his father figure's soured relationship. Many scholars have noted these points.[259] However, they have tended to overlook how the book testified to Malcolm's experiences in wrestling with a rapidly changing world of media in the 1960s and his attempts to defend himself against the NOI's robust media campaign following the split. He contended that he was possibly the most instrumental component in building the Nation to its public stature after working tirelessly for twelve years to "represent" Muhammad and his message at every chance. He accused NOI leaders of growing jealous of his extensive media presence, even as the Nation was putting its men on increased public display. The book also affirmed that *he* was the founder of *Muhammad Speaks*.[260]

Even still, Malcolm also explained his particular struggle with mass media after his departure. Noting this crucial point is critical to fully understanding the personal transformations he underwent and organizing efforts he undertook toward the end of his life. He had been trying to redeem his public image, but was hard pressed to shake the image he had built under the NOI and move his life and new goals forward by displaying a post-NOI public self. "One of the major troubles I was having in building the organization that I wanted," he wrote, "was that my earlier public image, my old so-called 'Black Muslim' image kept blocking me. I was trying gradually to reshape that image. I was trying to turn a corner, into a new regard by the public, especially Negroes."[261] His struggles to change his image spoke in many ways to the success of the NOI's media campaign and his role in it as spokesman. Malcolm had seemingly done his job so well that he had constructed and displayed a powerful public image of NOI manhood from which he was virtually inseparable despite his new political and religious out-looks.[262] Over the years, Malcolm had worked to learn how to navigate the vicissitudes of mass media and had succeeded in developing an approach that for the most part produced the results he sought when he was the NOI spokesman. He had prided himself on being a fast learner. But his use of television as a potent force in shaping images and the public sphere as much as, if not more than, newspapers long had, now worked to his disadvantage.[263] Undaunted, he tried to return to his roots as a publisher, using what had long been the mainstay and most reliable tool of black men's public vocalization and racial leadership. His OAAU started a newsletter, *Blacklash*. A sheet comprising around six pages, it featured crude, mostly handwritten headlines about the freedom struggle in America and abroad, a rudimentary style that probably reflected the rushed pace of its publisher at the time. But the paper was the start of the new organization's media initiative, which, under the direction of its "Public Relations and Propaganda Chief," was preparing to build a robust media campaign of its own.[264] *Blacklash* appeared to have a short run, however. Archival records indicate that two editions appeared in September 1964 and one in November of that year.[265] His proposed *Flaming Crescent* might have also helped him redeem his image, and promote his new organizations, new outlook, and new conceptions of black manhood. The name of the paper spoke to his new vision for igniting black, Islamic, third world, and African solidarities against white supremacy the world over, ideas that echoed parts of Robert F. Williams's internationalist outlook. Along these lines, he had tried to re-conceptualize the urban from a space in need of renewal to one in need of revolution, a cultural, political, and economic one, to be sure, that would be led by black men under a new vision of black masculinity vastly distinct from that of Muhammad's. Malcolm's new model was grounded in a "broth-erhood" that was active, was physical, and, similar to Marcus Garvey, worked to unite "people of African descent." Indeed, what he envisaged was decid-edly male-centered. For Malcolm, the gendered implications of this new vision amounted to one simple equation: "DIGNITY plus MANHOOD plus FREEDOM equal HUMAN RIGHTS." He had begun to construe the urban as a site for black political struggle, much like W. E. B. DuBois had during the Great Migration. And like many black male publishers that came before him, he saw a "crisis at hand." It was a "crisis of freedom," calling "black men, brown men, and yellow men" "to stand up as free men." Figuring Harlem as "our center of power," the launching pad for a new "united front," or even more pointedly, a "united force" of black people fighting an international black freedom struggle, Malcolm summarized the paper's name simply: "we want to set the world on fire."[266] The *Flaming Crescent* was never to be.[267]

Malcolm wrote in his autobiography, "My whole life had been a chronology of *changes*" (Malcolm's emphasis). This was one of Malcolm's many moments of deep introspection and self-discovery, similar to ones that had moved W. E. B. DuBois and Robert S. Abbott at the dawn of the twentieth century. And it was a challenge for him to write the book largely because of this, he told Haley. "How is it possible to write one's autobiography in a world so fast-changing as this?"[268] But Malcolm tried to be as observant as he was introspective, a voracious student of virtually everything from history to the rapidly changing developments of his own historical moment. And this moment situated him in a new world of media that impinged on the role of the black press in shaping black male leadership and the black freedom struggle.[269] It was a world he tried to learn. Mass media launched the NOI to national attention in a storm of controversy. First using the paper that Malcolm founded, the NOI unleashed a robust media campaign to promote Elijah Muhammad's vision for racial advancement and display his redeemed black men against the failures of urban black life both in print and in public. When Malcolm broadened that display to television, he troubled the black press as the voice of the race, helping expose limits in black men's long-standing efforts to speak for the race in a singular, masculine voice articulated through black newspapers. NOI leaders partly resolved this problem by turning *Muhammad Speaks* against its own founder, and then turning their campaign's promises of renewing black men's lives into warnings of death aimed at Malcolm.

Malcolm was cut short of his full publishing potential, which would have enabled him to assert an influential leadership role in vocalizing a new racial politics, as well as a new manly vision for racial advancement. Yet he believed in a certain kind of resurrection of the dead.[270] *Muhammad Speaks* helped herald the rise of the radical black press, and, indeed, more radical black papers followed by the late 1960s. Some of them bore the influence of the Nation and its paper. The *Black Panther Newspaper Intercommunal News Service* was one. Bobby Seale and Huey P. Newton founded the Black Panther Party for Self-Defense in October 1966 in Oakland, California, to address urban decay, black poverty, police brutality, and members of the black public, who now crystallized under "Black Power." The "mercurial moods of the black masses" that Malcolm had observed now trumpeted this powerfully sensational phrase. Seale and Newton launched the paper in

April 1967.[271] And many Panthers considered the NOI a harbinger of Black Power.[272] Like salesmen for *Muhammad Speaks*, the Panthers had working-class members, who made inner-city streets a public stage for selling the *Black Panther* and promoting their cause. Panthers elevated what they called "brothers on the block," as members donned a look, the "Panther uniform," that distinguished them before the public—a "black beret, black slacks, black shoes . . . blue shirt, and a black turtleneck," as Seale described it. Panthers were also often arrested for selling the paper. And they deployed militant, highly masculinized rhetoric and politics that reflected and rivaled the NOI's own, with the *Black Panther* featuring a ten-point agenda for racial advancement, "What We Want, What We Believe," inspired by the Nation's "What the Muslims Want, What the Muslims Believe." In fact, Newton used to attend one of the Nation's mosques in West Oakland. But as Newton later recalled, he and Seale "had been through many groups" before forming the Panthers, many of which "were so dedicated to rhetoric and artistic rituals that they had withdrawn from living in the Twentieth Century. Sometimes their analyses were beautiful, but they had no practical programs," Newton contended. "When they tried to develop practical programs, they often failed, because they lacked a systematic ideology which would help them do concrete analyses of concrete conditions to gain a full understanding of the community and its needs."[273] The NOI was among the groups Newton was describing, though the vision of its erstwhile spokesman did represent something concrete for the two Panther founders. According to historian Manning Marable, Seale had even requested a subscription to *Blacklash* from the OAAU in late 1964.

Panthers praised the NOI as forerunners to black radicalism, but they also distinguished themselves from the religious group and especially exalted Malcolm. At a time when some black militants refused to buy *Muhammad Speaks* after Malcolm was killed, the *Black Panther* elevated his voice, frequently printing statements he had made in sections titled "Remember the Words of Brother Malcolm."[274] Panthers extolled Malcolm as a martyr to the cause of black liberation and considered his autobiography to be the treatise of a visionary, revolutionary thinker, assigning it for members to read. And they considered themselves, as they put it, his "heirs," affirming a reproduction of Race Men under Malcolm in which they intended to continue his legacy. Whereas *Muhammad Speaks* had argued that Malcolm failed as a black leader in part for his inability to offer a proper black manhood, Panthers drew deep inspiration especially from his final model of masculinity, even his use of television, in addition to the vision of active and physical grassroots political engagement and internationalist politics that he promoted toward the end of his life. With the paper selling upward of 139,000 issues a week, and counting readers in the United States, Cuba, Europe, Africa, and Asia by the close of the decade, the *Black Panther* in part resurrected Malcolm, discursively and ideologically. Malcolm used to talk at length about his "'before' life." But the Panthers, along with many other Black Power advocates, helped herald Malcolm's "afterlife," stories about Malcolm that elevated him as the ultimate image of manly black leadership before a radical black public.[275]

NOI leaders accepted the credit Panthers gave them for helping inspire Black Power, and though the circulation of the *Black Panther* remained second only to that of *Muhammad Speaks*, the Nation still seemed threatened by them and their paper. The Panthers's and their paper's celebration of Malcolm probably did not help.[276] Sensing a radical competitor sold by an organization whose public displays were perhaps more provocative than that of the NOI's, *Muhammad Speaks* writers found it necessary to say that their publication had always been the only authentically black news organ. Writers pointed to the paper as part of the evidence that the NOI had indeed inspired Black Power, and Minister Louis Farrakhan, formerly Louis X, underscored the point further.[277] "While our black brothers and sisters in the civil rights movement were sitting-in, kneeling-in, etc., the Honorable Elijah Muhammad and his faithful followers were busy developing the only black newspaper whose policy is completely controlled by the black man," he said. Emphasizing its lead over the competition, *Muhammad Speaks* proudly declared that "more people than ever" were reading the paper "because we face the issue squarely." "The issue is Black survival in a changing world."[278]

Conclusion

Now a New Day Is upon Us

. . . .

In 1978, John Sengstacke was elected president of the National Newspaper Publishers Association, formerly the Negro Newspaper Publishers Association (NNPA). It would be his fifth time serving as president. Having founded the organization in 1940, he returned to the role with the ken of a veteran newspaperman, who also planned to scold his fellow publishers a bit.[1] "Forty years ago, a gathering of black publishers under the same roof would have been no more possible than a flight to the moon," he said in a speech that he prepared to deliver to the group. "But getting together is not enough. Are we building a solid future for the Black press and our readers? While we have made some progress, my candid reply is NO." Now a seasoned publisher, his tone disclosed a certain frustration, however. "All of us take certain pride as publishers and editors," he continued, but "we have allowed the white press to elbow us into the back seat and muffle our voices." "The black revolution of the 60's" compounded this, as Robert F. Williams had warned. It "produced embarrassing evidence of the lethargy of our editors in the area of neglected social action. We have abdicated our leadership. As a consequence, new organizations sprung up overnight to protest social abuses and economic denials that we should have stressed in bold type in our headlines." Activists had filled "an intellectual vacuum left by the black press," he affirmed, and "as a result, our circulation is limited to the restricted perimeter of the black community and our political influence is waning. . . . We are still doing business as usual."[2] Sengstacke was pointing to many of the sharp realities facing many mainstream black papers and their role, or the lack thereof, in shaping black leadership, the freedom struggle, and black manhood since the rise of black radicalism. Malcolm X, the NOI, and *Muhammad Speaks* had helped herald these realities, and as a result, Sengstacke and other observers saw a crisis approaching.

Nearly a month following Malcolm's assassination, Daniel Patrick Moynihan, assistant secretary of labor for policy planning and research under President Lyndon Johnson, completed *The Negro Family: The Case for National Action*. Moynihan argued in that report that black people suffered from abysmal employment rates in inner cities and dysfunctional family structures, especially among the black urban poor. But he also contended that "the Muslim doctrines . . . exert powerful influence," reflecting "a time when the possibility that the nations of the world will divide along color lines seems suddenly not only possible, but even immanent." For him, black unemployment, disorder in black families, and the NOI's influence, among other things, could be prevented in the United States through the cultivation of a manly black leadership that began first with black men leading their families. Matriarchal households had usurped black men's roles as fathers, husbands, and breadwinners, he argued, a role that he thought the nation and federal government could help restore. In many ways, Moynihan echoed the NOI's emphasis on combating the failures of the urban and redeeming the manhood of black men through gainful employment and manly self-assertion, even as he feared the Nation's influence.[3] Two months later, Robert Penn Warren, a highly acclaimed white writer, published *Who Speaks for the Negro?,* the title of which recalled the same point raised by *Jet* magazine in July 1961. Warren wrote the book to "find out something, first hand, about the people . . . who are making the Negro Revolution what it is." The book centered on a collection of interviews mostly with black male leaders, activists, and thinkers of the day. Here, again, black women's leadership, contributions, and voices were subsumed under black men's influence on and now narration of the black freedom struggle. In many ways, Warren spoke with the leaders that the black press had helped elevate. One of Warren's interviews was with Malcolm, but the interview was situated, among several other interviewees that bemoaned his leadership, the NOI and what they thought was the irresponsible role of the press in helping to give them a voice. For example, in an interview with Whitney Young, director of the Urban League, Young stated that one of the problems that the "Negro Revolution" confronted had to do with "the inability of the white person to distinguish significant Negro leadership." The white press in particular had a "great preoccupation" with would-be leaders like Malcolm. "Instead of talking about Whitney Young, let's play up the Black Muslims." Ironically, Malcolm leveled the same charge against the civil rights establishment at the time of his interview. "I don't think that anyone has been created more by the white press than the civil rights leaders," he said. Warren's volume was aptly titled, reflecting many of the critical questions the conflict between Malcolm, Elijah Muhammad, and *Muhammad Speaks* had pointed up. The book was "about to go on press" when Malcolm was killed, Warren wrote.[4]

Some members of the white press also recognized the kinds of issues Young had identified. It led them, along with some black journalists, to gather at the University of Missouri's School of Journalism in November 1965. Titled "The Racial Crisis and the News Media," the three-day conference brought together more than seventy-five journalists, representing, for example, the *Los Angeles Times*, the *Chicago Daily News*, *Life* magazine, the *New York Times*, the *Norfolk Journal and Guide*, and CBS News. "The racial crisis has presented news media with new problems regarding techniques, especially those involving the medium of television," they asserted. One problem rested on their coverage of black leaders. "A Negro 'leader' can be created overnight by the media if he makes statements that are extreme and sensational enough," one journalist complained, alluding to Malcolm, as well as the influence of the NOI's sensational rhetoric that underpinned its robust media campaign. "Playing up such sensationalists out of all proportion to their worth or meaning to the Negro revolution could lead to an unwitting fragmentation of the real Negro leadership," another added.[5] They proposed a set of "Guidelines for Newsmen," recommending that more black newspapermen be recruited to the "totally 'white'" press and that journalists "distinguish between the authentic and the 'phony' Negro leader" and "exercise caution in giving advance publicity to professional bigots and hatemongers of all races," among other things. Thomas Young, editor of the *Journal and Guide*, commended the black press on this score, however. "The Negro publisher knows who the Negro leaders are, the sources and the extent of their strength. The Negro press does not invent or create community leaders," he stated. "In that way, it is helping to prevent a proliferation of spokesmen and chieftains eager to lead a march at the drop of a hat or the click of a newsman's camera. Appraising Negro leaders is a responsibility that the Negro press takes seriously. The white press— and that includes radio and television—must assume its share of this responsibility," Young admonished.[6]

Social critic Harold Cruse also saw the sensationalism of certain black leaders in promoting the black freedom struggle that other observers had noticed, though differently. He asserted in his study *The Crisis of the Negro Intellectual* (1967) that activists and even the black press had not been revolutionary enough, too often advancing revolutionary rhetoric and slogans that obscured conservative tendencies that ultimately hampered truly revolutionary visions for racial advancement. The title of Cruse's work distilled the challenges now facing black leaders and their efforts in racial uplift just as much as Warren's had. But Cruse concluded that Malcolm was "the last outstanding leader," and perhaps for all of his exposure in the press, he was still misunderstood.[7]

To some extent, Sengstacke worked to keep pace with these developments and the crisis it appeared to unleash.[8] In fact, in 1966, he was optimistic about the future of the black press and its ability to address these issues. "In the jungle of unrelieved segregation, the voice of the Negro editor was strident and strong," he editorialized, recounting a glowing version of the halcyon days of black newspapers. "In the course of the post-Emancipation history, it was the Negro press which directed its efforts toward lifting the American black man out of the muck of subjugation," he waxed poetic. "Now a new day is upon us. And the question of the role of the Negro press once more comes to the fore." Sengstacke embraced the critical questions and challenges before the black freedom struggle and black newspapers as he had done during the Depression era. The "Racial Conference and the News Media" gathering signified the inroads racial issues had increasingly made into the white press and broader society, and in many ways, away from the domain of the black press. Yet, at the time, Sengstacke praised this change.

For Sengstacke, black newspapers had been one of the leading forces that fought hard for integration and racial equality, and that the walls of segregation were beginning to crumble testified to the successful work of the black press, as well as the possibilities of its future. Sengstacke thought that the "Negro press will function just as well in an integrated society as it has in the segregated community." "Its function, however, will not be to agitate for the removal of the impediments to full citizenship, for that issue will have been resolved. Its main role will be to seek a refinement of those instruments that keep the democratic process viable and vibrant," a hopeful Sengstacke declared.[9] This vision was a far cry from the global black liberation struggle that Malcolm had imagined for the black press toward the end of his life, and what some black radicals and their papers were promoting in revolutionary tones. But given that Sengstacke's influence and business leadership had attracted the support of some white leaders, he may have had a point about the prospects of integration for black people and their newspapers. For instance, in February 1968, the Illinois Academy of Criminology invited Sengstacke to speak on the urban rebellions of 1967. Three months later, the Illinois Commission for Economic Development, headed by state senator Arthur R. Gottschalk, wanted him to speak to their upcoming meeting on jobs and how to help "the ghettos of our urban areas."[10] Gottschalk had once publicly criticized the NOI.[11] Amid expanding black radicalism and urban unrest, Gottschalk was among many white leaders who now turned to black men like Sengstacke for "responsible" black male leadership. Sengstacke's model of black manhood, leadership, and publishing was cut from aspects of an era that may have seemed more familiar and more acceptable to white leaders like Gottschalk than that of men like Malcolm and the black militants his legacy helped inspire. Indeed, President-elect Richard Nixon followed Gottschalk by December 1968. Considering Sengstacke a "leader," Nixon tapped him to help in identifying "exceptional individuals" for his new administration.[12] Robert S. Abbott would have been proud.

Yet, perhaps to the chagrin of some of these white leaders, Sengstacke echoed some parts of the black radical argument.[13] The speech he gave to the Illinois Academy of Criminology indicated this, for example. Federal and local investigations into the urban rebellions of the 1960s were "couched in superb rhetoric," making "fascinating reading," but had a "common failing: they are long on pontifical deductions and short on the mechanics . . . for improving conditions." He was likely referring to the *Report of the National Advisory Commission on Civil Disorders* produced by the federally appointed Commission on Civil Disorders (also known as the Kerner Commission). Led by Otto Kerner, the governor of Illinois, the commission published the report in April 1968, declaring, "We are moving toward two societies, one black, one white—separate and unequal." But this growing racial gap was not "inevitable." It could be closed through a "commitment to national action—compassionate, massive, and sustained, backed by the resources of the most powerful and the richest nation on this earth. From every American it will require new attitudes, new understanding, and, above all, new will."[14] The report also criticized white media for helping exacerbate the racial divide, especially during the riots, by reporting "from the standpoint of a white man's world." It recommended that the white press hire more black journalists, "establish better lines of communication to their counterparts in the Negro press," and draw upon black newspapers as a resource "manned largely by people who live and work in the ghetto," which made the black press "a particularly useful source of information and guidance about activities in the black community." "To editors who say 'we have run thousands of inches on the ghetto which nobody reads' and to television executives who bemoan scores of underwatched documentaries, we say: find more ways of telling this story."[15]

For Sengstacke, such reports were compiled by "men with high ideals" but who "do not have the emotive feeling for that breed of black humanity whose ailments they are called upon to diagnose." He titled his speech "A Businessman Looks at Riots," showing that once again, for a time, Sengstacke merged the racial and economic politics of his moment with his entrepreneurial perspective. "Our present urban condition stems from a metropolitan system that concentrates the Negro and the poor in the inner city areas and maintains a suburban fringe bent on keeping relatively rich and untainted by the Negro and the poor." The exigencies of the riots demanded that the country mobilize its "human, material, and spiritual" resources no different than it had after the attack on Pearl Harbor, he said. And one way the country could start doing this was by "strengthening the fabric of Negro business," the "backbone" of any "thriving Negro community." Sengstacke's comments pointed to Nixon's campaign promises to empower black people through Black Capitalism, which some Black Power advocates endorsed.[16] However, there remained deeper problems at play that would require more than just a greater number of job opportunities for ghetto-dwellers. "The long years of social ostracism, of economic deprivation, rejection and segregation have created in the American black man a deep sense of inferiority complex—a malady that only a 'soul brother' can cure." He affirmed that "the Negro business . . . is better equipped psychologically to carry on the delicate task of economic, social as well as emotional rehabilitation of the black man."[17]

A decade later, however, Sengstacke was tired, visibly irritated, and even indignant, as evidenced in an interview he did with A. S. Doc Young, a black journalist, not too long after his fifth election to the helm of the NNPA.[18] The approaching crisis that observers noticed brewing years ago had palpably erupted, at least within the black press. Though the NNPA's membership had now grown to nearly 150 members, present challenges to black newspapers seemed to be taking a toll on Sengstacke. He had accepted his well-worn post as president reluctantly. He was the last man standing, so to speak, at least in the eyes of many black publishers, who wanted him to serve again in order to "straighten the organization [the NNPA] out," as he put it, in the ways that only he could apparently. "I founded the organization in 1940 and of all the publishers around today, they've got to ask me to come back." Perhaps he actually could fix the black press, given many of the professional capacities in which he had been leading. In addition to having built for himself an influential manly public image that reached social and political echelons as high as the president of the United States, he had grown the *Defender*'s publishing empire into several business ventures, including the ownership of ten papers and the founding of Amalgamated Publishers

Incorporated, a firm that managed advertising accounts for many black papers. Sengstacke had even purchased in 1965 one of the *Defender*'s long-time competitors, the *Pittsburgh Courier*. His *Daily Defender* was among only two daily black papers in the country, the other being the *Atlanta Daily World*. And not long before the interview took place, he had completed a business deal to get $50 million in state and federal funds to support the building of a new hospital in Chicago.[19] Clearly, Sengstacke was still a "'front' man," though his successful work in these areas had also made him "a little tired," he remarked in 1974.[20] Still, underlying these accomplishments was the fact that he had founded the NNPA after being groomed and trained by Abbott, the standard bearer of black journalism, who had helped inaugurate the modern black press. No one better than Sengstacke could recall his original goals in birthing the organization.

Sengstacke could also recall the "golden age" of the black press in serving as a powerful tool for black men's public vocalization and racial leadership that also shaped the leadership, rhetoric, and protest strategies of the twentieth-century black freedom struggle to construct and affirm a quest for black manhood. Here, Thomas Young's point that "the Negro press does not invent or create community leaders" was wrong. The black press did. It had created black male leaders, in particular, sometimes the publishers themselves, and elevated them and their manly visions for racial advancement before a vibrant black public sphere. At other times, it had helped destroy black male leaders and their visions through discursive contests of masculinity. The newly elected president could remember well this crucial role of black male publishers in being architects and amplifiers of an influential discourse and politics of black manhood intended to help restore black men to their rightful place as men. But Sengstacke believed that black publishers had now lost something. Ethel Payne, who wrote for the *Defender*, once described him as a "brooder."[21] The interviewer suggested that it was their "statesmanship" perhaps, a certain "quality of publishers, the past versus the present." Sengstacke agreed.[22]

"The NNPA is in trouble," he said bluntly. And the sources of the trouble were many. More local, community-based newspapers were giving mainstream black papers more and more competition. Indeed, in the 1970s, *Muhammad Speaks* and the *Black Panther* still held the lead over mainstream black papers.[23] In other areas, the mainstream black press was again struggling to attract white advertisers and penetrate newspaper stands in white areas. Sometimes a newspaper seller just "hides" the black papers at their newspaper stand, Sengstacke commented. Further, the white press had hired more talented black journalists away from the black press, as the "Racial Crisis and the News Media" and Kerner Commission had suggested, though few of these black journalists had decision-making positions. Sengstacke supported the hiring of black journalists by the white press, in fact, seeing it as a sign of racial progress. But he remained frustrated that the reverse was not also the case: "we [black newspapers] can't get into the white market."[24] Black newspapers were among many black institutions that were becoming casualties of integration, some of the unanticipated consequences of desegregation battles, as historian David S. Cecelski has noted, battles that much of the black press had helped promote.[25] And some black leaders had stopped supporting black newspapers, seeking publicity first through the white press. Only when a white-owned paper attacked them did they want a black paper to "run a headline on it" in their defense, Sengstacke argued, although they "don't even buy the doggone newspaper."[26] It seemed that dedicated readers like Cato Anderson were long gone. The optimism Sengstacke had in 1966 had gone too.

But other troubles in the black press stemmed from a younger generation of publishers and newspapermen, "young cats," as he put it, who "wouldn't do their homework." He had chastised his fellow newspapermen for distancing themselves from the black revolution, but he now distanced himself, at least rhetorically, from "those young publishers." Part of the reason he returned to the presidency was so that he could "use this term to develop some young people who can carry on the tradition of those who came before us." But they called him "old school." "I think these young people think that the world owes them something, and they don't want to do the labor that is necessary to accomplish themselves," he retorted. "I don't understand it. All of them are looking for money; well, fine, but you've got to work for money. I find that anything I've got, I had to work for. No. Nobody has given me anything." In many ways, Abbott gave him the *Defender*, but Sengstacke's emphasis on work here stemmed from his part in establishing a leadership of the paper all is his own over the years that had successfully grown the *Defender*'s empire and legacy. He deeply appreciated what his uncle had done for him and the race. And accepting the mantle of the black men who had solidified the black press in the same ways he had is what had escaped this young generation of publishers, he thought. "If you look at some of the newspapers today, when you consider the guys who started them, (you realize that) these guys today don't have the commitment of those guys who founded those newspapers and those who carried on after the founder passed. We just don't have the commitment."[27]

A nostalgic Sengstacke recalled the strong ties between black manhood and black media in what increasingly appeared to be a bygone era. Yet he also acknowledged, "We can't do the same thing that we did 20 years ago—as my uncle did in his time—because things have changed and we've got to change with the times." He was now around the same age Abbott was when his uncle began grooming him. Now, Sengstacke had been summoned in part to perform the same role of imparting to a new generation of black male publishers the imperatives of their position to the race, its models of proper black manhood and manly visions for racial advancement, past and present. This was the third time he had been elected to especially rescue the NNPA, and through it, black newspapers. But as this generation of newspapermen seemed to abandon these crucial foundations, Sengstacke struggled to fuse his entrepreneurial perspective with the exigencies of the racial politics of his current moment, as he had usually done. "It's a sad situation," but "I'm going to try once more," the senior publisher groaned. "You know, if they can't carry this thing on and I'm the only one who can save it then, hell, it may as well die."[28]

Notes

Abbreviations Used in Notes

ASFP   Abbott-Sengstacke Family Papers
MXC   The Malcolm X Collection
RFWP   Robert Franklin Williams Papers
UMC   Universal Negro Improvement Association Miscellaneous Collection

Introduction

1. *Courier*, "'Newspapers Should Take Up Race Leadership' Declares Baltimore Professor," June 4, 1927.

2. *Defender*, "'Make Men,' Rev. Austin Urges Air Audience in W. G. N. Noonday Sermon," December 7, 1935.

3. See, for instance, Gold, *Debates in the Digital Humanities*.

4. On racist pseudoscientific theories, see, for example, Frederickson, *Black Image in the White Mind*; Reverby, *Tuskegee's Truths*; Washington, *Medical Apartheid*; Barkan, *Retreat of Scientific Racism*. See also Chicago Commission on Race Relations, *Negro in Chicago*, 594.

5. See, for example, "Public Opinion in Race Relations," in Chicago Commission on Race Relations, *Negro in Chicago*, 436–596. See also Kerlin, *Voice of the Negro*, 3; Waters, *American Diary*, 266.

6. Lippmann, *Public Opinion*, 65, 220.

7. Detweiler, *Negro Press in the United States*, 79.

8. Detweiler, 236.

9. On social etiquette, see, for example, Kennedy, *Jim Crow Guide to the U.S.A.*; Doyle, *Etiquette of Race Relations*; Berrey, *Jim Crow Routine*.

10. See, for example, Rotundo, *American Manhood*; Kimmel, *Manhood in America*; Bederman, *Manliness and Civilization*; DiPiero, *White Men Aren't*; Estes, *I Am a Man!*.

11. See, for example, Gaines, *Uplifting the Race*.

12. See, for example, Summers, *Manliness and Its Discontents*; Hine and Jenkins, *Question of Manhood*; Wilder, *In the Company of Black Men*; Hornsby-Gutting, *Black Manhood*.

13. See, for example, Suggs, *P. B. Young, Newspaperman*, 9–10, 20–24.

14. Myrdal, *American Dilemma*, 908.

15. See, for instance, Tolnay and Beck, *Festival of Violence*; Wood, *Lynching and Spectacle*.

16. Oak, *Negro Newspaper*, 151–65; Detweiler, *Negro Press in the United States*, 132; Hill, *Who's Who in the American Negro Press*, 71–80. See also Gore, *Negro Journalism*, 27–32.

17. Quoted in Detweiler, *Negro Press in the United States*, 1.

18. See, for example, Kornweibel, *"Investigate Everything"*; Washburn, *Question of Sedition*.

19. See, for example, "Violence and Minority Media," in Nerone, *Violence against the Press*, 128–64. The southern black press was especially reluctant to protest militantly because threats of economic reprisals and violence were virtually certain to follow if it did. Consider the well-known instance of the white mob that destroyed the headquarters for Ida B. Wells's *Free Speech and Headlight* in Memphis, Tennessee, after she accused white business owners of motivating the lynching of three black men.

20. See, for instance, Rotundo, *American Manhood*; Kimmel, *Manhood in America*; Bederman, *Manliness and Civilization*. For histories of black manhood, see, for example, Summers, *Manliness and Its Discontents*; Wilder, *In the Company of Black Men*; Estes, *I Am a Man*; Hine and Jenkins, *Question of Manhood*; Williams, *Torchbearers of Democracy*; Buckner and Caster, *Fathers, Preachers, Rebels, Men*; Gilmore, *Gender and Jim Crow*.

21. Vogel, *Black Press*; "Editing and the Art of Forgetfulness in Social Science" and "Memory and Racial Humiliation in Popular Literature," in Holloway, *Jim Crow Wisdom*, 14–39, 40–66.

22. Kimmel, *Manhood in America*, ix. Here, I borrow from Kimmel, who argues that discourses on masculinity became widely articulated at the times in which there were perceived triumphs of and/or challenges to men's manhood, producing new ideas of men's masculinity, or reviving and/or reshaping old ones. See also Harper, *Are We Not Men?*, x.

23. Summers, *Manliness and Its Discontents*; Wilder, *In the Company of Black Men*; Estes, *I Am a Man*; Hine and Jenkins, *Question of Manhood*; Williams, *Torchbearers of Democracy*; Buckner and Caster, *Fathers, Preachers, Rebels, Men*; Gilmore, *Gender and Jim Crow*.

24. See Ross, *Manning the Race*, 1, 8. In my analyses of black male publishers, their newspapers, and the influence of both on different publics, I draw on Ross's insights that African American writings were "crucial sites of self-conscious theorizing on the concept of manhood" as well as his concerns about how black men were "marketed" and "have imagined and imaged themselves."

25. See also Michael Uebel, "Men in Color: Introducing Race and the Subject of Masculinities," in Stecopoulos and Uebel, *Race and the Subject of Masculinities*, 1–14. Uebel calls the consequences of the relationship between men of color's gendered subjectivities and their roles as historical actors "racial maleness." His concept of "identity politics" foregrounds the "effects of cultural forces on identities and the forms in which identities are imagined," and thus *racial maleness* becomes the "result and the potential agent" of the exchange between men's racial and gendered identities and their historical experiences.

26. See, for example, Brandt, *Harlem at War*; Miller, *Messman Chronicles*; Edgerton, *Hidden Heroism*; Williams, *Torchbearers of Democracy*.

27. See, for example, Pride and Wilson, *History of the Black Press*; Wolseley, *Black Press, USA*; Dann, *Black Press, 1827–1890*; Jordan, *Black Newspapers*; Simmons, *African American Press*; Finkle, *Forum for Protest*; Washburn, *African American Newspaper*; Farrar, *Baltimore Afro-American*; Suggs, *P. B. Young, Newspaperman*; Buni, *Robert L. Vann*; Michaeli, *Defender*; Booker, *Alone atop the Hill*; Morris, *Eyes on the Struggle*; Forss, *Black Print with a White Carnation*; Gardner, *Black Print Unbound*; Carrol, *Race News*; Gershenhorn, *Louis Austin and the* Carolina Times.

28. For examples of the part the black press played in responding to real and perceived attacks on black people, see Washburn, *African American Newspaper*; Simmons, *African American Press*; Jordan, *Black Newspapers*.

29. See, for example, Booker, *Alone atop the Hill*; Morris, *Eyes on the Struggle*; Forss, *Black Print with a White Carnation*. See also Streitmatter, *Raising Her Voice*.

30. For works on discourse theory and public spheres, see, for example, Foucault, *Archaeology of Knowledge*; Howarth and Torfing, *Discourse Theory in European Politics*; Foucault, *Discipline and Punish*; Habermas, *Structural Transformation of the Public Sphere*. On black public spheres, see, for example, Michael Huspek, "Transgressive Rhetoric in Deliberative Democracy: The Black Press," in Lacy and Ono, *Critical Rhetorics of Race*, 159–77; Catherine Squires, "The Black Press and the State: Attracting Unwanted(?) Attention," in Asen and Brouwer, *Counterpublics and the State*, 111–36; Savage, *Broadcasting Freedom*; Baker, "Critical Memory and the Black Public Sphere"; Fraser, "Rethinking the Public Sphere"; Black Public Sphere Collective, *Black Public Sphere*; Heitner, *Black Power TV*; Green, *Selling the Race*.

31. For example, see Hall, "Long Civil Rights Movement"; Sugrue, *Sweet Land of Liberty*; Theoharis and Woodard, *Freedom North*; Countryman, *Civil Rights and Black Power*; Biondi, *To Stand and Fight*; Gilmore, *Defying Dixie*; Murch, *Living for the City*.

32. For works that analyze the privileging of black men's leadership and plight at the expense of black women's, see, for example, Hine, *Hine Sight*; Kimberly Springer, "Black Feminists Respond to Black Power Masculinism," in Joseph, *Black Power Movement*, 105–18; Giddings, *When and Where I Enter*; Collier-Thomas and Franklin, *Sisters in the Struggle*; White, *Too Heavy a Load*; Gore et al., *Want to Start a Revolution?*; McGuire, *At the Dark End of the Street*.

33. Detweiler, *Negro Press in the United States*, 79–82; Oak, *Negro Newspaper*, 90.

34. Alfred Arteaga, "Foreword: The Red and the Black," in Aldama, *Violence and the Body*, vii–viii; "Turning White Space into Black Space," in Mullen, *Popular Fronts*, 44–74; Vogel, *Black Press*; Holloway, *Jim Crow Wisdom*, 22.

35. Oak, *Negro Newspaper*, 29.

36. Gore, *Negro Journalism*, 26. See also Muhammad, *Condemnation of Blackness*, 94–96.

37. See, for example, Fredrickson, *Black Image in the White Mind*; Detweiler, *Negro Press in the United States*, 11–12, 23; Oak, *Negro Newspaper*, 22. Hill, *Who's Who in the American Negro Press*, 50. See also Chicago Commission on Race Relations, *Negro in Chicago*, 497–98.

38. On these points, see, for example, Vogel, *Black Press*; Kreiling, "Making of Racial Identities."

39. See, for example, Hine and McCluskey, *Black Chicago Renaissance*; Guzman, *Black Writing from Chicago*; De Santis, *Langston Hughes and the* Chicago Defender; Dowd, *Negro in American Life*, 352. See also Kaye, "Colonel Roscoe Conkling Simmons." Consider also periodicals like the *Opportunity*, which regularly featured black literary work. See Wilson, *Opportunity Reader*.

40. "The Inside Story of the Chicago Defender 'World's Greatest Weekly,'" 1938, ASFP, box 11, fol. 7. A booklet titled "33 Years of Progress" said that "in order for our readers to get the news in first-class condition, photographs, drawings, entertaining and instructive features and cartoons, must be added to illustrate these news stories—all of which requires skill and effective coordination of each department." See also Eneil F. Simpson to Nathan K. McGill, August 23, 1933, ASFP, box 11, fol. 2. Simpson spoke of creating a "vigorous editorial campaign . . . in giving the utmost of re-employment to those our group" during the Depression and particular struggles the *Defender* faced at that time, as well as how to best present the layout of *Abbott's Monthly*, one of Abbott's journalistic ventures in the 1930s. "It is my belief that the present makeup," he wrote, "should be changed completely and instead of a 64-page magazine-finished book, we edit and compile a 32-page tabloid to sell at 5 cent per copy retail, printed solely in black and white ink with stories of a 'racketeer and sensational' type that would appeal to the lower masses and be of an understandable nature. The entire publication could be handled in our own Composing room and on our own presses with very little expense attached thereto." See also Gore, *Negro Journalism*, 15–16; Hill, *Who's Who in the American Negro Press*.

41. See Streitmatter, *Raising Her Voice*; Bass, *Forty Years*; Bates, *Long Shadow of Little Rock*; Booker, *Alone atop the Hill*; Morris, *Eyes on the Struggle*; Forss, *Black Print with a White Carnation*; Freer, "L.A. Race Woman"; see also Streitmatter, *Raising Her Voice*, 91. My point here is not to suggest that the "Woman's Page" or women's news was not serious news or politically and culturally important. It was, and historians Kim Gallon and Ula Y. Taylor, for example, have shown this. My intent here is to point out that in many cases, what was considered "serious news" at the time was usually handled by black men journalists. Streitmatter's book highlights notable black women journalists by profiling the careers of eleven women. Yet his book also demonstrates the paucity of black women journalists, who had opportunities to excel in the field and cover a range of issues. See also Gallon, "Silences Kept"; Taylor, *Veiled Garvey*.

42. Waters, *American Diary*, 149, 134–36, 154.

43. Waters, 266.

44. Bass, *Forty Years*; Forss, *Black Print with a White Carnation*, 2. Forss writes that Brown "holds the record for operating the longest-running black newspaper founded by a black woman in the United States," whereas "all the other twentieth century's black women newspaper owners inherited their weeklies from their husbands."

45. See Carby, *Race Men*, 5–6, 10–12. See also Cooper, *Beyond Respectability*; "Some Interesting Facts about a Great Newspaper," ASFP, box 11, fol. 4. This pro-

motional pamphlet for the *Defender* delineated "Why Men Prefer the *Chicago Defender*," based on sports coverage, editorials, and "timely topics of the day." "Why Women Prefer the *Chicago Defender*" involved news on "society" and "clubs."

46. For an example of the ways in which conceptions of black womanhood were articulated within a masculine framework, see Wolcott, *Remaking Respectability*.

47. Though conceptions of black men's manhood may have been different from conceptions of white men's manhood, the scholarship on black manhood has pointed out that black men argued not for a subversion of manhood as an idea or a factor in American life, but perhaps what Michael Kimmel calls a "democratic manhood," the idea that nonwhite men should be included and permitted to participate in the social, cultural, and political structures that allowed white men to express their manhood freely. Along these lines, black men's construction of black manhood contained an assent to patriarchy. See "Epilogue: Toward Democratic Manhood," in Kimmel, *Manhood in America*, 254–57.

48. Though one of the first studies on the black press, Penn, *Afro-American Press and Its Editors* appeared in 1891, I am referring here to the studies that began analyzing the twentieth-century black press around the 1920s. See, for example, Kerlin, *Voice of the Negro*; Detweiler, *Negro Press in the United States*; Gore, *Negro Journalism*; Gordon, "Negro Press." Others followed in ensuing decades. See, for example, Fleming, "108 Years of the Negro Press"; Detweiler, "Negro Press Today"; Young, "Objective Reader Interest Study"; Durr, *Negro Press*; Oak, *Negro Newspaper*; Pride, "Negro Newspapers." However, Salmon's encyclopedic studies of newspapers in the United States, providing a "sufficient number of examples," barley considered the black press though black newspapers were becoming a force among black Americans by the time of her studies. See Salmon, *Newspaper and the Historian*; and Salmon, *Newspaper and Authority*.

49. Kerlin, *Voice of the Negro*, v, ix–x.

50. Detweiler, *Negro Press in the United States*, 102, 126.

51. Quoted in Detweiler, *Negro Press in the United States*, 2–3.

52. Dowd, *Negro in American Life*, 353–54. See also Chicago Commission on Race Relations, *Negro in Chicago*, 558–60.

53. See, for instance, "Critical Evaluation of the Negro Newspaper (Unfavorable)" and "Suggestions for Improvement," in Oak, *Negro Newspaper*, 43–64, 133–37.

54. Detweiler, *Negro Press in the United States*, 76. See also Oak, *Negro Newspaper*, 28.

55. Gore, *Negro Journalism*, 21, 26, 35; Suggs, *P. B. Young, Newspaperman*, 9.

56. Oak, *Negro Newspaper*, 23–24; Hill, *Who's Who in the American Negro Press*, 40–41, 48.

57. See, for example, Robert S. Abbott to Emmett J. Scott, May 5, 1918, ASFP, box 8, fol. 29. In a letter asking for Scott's help in keeping members of his staff from being drafted into World War I, Abbott said that he had "exerted every possible effort to fully train them in all events to master details of journalism." See also Burns, *Nitty Gritty*, 3–4, 6, 10–13; Booker with Booker, *Shocking the Conscience*, 26, 38.

58. "Sensationalism, as a Major Criticism of the American Negro Press," in Hill, *Who's Who in the American Negro Press*, 50–56; "Critical Evaluation of the Negro

Newspaper (Unfavorable)," in Oak, *Negro Newspaper*, 43–64. See also Booker, *Shocking the Conscience*, 38.

59. Waters, *American Diary*, 232.

60. See, for example, Albert Kreiling, "The Commercialization of the Black Press and the Rise of Race News in Chicago," in Solomon and McChesney, *Ruthless Criticism*, 176–203.

61. Hill, *Who's Who in the American Negro Press*, 56.

62. Gallon, "Silences Kept."

63. Ottley, *New World A-Coming*, 280. See, for example, *Defender*, "Lost Manhood!," July 11, 1936; *Defender*, "Manhood Loss?," May 30, 1936; *Defender*, "Pure Herbs," October 9, 1920. See also Detweiler, *Negro Press in the United States*, 113–14, 122–26; Hill, *Who's Who in the American Negro Press*, 49; Oak, *Negro Newspaper*, 25; Davis, *Commerce in Color*, 175, 179.

64. See, for example, "Negro Press," in Myrdal, *American Dilemma*, 911. Myrdal wrote that the black press "defines the Negro group to the Negro themselves," having "created the Negro group as a social and psychological reality to the individual Negro" as the "chief agency of group control," suggesting that black readers were uncritical consumers, who patronized the black press because it "tells the individual how he should think and feel as an American Negro." But readers did not consume black papers because they told them what to think and feel. This they already knew how to do without the press. Rather, they consumed black papers because the papers often reflected what they thought and felt.

65. Detweiler, *Negro Press in the United States*, 103. See also "Some Interesting Facts about a Great Newspaper," ASFP, box 11, fol. 4. This promotional pamphlet on the part of the *Defender* showed the ways in which editors and writers for the paper thought very deliberately about how to attract and keep men, women, and children readers to the paper.

66. Oak, *Negro Newspaper*, 25.

67. Samuel Piggsford to Robert S. Abbott, August 8, 1934, ASFP, box 8, fol. 10.

68. Clifford, *Experience of Reading*, 16, 198.

69. Chiasso, *Press in Times of Crisis*, x; Benton and Frazier, "Agenda-Setting Function of Mass Media"; Protess and McCombs, *Agenda Setting*.

70. The black press's historic "Double V" campaign, launched by the *Pittsburgh Courier* during World War II, is probably the best-known example of this. Many of the critical racial issues that black people were trying to address then, particularly the March on Washington movement, the right of black soldiers to fight in combat positions without having to be segregated in the U.S. Army, and the right to work in defense industries unencumbered by racial discrimination—were boiled down into a pithy but provocative phrase: "Double Victory," a victory against fascism abroad and a victory against racial injustice at home. The paper took the phrase from the words of James G. Thompson, a black male reader working in a war industry. This illustrated how the black press provided a forum for black writers, thinkers, and publics to engage one another, as well as the ways in which there existed a special dialogue between black male readers and black male publishers. See also Vogel, *Black Press*. These agendas and their mutability over time point to what Vogel's

volume argues, that the black press was a "cultural production," in which, in its broader social context, one can observe "writers forming and reforming ideologies, creating and recreating a public sphere, and staging and restaging race itself. See also "Introduction," in Hutton, *Early Black Press in America*, ix–xviii; Kerlin, *Voice of the Negro*, 23; Finkle, *Forum for Protest*, 17–39; Ottley, *Lonely Warrior*, 126–27. For examples of these lists, see Detweiler, *Negro Press in the United States*, 107, 146. For examples in the *Defender*, see "American Race Prejudice Must Be Destroyed," August 25, 1928; "Renews Fight for U.S. Antilynching Law: Chicago *Defender* in Nation-Wide Drive," November 25, 1933; "Robert S. Abbott, 1870 1940," April 6, 1940.

71. See, for example, Mitchell, *Righteous Propagation*; Gaines, *Uplifting the Race.*

72. Kerlin, *Voice of the Negro*, v, ix–x.

73. See also Detweiler, *Negro Press in the United States*, 203; and Oak, *Negro Newspaper*, 17. Detweiler argued that "the deepest interest in the Negro press will spring from a desire to see as clearly and as intimately as possible the life there mirrored. . . . It must not be forgotten, of course, that no white man will be as greatly interested in journalistic glimpses of Negro life as the colored man himself will be. . . . Pictures, descriptions, and reports of others like himself are in demand." Yet Oak suggested that "the newspapers of today do not necessarily reflect public opinion and that what is normally passed on by them as such is often the reflection of the thinking of their editors or publishers." I argue that both were the case, and in fact formed a dialogic relationship.

Chapter 1

1. Lester, *Seventh Son*, 24. See also Carby, *Race Men*, 9–10.

2. Abbott started Hampton in 1890. See *Defender*, "Quest for Equality," Installment 3, March 30, 1940.

3. Abbott to Mr. Armstrong, June 6, 1888, ASFP, box 10, fol. 7; and lodging receipts in ASFP, box 6, fol. 2; *Defender*, "Quest for Equality," Installment 5, April 13, 1940.

4. Hornsby-Gutting, *Black Manhood*, 17–18.

5. Carby, *Race Men*, 25, 34.

6. For more on the Great Migration, see Gregory, *Southern Diaspora*; Grossman, *Land of Hope*; Trotter, *Great Migration in Historical Perspective*; Scott, *Negro Migration during the War*; Henri, *Black Migration*; Painter, *Exodusters*; Woodson, *Century of Negro Migration.*

7. Quoted in Suggs, *P. B. Young, Newspaperman*, 34–36.

8. Quoted in Simmons, *African American Press*, 37.

9. Quoted in Gregory, *Southern Diaspora*, 47.

10. Simmons, *African American Press*, 32.

11. "The Exodus," *Crisis* 14, no. 1 (May 1917).

12. *Defender*, "Somebody Lied," October 7, 1916.

13. On racist pseudoscientific theories, see, for example, Frederickson, *Black Image in the White Mind*; Reverby, *Tuskegee's Truths*; Washington, *Medical Apartheid*; Barkan, *Retreat of Scientific Racism.*

14. Logan, *Negro in American Life and Thought*.

15. See, for example, Gaines, *Uplifting the Race*, 29–31, 52. For the "nadir" of gender relations, historians Michelle Mitchell and Glenda Gilmore, for example, have shown the post-Emancipation and Jim Crow eras posed racial *and* gendered challenges to black Americans. Here, I borrow from Logan's oft-quoted phrase the "nadir" in order to speak to a "nadir of gender relations," or the deep intersections of race, gender, and politics at the time, and how those intersections negatively affected race relations and the lives of African Americans. See Mitchell, *Righteous Propagation*; and Gilmore, *Gender and Jim Crow*.

16. "The First Step in Nation Making" and "The Dilemmas of Nation Making," in White, *Too Heavy a Load*, 21–55, 56–86. Journalist, civil rights activists, vocal member of the National Association of Colored Women, and crusader against lynching Ida B. Wells was especially a leader in this regard. See, for example, Patricia A. Schecter, "Unsettled Business: Ida B. Wells against Lynching, or, How Antilynching Got Its Gender," in Brundage, *Under Sentence of Death*, 292–317.

17. Hornsby-Gutting, *Black Manhood*. See also Giddings, *When and Where I Enter*, 113–17.

18. Gaines, *Uplifting the Race*, 43–99. See also Carle, *Defining the Struggle*.

19. Washburn, *African American Newspaper*, 73–77.

20. Scott, *Negro Migration during the War*, 49.

21. Gregory, *Southern Diaspora*, 26.

22. For more on the nineteenth-century black press, see, for example, Pride and Wilson, *History of the Black Press*; Dann, *Black Press, 1827–1890*; Simmons, *African American Press*; Gardner, *Black Print Unbound*.

23. Grossman, *Land of Hope*, 66–97, 3–4.

24. See, for example, Gaines, *Uplifting the Race*.

25. Gaines, *Uplifting the Race*, 72. For more on this point, see "Urban Pathology and the Limits of Social Research: W. E. B. DuBois' The Philadelphia Negro," in Gaines, *Uplifting the Race*, 152–78.

26. Ovington, *Half a Man*, 1, 74, 88, 92.

27. DuBois, *Philadelphia Negro*. For another example of these studies, see Kelly Miller, *Race Adjustment*.

28. "Going over Niagara," in Lewis, *W. E. B. Dubois: Biography*, 297–342.

29. Aptheker, *Writings in Periodicals*, vii.

30. DuBois, *Dusk of Dawn*, 94, 268.

31. Aptheker, *Correspondence of W. E. B. DuBois*, 2:45. See also DuBois, *Darkwater*, 49.

32. DuBois, *Dusk of Dawn*, 94, 92.

33. Aptheker, *Writings and Periodicals*, viii; DuBois, *Dusk of Dawn*, 92–93. It should be noted that some NAACP officials initially resisted DuBois's efforts to create a paper for the organization. See Rudwick, *W. E. B. DuBois*, 150–51. Over the years, this resistance continued. See also Rudwick, *W. E. B. DuBois*, 165. See also Dan S. Green, "W. E. B. DuBois: His Journalistic Career," in Tinney and Rector, *Issues and Trends*, 61–85.

34. Marable, *W. E. B. DuBois*, 75, 84.

35. Quoted in Tinney and Rector, *Issues and Trends*, 64.

36. See also Kirschke and Sinitiere, *Protest and Propaganda*, 2.

37. "The Crisis," *Crisis* 1, no. 1 (November 1910).

38. DuBois, *Autobiography of W. E. B. DuBois*, 256.

39. DuBois, *Dusk of Dawn*, 226; Dan S. Green, "W. E. B. DuBois: His Journalistic Career," in Tinney and Rector, *Issues and Trends*, 62–63, 65.

40. Aptheker, *Documentary History*, 39.

41. DuBois, *Dusk of Dawn*, 226, 293. See also Rudwick, *W. E. B. DuBois*, 176.

42. DuBois, *Dusk of Dawn*, 226–28.

43. See "The Crisis," *Crisis* 1, no. 1 (November 1910); "Emigration to Canada," *Crisis* 2, no. 1 (May 1911). Yet it should be noted that the *Crisis*'s endorsement of the early stages of the migration came at a time when black professionals were mostly the ones moving northward, a demographic that fulfilled DuBois's desires for a social and political movement among the "Talented Tenth." See "The Migration of the Talented Tenth," in Woodson, *Century of Negro Migration*, 147–66.

44. DuBois, *Dusk of Dawn*, 258, 294.

45. Lewis, *W. E. B. DuBois, 1919–1963*, 2, 19, 25. See also "Rise of the Crisis, Decline of the Wizard," in Lewis, *W. E. B. DuBois: Biography*. See also DuBois, *Dusk of Dawn*, 293.

46. Scholars Hazel V. Carby and Monica L. Miller have made powerful arguments about DuBois's "dandyism," or how he used a certain style of clothing to represent himself as an intellectual and modern black man fit for proper and manly racial leadership. But examining DuBois's editorship of the *Crisis* as a claim on racial leadership reveals and complicates his intent to represent manly leadership through a range of influential public medias that included clothing and the *Crisis*. See Carby, *Race Men*, 21–23; and "W. E. B. DuBois' 'Different' Diasporic Race Man," in Miller, *Slaves to Fashion*, 137–75. See also "W. E. B. DuBois as Print Propagandist," in Kirschke and Sinitiere, *Protest and Propaganda*, 28–48; see also DuBois, *Dusk of Dawn*, 282–83.

47. Zuckerman, *Social Theory of W. E. B. DuBois*, 185.

48. "World War One and David Wark Griffith," in Nesteby, *Black Images in American Films*, 27–42. See also Wallace-Sanders, *Skin Deep Spirit Strong*; Fredrickson, *Black Image in the White Mind*; "Birth of a Cultural Strategy" and "Du Bois's *Crisis* and the Black Image on the Page," in Woodley, *Art for Equality*, 11–34, 63–96.

49. "The Souls of Black Men," in Carby, *Race Men*, 9–41.

50. "The Crisis," *Crisis* 1, no. 1 (November 1910).

51. See, for example, Scott, *Negro Migration during the War*, 29–33; Washburn, *African American Newspaper*, 111; Simmons, *African American Press*, 32.

52. "The Migration of Negroes," *Crisis* 14, no. 2 (June 1917). See also Robert W. Williams, "W. E. B. DuBois and Positive Propaganda: A Philosophical Prelude to His Editorship of the Crisis," in Kirschke and Sinitiere, *Protest and Propaganda*, 16–27.

53. Gregory, *Southern Diaspora*, 128. See also "The Greater Crisis," *Crisis* 16, no. 5 (September 1918). See also DuBois, *Dusk of Dawn*, 258.

54. Anderson, *Agitations*, 44–45. See also Rudwick, *W. E. B. DuBois*, 152.

55. *Defender*, "Quest for Equality," Installment 1, March 16, 1940; "John H. Seng-stacke III: America's Black Press Lord," ASFP, box 22, fol. 9, p. 13. See also Michaeli, *Defender*, 5, 16.

56. For more on a discussion of the out-migration of black professionals in the later nineteenth and early twentieth centuries, see Gaines, *Uplifting the Race*, 24; and "The Migration of the Talented Tenth," in Woodson, *Century of Negro Migration*, 147–66.

57. *Defender*, "Quest for Equality," Installment 6, April 20, 1940.

58. *Defender*, "A Recapitulation of 25 Years Work: Editor Robt. S. Abbott's Story of Early Struggles and Success of the World's Greatest Weekly," *Defender*, May 3, 1930; Waters, *American Diary*, 113.

59. *Defender*, "Quest for Equality," Installment 7, April 27, 1940.

60. "A Bit about Chicago: Where to Go What to See How to Get There," ASFP, box 11, fol. 1.

61. Butler, *Entrepreneurship and Self-Help*, 64–71. See also Green, *Selling the Race*; and Gaines, *Uplifting the Race*.

62. *Defender*, "The Chicago Defender's Salutation to Its Readers," December 26, 1908, reprinted May 3, 1930. Interestingly enough, Abbott had the help of a small staff that he had assembled under his employ by 1907. For a discussion of some of Abbott's staff, see Albert Kreiling, "The Commercialization of the Black Press and the Rise of Race News in Chicago," in Solomon and McChesney, *Ruthless Criticism*, 179–82. See also Ottley, *Lonely Warrior*, 95. See *Defender*, "Editor Robt. S. Abbott's Story of Early Struggles and Success of . . . the World's Greatest Weekly," May 3, 1930. Abbott explained that when "the struggle to manage all the departments of [the *Defender*], which had extended its activities in so many fields, had reached the point where help in the management of it was necessary," he "decided to look around for a man competent to take over the task." See also Waters, *American Diary*, 136.

63. "The Struggle for Homes and Jobs," in Spear, *Black Chicago*, 147–66.

64. Abbott likely admired Washington. See, for example, *Defender*, "Black Men Founders of Civilization," November 27, 1915; *Defender*, "Washington and Dubois," February 27, 1915. See also *Defender*, Quest for Equality, Installment 6, April 20, 1940. Like Washington, Abbott attended Hampton and imbibed its educational philosophy of industrial training. He wrote, "[Hampton's] stressing of industrial training for a race that had just emerged from slavery was, to my mind a very important and necessary step."

65. Grossman, *Land of Hope*, 82.

66. Quoted in Grossman, *Land of Hope*, 81. See also *Defender*, "Making Good Employees," July 31, 1915.

67. Spear, *Black Chicago*, 81.

68. Gaines, *Uplifting the Race*, 21. For more on Washington along these lines, see Gaines, 37–41. As Gaines shows, this approach to race progress formed one component of a broader strategy of racial advancement expressed and promoted as "uplift" in the early twentieth century, a complex, class-based ideology that Washington and his critics both advocated as they grappled with the new racial order. For more on Washington and his ideology, see, for example, Smock, *Booker T. Washington*;

Cunnigen et al., *Racial Politics of Booker T. Washington*; Brundage, *Booker T. Washington and Black Progress*; Verney, *Art of the Possible*.

69. Gaines, *Uplifting the Race*, 63.

70. Suggs, *P. B. Young, Newspaperman*, 34–36.

71. Gaines, *Uplifting the Race*, 63. See also Aptheker, *Documentary History of the Negro People*, 848–51, 877–86; DuBois, *Dusk of Dawn*, 94.

72. DuBois, *Souls of Black Folk*, 40–42. See also Carby, *Race Men*, 39–41.

73. DuBois, *Dusk of Dawn*, 86, 93–94; Dan S. Green, "W. E. B. DuBois: His Journalistic Career," in Tinney and Rector, *Issues and Trends*, 63–64.

74. Litwack, *Trouble in Mind*, 429. See also Simmons, *African American Press*, 65–67.

75. Gaines, *Uplifting the Race*, 60–66; *Voice of the Negro*, 2, 33.

76. Gaines, *Uplifting the Race*, 41–46; Washburn, *African American Newspaper*, 69. See also "The Platform, the Pamphlet, and the Press: Ida B. Wells's Pedagogy of American Lynching," in Zackodnik, *Press, Platform, Pulpit*, 131–66.

77. Gregory, *Southern Diaspora*, 14.

78. Though it seemed more concerned with black southerners' movement to the North, the *Defender* acknowledged that black southerners were also going west, as well as immigrating to Africa. See *Defender*, "Negroes Fleeing Southern Plantations for West," January 28, 1911, and *Defender*, "Predicts Exodus of Race," February 19, 1916; Grossman, *Land of Hope*, 13–19, 37; Scott, *Negro Migration during the War*, 14–16.

79. "The Immediate Program of the American Negro," *Crisis* 9, no. 6 (April 1915). It is important to note, as Grossman has argued, that labor agents, informal networks of communication among black southerners, and the reality of life for blacks in the South were motivating factors enough with or without the black press. The death of Washington in November 1915 was also significant, representing for some a symbolic end to the policy that blacks should remain in the South. The *Crisis* celebrated "what this great figure gave of good," while "silently rejecting all else." "Let the Negro race," continued the *Crisis*, "march steadily on, determined as never before . . . [for] . . . the right to vote, the right to know, and the right to stand as men among men throughout the world." See "Booker T. Washington," *Crisis* 2, no. 3 (December 1915).

80. Grossman, *Land of Hope*, 16. See also Gregory, *Southern Diaspora*, 45.

81. Kimmel, *Manhood in America*, 103. According to Kimmel, the ideal of the self-made man was a popular one in both the eighteenth and nineteenth centuries, though whites constructed the ideal as a white man in particular that was "frugal and productive," while black men were seen as the contrary, embodying "laziness and license." Abbott's emulation of the ideal of the self-made man shows not only how the image and ideal of the self-made man prevailed among some black men but also how the ideal was used by black men to show the industriousness of black men and the race.

82. Burns, *Nitty Gritty*, 4.

83. Campbell, *Yellow Journalism*, 8–12, 38–39.

84. Washburn, *African American Press*, 83; Ottley, *Lonely Warrior*, 104–6.

85. "The Printed Page, Racial Style," in Ottley, *Lonely Warrior,* 121–39.

86. Grossman, *Land of Hope,* 82–83; Washburn, *African American Press,* 89.

87. Gregory, *Southern Diaspora,* 51.

88. Washburn, *African American Press,* 97–98.

89. Gregory, *Southern Diaspora,* 126; Kornweibel, *"Investigate Everything,"* 120. See also Chicago Commission on Race Relations, *Negro in Chicago,* 564.

90. Ottley, *Lonely Warrior,* 106; see also Waters, *American Diary,* 169.

91. Detweiler, *Negro Press in the United States,* 60–61.

92. DuBois, *Autobiography,* 257.

93. Quoted in Rudwick, *W. E. B. DuBois,* 168. See also Rudwick's discussion of the spat between DuBois and black publishers that followed those comments. See also Schuyler, *Black and Conservative,* 228.

94. Quoted in Scott, *Negro Migration during the War,* 32. See also "Stimulation of the Movement," in Scott, *Negro Migration during the War,* 26–37.

95. Gallon, "Silences Kept."

96. *Defender,* "A Recapitulation of 25 Years Work: Editor Robt. S. Abbott's Story of Early Struggles and Success of the World's Greatest Weekly," May 3, 1930.

97. Baldwin, *Chicago's New Negroes,* 29, 44–52, 195–204.

98. "The Dilemmas of Nation Making," in White, *Too Heavy a Load,* 56–86; see also Hornsby-Gutting, *Black Manhood,* 17–18.

99. *Defender,* "Unenforced Laws," October 14, 1916.

100. For an analysis on the significance of this case to American race relations and blacks' relationship to the law, see, for example, Fehrenbacher, *Dred Scott Case*; and Fehrenbacher, *Slavery, Law, and Politics.*

101. Scott, *Negro Migration during the War,* 19–20.

102. Black land ownership, a vehicle for black individual uplift and autonomy, grew tremendously immediately following the Civil War, but dropped precipitously along with blacks' incomes by the time of the migration. See Manning Marable, "The Politics of Black Land Tenure, 1877–1915," in Hine and Jenkins, *Question of Manhood,* 131–37.

103. Patricia A. Schecter, "Unsettled Business: Ida B. Wells against Lynching, or, How Antilynching Got Its Gender," in Brundage, *Under Sentence of Death,* 294–310. On social etiquette, see, for example, Kennedy, *Jim Crow Guide to the U.S.A.*; Doyle, *Etiquette of Race Relations,* 137. Doyle argued that whites used racial etiquette as a form of social control against blacks. Doyle asserted that following emancipation, "laws were passed to enforce what had, prior to emancipation, enforced itself, namely, a code of etiquette in race relations." See also Berrey, *Jim Crow Routine.*

104. Litwack, *Trouble in Mind,* 4, 8, 10; Gilmore, *Gender and Jim Crow,* 3. Consider also how whites did not call black men "Sir" or "Mister," and instead called them "uncle" or "boy." Whites referred to black women as "auntie" and "girl," hardly ever "Miss" or "Mrs." "Sir," "Mister," "Miss," and "Mrs." were terms of respectability reserved only for white men and women.

105. *Defender,* "One White Man's Nigger and Two Southern Editors," December 30, 1916.

106. Though black women were also lynched, black men were lynched far more often and for reasons that buttressed the tenets of white supremacy that commonly accused black men of sexually molesting or raping white women. Brundage, *Lynching in the New South*, 80. See also Feimster, *Southern Horrors*; Kris DuRocher, "Violent Masculinity: Learning Ritual and Performance in Southern Lynchings," in Friend, *Southern Masculinity*, 47; Robyn Wiegman, "The Anatomy of Lynching," in Hine and Jenkins, *Question of Manhood*, 349–69.

107. Kris DuRocher, "Violent Masculinity: Learning Ritual and Performance in Southern Lynchings," in Friend, *Southern Masculinity*, 56, 59.

108. Patricia A. Schecter, "Unsettled Business: Ida B. Wells against Lynching, or, How Antilynching Got Its Gender," in Brundage, *Under Sentence of Death*, 294.

109. Scott, *Negro Migration during the War*, 22. Scott found that "both whites and negroes in mentioning the reasons for the movement generally give lynching as one of the most important causes and state that the fear of the mob has greatly accelerated the exodus."

110. *Defender*, "Big Dailies Worried by Recent Migration," March 24, 1917.

111. Quoted in Grossman, *Land of Hope*, 75; *Defender*, "Why They Leave South," January 6, 1917; "The South and the Negro," February 24, 1917; "Would Stop Exodus; Forget Lynchings," July 28, 1917; "One Reason!," September 30, 1916.

112. *Defender*, "Remember This Scene Tuesday," November 4, 1916; "White Men and Party Held," March 24, 1917; *Defender*, "Unenforced Laws," October 14, 1916.

113. Quoted in Simmons, *African American Press*, 33. See also Litwack, *Trouble in Mind*, 346–47.

114. *Defender*, "The Race's Magna Charta," December 2, 1916.

115. *Defender*, "The Exodus," September 2, 1916. A front-page image of black male laborers, awaiting a labor train going north, proclaimed that the men were "tired of being kicked and cursed," and therefore, "leaving by the thousands."

116. *Defender*, Robert S. Abbott, "I Appeal to All the Members of My Race throughout the United States to Crush This Damnable Disgrace," August 4, 1917.

117. White, *Too Heavy a Load*, 52–53.

118. *Defender*, "Editor's Mail," July 14, 1917.

119. *Defender*, "Fostering Trouble," July 17, 1918.

120. *Defender*, "W. Allison Sweeny Wants to Know If the *Chicago Defender*'s Backbone Tonic Is Not Needed in the North as Well as the South," February 24, 1917. Interestingly, the *Defender*'s illustrations of the black southerner or black migrant were usually depicted as a black man. See, for example, "The Awakening," August 19, 1916.

121. Grossman, *Land of Hope*, 19–27. Grossman argues that migration and "spatial mobility" symbolized freedom and independence to blacks, especially after slavery.

122. *Defender*, "Fostering Trouble," July 17, 1918; *Defender*, "Migration," August 26, 1916; *Defender*, "Migration and Its Effect," April 20, 1918.

123. *Defender*, "Getting the South Told," November 25, 1916.

124. "Black Migration to the Urban Midwest: The Gender Dimension, 1915–1945," in Hine, *Hine Sight*, 87–107.

125. "Burden of the Black Woman," *Crisis* 9, no. 1 (November 1914) and "Votes for Women," *Crisis* 10, no. 4 (August 1915). See also "Gaining Strength in South," *Crisis* 13, no. 3 (January 1917).

126. "New Education in the New South: Domestic Science for Colored Girls Only," *Crisis* 16, no. 5 (September 1913). See also "The Next Colored Delegation to the White House," *Crisis* 10, no. 2 (June 1915).

127. "Colored Woman in Industry," *Crisis* 17, no. 1 (November 1918).

128. Spear, *Black Chicago*, 135.

129. *Defender*, "Slavery Still Exists," February 17, 1917; Scott, *Negro Migration during the War*, 24. One *Defender* article reported that in one instance in Jacksonville, Florida, black women forced their husbands to leave the South when the men hesitated to take a train north. See *Defender*, "Southerners Plan to Stop Exodus," August 12, 1916. See also Scott, *Negro Migration during the War*, 24.

130. For example, "Tell Me about the Place," in Grossman, *Land of Hope*, 66–97; Best, *Passionately Human, No Less Divine*, 19.

131. *Defender*, "Conditions Good in North," December 2, 1916; *Defender*, "Forced Labor," December 2, 1916; Washburn, *African American Newspaper*, 92.

132. "The Booster Press," in Cloud, *Coming of the Frontier Press*, 67–83.

133. Grossman, *Land of Hope*, 67–68.

134. "Urban Symbolic Ecology and the Hypercity: State of the Art and Challenges for the Future," in Nas and Samuels, *Hypercity*, 7–15; Baldwin, *Chicago's New Negroes*, 8.

135. Spear, *Black Chicago*, 137.

136. *Defender*, "Read This and Laugh," September 15, 1917.

137. Grossman, *Land of Hope*, 86–87, 89. See also Pride and Wilson, *History of the Black Press*, 136.

138. For a theoretical exploration of the gendering of space, particularly "geographies of men and masculinities," see "Introduction," in Hoven and Horschelmann, *Spaces of Masculinities*.

139. Suggs, *P. B. Young, Newspaperman*, 33–34.

140. "The Sporting Life," in Baldwin, *Chicago's New Negroes*, 193–232; Manning Marable, "The Politics of Black Land Tenure, 1877–1915," in Hine and Jenkins, *Question of Manhood*, 131–37. The *Defender*'s promotion of this new model of masculinity that did not hinge on older, agricultural models may have appealed to black farmers looking for better conditions especially at this time when black agriculture and land tenure dropped into a sharp decline.

141. *Defender*, "The Race's Magna Charta," December 2, 1916; *Defender*, "The Eternal Question," August 12, 1916.

142. Best, *Passionately Human, No Less Divine*.

143. *Defender*, "Our Part in the Exodus," March 17, 1917; *Defender*, "South Howls!," September 23, 1916.

144. *Defender*, "Wake Up Brothers," December 8, 1917; "Migration and Its Effect," April 20, 1918; "Savannah Alarmed over Labor Exodus," October 14, 1916; "Conditions Good in North," December 2, 1916. The young man was indeed determined never to return south. He even insisted that though his parents were still in Ala-

bama, they would have to go north before they saw him again. He was nonetheless "working hard" to earn enough money to bring them north. Grossman writes that transferring families northward after one family member had already established themselves "ensured continuity in their lives as well as in the Great Migration itself." See Grossman, *Land of Hope*, 67.

145. *Defender*, "Keep up the Good Work," November 25, 1916.

146. "The Struggle for Homes and Jobs," in Spear, *Black Chicago*, 147–66. The *Defender*'s emphasis on job opportunities for black males overshadowed the degree to which black women contributed to the industrial economy of the North. In fact, according to Henri, there were more black women industrial workers than there were men industrial workers between 1900 and 1920. See Henri, *Black Migration*, 95; see also "Black Migration to the Urban Midwest: The Gender Dimension, 1915–1945," in Hine, *Hine Sight*, 87–107.

147. *Defender*, "Our Part in the Exodus," March 17, 1917.

148. Grossman, *Land of Hope*, 145; Baldwin, *Chicago's New Negroes*, 29. See also Gaines, *Uplifting the Race*, 93.

149. Grossman, *Land of Hope*, 82, 88.

150. Gregory, *Southern Diaspora*, 24.

151. Quoted in Buni, *Robert L. Vann*, 71.

152. "The Migration," *Crisis* 14, no. 1 (May 1917).

153. *Defender*, "Northern Drive to Start," February 10, 1917.

154. Scott, *Negro Migration during the War*, 33.

155. Grossman, *Land of Hope*, 87–88, 96. Grossman argues that black southerners' "informal networks," in particular, served to provide black southerners with the information necessary to convince them to go north. Yet the *Defender* became a part of these informal networks. See Grossman, *Land of Hope*, 68–69, 73, 88.

156. Scott, *Negro Migration during the War*, 33.

157. *Defender*, "What the Defender Has Done," February 2, 1918.

158. "The Migration," *Crisis* 14, no. 1 (May 1917).

159. *Defender*, "Somebody Lied," October 7, 1916. See also *Defender*, "Editorials Worth Mentioning," April 28, 1917. For examples of some of the articles that the white press published about the cold killing of black migrants, see Ottley, *Lonely Warrior*, 169–70. See also Gregory, *Southern Diaspora*, 53. Gregory argues that though the white southern press and black northern press discussed the migration differently, the presses were "collaborative" because they both acknowledged the historic precedence of the migration.

160. *Defender*, "Slavery Still Exists," February 17, 1917; *Defender*, "Urban League Report Shows Much Progress," December 29, 1917; Strickland, *History of the Chicago Urban League*, 24.

161. *Defender*, "Northern Drive to Start," February 10, 1917; *Defender*, "Somebody Lied," October 7, 1917. Grossman, *Land of Hope*, 88. For more on the *Defender*'s use of biblical imagery to promote the migration, see Washburn, *African American Newspaper*, 92.

162. Scott, *Negro Migration during the War*, 31; *Defender*, "South Howls," September 23, 1916; "Freezing to Death in the South," February 24, 1917.

163. Ottley, *Lonely Warrior*, 140–41.

164. *Defender*, "The Chicago Defender Entirely Owned by R. S. Abbott," May 4, 1918.

165. *Defender*, "Editor's Mail," January 22, 1916.

166. *Defender*, "The Chicago Defender Entirely Owned by R. S. Abbott," May 4, 1918.

167. Ottley, *Lonely Warrior*, 141. See also Simmons, *African American Press*, 30.

168. Ottley, *Lonely Warrior*, 109.

169. "Efforts to Check the Movement," in Scott, *Negro Migration during the War*, 72–85.

170. Simmons, *African American Press*, 36.

171. Grossman, *Land of Hope*, 44, 86.

172. The *Defender*, in one article, lampooned the efforts to stop its sale in the South. See *Defender*, "Read This, Then Laugh," September 15, 1917; Grossman, *Land of Hope*, 74, 86; Simmons, *African American Press*, 36–37. Simmons writes that whites saw the *Defender* as such a subversive force that the Ku Klux Klan threatened anyone seen with a copy. To add, two distributors of the paper were killed.

173. DuBois, *Dusk of Dawn*, 246, 262.

174. Jordan, *Black Newspapers*, 118–22. See also "The Most Dangerous of All Negro Journals: Federal Efforts to Silence the *Chicago Defender*," in Kornweibel, *"Investigate Everything*," 118–31.

175. Abbott to Emmett J. Scott, May 5, 1918, ASFP, box 8, fol. 29.

176. *Defender*, "A Greater Chicago Defender to the Public," February 2, 1918. Reprinted May 3, 1930.

177. Kornweibel, *"Investigate Everything*," 125–26. See also Jordan, *Black Newspapers*, 122–33. See also *Defender*, "Newspaper Men and Leaders in Important Conference," June 6, 1918.

178. *Defender*, "Getting Scared," September 9, 1916.

179. *Defender*, "Dr. Holloway Interviewed," August 11, 1917; *Defender*, "Editorials Worth Mentioning," April 28, 1917.

180. *Defender*, "Richest Woman of the Race in United States," December 29, 1917; *Defender*, "Thousands Hear Madame Walker Tell Story of Her Rise to Fame and Riches," March 16, 1918. See also "Making Do," in Baldwin, *Chicago's New Negroes*, 53–90.

181. Farr, *Black Champion*, 83–84; Ward, *Unforgivable Blackness*, 236–37; Roberts, *Papa Jack*.

182. Baldwin, *Chicago's New Negroes*, 195–204.

183. *Defender*, "Jack Johnson, Self-Made Man," May 15, 1920.

184. *Defender*, "Race Man, Wake Up," October 6, 1917.

185. *Defender*, "Editor's Mail," January 22, 1916.

186. *Defender*, "Quest for Equality," Installment 7, April 27, 1940.

187. Detweiler, *Negro Press in the United States*, 60.

188. Butler, *Entrepreneurship*, 64–71. See also Green, *Selling the Race*; and Gaines, *Uplifting the Race*.

189. See also Reed, *Rise of Chicago's Black Metropolis*, 39–41.

190. ASFP, box 2, fol. 6; Reed, *Rise of Chicago's Black Metropolis*, 41. See also Burns, *Nitty Gritty*, 12. One of Abbott's chauffeurs, David Kellum, became a staff member and later editor of the Bud Billiken children's page, after he had "sideswiped another car."

191. *Defender*, "Abbott of the Defender," reprinted May 3, 1930.

192. Metz P. Lochard, "Phylon Profile XII: Robert S. Abbott—'Race Leader,'" *Phylon* 8 (1947): 124–32. See also Burns, *Nitty Gritty*, 4–5; Waters, *American Diary*, 147; Reed, *Black Chicago's First Century*, 389, 441–42.

193. *Defender*, "South Howls," September 23, 1916; *Defender*, "Sympathy," August 25, 1917; *Defender*, "Talks on Migration," August 11, 1917. See also *Defender*, "Migration and Its Effect," August 26, 1918.

194. Ottley, *Lonely Warrior*, 109–10.

195. Drake and Cayton, *Black Metropolis*, 392–95. See also Baldwin, *Chicago's New Negroes*, 7. For more on Race Men and Race Women, especially in varying contexts, see, for instance, Mitchell, *Righteous Propagation*; and Carby, *Race Men*.

196. The *Defender* maintained that the economy of the South depended on the labor of black men. In fact, its economy rested on their "backs." See *Defender*, "Unenforced Laws," October 14, 1916; *Defender*, "Race Labor Leaving," February 5, 1916; *Defender*, "Our Part in the Exodus," March 17, 1917.

197. Spear, *Black Chicago*, 168; Gaines, *Uplifting the Race*, 72, 88–93; Grossman, *Land of Hope*, 145; Baldwin, *Chicago's New Negroes*, 29. See also Best, *Passionately Human, No Less Divine*; Gaines, *Uplifting the Race*, 67–99. Implicit in the *Defender*'s charge for black northerners to help southern migrants was a degree of elitism and disdain for what was a perceived backwardness about black migrants. While it advised "ambitious" black southerners to go north, it discouraged the migration of "shiftless" black migrants. Abbott wrote one article that advised black southerners on public decorum and manners in the North. See *Defender*, "Conditions Good in North," December 2, 1916; "Things That Should Be Considered," October 20, 1917. See Washburn, *African American Newspaper*, 92–93. See also "Migration and Help," *Crisis* 13, no. 3 (January 1917).

198. *Defender*, "Our Part in the Exodus," March 17, 1917. *Defender*, "Urban League Adopts Migration Resolutions," February 3, 1917.

199. *Defender*, "Still They Come," February 10, 1917.

200. *Defender*, "What the Defender Has Done," February 2, 1918.

201. "Preface," in Woodson, *Century of Negro Migration*,192. See also Scott, *Negro Migration during the War*.

202. *Defender*, "Still They Come," February 10, 1917; *Defender*, "The Eternal Question," August 12, 1916.

203. Tuttle, *Race Riot*, 14. See also Krugler, *1919, the Year of Racial Violence*.

204. For more on this point, see, for example, Williams, *Torchbearers of Democracy*.

205. "Returning Soldiers," *Crisis* 18, no. 1 (May 1919).

206. Spear, *Black Chicago*, 214–22; Tuttle, *Race Riot*, 210.

207. Jordan, *Black Newspapers and America's War for Democracy*, 150.

208. See, for example, *Defender*, "Home, Sweet Home," August 30, 1919; *Defender*, "Riot Sweeps Chicago," August 2, 1919; *Defender*, "Ghastly Deeds of Race Rioters Told," August 2, 1919.

209. Spear, *Black Chicago*, 214–22. *Defender*, "Ghastly Deeds of Race Rioters Told," August 2, 1919. See Tuttle, *Race Riot*, 49. Black news wire services picked the story up and carried it across the country to other members of the black press. Black leaders such as Walter White, a national staff member of the NAACP, repeated the story as evidence of the callous racial violence sweeping the nation. To be sure, white papers were also guilty of reporting false accounts that helped inflame reactions. See Krugler, *1919, the Year of Racial Violence*, 123–24.

210. *Defender*, "Paying the Penalty," October 4, 1919.

211. "A Case of Ambivalence," in Ottley, *Lonely Warrior*, 173–87.

212. Chicago Commission on Race Relations, *Negro in Chicago*, 646–47, 650–51; Spear, *Black Chicago*, 218–19.

213. Waters, *American Diary*, 152.

214. Ottley, *Lonely Warrior*, 185.

215. "Let Us Reason Together," *Crisis* 18, no. 5 (September 1919).

216. Tuttle, *Race Riot*, 210; White, *Too Heavy a Load*, 52–53.

217. Detweiler, *Negro Press in the United States*, 170.

218. Aptheker, *Documentary History of the Negro People*, 278.

219. Kerlin, *Voice of the Negro*, x–xi, 185. See also "The New Era," in Kerlin, *Voice of the Negro*, 24–30.

220. *Defender*, "Self-Appointed Spokesman," November 1, 1919.

221. Du, *Autobiography*, 260; DuBois, *Darkwater*, 48–50; Broderick, *W. E. B. DuBois*, 120.

222. *Defender*, "Quest for Equality," Installment 8, May 4, 1940, and Installment 10, May 18, 1940.

Chapter 2

1. Jacques-Garvey, *Philosophy and Opinions of Marcus Garvey*, 124–26.

2. Martin, *Race First*, 91.

3. Jacques-Garvey, *Philosophy and Opinions*, 126; Jacques-Garvey, *Garvey and Garveyism*, 8–10.

4. For more on Barnett, see, for example, "The Ends of Clientage," in Green, *Selling the Race*, 93–127.

5. Summers, *Manliness and Its Discontents*, 68. See also Aptheker, *Correspondence of W. E. B. DuBois*, 1:262. In a letter to Dubois dated January 5, 1923, Robert S. Abbott told DuBois that the "Y. M. C. A., Y. W. C. A., the Urban League and N. A. A. C. P. must not only see to it that [migrants] are guided to freedom but take steps to adjust them to northern environment and conditions."

6. Gaines, *Uplifting the Race*, 89–93.

7. Weiss, *National Urban League*, 220.

8. See Ewing, *Age of Garvey*.

9. See, for example, "A Spirit of Manliness," in Summers, *Manliness and Its Discontents*, 66–110.

10. Miller, *Slaves to Fashion*, 138.

11. Scholarship on the black press mostly celebrates the advocacy and protest campaigns of black newspapers but hardly treats the ideological conflicts waged by black leaders and journalists in the press. These conflicts in general are important to investigate, for, as Todd Vogel has argued, one can observe in the black press, as it engaged with the broader social context, "writers forming and reforming ideologies, creating and recreating a public sphere, and staging and restaging race itself." See "Introduction," in Vogel, *Black Press*, 1–14.

12. Hill, *Marcus Garvey and UNIA Papers*, 1:xxxix–xl.

13. Rolinson, *Grassroots Garveyism*, 48–71. See also "The Origins of the UNIA," in Vincent, *Black Power and the Garvey Movement*, 91–98.

14. Gates, "Trope of a New Negro."

15. Ogbar, *Harlem Renaissance Revisited*, 246. See also Lewis, *When Harlem Was in Vogue*; Watson, *Harlem Renaissance*.

16. For the Negro Renaissance and New Negro movement outside of Harlem, see, for example, Baldwin, *Chicago's New Negroes*; Hine and McCluskey, *Black Chicago Renaissance*; Glasrud and Wintz, *Harlem Renaissance in the American West*.

17. See, for instance, James, *Holding aloft the Banner of Ethiopia*.

18. Stephens, *Black Empire*, 84–91.

19. Stein, *World of Marcus Garvey*, 42–50. See also Martin, *Race First*, 8–11.

20. Martin, *Race First*, 9–10; Gaines, *Uplifting the Race*, 237–39; Foner, *American Socialism and Black Americans*, 325.

21. Stein, *World of Marcus Garvey*, 49.

22. Martin, *Race First*, 11. See also Hill, *Marcus Garvey and UNIA Papers*, 1:428, May 3, 1919.

23. Hill, *Marcus Garvey and UNIA Papers*, 1:281, 285–93. Garvey came to the attention of the BOI as early as September 1918. See also Stein, *World of Marcus Garvey*, 186. As early as 1919, officials in the Justice Department wanted to take action against Garvey.

24. Kornweibel, *Investigate Everything*.

25. Kornweibel, 148.

26. Garvey, *Garvey and Garveyism*, 32.

27. For a discussion on these editors, see Rolinson, *Grassroots Garveyism*, 77–85.

28. James, *Holding aloft the Banner of Ethiopia*, 156, 270.

29. Gaines, *Uplifting the Race*, 85–86, 239–40, 100–103.

30. "Black Star Line and the Negro Ship of State," in Stephens, *Black Empire*, 102–125.

31. Jacques-Garvey, *Philosophy and Opinions*, 78–79. Also quoted in Martin, *Race First*, 103.

32. Martin, *Race First*, 92; Garvey, *Garvey and Garveyism*, 32.

33. Garvey's use of the *Negro World* as a propaganda machine for the UNIA has led older scholarship on Garvey to wrongly conclude that it indicates how much

Garvey's leadership had fascist tendencies. These scholars tend to discount other black leaders using their papers as tools of propaganda at the same time in order to build mass support too. For examples of this scholarship, see Cronon, *Black Moses*. Newer scholarship rejects the idea that the paper's propagandistic function was tantamount to fascism or demagoguery. See, for example, Rolinson, *Grassroots Garveyism*; Hahn, *Political Worlds of Slavery and Freedom*.

34. The French and Spanish sections of the *Negro World* helped Garvey build UNIA support in certain parts of the black Diaspora. See Hill, *Marcus Garvey and UNIA Papers*, 1:cxv.

35. Jacques-Garvey, *Garvey and Garveyism*, 131.

36. See Stein, *World of Marcus Garvey*, 193. Hubert Harrison, one of the editors of the *Negro World*, told U.S. agents that Garvey had used revenue from the *Negro World* to help fund the BSL.

37. Jacques-Garvey, *Garvey and Garveyism*, 131, 46.

38. Martin, *Race First*, 94–100.

39. Martin, 93. See also Grant, *Negro with a Hat*, 307; "Africa for the Africans," in Ewing, *Age of Garvey*, 76–106.

40. Rolinson, *Grassroots Garveyism*, 72–75, 78.

41. Garvey, *Garvey and Garveyism*, 228.

42. Hahn, *Nation under Our Feet*, 469–72.

43. Detweiler, *Negro Press in the United States*, 9.

44. Aptheker, *Documentary History of the Negro People*, 398.

45. Rolinson, *Grassroots Garveyism*, 17, 73–75. The rural black South claimed about half of UNIA divisions, more than the Northeast and Midwest put together.

46. Martin, *Race First*, 91–100; Vincent, *Black Power and the Garvey Movement*, 19.

47. "Garvey and the Politics of Agitation," in Stein, *World of Marcus Garvey*, 38–60.

48. Farrar, *Baltimore Afro-American*, 146; Freer, "L.A. Race Woman."

49. Hill, *Marcus Garvey and UNIA Papers*, 1:282–83, September 28, 1918, and November 2, 1918.

50. Quoted in Stein, *World of Marcus Garvey*, 64.

51. See Baldwin, *Chicago's New Negroes*; and Summers, *Manliness and Its Discontents*.

52. Stein, *World of Marcus Garvey*, 63–64.

53. Hill, *Marcus Garvey and UNIA Papers*, 2:85–88, *Negro World*, October 20, 1919.

54. Stein, *World of Marcus Garvey*, 67, 74.

55. Ottley, *New World A-Coming*, 72; Rolinson, *Grassroots Garveyism*, 86.

56. Summers, *Manliness and Its Discontents*, 67, 79–83; Campbell, *Middle Passages*, 236.

57. Hill, *Marcus Garvey and UNIA Papers*, 1:351, *Negro World*, February 1, 1919.

58. See, for example, "The Negro Should Be a Party to the Commercial Conquest of the World Wake Up You Lazy Men of the World—This Is the Time of Preparation for All," in Hill, *Marcus Garvey and UNIA Papers*, 1:351, *Negro World*, February 1,

1919. See also Hill, *Marcus Garvey and UNIA Papers*, 1:460, *Negro World*, July 19, 1919. See also Stein, *World of Marcus Garvey*, 64.

59. Hill, *Marcus Garvey and UNIA Papers*, 2:160, *Negro World*, December 12, 1919.

60. See Bederman, *Manliness and Civilization*.

61. White, *Too Heavy a Load*, 116–21.

62. Hill, *Marcus Garvey and UNIA Papers*, 4:51–55, *Negro World*, November 5, 1921. See also Stephens, *Black Empire*, 80–83, 91, 110–12. Stephens argues that the ships represented and facilitated the unencumbered movement of actual black men as sailors, and the New Negro, which was culturally figured as male, to engage the black diaspora. Among the many demands of the "Declaration of Rights of Negro Peoples," for example, number thirty-six read: "We declare that all Negroes are entitled to the same right to travel over the world as other men."

63. Hill, *Marcus Garvey and UNIA Papers*, 2:14, *Defender*, September 6, 1919. See also Stein, *World of Marcus Garvey*, 88. The *New York Age* also made negative assessments of Garvey and the BSL, calling him a "dangerous Negro." Other papers, such as the *New York Tribune* and Cyril Briggs's *Crusader*, simply questioned Garvey's ability to keep the UNIA organized.

64. Hill, *Marcus Garvey and UNIA Papers*, 1:325. The speech was advertised for January 13, 1918, but scheduled for January 16.

65. Hill, *Marcus Garvey and UNIA Papers*, 2:122, November 1, 1919. See also Hill, *Marcus Garvey and UNIA Papers*, 2:298, *Negro World*, May 8, 1920; Hill, *Marcus Garvey and UNIA Papers*, 1:466, *Negro World*, July 19, 1919. A *Negro World* headline began, "Wanted 10,000 Intelligent Young Negro Men and Women of Ambition to Take Advantage of the Following: The Universal Negro Improvement Association 10,000 Leaders to Send into New Fields." Yet in response to critics in 1923, Garvey said that "the African liberation program . . . is a big job, and it is [a] man's job, and [other black movements] are not prepared for a man's job." See also Hill, *Marcus Garvey and UNIA*, 5:250.

66. Summers, *Manliness and Its Discontents*, 19, 23.

67. Barbara Bair, "True Women, Real Men," in Helly and Reverby, *Gendered Domains*, 155–62. For example, the UNIA constitution made provisions for a "Male President" and a "Lady President." The Male President had more formal authority and was responsible to the parent body. On the other hand, the Lady President was responsible to the Male President. She could call meetings and had control over "those departments of the organization over which she may be able to exercise better control than the Male President," but "all her reports shall be submitted to the Male President for representation to the general membership. See Hill, *Marcus Garvey and UNIA Papers*, 1:269.

68. Hill, *Marcus Garvey and UNIA Papers*, 1:42, *Negro World*, October 11, 1919.

69. White, *Too Heavy a Load*, 121, 135–36. See also Taylor, *Veiled Garvey*, 42–46.

70. Barbara Bair, "True Women, Real Men," in Helly and Reverby, *Gendered Domains*, 160, 161–66. Women delegates at the 1922 UNIA convention protested gendered restrictions on women by taking over the stage after Garvey left the room to propose five resolutions that demanded more leadership opportunities. See also Rolinson, *Grassroots Garveyism*, 18. Rolinson argues that the rural South offered

women more opportunities for involvement than did urban centers, though the organization remained overwhelmingly patriarchal. See also "Our Women and What They Think," in Taylor, *Veiled Garvey*, 64–90.

71. Barbara Bair, "True Women, Real Men," in Helly and Reverby, *Gendered Domains*, 161.

72. Hill, *Marcus Garvey and UNIA Papers*, 3:51, *Negro World*, November 1, 1919. See also Hill, *Marcus Garvey and UNIA*, 2:298, *Negro World*, May 8, 1920; and Hill, *Marcus Garvey and UNIA Papers*, 4:150–51, *Negro World*, November 5, 1921. See also White, *Too Heavy a Load*, 121–23.

73. White, *Too Heavy a Load*, 112–20.

74. Barbara Bair, "True Women, Real Men," in Helly and Reverby, *Gendered Domains*, 159.

75. Vincent, *Black Power and the Garvey Movement*, 114.

76. Hill, *Marcus Garvey and UNIA Papers*, 3:51, *Negro World*, October 23, 1920; Barbara Bair, "True Women, Real Men," in Helly and Reverby, *Gendered Domains*, 159, 166.

77. Stein, *World of Marcus Garvey*, 72–74. Hill, *Marcus Garvey and UNIA Papers*, 1:429–31, 445, 447, *Negro World*, June 21, 1919. See also *Defender*, "Law Is Still on Mark Garvey's Trail," September 27, 1919. The *Defender* had a reporter attend the meeting between Garvey and the officers in order to report on the dispute between Garvey and his employees.

78. Stein, *World of Marcus Garvey*, 74–75. Hill, *Marcus Garvey and UNIA Papers*, 1:474–75, *Negro World*, August 2, 1919. For Grey's and Warner's statements, see Hill, *Marcus Garvey and UNIA Papers*, 1:462–65.

79. Hill, *Marcus Garvey and UNIA Papers*, 1:475, *Negro World*, August 2, 1919 and 2:4–7.

80. Hill, 2:568.

81. Hill, 1:431–32, 450.

82. Stein, *World of Marcus Garvey*, 79; Examples in the *Defender* include "Brundage 'Sinks' Black Star Line," October 4, 1919; "Seeks $200,000 Damages; Gets Only Six Cents," June 19, 1920; "Garvey Dodges Libel Suit but Loses in End," May 21, 1921; Martin, *Race First*, 316. See also Garvey, "Why I HAVE NOT SPOKEN IN Chicago since 1919," in Jacques-Garvey, *Philosophy and Opinions*, 321–23.

83. Aptheker, *Documentary History*, 399; Stein, *World of Marcus Garvey*, 164.

84. Hill, *Marcus Garvey and UNIA Papers*, 2:86–87, 99, *Negro World*, October 25, 1919.

85. For an evaluation on the historiography of Garvey and its evaluation of his movement and leadership, see "Introduction: The Problem of Garvey and Garveyism" and "Ethnic Politics as Pan-Africanism: The Locals of the UNIA," in Stein, *World of Marcus Garvey*, 1–6, 223–47. See also Martin, *Race First*, 164.

86. Stein, *World of Marcus Garvey*, 93–97; Lewis, *W. E. B. DuBois*, 74.

87. Stein, *World of Marcus Garvey*, 79.

88. See Hill, *Marcus Garvey and UNIA Papers*, 2:18, Frank Burke to George Lamb, September 15, 1919.

89. Hill, *Marcus Garvey and UNIA Papers*, 2:271–79. Growing criticism of him compelled Garvey to appeal in the *Washington Bee* to the black press for a "fairer estimate of his movement." See Hill, *Marcus Garvey and UNIA Papers,* 4:131, *Washington Bee*, October 25, 1921.

90. Though he wanted to publish a fair evaluation on Garvey in the *Crisis*, DuBois might have been more interested in Garvey's answers than were *Crisis* readers. DuBois's letter to Garvey was perhaps the first of many attempts he made to investigate Garvey with or without Garvey's knowledge. DuBois believed that Garvey was "more or less a fraud," and by July 1920, DuBois began asking his own associates for any information they could share about Garvey and his business operations. Further, DuBois also appealed to the North American Shipping Corporation, the New York State Department of Commerce, the American Bureau of Shipping, and corporations selling ships and doing business with the BSL for information on Garvey. See Hill, *Marcus Garvey and UNIA Papers*, 1:394–99, *Negro World*, April 5, 1919; Hill, *Marcus Garvey and UNIA Papers*, 2:3, 153, 431–32, 434–35, DuBois to James Burghardt, August 27, 1919, DuBois to A. H. May, November 8, 1919, DuBois to Garvey, July 22, 1920, Truman K. Gibson to DuBois, July 24, 1920, DuBois to H. L. Stone, July 24, 1920; Hill, *Marcus Garvey and UNIA Papers*, 3:72–73, 90–93, DuBois to Lloyd's Register, November 6, 1920, DuBois to North American Shipping Corporation, DuBois to the New York State Department of Commerce, November 22, 1920, DuBois to the American Bureau of Shipping, November 23, 1920.

91. Vincent, *Voices*, 95.

92. Vincent, 95–96.

93. Quoted in Tinney and Rector, *Issues and Trends*, 71.

94. Hill, *Marcus Garvey and UNIA Papers*, 3:124, "Meeting Announcement." The speech was scheduled for January 2, 1921.

95. Vincent, *Voices*, 97–98. For a discussion of DuBois's journalism before the *Crisis*, see Dan S. Green, "W. E. B. DuBois: His Journalistic Career," in Tinney and Rector, *Issues and Trends*, 61–85.

96. Carby, *Race Men*, 39–41.

97. Vincent, *Voices*, 97.

98. Hill, *Marcus Garvey and UNIA Papers*, 3:172–73, Arthur B. Spingarn to Wilford Smith, February 10, 1921. See also n1.

99. Hill, *Marcus Garvey and UNIA Papers*, 1:450, *Negro World*, June 28, 1919.

100. Hill, 2:215, "News Report in Baltimore Afro-American," February 25, 1920.

101. Hill, 5:255, February 24, 1923.

102. *Defender*, "Garvey Backs Down in Fight with Defender," August 6, 1921.

103. For more on the scramble for Africa, see Forster et al., *Bismarck, Europe, and Africa*.

104. Vincent, *Voices*, 114–17. See also Kornweibel, *No Crystal Stair*, 135–36.

105. Foner, *American Socialism*, 325; Kornweibel, *No Crystal Stair*, 134, 139. Randolph first criticized Garvey in the 1921 *Messenger* issue, though he had long been alarmed by Garvey's black nationalism. See Vincent, *Voices*, 113–21. Randolph, writing in 1922, turned his introduction of Garvey against him, insisting that the

"Garvey movement could only have begun in New York City where the field had been prepared by Owen and Randolph for the reception of new ideas, presented through the vehicle of radicalism. It is well known that Garvey began his propaganda in harmony with the Messenger's principles in order to get a hearing."

106. Kornweibel, *No Crystal Stair*, 134–36, 169. Kornweibel further argues that opposition to Garvey had to do with a petty jealousy of his incredible success at organizing a mass movement so fast as much as critics' differences with him in terms of ideology and strategy. See also Detweiler, *Negro Press in the United States*, 188–89, 195–96.

107. Summers, *Manliness and Its Discontents*, 72–73. See also Gaines, *Uplifting the Race*.

108. Quoted in Summers, *Manliness and Its Discontents*, 87, 83.

109. Quoted in Baldwin, *Chicago's New Negroes*, 194–95. See also Summers, *Manliness and Its Discontents*, 92–101. Summers makes the point that Garvey and Garveyites performed a proper black manhood through certain rituals both in private and public, including in UNIA meetings and parades. But Garvey's sensational public behavior that his critics harped on should also be seen as another part of these rituals.

110. Quoted in Wolters, *DuBois and His Rivals*, 153.

111. Vincent, *Voices*, 108; Grant, *Negro with a Hat*, 312–13, 306; Vincent, *Black Power and the Garvey Movement*, 192. For examples of Johnson's articles, see Wilson, *Selected Writings of James Weldon Johnson*, 130–35. For more on the conflict between Garvey and Briggs, see Stephens, *Black Empire*, 117–25, and Martin, *Race First*, 240–43.

112. See *Defender*, "Lynching Good for My People—Mr. Garvey," February 17, 1923; *Defender*, "Government Ready to Try Garvey," October 14, 1922. For examples of fair treatments of Garvey, see Vincent, *Voices*, 95–97, 108–10, 114–17. Some of Garvey's critics harped on his being West Indian, intending it as a pejorative. In a *Messenger* article by Owen, Hill, *Marcus Garvey and UNIA Papers*, 4:758. Owen says, "This tool talk, too, emanates from a blustering West Indian demagogue who preys upon the ignorant, unsuspecting poor West Indian working men and women who believe Garvey is some sort of Moses." Emphasizing Garvey's West Indian background in this negative way tried to elevate not only homegrown black leadership but also the black American experience with racial oppression as too special a case to be handled by anyone other than native black American citizens. On this point, see "The Peculiarities of the Caribbeans," in James, *Holding aloft the Banner of Ethiopia*, 50–91.

113. See, for instance, *Defender*, "Law Still on Mark Garvey's Trail," September 27, 1919; *Defender*, "District Attorney Swan Now Handling Garvey Case," September 6, 1919; *Defender*, "Attorney Bares N. Y. Editor's Plot," September 20, 1919; *Defender*, "Black Star Line at Bottom of the Deep Blue Sea," November 4, 1922; *Defender*, "Thompson Not Fooled," February 4, 1922; *Defender*, "Garvey Cruel and Unfaithful Says Wife," September 11, 1920; *Defender*, "Marcus Garvey's Move Is Scored by Dean Pickens," July 29, 1922; *Defender*, "A Pioneer of Negro Culture," August 20, 1921; *Defender*, "Phillip Randolph Stamps Garvey Little Half-Wit," August 12, 1922. For more on conflicts within the UNIA, see Stein, *World of Marcus Garvey*, 142–50.

114. Ottley, *Lonely Warrior*, 213–14; Jordan, *Black Newspapers and America's War for Democracy*, 79; Jacques-Garvey, *Philosophy and Opinions*, 321.

115. Hill, *Marcus Garvey and UNIA Papers*, 4:479, *Negro World*, February 11, 1922. See also Stein, *World of Marcus Garvey*, 186, 189, 194.

116. Stein, *World of Marcus Garvey*, 188–92.

117. Aptheker, *Documentary History of the Negro People*, 370.

118. Pegram, *One Hundred Percent American*; Hill, *Marcus Garvey and UNIA Papers*, 6:186.

119. Hill, *Marcus Garvey and UNIA Papers*, 4:707, *Negro World*, July 9, 1922.

120. Hill, 4:707–12, *Negro World*, July 15, 1922. See also Jacques-Garvey, *Garvey and Garveyism*, 100. For more on the meeting between Garvey and Clarke, see "The Ku Klux Klan, White Supremacy, and Garvey—A Symbiotic Relationship," in Martin, *Race First*. Martin argues that it was because of the history of conflict and violence between the KKK and black people, particularly episodes of violent attacks on UNIA members by the KKK, as well as the fact that Clarke extended the invitation to meet, that the two met.

121. Kornweibel, *No Crystal Stair*, 137–39. Kornweibel writes that it was ironic that Randolph and Owen, who denounced the deportation of Socialist immigrants during the Red Scare, now promoted the deportation of Garvey on the basis that he was an anarchist, though Garvey was nothing of the sort.

122. See, for example, Hill, *Marcus Garvey and UNIA Papers*, 4:816, 856, 932.

123. Kornweibel, *No Crystal Stair*, 134–36, 169; Vincent, *Black Power and the Garvey Movement*, 192.

124. Moses, *Black Messiahs and Uncle Toms*, 350–54.

125. Quoted in Martin, *Race First*, 92.

126. Hill, *Marcus Garvey and UNIA Papers*, 4:999, 924, *Negro World*, August, 26, 1922.

127. Hill, 4:619–20, "Confidential Informant 800 to George F. Ruch," April 28, 1922.

128. White, *Too Heavy a Load*, 116–21; "The Sporting Life: Recreation, Self-Reliance, and Competing Visions of Race Manhood," in Baldwin, *Chicago's New Negroes*, 193–232.

129. Vincent, *Voices*, 65–66.

130. Quoted in Lewis, *When Harlem Was in Vogue*, 24. Quoted in Whalan, *Great War and the Culture of the New Negro*, 111.

131. Hill, *Marcus Garvey and UNIA Papers*, 4:364, *Negro World*, January 15, 1922.

132. Hill, 4:344–45, *Negro World*, January 21, 1922. See also Stein, *World of Marcus Garvey*, 194.

133. Hill, *Marcus Garvey and UNIA Papers*, 4:363–69.

134. Hill, 4:363, *Negro World*, January 21, 1922.

135. Hill, 4:445–46, *Negro World*, January 28, 1922.

136. Hill, 4:368–69, *Negro World*, January 15, 1922. For an example of coverage by the white press, see Hill, *Marcus Garvey and UNIA Papers*, 4:816, *New York Times*, August 7, 1922.

137. Martin, *Race First*, 103.

138. See Hill, *Marcus Garvey and UNIA Papers*, 4:884–87, 878, 1007–8.

139. Frazier, *Negro in the United States*, 515–16; Ottley, *Lonely Warrior*, 341–42; Ottley, *New World A-Coming*, 71. See also Detweiler, *Negro Press in the United States*, 182.

140. Quoted in Pride and Wilson, *History of the Black Press*, 218; Detweiler, *Negro Press in the United States*, 97. See also Frazier, *Negro in the United States*, 515–16.

141. Hill, *Marcus Garvey and UNIA Papers*, 4:878, *Negro World*, August 26, 1922. On the *Negro World*'s crime stories, see "What a Pure, Healthy, Unified Race Can Accomplish: Collective Reproduction and the Sexual Politics of Black Nationalism," in Mitchell, *Righteous Propagation*, 218–39.

142. Aptheker, *Documentary History of the Negro People*, 371–77; Stein, *World of Marcus Garvey*, 166.

143. Hill, *Marcus Garvey and UNIA Papers*, 4:481–84, *Negro World*, February 5, 1922.

144. Stein, *World of Marcus Garvey*, 201. For example, in a speech that he gave in Raleigh, North Carolina, in 1923, Garvey's rhetoric shifted from condemning white supremacy as he had in years past to condemning black people for their supposed failures as a race, and citing those failures as the reason why whites did not give black people a chance. In the latter article, Garvey again shifted from his usual wholesale condemnations of white supremacy and proposing world war to combat it to explaining that he and the UNIA preferred a separation of the races and building up Africa. Still, Garvey's bombastic gendered rhetoric did not tone down.

145. Hill, *Marcus Garvey and UNIA Papers*, 4:479–88, *Negro World*, February 11, 1922; White, *Too Heavy a Load*, 116–21.

146. Stein, *World of Marcus Garvey*, 79–80.

147. Bederman, *Manliness and Civilization*, 8. See also Hill, *Marcus Garvey and UNIA Papers*, 5:360–62, *Negro World*, June 23, 1923.

148. Hill, *Marcus Garvey and UNIA Papers*, 4:350, *Negro World*, January 21, 1922.

149. Hill, 4:379, *Negro World*, January 21, 1922.

150. Hill, 4:448, *Negro World*, January 28, 1922.

151. Hill, 4:353, *New York World*, January 13, 1922; Vincent, *Voices*, 99.

152. Garvey, *Garvey and Garveyism*, 70; Hill, *Marcus Garvey and UNIA Papers*, 4:479, *Negro World*, February 5, 1922.

153. For Johnson as a symbol of New Negro masculinity, see, for example, "Between the Ropes: Staging the Black Body in American Boxing," in Young, *Embodying Black Experience*, 76–118; Baldwin, *Chicago's New Negroes*, 195–204.

154. Hill, *Marcus Garvey and UNIA Papers*, 4:456, *Negro World*, February 4, 1922.

155. Vincent, *Voices*, 122. See Lewis, *DuBois, 1919–1963*, 82.

156. Hill, *Marcus Garvey and UNIA Papers*, 4:448, *Negro World*, January 28, 1922.

157. Hill, 4:924–31, *Negro World*, August 26, 1922. See also Stein, *World of Marcus Garvey*, 74. Stein argues that "the assertion of racial independence was simultaneously a substantive criticism of leadership and a democratic defense of the new popular politics."

158. Hill, *Marcus Garvey and UNIA Papers*, 4:488, *Negro World*, February 5, 1922.

159. Hill, 4:450, January 28, 1922.

160. See, for instance, Hill, *Marcus Garvey and UNIA Papers*, 4:31–42, 45–46, 277, 682–86, *Negro World*, September 17, 1921; Hill, *Marcus Garvey and UNIA Papers*, 5:248, *Negro World*, March 3, 1923; Vincent, *Voices*, 99–105. Amy Jacques shared Garvey's belief that DuBois was his greatest foe. See Garvey, *Garvey and Garveyism*, 80, 136.

161. Summers, *Manliness and Its Discontents*, 107–9.

162. Hill, *Marcus Garvey and UNIA Papers*, 5:204, "Marcus Garvey to the White Press of the World," 1923.

163. Hill, 5:240, February 17, 1923.

164. Vincent, *Voices*, 101; Hill, *Marcus Garvey and UNIA Papers*, 3:581, *Negro World*, August 6, 1921, and Hill, *Marcus Garvey and UNIA Papers*, 5:237, *Negro World*, February 17, 1923. For a brief biographical history of DuBois, as well as an evaluation of NAACP leadership, see Moore, *W. E. B. DuBois*, 18, 22–24, 86–87. It should be noted that Garvey had a deep resentment for light-skinned blacks that stemmed from his racial and class experiences in Jamaica. See Wolters, *DuBois and His Rivals*, 146–47, 155–56, 159.

165. See, for instance, Hill, *Marcus Garvey and UNIA Papers*, 3:549–53; Hill, 4:366; Hill, 5:119–20.

166. Gates, "Trope of a New Negro."

167. Hill, *Marcus Garvey and UNIA Papers*, 4:466–68, *Negro World*, February 4, 1922.

168. Martin, *Race First*, 284–305. Garvey's constant references to the NAACP prompted James Weldon Johnson to write him asking him to refrain from intimating that the NAACP was responsible for the UNIA's hardships. Garvey responded, promising only to continue rebuking the NAACP. See Hill, *Marcus Garvey and UNIA Papers*, 4:437, 526, Johnson to Garvey, January 20, 1922, and *Negro World*, February 25, 1922; Hill, 4:437, Johnson to Garvey, January 20, 1922. See also Hill, 5:598.

169. Hill, *Marcus Garvey and UNIA Papers*, 4:526, *Negro World*, February 25, 1922. Garvey said, "It is my duty to know men and to analyze them, especially if they are competitors in any way."

170. Hill, 4:466–68, *Negro World*, February 4, 1922. Garvey's ridicule of DuBois's clothing was no trivial matter. As Hazel V. Carby and Monica L. Miller have argued, DuBois used his clothing to embody and model a certain masculinity that projected the ideal modern, cosmopolitan, and intellectual black man, as he saw it in terms of proper racial leadership. See Carby, *Race Men*, 21–23; and "W. E. B. DuBois' 'Different' Diasporic Race Man," in Miller, *Slaves to Fashion*, 137–75.

171. Quoted in Campbell, *Middle Passages*, 237.

172. Hill, *Marcus Garvey and UNIA Papers*, 4:366, *Negro World*, January 21, 1922.

173. Martin, *Race First*, 284. Hill, *Marcus Garvey and UNIA Papers*, 4:468, *Negro World*, February 4, 1922.

174. Vincent, *Voices*, 99–104. Hill, *Marcus Garvey and UNIA Papers*, 5:257, 205, "Marcus Garvey to the White Press of the World," January 1923. For more on the conflict between DuBois and Garvey, see "DuBois and Garvey: Two 'Pan-Africas,'" in Lewis, *W. E. B. DuBois, 1919–1963*, 37–84.

175. In one reported incident, around 1923 or 1924, DuBois and Garvey encountered one another on their way to a public meeting and had to share an elevator. On the ride up, observers said the two men showed visible physical signs that they were agitated: Garvey trembled, while DuBois's nostrils flared. See Campbell, *Middle Passages*, 226–27.

176. Stein, *World of Marcus Garvey*, 190, 193–95.

177. See also Vincent, *Black Power and the Garvey Movement*, 191, 160.

178. Stein, *World of Marcus Garvey*, 79–80.

179. Garvey, *Garvey and Garveyism*, 101; Hill, *Marcus Garvey and UNIA Papers*, 4:672, June 12, 1922; Gloster Armstrong, January 5, 1923, UMC, folder labeled British Colonial Office UNIA Documents.

180. Hill, *Marcus Garvey and UNIA Papers*, 5:115, *Savannah Tribune*, October 30, 1922.

181. Vincent, *Voices*, 107. See also Ewing, *Age of Garvey*, 118–20.

182. Stein, *World of Marcus Garvey*, 166, 193.

183. Hill, *Marcus Garvey and UNIA Papers*, 5:xxxv. The second volume appeared in 1926. See, for example, Hill, 4:357. See also Taylor, *Veiled Garvey*, 46–47.

184. Stein, *World of Marcus Garvey*, 171–85; Summers, *Manliness and Its Discontents*, 74–75; see also "Dissensions and the Decline of Garveyism," in Vincent, *Black Power and the Garvey Movement*, 187–214.

185. Kornweibel, *No Crystal Stair*, 142; Stein, *World of Marcus Garvey*, 166–67; quoted in Summers, *Manliness and Its Discontents*, 72. Upon his discovery of the letter, Garvey wrote Harry M. Daugherty on February 4, 1923, to explain his side of things and assure Daugherty that there was "absolutely no truth" to their statements because they were his "avowed enemies." See Hill, *Marcus Garvey and UNIA Papers*, 5:217–19. Garvey then publicly responded to the letter in his own editorial on February 6, 1923. See Hill, *Marcus Garvey and UNIA Papers*, 5:220–28.

186. See Kornweibel, *Investigate Everything*; Hill, *Marcus Garvey and UNIA Papers*, 5:212–13, Perry W. Howard to William J. Burns, February 3, 1923.

187. Lewis, *DuBois, 1919–1963*, 81. See also Farrar, *Baltimore Afro-American*, 147.

188. Vincent, *Black Power and the Garvey Movement*, 200.

189. Aptheker, *Correspondence of W. E. B. DuBois*, 1:263–64, DuBois to W. A. Domingo, January 18, 1923.

190. Hill, *Marcus Garvey and UNIA Papers*, 5:302–5, May 14, 1923.

191. Stein, *World of Marcus Garvey*, 200.

192. Hill, *Marcus Garvey and UNIA Papers*, 5:309, 311, 332–33, *Negro World*, May 26, 1923.

193. Hill, 5:357n10.

194. Hill, 5:332–33. See also Stein, *World of Marcus Garvey*, 198.

195. See, for instance, Taylor, *Veiled Garvey*, 49.

196. Hill, *Marcus Garvey and UNIA Papers*, 5:333–44, June 23, 1923.

197. Hill, 5:344, June 23, 1923. See also Garvey, *Garvey and Garveyism*, 88. See also Tinney and Rector, *Issues and Trends*, 91.

198. Hill, *Marcus Garvey and UNIA Papers*, 5:355–56, 308–16, June 23, 1923.

199. Hill, 5:360–62, *Negro World*, June 23, 1923. See also Taylor, *Veiled Garvey*, 52.

200. Wilkins with Mathews, *Standing Fast*, 52.

201. Hill, *Marcus Garvey and UNIA Papers*, 5:375, June 22, 1923.

202. Hill, 5:375, June 22, 1923.

203. In November 1927, Garvey's sentence was commuted and he was deported to Jamaica in December. For a good evaluation of the ways in which Garvey's trial was politically driven by the BOI to have him neutralized, see "The Politics of Fraud, J. Edgar Hoover versus Marcus Garvey," in Stein, *World of Marcus Garvey*, 186–208.

204. Hill, *Marcus Garvey and UNIA Papers*, 5:376, June 22, 1923.

205. Hill, *Marcus Garvey and UNIA Papers*, 5:376–77, June 23, 1923.

206. Vincent, *Voices*, 105–7.

207. Cronon, *Black Moses*, 118.

208. Aptheker, *Correspondence of W. E. B. DuBois*, 1:271–72; Aptheker, *Correspondence of W. E. B. DuBois*, 3:424–25.

209. Vincent, *Black Power and the Garvey Movement*, 203–4.

210. For example, see Cronon, *Black Moses*, 115–17; Martin, *Race First*, 191–92; Stein, *World of Marcus Garvey*, 196–200.

211. See, for example, Hill, *Marcus Garvey and UNIA Papers*, 4:151, 376, 658, 663.

212. See, for example, "Messages Set to the Negro Peoples of the World from the Tombs Prison, New York City, U. S. A.," in Jacques-Garvey, *Philosophy and Opinions*, 217–27. See also Menzise, *J. A. Rogers' Rambling Ruminations*, 73. In an interview with an incarcerated Garvey in 1926, Rogers said, "When I suggested that he would have fared better had he got a lawyer, he insisted that here for once the maxim that the man who is his own lawyer has a fool for a client was wrong, as if he had not done so he would have got 'sixty years' as there was much on the inside that an onlooker would never have understood."

213. Hill, *Marcus Garvey and UNIA Papers*, 5:308–13, *Negro World*, May 26, 1923. See also Hill, *Marcus Garvey and UNIA Papers*, 4:922, "Enemies Plot to Do Away with Hon. Marcus Garvey," August 19, 1922; Martin, *Race First*, 56; Grant, *Negro with a Hat*, 332. Here, Garvey likened himself to other martyrs throughout history.

214. Gates, "Trope of a New Negro."

215. See, for example, Vincent, *Voices*; and Wilson, *Crisis Reader*.

216. Quoted in Farrar, *Baltimore Afro-American*, 147.

217. See "Preface: Struggle, Challenge, and History" and "Introduction: Reality and Contradiction," in Moses, *Creative Conflict in African American Thought*, xi–xviii, 1–18. See esp. 2.

218. Aptheker, *Documentary History of the Negro People*, 393, 400.

219. Jacques-Garvey, *Philosophy and Opinions*, 126. See also Jacques-Garvey, *Garvey and Garveyism*, 1.

220. Hill, *Marcus Garvey and UNIA Papers*, 5:360, *Negro World*, June 23, 1923. In this same speech printed in the *Negro World*, Garvey proclaimed that he was "only the first Marcus Garvey," again pointing to his belief that he and his movement had succeeded in producing proper Race Men for the future. See also Jacques-Garvey, *Philosophy and Opinions*, 180. For more on the aftermath of the UNIA following

Garvey's imprisonment, see "Garvey and Pan-Africanism, The Last Years," in Stein, *World of Marcus Garvey*, 248–72. Garvey struggled to hold the UNIA together while he was imprisoned, and he struggled to regain power and influence after his deportation. The UNIA was too riddled with reeling local chapters, internal dissension, embattled leaders, and Garvey's own inability to generate new ideas for racial advancement that did not repeat his earlier failures in business and shipping. However, Adam Ewing argues that the politics, organizing, and black diasporic consciousness that Garvey promoted did not wane but continued in places outside the United States. See Ewing, *Age of Garvey*.

Chapter 3

1. Martin, *Race First*, 195–96; See also Cronon, *Black Moses*, 140–41.
2. Michaeli, *Defender*, 171.
3. Martin, *Race First*, 197.
4. "A Bit about Chicago Where to Go What to See How to Get There," ASFP, box 11, fol. 1.
5. *Defender*, "Abbott's Monthly to Appear in October," August 9, 1930; Rice, *Chicago Defender*, 63.
6. Hogan, *Black National News Service*, 27–28. See also Waters, *American Diary*, 146–47.
7. ASFP, box 18, fol. 23.
8. "The Golden Decade of Black Business," in Reed, *Rise of Chicago's Black Metropolis*, 71, 102–4. See also Woodard, *Black Entrepreneurs in America*, 17.
9. Waters, *American Diary*, 125; Spear, *Black Chicago*, 184.
10. ASFP, box 18, fol. 23.
11. See, for example, Albert Kreiling, "The Commercialization of the Black Press and the Rise of Race News in Chicago," in Solomon and McChesney, *Ruthless Criticism*, 177; Tinney and Rector, *Issues and Trends*, 20; Hogan, *Black National News Service*, 56.
12. Wolcott, *Remaking Respectability*, 242–43. See also Vincent, *Voices*, 218–20.
13. Wolters, *Negroes and the Great Depression*, 91, 94, 79; Drake and Cayton, *Black Metropolis*, 83–88.
14. For more on the boycott, see "Don't Buy Where You Can't Work," in Greenberg, *"Or Does It Explode?,"* 114–39. See Drake and Cayton, *Black Metropolis*, 412.
15. See, for example, Anderson, *Puzzled America*, 39–42, 46, 53; Dubbert, *Man's Place*, 208–25. See also Filene, *Him/Her/Self*, 158–90; Leuchtenburg, *Franklin D. Roosevelt*, 118–19.
16. See, for example, Summers, *Manliness and Its Discontents*; Estes, *I Am a Man!*; Hornby-Gutting, *Black Manhood and Community Building*.
17. Many cultural, social, and political images would emerge during the 1930s and 1940s, representing black people's aspirations for racial progress. See, for instance, Sklaroff, *Black Culture and the New Deal*.
18. See also Drake and Cayton, *Black Metropolis*, 506–19. Many historians have argued that the modern civil rights era emerged out of black people's organizing

during the Depression era. See, for example, Hall, "Long Civil Rights Movement"; Sitkoff, *New Deal for Blacks*; Gellman, *Death Blow to Jim Crow*.

19. Scholarship on the black press has paid greater attention to what the newspapers published largely because it was the paper in printed form that directly engaged the public, rather than the business decisions that influenced an edition. At the heart of any analysis of black papers' impact on the black public sphere must be an analysis of the exchange between the paper and the public. Some scholars of the black press, such as Hayward Farrar, have noted the paucity of extant archival records from publishers, writers, and business managers. See "A Note on Sources," in Farrar, *Baltimore Afro-American*, 201–2. Some exceptions to this point include, however, Buni, *Robert L. Vann*; Suggs, *P. B. Young, Newspaperman*; Forss, *Black Print with a White Carnation*. Some publishers' published autobiographies and memoirs, such as that of W. E. B. DuBois, Charlotta Bass, Daisy Bates, and Robert F. Williams, present a few exceptions to this too.

20. "The Souls of Black Men," in Carby, *Race Men*, 25, 34. My interpretation here draws on Carby's analysis of DuBois's *Souls of Black Folk*. She argues that DuBois "was obviously concerned about the continuity of intellectual generations, what I would call the reproduction of Race men. . . . The map of intellectual mentors he draws for us is a map of male production and reproduction that traces in its form, but displaced through its content, biological and sexual reproduction. It is reproduction without women." I am interested in how Abbott and the *Defender* discussed his publishing of the paper within a similar context, and how this context mapped on to his exchanges with Sengstacke.

21. For illustrated examples of Abbott's paperboys, see Rice, *Chicago Defender*, 21–23. Rice writes that "there was even a *Chicago Defender* newsboy band." Ottley, *Lonely Warrior*, 351–54; Michaeli, *Defender*, 132–34. See also "Some Interesting Facts about a Great Newspaper," ASFP, box 11, fol. 4. A promotional pamphlet argued that older children enjoyed the *Defender* because its editorial pages helped them "in their history, geography and economics studies in school," that "Boys" liked "the snappy accounts of their particular football heroes," and that "upwards of fifty thousand poems, pictures and stories of ambitious youngsters are received annually by Bud [Billiken]." See also *Defender*, "Billikens Saddened by Death of Editor Abbott," May 9, 1940.

22. "An Old Deal, A Raw Deal," in Sitkoff, *New Deal for Blacks*, 34–57.

23. *Defender*, "Hold Your Jobs," December 7, 1929.

24. *Defender*, "What Is Your Plan for Economic Security?," July 9, 1932.

25. *Defender*, "Job Wanted: Male," January 17, 1931. It is interesting that against this background of the Depression and the enervating effects it was thought to have on black men, Sterling Brown published the poem "Strong Men," which described the remarkable ability of blacks to prevail in the face of oppression. See Harper, *Collected Poems of Sterling A. Brown*, 56–58.

26. *Defender*, "Capital vs. Labor," November 29, 1930; "What the People Say," August 23, 1930.

27. *Defender*, "The News of a Quarter Century," May 3, 1930.

28. *Defender*, "Twenty Five Years of Service," May 3, 1930.

29. *Defender*, "Mother of Defender," May 3, 1930; "Twenty Five Years of Service," May 3, 1930.

30. *Defender*, "Throughout the Years She Has Carried the Beacon—Calling Men to Higher Hopes and a Greater Understanding," May 3, 1930.

31. *Defender*, "Twenty Five Years of Service," May 3, 1930.

32. *Defender*, "A Recapitulation of 25 Years Work: Editor Robt. S. Abbott's Story of Early Struggles and Success of the World's Greatest Weekly," May 3, 1930.

33. *Defender*, "A Recapitulation of 25 Years Work: Editor Robt. S. Abbott's Story of Early Struggles and Success of the World's Greatest Weekly," May 3, 1930. One caption in this edition called Abbott's mother his "inspiration" also. But the import of the relationship between black fathers and their sons, as well as the social, economic, political, and gendered implications it has raised for black people historically, has in many ways developed as a complicated trope in black culture and politics. Black men have tended to share their inspiration from and/or resentment for their fathers as a real person and/or idealized image, in addition to their desires to adopt and/or reject their father's example of manhood. For examples of the trope in history and in black men's literature, see "The Moynihan Report," in Estes, *I Am a Man!*; "Solving the Boy Problem," in Hornsby-Gutting, *Black Manhood*, 52–94; Frazier, *Negro Family*; Dudley, *My Father's Shadow*; Carby, *Race Men*, 25–26. For another black male publisher who discussed his relationship with his stepfather, see Buni, *Robert L. Vann*, 8.

34. *Defender*, "A Recapitulation of 25 Years Work: Editor Robt. S. Abbott's Story of Early Struggles and Success of the World's Greatest Weekly," May 3, 1930.

35. *Defender*, "Rev. J. H. H. Sengstacke," May 3, 1930.

36. *Defender*, "My Message," May 3, 1930.

37. Waters, *American Diary*, 125; Spear, *Black Chicago*, 184. See also Detweiler, *Negro Press in the United States*, 26–27, 64–65; Reed, *Rise of Chicago's Black Metropolis*, 71, 74, 102; Spear, *Black Chicago*, 185; Baldwin, *Chicago's New Negroes*, 7–8. Baldwin argues that the black metropolis formed because of the efforts of "Black entrepreneurs, war veterans, laborers, artists, entertainers, politicians, and intellectuals" to "build a separate economic and institutional world—and worldview." See also Burns, *Nitty Gritty*, 4.

38. Ellis, "Robert S. Abbott's Response to Education for African Americans via the Chicago Defender, 1909–1940," 59; *Defender*, "Quest for Equality," Installment 7–8, *Defender*, May 4, 1940; Spear, *Black Chicago*, 185; Michaeli, *Defender*, 19.

39. Kimmel, *American Manhood*, 67, 72, 80. See also Wallace, *Constructing the Black Masculine*, 111–19. His examination of the forms of architecture that shape black male subjectivity provides several insights here. He argues that "mimetic architectures of black male inhabitation . . . project a material form of self" that house "black male bodies in individualistic solitude" and serve to "structure" black male subjectivity in empowering and problematic ways. The publisher's office can be construed in much the same way, for, in addition to serving as a space in which they actually worked, it was also a space in which they cultivated their gender identities as Race leaders and Race Men.

40. Michaeli, *Defender*, 189, 134–36; Waters, *American Diary*, 195. See also Rice, *Chicago Defender*, 30, 32, 38.

41. *Defender*, "A Recapitulation of 25 Years Work: Editor Robt. S. Abbott's Story of Early Struggles and Success of the World's Greatest Weekly," May 3, 1930.

42. Defender Promotional Pamphlet, ASFP, box 11, fol. 7; see also Detweiler, *Negro Press in the United States*, 26, 65; Waters, *American Diary*, 125. Waters, who joined the staff in 1935, wrote that the *Defender*'s staff was the largest he had ever seen of any black newspaper. Abbott's top-of-the-line printing press meant a great deal to him in terms of his professional journey. He gloated years later, "They said that I could not own a commercial press. . . . But, today, I own two commercial presses." See *Defender*, "This Press Prints World's Greatest Weekly," May 3, 1930; see also "A Busy Life Comes to a Close," March 9, 1940; "From Notebook to Newspaper: Making the Chicago Defender Is No Child's Occupation," May 4, 1935. Even after his death, one article commented that he "was the first publisher of his race to purchase a high speed rotary press." See also *Defender*, "Robert S. Abbott Dies after Long Illness: Death Comes during Sleep at His Home," March 9, 1940; Ottley, *Lonely Warrior*, 83, 94.

43. "Some Interesting Facts about a Great Newspaper," ASFP, box 11, fol. 4; Gore, *Negro Journalism*, 16–17.

44. *Defender*, "A Recapitulation of 25 Years Work: Editor Robt. S. Abbott's Story of Early Struggles and Success of the World's Greatest Weekly," May 3, 1930. Abbott's actual mother, Flora Sengstacke, also did her part to help launch the *Defender* on its way. She "pushed the switch that started the *Defender* on its first 100,000 run" in 1921. The *Defender* also featured another woman essential to Abbott's initial success: Elnora Claytor. Claytor and Abbott were both members of a singing club in Chicago. When Abbott decided to create the *Defender*, he asked the singing group to help him gather news and sell the paper. Claytor volunteered and helped him gather news items, as well as ads and subscriptions. She even became the first agent to sell the paper from a newsstand. Years later, she worked as a member of the staff. See *Defender*, "The Editor's Inspiration," May 3, 1930. See also Elnora Claytor to John Sengstacke, May 20, 1955, ASFP, box 27, fol. 1. Claytor was secretary of the editorial department and four weeks later was removed to the Billiken Department under editor David Kellum.

45. *Defender*, May 3, 1930, p. 2. See also "We Are 20 Years Old," May 9, 1925; Reed, *Rise of Chicago's Black Metropolis*, 81–82, 102.

46. *Defender*, May 3, 1930.

47. "The Souls of Black Men," in Carby, *Race Men*, 9–41.

48. See Bass, *Forty Years*, 177, 28. Some black women publishers seemed to have had little concern for this distinction. Certainly, they wanted their papers to be commercially successful, but their work as publishers seemed to hinge less on being self-made race figures. Charlotta A. Bass, publisher of the *California Eagle*, called herself a "highly inspired young woman who was destined to occupy a peculiar place in the realm of newspaper publishing." But Bass construed her role as a publisher in terms of being a servant of the race, rather than its leader. In her memoirs,

for example, she did more to recount the history, struggles, and successes of black people in Los Angeles, as well as the part the *Eagle* played in Los Angeles' black communities, than to recount her own experiences as a publisher. Her memoirs also paid a good deal of attention to people who helped build the *Eagle* into an institution, such as its original founder, John Neimore, and her husband, Joseph Bass. Bass's memoir suggests that she saw her paper not in terms of a singular charismatic personality guiding the paper as they cultivated a proper gendered subjectivity, like some black male publishers did, but as a democratic instrument that she and others could use to influence change for black people in Los Angeles.

49. Buni, *Robert L. Vann*, xii–xiii, 8–9, 12, 35, 61, 314; Hogan, *Black National News Service*, 49.

50. ASFP, box 8, fol. 7.

51. ASFP, box 11, fol. 2. See also ASFP, box 11, fol. 5; "The Totem Pole of Negro Woes," in Ottley, *Lonely Warrior*, 291–310.

52. Robert S. Abbott to John Sengstacke, October 13, 1933, ASFP, box 8, fol. 33.

53. For more on McGill, see the profiles of key staff members in the *Defender*, May 3, 1930. *Defender*, "A Recapitulation of 25 Years Work: Editor Robt. S. Abbott's Story of Early Struggles and Success of the World's Greatest Weekly," May 3, 1930.

54. Robert S. Abbott to John Sengstacke, February 17, 1934, ASFP, box 8, fol. 33. For more on McGill, see the profiles of key staff members in the *Defender*, May 3, 1940.

55. *Defender*, "Rev. J. H. H. Sengstacke," May 3, 1930.

56. Robert S. Abbott to John Sengstacke, October 6, 1933, ASFP, box 8, fol. 33. See also the letter from Ethel, Abbott's niece. Ethel to Abbott, April 11, 1934, ASFP, box 8, fol. 30.

57. Eneil F. Simpson to Nathan K. McGill, August 23, 1933, ASFP, box 11, fol. 2.

58. Hogan, *Black National News Service*, 197.

59. "Annual Meeting of the Directors of the Robert S. Abbott Publishing Company," January 28, 1933, ASFP, box 11, fol. 2; See also Michaeli, *Defender*, 158, 190.

60. Vincent, *Black Power and the Garvey Movement*, 219; Ottley, *Lonely Warrior*, 298.

61. Washburn, *African American Newspaper*, 126, 133–40; Hogan, *Black National News Service*, 216. See also, for example, *Atlanta Daily World*, "Depression Hits Harlem Press," June 10, 1932. The *Baltimore Afro-American* was one of the few papers that did well during the Depression, according to historian Hayward Farrar. See Farrar, *Baltimore Afro-American*, 16–19.

62. Aptheker, *Correspondence of W. E. B. Dubois*, Vol. 2, 115–19.

63. Dubois, *Dusk of Dawn*, 295.

64. Meier et al., *Black Protest Thought*, 154–57.

65. DuBois, *Dusk of Dawn*, 295.

66. Quoted in Sitkoff, *New Deal for Blacks*, 189.

67. Meir et al., *Black Protest Thought*, 158–64.

68. DuBois, *Dusk of Dawn*, 295; Dan S. Green, "W. E. B. DuBois: His Journalistic Career," in Tinney and Rector, *Issues and Trends*, 62–63, 65.

69. DuBois, *Dusk of Dawn*, 312.

70. Sitkoff, *New Deal for Blacks*, 189–91. See also Aptheker, *Correspondence of W. E. B. DuBois*, 1:478–81.

71. DuBois, *Autobiography of W. E. B. DuBois*, 258; DuBois, *Dusk of Dawn*, 311–12. It should be noted that the journalist within him did not retire. Because black media had long played a crucial role in his leadership and scholarship by providing him a powerful and consistent public platform to share his ideas, he continued to contemplate publishing columns after parting ways with the NAACP and *Crisis*. He fielded some offers and wrote some for the *Amsterdam News*. Offers continued to come, including one from Robert L. Vann, publisher of the *Pittsburgh Courier*, in December 1935. By February 1936, DuBois served as an independent columnist for the paper. See Aptheker, *Correspondence of W. E. B. DuBois*, 1:478.

72. For examples of the anxieties that black leaders shared, see Vincent, *Voices*, 57–59; Marable and Mullings, *Let Nobody Turn Us Around*, 298–300.

73. *Defender*, "Timely Topics," April 5, 1930. There were numerous articles that advised blacks to be thrifty at this time. It is interesting that some of these articles placed blame on black people for not being thrifty before the Depression began, that if they had avoided buying frivolous things and saved money in years past, their lot would be better. These writers ignored the reality of America's economic collapse, black poverty, and job discrimination.

74. *New York Amsterdam News*, "Poverty Should Not Be Alarming," March 30, 1933.

75. *Defender*, "'Make Men,' Rev. Austin urges Air Audience in W. G. N. Noonday Sermon," December 7, 1935.

76. *Defender*, "Slave Mentality," August 1, 1931; "Why Slavery Persists," March 21, 1931; "There Is No Other Way!," August 22, 1931; "Free Yet Slaves," April 8, 1933.

77. *Defender*, "The Race and Work Relief: Urban League Urges Citizens to Take Active Interest in Administration of Various Projects," August 17, 1935.

78. *Atlanta Daily World*, "An Opportunity of Service," August 24, 1934.

79. *Courier*, "Miss Burroughs Plans a 'New Deal' to Conserve Girlhood of the Race," August 26, 1933.

80. "The Housewives League of Detroit: Black Women and Economic Nationalism," in Hine, *Hine Sight*, 134. See also Drake and Cayton, *Black Metropolis*, 499; White, *Too Heavy a Load*, 144–45; Frazier, *Afro-American History*, 291.

81. Frazier, *Afro-American History*, 295–302.

82. *Courier*, "Streetwalkers," January 7, 1933. See also Wolcott, *Remaking Responsibility*, 175–76. See also Wolcott, "Culture of the Informal Economy." As historian Victoria Wolcott has argued, the informal economy included prostitution, as well as gambling and numbers-running, all of which helped some black women and men eke out an existence during the Depression. Through this subculture, the urban poor redefined respectability to adapt to the exigencies of the Depression. Still, the preservation of black womanhood by keeping black women from resorting to prostitution encouraged popular demands for black men to find work. Black men's gainful employment could protect black women from such a shameful prospect, it was thought. See also *Defender*, "Lights and Shadows," October 13, 1934.

83. "The Housewives League of Detroit: Black Women and Economic Nationalism," in Hine, *Hine Sight*, 129–45; Wolcott, *Remaking Respectability*, 167–240.

84. For the long-standing idea of men as the breadwinner and source of economic stability, see, for example, Rotundo, *American Manhood*; Kimmel, *Manhood in America*.

85. See Bates, *Pullman Porters*, 65–74. Bates shows that as early as the late nineteenth century, black women involved in the club movement considered manhood rights a part of universal suffrage rights for all people, regardless of race or sex.

86. *Defender*, "An Editorial," October 2, 1937; "Activities of Women's National Organizations," November 25, 1939. Another concern of Taylor's was that black women were increasingly becoming "breadwinners of their families" and lacked representation in the Women's Bureau.

87. *Defender*, "A Woman's Creed," September 11, 1937; *Courier*, "Manhood Going out of Style," March 12, 1932; *Courier*, "Men Don't Respect Women," December 12, 1932.

88. McElvaine, *Depression and the New Deal*, 170.

89. Sitkoff, *New Deal for Blacks*, 42, 106–7. See, for example, *Courier*, "Truly the Forgotten Man Is Negro Farmer," March 16, 1940; *Courier*, Emmett J. Scott, "'Man Farthest Down' Is Real Savior of Democrats: Race Will Support Democrats because of Roosevelt Ideal," June 20, 1936. The *Defender* declared that black men were the "real forgotten man" because of lynching, that the neglect of lynching as a national issue showed how "forgotten" they really were. See *Defender*, "An Appeal to the President," May 9, 1936.

90. Rauch, *Roosevelt Reader*, 72; Wolters, *Negroes and the Great Depression*, 94. In his 1932 acceptance speech for the Democratic presidential ticket, for example, Roosevelt was speaking to a national audience, and therefore referred to "men and women" as he discussed the conditions of America's listless economy, while at other times conflating economic recovery with employment for men and men in particular. For instance, when Roosevelt affirmed that Americans wanted work with a "reasonable measure of security," this security was of specific importance to Americans who wanted "security for themselves and for their wives and children."

91. Smith, *Building New Deal Liberalism*, 15. See also McEntee, *Now They Are Men*, 57.

92. Bryant Simon, "'New Men in Body and Soul': The Civilian Conservation Corps and the Transformation of Male Bodies and the Body Politic," in Scharff, *Seeing Nature through Gender*, 80–102.

93. Kirby, *Black Americans in the Roosevelt Era*, 31; Wolters, *Negroes and the Great Depression*, 94; see also Weiss, *Farewell to the Party of Lincoln*, 50. See also Sullivan, *Days of Hope*. There were definite anxieties in the press as to whether black people would be included equally in New Deal programs. See, for instance, *Defender*, "Waiting for the New Deal," March 18, 1933; *Defender*, "Promise 'No Color Line' in Federal Relief Jobs," April 8, 1933; *Defender*, "Race Fares Badly in U.S. Employment, What Roosevelt Will Do for Race in Way of Government Positions Is Speculative Question, Group Started Losing with Harding," March 11, 1933.

94. *Defender*, "Mayors, Governors Meet to Discuss Big Federal Program," November 18, 1933; *Defender*, "That New Deal," May 27, 1933.

95. Sitkoff, *New Deal for Blacks*, 36–43; *Defender*, "Race Fares Badly in U.S. Employment, What Roosevelt Will Do for Race in Way of Government Positions Is Speculative Question, Group Started Losing with Harding," March 11, 1933. See also "Challenge to the Solid South," in Sullivan, *Days of Hope*, 41–67. For a discussion of some papers' views on Roosevelt and the New Deal, see Oak, *Negro Newspaper*, 52–62.

96. *Defender*, "What Is Your Plan for Economic Security," April 8, 1933; Leuchtenberg, *Franklin D. Roosevelt and the New Deal*, 118, 122, 124; *Defender*, "'Make Men,' Rev. Austin Urges Air Audience in W. G. N. Noonday Sermon," December 7, 1935; *Defender*, "Returning to the Soil," January 12, 1935; see also Wolcott, *Remaking Respectability*, 232. Wolcott writes that the WPA's "practice house" employed black men in emasculating domestic roles as butlers and cooks. These occupations "brought back a vision of a servile African American male workforce not seen since the Great Migration." For discussions that foreground the experiences of black men in New Deal programs, see Salmond, *Civilian Conservation Corps*, 88–101; Jones, *Tribe of Black Ulysses*; Cole, *African-American Experience*. By the 1936 presidential election, black people would make a historic political shift to vote for Roosevelt and the Democrats for the first time.

97. "John H. Sengstacke III: America's Black Press Lord," ASFP, box 22, fol. 9, p. 13; ASFP, box 22, fol. 6, Untitled Manuscript by Walter Lee Lowe, n.d.

98. "John H. Sengstacke III: America's Black Press Lord," ASFP, box 22, fol. 9, p. 14.

99. See, for instance, Hornsby-Gutting, *Black Manhood*; Summers, *Manliness and Its Discontents*; Kimmel, *Manhood in America*; Rotundo, *American Manhood*.

100. Robert S. Abbott to John Sengstacke, October 8, 1931, ASFP, box 8, fol. 33.

101. "John H. Sengstacke III: America's Black Press Lord," ASFP, box 22, fol. 9, p. 15.

102. John Sengstacke to Robert S. Abbott, January 31, 1932, ASFP, box 8, fol. 33. See also Michaeli, *Defender*, 181.

103. John Sengstacke to Robert S. Abbott, March 21, 1932, ASFP, box 8, fol. 33.

104. John Sengstacke to Robert S. Abbott, April 5, 1932, ASFP, box 8, fol. 33.

105. "John H. Sengstacke III: America's Black Press Lord," ASFP, box 22, fol. 9, p. 14.

106. Robert S. Abbott to John Sengstacke, October 6, 1933, ASFP, box 8, fol. 33.

107. Robert S. Abbott to John Sengstacke, October 13, 1933, ASFP, box 8, fol. 33.

108. "John H. Sengstacke III: America's Black Press Lord," ASFP, box 22, fol. 9, p. 15.

109. Robert S. Abbott to John Sengstacke, April 17, 1934, ASFP, box 8, fol. 33.

110. Robert S. Abbott to John Sengstacke, April 17, 1934, ASFP, box 8, fol. 33.

111. Robert S. Abbott to John Sengstacke, April 17, 1934, ASFP, box 8, fol. 33.

112. Robert S. Abbott to John Sengtsacke, May 4, 1934, ASFP, box 8, fol. 33.

113. John Sengstacke to Robert S. Abbott, May 23, 1934, ASFP, box 8, fol. 33.

114. Waters, *American Diary*, 153.

115. Sitkoff, *New Deal for Blacks*, 106–7.

116. For the relationship between blacks and Communists during the Depression era, see Korstad, *Civil Rights Unionism*; Greenberg, *"Or Does It Explode?"*; Kelley, *Hammer and Hoe*; Naison, *Communists in Harlem*; Maxwell, *New Negro, Old Left*.

117. Denning, *Cultural Front*, xvi–xvii.

118. See, for example, "The Red and the Black," in Sitkoff, *New Deal*, 139–68; Kelley, *Hammer and Hoe*; Greenberg, *"Or Does It Explode?."*

119. Aptheker, *Correspondence of W. E. B. DuBois*, 2:115–20.

120. Quoted in Gellman, *Death Blow to Jim Crow*, 16, 2–5, 7.

121. Quoted in Gellman, 29.

122. John Sengstacke, "How I Depend on Others," April 27, 1932, ASFP, box 24, fol. 4; ASFP, box 24, fol. 4. See also "Waiting for a Leader," ASFP, box 24, fol. 17.

123. Robert S. Abbott to John Sengstacke, October 8, 1931, ASFP, box 8, fol. 33.

124. Waters, *American Diary*, 153–54. For another example of Sengstacke's embrace of worker consciousness, see *Defender*, "Today and Tomorrow," August 3, 1940.

125. Gellman, *Death Blow to Jim Crow*, 16; DuBois, *Dusk of Dawn*, 312–13.

126. ASFP, box 22, fol. 19.

127. "John H. Sengstacke III: America's Black Press Lord," ASFP, box 22, fol. 9, p. 6.

128. "John H. Sengstacke III: America's Black Press Lord," ASFP, box 22, fol. 9, p. 15–17; June 8, 1936, ASFP, box 11, fol. 5. See also Hogan, *Black National News Service*, 197–98; Michaeli, *Defender*, 204–5; Ottley, *Lonely Warrior*, 333–36.

129. Eniel F. Simpson to Robert S. Abbott, October 23, 1934, ASFP, box 11, fol. 3.

130. "Notice to All Departments," n.d., ASFP, box 11, fol. 3.

131. January 28, 1935, ASFP, box 11, fol. 2; "Annual Meeting of the Directors of the Robert S. Abbott Publishing Company," January 26, 1935, ASFP, box 11, fol. 4.

132. "The Inside Story of the Chicago Defender," ASFP, box 11, fol. 7, pp. 6–7.

133. "The Inside Story of the Chicago Defender," ASFP, box 11, fol. 7, pp. 6–7, 10, 8, 26.

134. "The Inside Story of the Chicago Defender," ASFP, box 11, fol. 7, p. 10.

135. ASFP, box 11, fol. 9, ca. 1930s.

136. Rayford W. Lemly Co., C. P. A., June 8, 1936, ASFP, box 11, fol. 5.

137. "Second Notice and Demand for Income Tax," ASFP, box 11, fol. 7; John Sengstacke to Carter H. Harrison, Collector of Internal Revenue, July 7, 1938, ASFP, box 11, fol. 7.

138. Treasury Department to Abbott Publishing Company, August 11, 1938, ASFP, box 11, fol. 7.

139. John Sengstacke to All Employees, n.d., ASFP, box 11, fol. 7. See also "Continental Illinois National Bank and Trust Company to the Robert S. Abbott Publishing Co., September 13, 1938, ASFP, box 11, fol. 7. See also other financial records that indicate the company's growing debts in ASFP, box 11, fol. 7. A letter from Charles A. Beckett to John Sengstacke on August 30, 1939, even joked some about the rising debts. It said, "Everything is going on very well here. Things seem to be quiet. Somebody must have told the creditors that you [Sengstacke] were out of town because they haven't called, with the exception of one or two minor cases which were easy to pacify." See Beckett to Sengstacke, August 30, 1939, ASFP, box 11, fol. 8.

140. John Sengstacke to All Employees, October 5, 1938, ASFP, box 11, fol. 7.

141. "Notice of Attorney's Lien," May 24, 1939, ASFP, box 1, fol. 24.

142. Memorandum to John Sengstacke, n.d., ASFP, box 11, fol. 9; John Sengstacke to Al Monroe, February 19, 1940, ASFP, box 11, fol. 9.

143. "Report of Circulation Conditions in Eastern Territory," ASFP, box 11, fol. 10, n.d.

144. W. B. Abbott to John Sengstacke, February 13, 1940, ASFP, box 11, fol. 9. W. B. Abbott was likely Walter B. Abbott of New York, a cousin. See *Defender*, "Defender Swamped by Congratulations," May 17, 1930.

145. W. B. Abbott to John Sengstacke, February 21, 1940, ASFP, box 11, fol. 9.

146. John Sengstacke to W. B. Abbott, February 19, 1940, ASFP, box 11, fol. 9.

147. John Sengstacke to Claude Barnett, January 6, 1940, Barnett Papers, box 149, fol. 7.

148. Hogan, *Black National News Service*, 44, 198–201. See also, Horne, *Rise and Fall of the Associated Negro Press*.

149. Hogan, *Black National News Service*, 215–18; Pride and Wilson, *History of the Black Press*, 174–78.

150. Quoted in Mullen, *Popular Fronts*, 49.

151. *Defender*, "A Recapitulation of 25 Years Work: Editor Robt. S. Abbott's Story of Early Struggles and Success of the World's Greatest Weekly," May 3, 1930. See also Michaeli, *Defender*, 157.

152. Waters, *American Diary*, 136, 147–49, 135. See also Ottley, *Lonely Warrior*, 84.

153. Barnett Papers, Sengstacke to Barnett, January 6, 1940, box 149, fol. 7.

154. Quoted in Hogan, *Black National News Service*, 217.

155. John Sengstacke to Claude Barnett, January 6, 1940, Barnett Papers, box 149, fol. 7.

156. Quoted in Gellman, *Death Blow to Jim Crow*, 29. Scholars have also identified a militant ethic of women's activism that came out of the Communist orbit and influenced second-wave feminism. See, for example, McDuffie, *Sojourning for Freedom*; Gore, *Radicalism at the Crossroads*; Gore et al., *Want to Start a Revolution?*.

157. "Fellow Publishers and Editors," ASFP, box 26, fol. 11.

158. Hogan, *Black National News Service*, 198, 49–51, 45–47. See also Waters, *American Diary*, 419, 423.

159. See also Summers, *Manliness and Its Discontents*; Wilder, *In the Company of Black Men*.

160. *Defender*, "Robert S. Abbott Dies after Long Illness: Death Comes during Sleep at His Home," March 9, 1940.

161. ASFP, box 22, fol. 6.

162. Detweiler, *Negro Press in the United States*, 4, 127; Hill, *Who's Who in the American Negro Press*, 13–37, 65. See also Booker with Booker, *Shocking the Conscience*, 29, 31.

163. John Sengstacke to Claude Barnett, February 7, 1940, Barnett Papers, box 149, fol. 7.

164. Kimmel, *Manhood in America*, 172. Though Kimmel analyzes the many meanings of manhood mainly for white men, he writes that "fraternal orders allowed men to reinvent themselves as men, to experience the pleasures and comforts of each other's company and cultural and domestic life without feeling feminized."

165. Quoted in White, *Too Heavy a Load*, 149; Giddings, *When and Where I Enter*, 229–30.

166. Giddings, *In Search of Sisterhood*, 69, 109; White, *Too Heavy a Load*, 149, 152, 155; Clarenda M. Phillips, "Sisterly Bonds: African American Sororities Rising to Overcome Obstacles," in Brown, Parks, and Phillips, *African American Fraternities and Sororities*, 348, 350.

167. Wolcott, *Remaking Respectability*, 168–69, 204, 216.

168. Morris, *Eye on the Struggle*, 112, 114. See also Bradley, *Women and the Press*, 132, 192–93; "Crossing the Threshold," in Cairns, *Front-Page Women Journalists*, 14. As Cairns argues, the office could be considered a masculine space. Cairns calls the newsroom an "inviolate male space" that both white and black women journalists sometimes struggled to navigate.

169. Wolcott, *Remaking Respectability*, 168, 209; White, *Too Heavy a Load*, 163–66.

170. Giddings, *In Search of Sisterhood*, 49, 66–67; Andre McKenzie, "In the Beginning: The Early History of the Divine Nine," in Brown, Parks, and Phillips, *African American Fraternities and Sororities*, 192, 184.

171. Marable and Mullings, *Let Nobody Turn Us Around*, 294–97. It should be noted that, as Giddings argues, Bethune was adept at public relations, having, as Giddings put it, a "silver tongue." See Giddings, *When and Where I Enter*, 226–27.

172. Giddings, *When and Where I Enter*, 204–5.

173. *Defender*, "Publishers Favor Forming News Service," March 9, 1940. See also Mullen, *Popular Fronts*, 47–52.

174. Waters, *American Diary*, 141.

175. Hogan, *Black National News Service*, 217–18.

176. Quoted in Pride and Wilson, *History of the Black Press*, 186.

177. Program Agenda and "Agenda and Organization of the Conference of Negro Publishers and Editors," Barnett Papers, box 149, fol. 7. See also Simmons, *African American Press*, 69.

178. Waters, *American Diary*, 134–36. For scholars who echo this point, see also Tinney and Rector, *Issues and Trends*, 20; Hogan, *Black National News Service*, 56, 45; *Defender*, "Random Thoughts," March 9, 1940. "Turning White Space into Black Space: The Chicago Defender and the Creation of the Cultural Front," in Mullen, *Popular Fronts*, 47–48, 51–52.

179. *Defender*, "Race Publishers Pause to Pay Tribute to Editor Abbott," March 9 1940.

180. Michaeli, *Defender*, 232; *Defender*, "Publishers Favor Forming News Service," March 9, 1940.

181. "Turning White Space into Black Space: The *Chicago Defender* and the Creation of the Cultural Front," in Mullen, *Popular Fronts*, 47–48, 51–52.

182. John Sengstacke to D. Arnett Murphy, March 14, 1940, ASFP, box 67, fol. 12.

183. Hogan, *Black National News Service*, 215–18; Mullen, *Popular Fronts*, 51; *Defender*, "Random Thoughts," March 9, 1940; *Defender*, "Publishers Favor Forming News Service," March 9, 1940.

184. *Defender*, "A Titan Passes," March 16, 1940; *Defender*, "The Bridge Is Built," March 16, 1940; *Defender*, "Robert S. Abbott Dies after Long Illness: Death Comes during Sleep at His Home," March 9, 1940.

185. *Defender*, "Dustin' Off the News: Robert S. Abbott 'Toiled Upward thru the Night,'" March 9, 1940.

186. *Defender*, "The Observation Post," March 16, 1940.

187. *Defender*, "What's Going on in Hollywood," March 16, 1940.

188. *Defender*, "Quest for Equality" series.

189. Dudley, *My Father's Shadow*, 8.

190. Waters, *American Diary*, 135, 153.

191. *Defender*, "File Will of Editor Abbott for Probate," March 16, 1940.

192. *Defender*, "File Will of Editor Abbott for Probate," March 16, 1940. See also John Sengstacke, ASFP, box 1, fol. 1. Sengstacke, as owner and publisher following his uncle's death, promised to carry on what he had gained from Abbott: "As I knew Robert S. Abbott, he had the utmost joy from his work and it was his chief happiness and reward. His greatest love was helping others to grow and prosper. I dedicated myself to this philosophy and have enjoyed every moment I have spent in this service to America."

193. *Defender*, "Hundreds Express Grief at Editor Abbott's Death," March 9, 1940.

194. "John H. Sengstacke III: America's Black Press Lord," ASFP, box 22, fol. 9, p. 23; Ottley, *Lonely Warrior*, 351–54. See also Burns, *Nitty Gritty*, 7.

195. See, for example, *Defender*, "John Sengstacke, Abbott's Nephew, Replaces Widow as Head of *Defender*," February 7, 1942; *Defender*, "File Will of Editor Abbott for Probate," March 16, 1940; "Court Petition Names Sengstacke Principal Owner of Abbott Stock," May 7, 1942; *Defender*, "File Will of Editor Abbott for Probate," March 16, 1940. See also Michaeli, *Defender*, 238; and Waters, *American Diary*, 154–55.

196. D. Arnett Murphy to John Sengstacke, March 19, 1940, ASFP, box 67, fol. 12; D. Arnett Murphy to John Sengstacke, May 27, 1940, ASFP, box 67, fol. 12; *Defender*, "Publishers Favor Forming News Service," March 9, 1940. See also Pride and Wilson, *History of the Black Press*, 195. While the organization's by-laws were revised in 1970, it reiterated its fraternal goals. It intended to "encourage and foster co-operation and fraternal fellowship," among other things.

197. Pride and Wilson, *History of the Black Press*, 190–92; John Sengstacke, January 23, 1943, ASFP, box 24, fol. 11. See also "What Newspapers Can Do to Help National Unity," 1943, ASFP, box 24, fol. 23; Wiggins, "Wendell Smith, the *Pittsburgh Courier-Journal*, and the Campaign to Include Blacks in Organized Baseball, 1933–1945"; *Defender*, "Today and Tomorrow," August 3, 1940; Mullen, *Popular Fronts*, 47–48, 51–52; "Victory through Unity," in Michaeli, *Defender*; Washburn, *African American Newspaper*, 157–59, 172–76.

198. ASFP, box 24, fol. 15; Pride and Wilson, *History of the Black Press*, 187.

199. "The Struggle," in Sitkoff, *New Deal for Blacks*, 244–67. See also Gellman, *Death Blow to Jim Crow*; Sullivan, *Days of Hope*.

200. Lichtenstein, *State of the Union*, 34–35; Cohen, *Making a New Deal*, 5; Denning, *Cultural Front*, xvi–50. See also Nancy MacLean, "Postwar Women's History: The "Second Wave" or the End of the Family Wage?," in Agnew and Rosenzweig, *Companion to Post-1945 America*, 235–59.

201. Cohen, *Making a New Deal*, 246–49; Leuchtenburg, *Franklin D. Roosevelt*, 118–19.

202. "Confidential Memorandum," n.d., ASFP, box 58, fol. 2; Drake and Cayton, *Black Metropolis*, 400–401.

Chapter 4

1. Washburn, *African American Newspaper*, 177.

2. Quoted in Pride and Wilson, *History of the Black Press*, 188, 193–94.

3. Myrdal, *American Dilemma*, 923, 911. Also quoted in Washburn, *African American Newspaper*, 181.

4. Washburn, *African American Newspaper*, 181.

5. Washburn, 179–81.

6. Washburn, 179–81.

7. Green, *Selling the Race*, 191–93.

8. Roberts and Klibanoff, *Race Beat*, 94–96.

9. Ottley, *Lonely Warrior*.

10. Simmons, *African American Press*, 80–81.

11. *Courier*, "Fifty Years of Progress in Negro Journalism," June 17, 1950.

12. Quoted in Washburn, *African American Newspaper*, 199.

13. Klarman, "How Brown Changed Race Relations."

14. Green, *Selling the Race*, 196–97. See also Booker with Booker, *Shocking the Conscience*; Raiford, *Imprisoned in a Luminous Glare*, 88. See also Ruth Feldstein, "I Wanted the Whole World to See: Race, Gender, and Constructions of Motherhood in the Death of Emmett Till," in Meyerowitz, *Not June Cleaver*, 263–303, for the gendered and contested treatment of Till's mother, Mamie Till Bradley, in the press. See also Tyson, *Blood of Emmett Till*.

15. *Defender*, "Readers Flood *Defender* with Letters about Till," September 24, 1955. See also *Los Angeles Sentinel*, "Emmett Till Case Gains All Out Aid for NAACP," September 29, 1955. According to the latter article, NAACP membership and funds had jumped as a result of Till's lynching.

16. See Tyson, *Radio Free Dixie*, 20.

17. See, for instance, Parker, *Fighting for Democracy*.

18. Tyson, *Radio Free Dixie*; Barksdale, "Robert F. Williams."

19. Myrdal, *American Dilemma*, 910. See also Gershenhorn, *Louis Austin and the Carolina Times*.

20. See also Umoja's definition of "armed resistance," in Umoja, *We Will Shoot Back*, 7.

21. Williams, *Negroes with Guns*, 51; Tyson, *Radio Free Dixie*, 38–48.

22. Williams, *Negroes with Guns*, 57; Tyson, *Radio Free Dixie*, 48–72.

23. Williams, *Negroes with Guns*, 110. Williams stated, for example, that "the principle of self-defense is an American tradition that began at Lexington and Concord."

24. Stephens, "Narrating Acts of Resistance." For more on the resurgence of the KKK during the civil rights era, see, for example, Greenhaw, *Fighting the Devil in Dixie*; Williams, *Negroes with Guns*, 41, 39, 54, 74, 99, 114.

25. Williams, *Negroes with Guns*, 50.

26. Klarman, "How Brown Changed Race Relations."

27. Tyson, *Radio Free Dixie*, 80.

28. Williams, *Negroes with Guns*, 73, 95. See also Tyson, *Radio Free Dixie*, 80. The group was well armed and well trained, in part because many of them were veterans. They started building their own rifle range and an arsenal that included M-Is, German semiautomatic weapons, and steel helmets. Monroe black women, many the wives of these men, participated too as a phone patrol that called neighbors to alert them to trouble.

29. Cohen, *Black Crusader*, 97–101.

30. Williams, *Negroes with Guns*, 51. See also Tyson, *Radio Free Dixie*, 81; Reed, *Chicago NAACP*.

31. Tyson, *Radio Free Dixie*, 82. It must be noted that this number may have been greater because some members did not want their names recorded lest they face reprisals from whites. See Strain, *Pure Fire*, 54.

32. Barksdale, "Robert F. Williams."

33. Payne, *I've Got the Light of Freedom*. See also Stephens, "Narrating Acts of Resistance." Stephens argues that in the last twenty-four years of his life, Williams remained committed to empowering local people to become local leaders, evidenced by his organizing efforts in the black community of Lake County, Michigan, where Williams moved in 1974. See also Ransby, *Ella Baker*.

34. Tyson, *Radio Free Dixie*, 87, 206. See also Gaines, *Uplifting the Race*.

35. Tyson, *Radio Free Dixie*, 39, 70. See Hall, "Long Civil Rights Movement"; Sugrue, *Sweet Land of Liberty*; Theoharis and Woodard, *Freedom North*; Countryman, *Civil Rights and Black Power*; Biondi, *To Stand and Fight*; Gilmore, *Defying Dixie*.

36. Williams, *Negroes with Guns*, 52.

37. Williams, 54–58; Tyson, *Radio Free Dixie*, 87–89.

38. Strain, *Pure Fire*, 56–57; Williams, *Negroes with Guns*, 57.

39. McGuire, *At the Dark End of the Street*, 80, 98, 110.

40. Quoted in Morris, *Eye on the Struggle*, 182; Streitmatter, *Raising Her Voice*, 124.

41. *Atlanta Daily World*, "Huge Blow to Bias" and "Bus Segregation Loses," November 20, 1956.

42. *Los Angeles Sentinel*, "A New Kind of Negro Leader," October 31, 1957.

43. *Courier*, "Martin Luther King Jr.: A Young Minister Marked for Leadership," April 7, 1956; King, *My Life with Martin Luther King, Jr.*, 153–54.

44. Wendt, *Spirit and the Shotgun*, 25; Washington, *Testament of Hope*, 38.

45. Strain, *Pure Fire*, 37.

46. Washington, *Testament of Hope*, 75–76, 17.

47. Strain, *Pure Fire*, 38–42; Washington, *Testament of Hope*, 10.

48. Raiford, *Imprisoned in a Luminous Glare*, 75.

49. Marisa Chappell, Jenny Hutchinson, and Brian Ward, "'Dress Modestly, Neatly . . . As If You Were Going to Church': Respectability, Class and Gender in the Montgomery Bus Boycott and the Early Civil Rights Movement," in Ling and Montieth, *Gender and the Civil Rights Movement*, 92, 95.

50. *New York Times*, "Non-Violence Held Aid to Integration," August 16, 1958; *Washington Post and Times*, "Exemplary Race Relations," February 24, 1956; *Courier*, "Non-Violence Plan Wins White Friends," November 1, 1958.

51. Marissa Chapell et al., "'Dress Modestly, Neatly . . . As If You Were Going to Church'," in Ling and Montieth, *Gender and the Civil Rights Movement*, 92, 95.

52. Quoted in Tyson, *Radio Free Dixie*, 78.

53. "Designed to Harass" and "Black, White, and Red All Over," in Woods, *Black Struggle, Red Scare*; Dudziak, *Cold War Civil Rights*, 11–13; "Domesticating Anticolonialism," in Von Eschen, *Race against Empire*.

54. Sullivan, *Lift Every Voice*, 425–26.

55. Williams, *Negroes with Guns*, 50.

56. Cruse, *Crisis of the Negro Intellectual*, 353.

57. Williams, *Negroes with Guns*, 61–63.

58. *New York Times*, "N. A. A. C. P. Leader Urges Violence," May 7, 1959; Wendt, *Spirit and the Shotgun*, 29–31.

59. Wilkins, *Standing Fast*, 39, 46–50, 55–58, 155–56, 265.

60. For a more dramatic exchange of words between the two men, see Tyson, *Radio Free Dixie*, 150–51.

61. *New York Times*, "N. A. A. C. P. Leader Urges Violence," May 7, 1959.

62. Marissa Chapell et al., "'Dress Modestly, Neatly . . . As If You Were Going to Church'," in Ling and Montieth, *Gender and the Civil Rights Movement*, 78.

63. Quoted in Wendt, *Spirit and the Shotgun*, 31. See also *Defender*, "NAACP Aides Disagree," May 23, 1959; *New York Amsterdam News*, "Williams Case Up Next Wednesday," May 30, 1959; *Defender*, "NAACP's Policy Faces Challenge," June 6, 1959; *Atlanta Daily World*, "NAACP Directors Upheld in Robert F. Williams Case," July 21, 1959.

64. *Daily Defender*, "Violence Advocate Tries to Get Sons in White School," June 2, 1959.

65. *Defender*, "Carolina Leader Lashes Critics," May 23, 1959.

66. *Daily Defender*, "Watch on the Potomac," May 13, 1959.

67. *Courier*, "'We Must Fight Back' But . . . With What and How?," May 30, 1959.

68. Quoted in Tyson, *Radio Free Dixie*, 154.

69. Roberts and Klibanoff, *Race Beat*, 151.

70. Bates, *Long Shadow of Little Rock*, 3, 33–34; Pride and Wilson, *History of the Black Press*, 215. On black women publishers, see, for example, Streitmatter, *Raising Her Voice*.

71. For more on the Little Rock crisis, see, for example, Kirk, *Beyond Little Rock*. See also Bullock, "'Freedom Is a Job for All of Us.'"

72. *Arkansas State Press*, "Be Calm . . . Don't Compromise Watch Your Conduct . . . ," August 16, 1957; Quoted in Tyson, *Radio Free Dixie*, 154.

73. See Tyson, *Radio Free Dixie*, 152. Wilkins wrote Prattis, arguing that Williams's couching of black armed resistance in terms of self-defense was a "façade," that William was instead in support of outright violence.

74. *Courier*, "Horizon: Non-Violence," November 30, 1957.

75. *Courier*, "Horizon: Non-Violence," December 7, 1957. See also *Courier*, "Horizon: King's Alchemy," November 22, 1958.

76. *Courier*, "Horizon: Truth on Scaffold," May 30, 1959. See also Strain, *Pure Fire*, 50–51.

77. *New York Amsterdam News*, "They Lynched Us All," May 16, 1959.

78. Wilkins, *Standing Fast*, 265.

79. Williams, *Negroes with Guns*, 66; Tyson, *Radio Free Dixie*, 193–96.

80. Williams, *Negroes with Guns*, 66, 117.

81. Williams, 66, 73, 54, 110.

82. Quoted in Tyson, *Radio Free Dixie*, 193.

83. Williams, *Negroes with Guns*, 73.

84. *Crusader* 1, no. 1 (June 26, 1959), RFWP, box 5.

85. Detweiler, *Negro Press in the United States*, 53–58.

86. Tyson, *Radio Free Dixie*, 193–95; Williams, *Negroes with Guns*, 65.

87. McMillan, *Smoking Typewriters*, 7, 10–11.

88. Tyson, *Radio Free Dixie*, 194–96.

89. *Defender*, "Publishers Favor Forming News Service," March 9, 1940.

90. Tyson, *Radio Free Dixie*, 88. As Williams stated, the men began "getting organized and setting up, digging foxholes and started getting up ammunition and training guys." They "started building our own rifle range, and we got our own M-1's and got our own Mausers and German semi-automatic rifles, and steel helmets. We had everything."

91. Quoted in Tyson, *Radio Free Dixie*, 141; McGuire, *At the Dark End of the Street*, 76, 65.

92. See also "A Question of Honor," in Estes, *I Am a Man*, 39–59.

93. Tyson, *Radio Free Dixie*, 141–42. It must be noted, however, as historian Christopher Strain has pointed out, that when women wanted to participate in the armed guard, even Williams's wife, he kept them from doing so. See Strain, *Pure Fire*, 74–75.

94. Williams, *Negroes with Guns*, 121; Strain, *Pure Fire*, 56.

95. *Crusader* 1, no. 5 (July 18, 1959), RFWP, box 5.

96. *Crusader* 1, no. 5, (July 25, 1959), RFWP, box 5.

97. "Armed Resistance and the Mississippi Movement" in Wendt, *Spirit and the Shotgun*, 100–30.

98. Umoja, *We Will Shoot Back*, 8.

99. Wendt, *Spirit and the Shotgun*, 101, 104–5.

100. Tyson, *Radio Free Dixie*, 3; "Gon' Be Treated Right: Self-Defense in Black History," in Strain, *Pure Fire*; "Conclusion: The Myth of Nonviolence," in Hill, *Deacons for Defense*, 258–73. See also Umoja, *We Will Shoot Back*.

101. *Atlanta Daily World*, "NAACP Approves Suspension of 'Fire with Fire' Branch Head," June 11, 1959; *Courier*, "NAACP Maverick Plans Fight over Ouster at Convention," June 10, 1959.

102. Quoted in Barksdale, "Robert F. Williams."

103. *Courier*, "2000 Delegates Take Part in NAACP's 50th Convention," July 25, 1959; *Atlanta Daily World*, "NAACP Case Upheld in Robert F. Williams Case," July 21, 1959.

104. *Washington Post and Times Herald*, "NAACP Convention Approves Suspension of Carolina Leader," July 18, 1959.

105. Peter J. Ling, "Gender and Generation: Manhood at the Southern Christian Leadership Conference," in Ling and Montieth, *Gender and the Civil Rights Movement*, 113.

106. See, for example, *Arkansas State Press*, "NAACP Committee to Hear Charges against Williams," May 22, 1959; "NAACP Continues Suspension of Branch President, but Stands Firmly behind Those Who Will Protect Themselves," June 12, 1959.

107. Tyson, *Radio Free Dixie*, 159–65; Bates, *Long Shadow of Little Rock*, 200, 202, 221; Pride and Wilson, *History of the Black Press*, 215–16.

108. *Crusader* 1, no. 17 (October 17, 1959), RFWP, box 5; Tyson, *Radio Free Dixie*, 199.

109. *New York Times*, "N. A. A. C. P. Upholds Stand by Wilkins," May 12, 1959. See also *Defender*, "The People Speak: Williams and NAACP," July 8, 1959.

110. *Crusader* 1, no. 3 (July 25, 1959), RFWP, box 5; See also *Courier*, "NAACP Maverick Plans Eight over Ouster at Convention," June 20, 1959.

111. Von Eschen, *Race against Empire*, 77–85, 99–107; See also Meriwether, *Proudly We Can Be Africans*.

112. Lewis, *W. E. B. DuBois, 1919–1963*, 563–68; Tyson, *Radio Free Dixie*, 244.

113. *Crusader* 1, no. 8 (August 15, 1959), RFWP, box 5.

114. *Crusader* 1, no. 14 (September 26, 1959), RFWP, box 5.

115. "A Question of Honor," in Estes, *I Am a Man*.

116. Tyson, *Radio Free Dixie*, 194–95.

117. Tyson, 141–42.

118. Tyson, 142; Peter J. Ling, "Gender and Generation: Manhood and the Southern Christian Leadership Conference," in Ling and Montieth, *Gender and the Civil Rights Movement*, 113.

119. Strain, *Pure Fire*, 74–75. See also Farah Jasmine Griffin, "'Ironies of the Saint': Malcolm X, Black Women, and the Price of Protection," in Collier-Thomas and Franklin, *Sisters in the Struggle*, 214–29. Griffin argues that black men's "promise of protection" has been a problematic proposition that, while perhaps sincere, enforced patriarchy and women's dependence on men.

120. See, for example, Collier-Thomas and Franklin, *Sisters in the Struggle*; Susan M. Hartman, "Women's Employment and the Domestic Ideal in the Early Cold War Years," in Meyerowitz, *Not June Cleaver*, 86.

121. King, *My Life with Martin Luther King, Jr.*, 153.

122. Peter J. Ling, "Gender and Generation: Manhood at the Southern Christian Leadership Conference," in Ling and Montieth, *Gender and the Civil Rights Movement*, 105–8.

123. Peter J. Ling, "Gender and Generation," in Ling and Montieth, *Gender and the Civil Rights Movement*, 114.

124. Strain, *Pure Fire*, 46.

125. Carson, *Eyes on the Prize*, 110–12.

126. See, for instance, "Sissy Race of All Mankind," in Tyson, *Radio Free Dixie*, 137–65.

127. *Crusader* 1, no. 19 (October 31, 1959), RFWP, box 5.

128. *Crusader* 1, no. 13 (September 19, 1959), RFWP, box 5.

129. *Crusader* 2, no. 32 (July 19, 1961), RFWP, box 5.

130. *Crusader* 1, no. 19 (October 31, 1959), RFWP, box 5.

131. *Los Angeles Sentinel*, "A New Kind of Negro Leader," October 31, 1957.

132. *Atlanta Daily World*, "Non-Violent 'New Attitude,' Not Weakness, Leaders Told," July 24, 1959.

133. *Defender*, "Say Non-Violence Shows Strength, Not Weakness," August 8, 1959.

134. Miller, *Messman Chronicles*; Allen, *Port Chicago Mutiny*, 33–34; Washburn, *African American Newspaper*, 147–48, 161. For examples of this in the *Courier's* campaign, see *Courier*, "A Hero?," February 14, 1942; *Courier*, "The Naval Disgrace," November 16, 1940; *Courier*, "Score Navy 'Do Nothing' Policy," February 27, 1943; *Courier*, "Another Navy Hero!," May 20, 1944; *Courier*, "All He Can Be Is a Mess Attendant," September 23, 1939.

135. Dowd, *Negro in American Life*, 353.

136. Myrdal, *American Dilemma*, 908; Oak, *Negro Newspaper*, 20, 136–37; Waters, *American Diary*, 140; Ottley, *"New World A-Coming,"* 268; Frazier quoted in Simmons, *African American Press*, 71.

137. Von Eschen, *Race against Empire*, 147–59.

138. Peter J. Ling, "Gender and Generation," in Ling and Montieth, *Gender and the Civil Rights Movement*, 114.

139. Carson, *Papers of Martin Luther King Jr.*, 4:118.

140. Washington, *Testament of Hope*, 5–9.

141. Williams, *Negroes with Guns*, 122.

142. Strain, *Pure Fire*, 47.

143. King, *Stride toward Freedom*, 202.

144. King Jr., *Measure of a Man*, 16–21. See also Wendt, *Spirit and the Shotgun*, 39–41.

145. Ellwood, *Fifties Spiritual Marketplace*, 9, 25; Tyson, *Radio Free Dixie*, 213. See also Calloway-Thomas and Lucaites, *Martin Luther King, Jr.*

146. King, *My Life with Martin Luther King, Jr.*, 91.

147. Martin Luther King Jr., "The Social Organization of Non-Violence," in Carson, *Eyes on the Prize*, 112–14. See also King's essay reprinted in Williams, *Negroes with Guns*, 13–14. The debate between King and Williams was intense and well publicized, namely, within the *Liberation* magazine. Even contemporary observers treated the two men as foils. For instance, a 1959 biography of King was titled

Crusader without Violence. See Strain, *Pure Fire*, 60. See also Tyson, *Radio Free Dixie*, 213–16. The same month that King published his rebuttal to Williams, non-violent advocates Bayard Rustin, A. J. Muste, and David Dellinger took Williams on in a public debate. Dellinger edited *Liberation* and allowed Williams to publish first so that King could respond later and at length, deliberately stacking the odds in King's favor.

148. Washington, *Testament of Hope*, 39.

149. Peter J. Ling, "Gender and Generation," in Ling and Montieth, *Gender and the Civil Rights Movement*, 114, 117; Carson, *Eyes on the Prize*, 131–32.

150. Washington, *Testament of Hope*, 12; King, *My Life, My Love, My Legacy*, 66. See also King, *Stride toward Freedom*, 80, 85.

151. King, *My Life, My Love, My Legacy*, 66; King, *My Life with Martin Luther King, Jr.*, 160.

152. Woods, *Black Struggle Red Scare*, 143, 168.

153. "The Civil Rights Era and the Black Press," in Washburn, *African American Newspaper*, 197–205. See also, "Questionable Leanings," in Carrol, *Race News* 117–51.

154. Quoted in McGuire, *At the Dark End of the Street*, 105.

155. McGuire, 107–10.

156. Quoted in Simmons, *African American Press*, 97–98.

157. Quoted in Morgan and Davies, *From Sit-Ins to SNCC*, 13.

158. Iwan Morgan, "The New Movement: The Student Sit-ins in 1960," in Morgan and Davies, *From Sit-Ins to SNCC*, 1–22. See also Robert E. Luckett Jr., "Charles Sherrod and Martin Luther King Jr.: Mass Action and Nonviolence in Albany," in Glisson, *Human Tradition in the Civil Rights Movement*, 181–95.

159. Quoted in Morgan and Davies, *From Sit-Ins to SNCC*, 12.

160. *Defender*, "Movement Guided by Non-Violence," March 24, 1960.

161. *New York Amsterdam News*, "Heed Their Rising Voices," April 9, 1960. The paper's request for financial support from black celebrities was not farfetched necessarily, for several of them came to support the movement often as spokespersons and fundraisers. See Raymond, *Stars for Freedom*.

162. Morgan and Davies, *From Sit-Ins to SNCC*, 8. See also Roberts and Klibanoff, *Race Beat*, 222–23.

163. Quoted in Simmons, *African American Press*, 102–9. See also Caryl A. Cooper, "Percy Greene and the Jackson Advocate," in Davies, ed., *Press and Race*, 55–84. On racial violence in Mississippi, see, for example, Umoja, *We Will Shoot Back*; Simmons, *African American Press*, 102–4.

164. *Crusader* 1, no. 36 (March 5, 1960), RFWP, box 5. Used with the permission of the Bentley Historical Library, University of Michigan.

165. Tyson, *Radio Free Dixie*, 265.

166. Quoted in Tyson, 266.

167. Tyson, 268–77.

168. See, for example, *Daily Defender*, "Heavily Armed Cops Roam Tense, Riot Torn Streets," August 29, 1961; *Chicago Daily Defender*, "Monroe Race Riot Brewed

for Months," August 29, 1961; *Atlanta Daily World*, "Kennedy Calls for Prosecution of Those Behind Riot," August 29, 1961.

169. *Chicago Daily Defender*, "'Riders' Carry On Civil Rights Battle in N. Car.," August 24, 1961.

170. *Daily Defender*, "Integrationists 'Passive' Resistance Plan Explodes," August 29, 1961.

171. *Defender*, "N. C. Leader Who Held 2 Whites Flees," August 30, 1961.

172. Williams, *Negroes with Guns,* 85–90. For its historical context of the Freedom Rides in Monroe and more on the so-called kidnapping incident, see Tyson, *Radio Free Dixie*, 278–86. It must be noted that Williams was expelled from the NAACP after the Freedom Riders came to Monroe because he resorted to self-defense to protect the riders from racial violence. See Strain, *Pure Fire*, 62. For more on the Freedom Rides, see Arsenault, *Freedom Riders*.

173. Williams, *Negroes with Guns*, 109, 120.

174. *Courier*, "FBI Seeking Hideout of Fiery NAACP Leader," September 9, 1961.

175. *New York Amsterdam News*, "FBI Hunts NAACP Leader," September 23, 1961. See also Williams, *Negroes with Guns*, 91.

176. *Chicago Daily Defender*, "N. C. NAACP Leader Williams Claims His Innocence from Havana Sanctuary," October 11, 1961; *Chicago Daily Defender*, "Monroe Integrationist Asks Asylum in Cuba," October 2, 1961.

177. Williams, *Negroes with Guns*, 109, 120; Tyson, *Radio Free Dixie*, 290; Pohlmann, ed., *African American Political Thought*, 174.

178. Quoted in Williams, *George S. Schuyler*, 138–45.

179. On Williams's years in exile, see "Conclusion: Radio Free Dixie," in Tyson, *Radio Free Dixie*, 287–308.

180. "The Negro Press in America," n.d., RFWP, reel 5. Though undated, it is clear that Williams wrote this document while exiled in Cuba. He indicated the address from which it was written as "La Havana, Cuba."

181. Frazier, *Black Bourgeoisie*, 174, 178–79.

182. "The Negro Press in America," n.d., RFWP, reel 5.

183. Simmons, *African American Press*, 91, 102–3. See also "What Price, Integration?: 1970–1990s," and "The Kerner Report as Catalyst," in Wilson, *Black Journalists in Paradox*, 101–16.

184. Washburn, *African American Newspaper*, 185; Wilson, *Black Journalists in Paradox*, 86–88, see also 78.

185. Washburn, *African American Newspaper*, 200. See also Simmons, *African American Press*, 102.

186. Bates, *Long Shadow of Little Rock*, 200, 202, 221; Pride and Wilson, *History of the Black Press*, 215–16.

187. Pride and Wilson, *History of the Black Press*, 215–16.

188. *Atlanta Daily World*, "Miss. Publishers Discuss Race in the News," June 14, 1950.

189. Davies, *Press and Race*, 5–14.

190. See Roberts and Klibanoff, *Race Beat*.

191. "The Civil Rights Era and the Black Press," in Washburn, *African American Newspaper*, 197–205.

192. Simmons, *African American Press*, 101–8; Washburn, *African American Newspaper*, 200.

193. Washburn, *African American Newspaper*, 201.

194. "The Negro Press in America," n.d., RFWP, reel 5.

195. Williams, *Negroes with Guns*, 40, 116–17, 120–21.

196. Williams, 91.

197. Simmons, *African American Press*, 102–3.

198. Quoted in Washburn, *African American Newspaper*, 200.

199. Williams, *Negroes with Guns*, 121.

Chapter 5

1. *Muhammad Speaks*, "Brother Lopez Broke with Old Order, Joined Islam," February 19, 1965.

2. "The Negro Press in America," n.d., RFWP, reel 5.

3. Tyson, *Radio Free Dixie*, 2, 145, 205, 296–97. See also Williams, *Negroes with Guns*, 112.

4. Marable, *Malcolm X*, 20–36, 42–45, 75–79, 98; Clegg, *Original Man*, 116.

5. Lomax, *Negro Revolt*, 167.

6. Lincoln, *Black Muslims in America*, 128, 137; *Muhammad Speaks*, "Mr. Muhammad Addresses 15,000 in New York," October–November 1961.

7. For more on Muhammad's religious and social beliefs, see, for example, Curtis, *Black Muslim Religion*; Lincoln, *Black Muslims in America*; Muhammad, *Message to the Blackman in America*.

8. *Muhammad Speaks*, "Mr. Muhammad Addresses 15,000 in New York," October–November 1961; "Wasted Genius of Black Man," December 1961.

9. *Muhammad Speaks*, "Self Help or Oblivion for the Negro," October–November 1961.

10. "The Moynihan Report," in Estes, *I Am a Man*, 107–29. See also Geary, *Beyond Civil Rights*; *Report of the National Advisory Commission on Civil Disorders*.

11. See, for instance, Murch, *Living for the City*. For more on the rebellions, see, for example, McLaughlin, *Long Hot Summer of 1967*.

12. See, for example, *Muhammad Speaks*, "Says God, Hell, Heaven on Earth," October 31, 1962; *Muhammad Speaks*, "Black Citizens Caught in Squeeze of Poverty Powder Kegs Looking for a Match," August 27, 1965; *Muhammad Speaks*, "Congressman Powell Warns: Every Black Ghetto a Potential Los Angeles!," August 27, 1965.

13. Lomax, *When the Word Is Given*, 56–57. Also see, *Muhammad Speaks*, "Some of This Earth for Our Own or Else!," October–November 1961; *Muhammad Speaks*, "Don't Want Integration, Give Us Separation!," December 1961; *Muhammad Speaks*, "Separation or Integration?," April 1962; *Muhammad Speaks*, "The Integration Game . . . ," April 1962; *Muhammad Speaks*, "Separation or Integration?," April 1962; *Muhammad Speaks*, "Hell Will Not Stand," July 19, 1963; *Muhammad Speaks*, "Out of the Lion's Den," January 1, 1965; *Muhammad Speaks*, "Most Beautiful Woman in

the World," December 1961; *Muhammad Speaks*, "Says God, Hell, Heaven on Earth," October 31, 1962. See also *Muhammad Speaks*, "The Ol' Integrator," May 1962. Integration had specific gendered and sexual overtones in which black women would become vulnerable to white men's sexual advances.

14. Malcolm X with Haley, *Autobiography*, 293; Lomax, *When the Word Is Given*, 26, 59–60.

15. Most scholars of the NOI usually mine the paper for comments made by or about Nation ministers, particularly by or about Malcolm X, especially in terms of tensions between him and other NOI leaders. Similarly, scholarship on the black press usually overlooks *Muhammad Speaks*. For scholars who have examined some of the cultural, religious, and gendered aspects of the paper, see, for example, Jeffries, *Nation Can Rise No Higher*; and Curtis, *Black Muslim Religion*.

16. See, for example, Joseph, *Waiting til the Midnight Hour*.

17. Rocksborough-Smith, "'Filling the Gap'"; Simmons, *African American Press*, 91; Tinson, *Radical Intellect*. See also Ogbar, *Black Power*, 79.

18. See, for example, Murch, *Living for the City*, 154–55; Bloom and Martin, *Black against Empire*, 10, 79–80. See also, Tinson, *Radical Intellect*.

19. See, for instance, Wolseley, *Black Press U.S.A.*, 3–4, 90–91, 141. In Wolseley's definition of the black press, *Muhammad Speaks* and the *Black Panther* did not represent "conventional commercial papers, but actually quasi magazines. . . . They were not standard, major newspapers to be lined or equated with the *Afro* or the *Chicago Defender*. They were organs of groups and cause or advocacy journals." To say that these publications were "not standard, major newspapers" equal to the "*Afro* or the *Chicago Defender*" is to deny their composition and impact. It also denies the rich black political thought, concerns of readers and writers, editorial crusades, and critical historical moments that otherwise characterized what older black press scholarship would call the black press. This stance by older black press scholarship may have more to do with the racial politics of the time in which they were writing. Attempting to distance themselves from both groups' takes on black nationalism and radicalism, the scholarship seemed reluctant to credit groups and papers that departed from black middle-class, integrationist, and so-called respectable protest.

20. Ogbar, *Black Power*, 2.

21. Malcolm X with Haley, *Autobiography*, 290, 297, 211.

22. Curtis, *Black Muslim Religion*, 7.

23. Biographies and analyses of Malcolm abound. A few include Marable, *Malcolm X*; Perry, *Malcolm*; Boyd et al., *By Any Means Necessary*; DeCaro, *On the Side of My People*.

24. See, for instance, Bassey, *Malcolm X and African American Self-Consciousness*; DeCaro, *On the Side of My People*; Wood, *Malcolm X in Our Own Image*; Terrill, *Malcolm X*; Karim with Skutches and Gallen, *Remembering Malcolm*.

25. Tucker, "Malcolm X, the Prison Years."

26. For examples in the *Defender*, see "Tells Court His Allegiance Pledged to 'Islam'; Not U.S.," August 8, 1942; "D.C. Cultist Convicted of Draft Dodge," October 24, 1942; "Indicts 12 on Sedition," October 24, 1942; "U.S. Gets Rough with

Moslems on Draft Issue," May 30, 1942; "2 Draft Foes Arrested," November 8, 1950. See also Essien-Udom, *Black Nationalism*, 63–68.

27. Clarke, *Malcolm X*, 109. See also Wilson, "Come Down off the Cross."

28. Malcolm X with Haley, *Autobiography*, 272; DeCaro, *On the Side of My People*, 107–8; see also Perry, *Malcolm*, 214.

29. *Muhammad Speaks*, "Our Platform," October–November 1961.

30. Nance, "Mystery of the Moorish Science Temple"; Gomez, *Black Crescent*, 276, 295.

31. Clegg, *Original Man*, 6, 14–25, 29–40, 116. For more on Muhammad's short-lived papers, see Jeffries, *Nation Can Rise No Higher*, 79; Lincoln, *Black Muslims*, 127–28; Evanzz, *Messenger*, 206, 221, 271. See also Lomax, *When the Word Is Given*, 45–46. For more on Johnson, see "Selling the Race," in Green, *Selling the Race*, 129–77.

32. Malcolm X with Haley, *Autobiography*, 272, 251. For more on Malcolm's affinity for words, see, for example, Terrill, *Malcolm X*.

33. For more on J. A. Rogers, see, for example, Asukile, "Joel Augustus Rogers."

34. Malcolm X with Haley, *Autobiography*, 206, 207, 201, 212, 199.

35. *Defender*, "Moslem Set for Meeting February 23," February 22, 1958. See also *Defender*, "Devoutness Key to Islam Success," April 5, 1956, and *Defender*, "University, Temple Center of Moslems in Chicagoland," February 22, 1958. The *Defender* continued to report on NOI members and draft-dodging, however. See, for example, *Defender*, "Convict Moslem Leader's Son," May 2, 1958. For more on their improved public image at this time, see also Abernethy, *Iconography of Malcolm X*, 28, 31.

36. Malcolm X with Haley, *Autobiography*, 272; Marable, *Malcolm X*, 52.

37. Malcolm X with Haley, *Autobiography*, 272–73, 258, 251. See also Lomax, *When the Word Is Given*, 24–25. "Limited" as Malcolm's efforts may have been, the FBI still followed his and Muhammad's articles. See, for instance, Carson, *Malcolm X*, 137–48.

38. Malcolm X with Haley, *Autobiography*, 271; Lomax, *Negro Revolt*, 164, 167, 203. See also "About the Author," in Lomax, *Negro Revolt*; Wallace and Gates, *Close Encounters*, 136; Wallace with Gates, *Between You and Me*, 86, 67. See also MacDonald, *Blacks and White TV*, 100–102, 93, 103–10; Barnouw, *Tube of Plenty*, 269; see also "'The Double Life of 'Sit-In'," in Torres, *Black, White, and in Color*.

39. See, for example, Carson, *Malcolm X*, 146–48.

40. Kellner, *Television and the Crisis of Democracy*, 37–45; Bodroghkozy, *Equal Time*, 2.

41. Malcolm X with Haley, *Autobiography*, 272.

42. Wallace and Gates, *Close Encounters*, 136–37; Marable, *Malcolm X*, 161; Mike Wallace with Gates, *Between You and Me*, 87; Malcolm X with Haley, *Autobiography*, 274.

43. Malcolm X with Haley, *Autobiography*, 279.

44. Ogbar, *Black Power*, 45; Essien-Udom, *Black Nationalism*, 307–9, 313–17. See also Malcolm X with Haley, *Autobiography*, 273–80. See also Curtis, *Black Muslim Religion*, 4; Lincoln, *Black Muslims*, 102–3, 136–40. See also Gardell, *In the Name of*

Elijah Muhammad, 53. The FBI fed propaganda to several newspapers in order to discredit the NOI.

45. *Defender*, "Portrait of a Shrewd Cult Leader," August 22, 1959; *Muhammad Speaks*, "Onetime Proud Weekly Being Bossed by White 'Brainwashers of Blackmen,'" May 1962. See also *Muhammad Speaks*, "Marty Faye Gets Reckless," April 1962; Lincoln, *Black Muslims*, 125–26, 137. The *Courier* received a number of complaints from orthodox Muslims about Muhammad's column. See DeCaro, *On the Side of My People*, 146, 155; Essien-Udom, *Black Nationalism*, 72–73, 307–9, 313–17. Muhammad's last column in the *Courier* appears to have been published on August 22, 1959. The *Courier* awarded Muhammad the "Courier Achievement Award" in 1957, which might have indicated its popularity. He was also awarded the "highest Achievement Award ever given to an individual" by the *Herald Dispatch*.

46. Malcolm X with Haley, *Autobiography*, 279. See also Essien-Udom, *Black Nationalism*, 189–90.

47. Malcolm X with Haley, *Autobiography*, 273. See also *Muhammad Speaks*, "White Man Gives 'Frank' Opinion," April 1962.

48. Gallen, *Malcolm X*, 96; Malcolm X with Haley, *Autobiography*, 273, 304.

49. *Muhammad Speaks*, "Onetime Proud Weekly Being Bossed by White 'Brainwashers of Blackmen,'" May 1962.

50. *Muhammad Speaks*, "Our Platform," October–November 1961.

51. Malcolm X with Haley, *Autobiography*, 273. See also *Muhammad Speaks*, "Letter to the Editor," April 1962. One reader stated, "I have read with serious profound interest Muhammad Speaks. For a long time I have been reading His [other] Articles in the Courier, Herald Dispatch, and the New Crusader. . . . I am mindful of the great good Mr. Muhammad has done for us Negroes."

52. Quoted in Gallen, *Malcolm X*, 78. See also *Muhammad Speaks*, "Who Speaks for Negro?," October–November 1961; Lomax, *Negro Revolt*, 203.

53. Malcolm X with Haley, *Autobiography*, 237; *Muhammad Speaks*, "In the Future," October–November 1961; "Our Platform," October–November 1961; see also *Muhammad Speaks*, "Would You Like to Be an Expert?," April 1962; *Muhammad Speaks*, "Who Speaks for Negro?," October–November 1961. Lomax also pointed out that Muhammad "speaks with a disturbing lisp." See Lomax, *Negro Revolt*, 168. See also Essien-Udom, *Black Nationalism*, 77.

54. Curtis, *Black Muslim Religion*, 136–46; Essien-Udom, *Black Nationalism*, 149–57. See also Farrakhan, *Meaning of F. O. I.*; Malcolm X with Haley, *Autobiography*, 332, 261; "A Tribute to a Great Man in our Midst Mr. Elijah Muhammad," MXC, box 11, fol. 3.

55. Malcolm X with Haley, *Autobiography*, 273; *Muhammad Speaks*, February 1962; Lomax, *When the Word Is Given*, 69, 71. For more on their being required to sell the paper, see Curtis, *Black Muslim Religion*, 136–46.

56. *Muhammad Speaks*, "The Fruit of Islam," February 1962.

57. *Muhammad Speaks*, "Coast-to-Coast Subscription Drive Under Way," July 1962. See also "Would You Like to Be an Expert?," April 1962.

58. *Muhammad Speaks*, "Coast-to-Coast Subscription Drive Under Way," July 1962; "Subscription Drive Picks up Momentum," July 15, 1962. See also Curtis,

Black Muslim Religion, 139; Malcolm X with Haley, *Autobiography*, 258–59; Perry, *Malcolm*, 220–21; Terrill, *Malcolm X*, 94.

59. *Muhammad Speaks*, "Your Subscription," July 1962; "Subscribe Today! Muhammad Speaks Newspaper," April 10, 1964; *Muhammad Speaks*, "Onetime Proud Weekly Being Bossed by White 'Brainwashers of Blackmen,'" May 1962.

60. *Muhammad Speaks*, "Sells 15,000 Muhammad Speaks for Trophy," August 18, 1967; *Muhammad Speaks*, "Readers of [Varied] Religions Aid MS Subscriptions," August 15, 1962; *Muhammad Speaks*, "Setting a Blazing 700-copies . . .", December 30, 1962; *Muhammad Speaks*, "Salesmen from Los Angeles Take Prizes in Contest," October 29, 1965; *Muhammad Speaks*, "When Lights Went Out He Sold Muhammad Speaks by Way of Candlelight," December 3, 1965; *Muhammad Speaks*, "Outstanding Salesman of Muhammad Speaks," August 18, 1967; *Muhammad Speaks*, "THE RUSSWURM PLAQUE being presented . . . ," March 26, 1965.

61. *Muhammad Speaks*, "Sells 15,000 Muhammad Speaks for Trophy," August 31, 1962.

62. *Muhammad Speaks*, October–November 1961; "In the Future," October–November 1961.

63. *Muhammad Speaks*, "Muhammad Speaks Is His Favorite Source of News," June 25, 1965.

64. *Muhammad Speaks*, "In the Future," October–November 1961. See also *Muhammad Speaks*, "Would You Like to Be an Expert?," April 1962.

65. *Muhammad Speaks*, "Would You Like to Be an Expert?," April 1962.

66. *Muhammad Speaks*, "Would You Like to Be an Expert?."

67. Ogbar, *Black Power*, 44; Perry, *Malcolm*, 220–21. See also *Muhammad Speaks*, "Reach," December 1961.

68. See also the letters from VIP news services and Asian-African press service in MXC, box 4, fol. 4 and box 11, fol. 5. *Muhammad Speaks* gathered much of its international news from news-clipping services like these. Abdul Basit Naeem, who wrote for *Muhammad Speaks*, was also the director of the Asian-African clipping service. See also Evanzz, *Messenger*, 421. For examples of coverage of Robert F. Williams, see *Muhammad Speaks*, "The Odyssey of Robert Williams," June 5, 1964.

69. Malcolm X with Haley, *Autobiography*, 284–86. See also Essien-Udom, *Black Nationalism*, 192–99.

70. Malcolm X with Haley, *Autobiography*, 286, 295. See also Marable and Felber, *Portable Malcolm X Reader*, 147–48.

71. Clegg, *Original Man*, 118; Essien-Udom, *Black Nationalism*, 70.

72. *Muhammad Speaks*, "16,000 Told So-Called Negro Must Have Home of Own! In Nation's Capital," October–November 1961; see also "Muhammad Thrills New York Audience," October–November 1961; "Underscores the Muslim Program," August 15, 1962; "Awake and See Truth," April 1, 1963; "Underscores the Muslim Program," August 13, 1962. See also Lincoln, *Black Muslims*, 27–29, 72, 130–31.

73. Lincoln, *Black Muslims*, 128; Clegg, *Original Man*, 127–28.

74. Elijah Muhammad to Malcolm X, February 8, 1962, MXC, box 3, fol. 8; Memorandum, April 25, 1963, MXC, box 3, fol. 8; "Recognize all Laborers," MXC, box 11, fol. 3.

75. Essien-Udom, *Black Nationalism*, 288–89. For more on Muhammad's eschatological beliefs, see, for example, "The Eschatology," in Essien-Udom, *Black Nationalism*, 122–42.

76. "'There Go My People': The Black Freedom Movement and the Rise of the Black Panther Party," in Ogbar, *Black Power*, 37–67; Estes, *I Am a Man!*, 97. See also Warren, *Who Speaks for the Negro?*.

77. *Muhammad Speaks*, "Martin Luther King Squirming," February 1962; *Muhammad Speaks*, December 1961; MXC, box 6, fol. 6; Lomax, *Negro Revolt*, 174.

78. Bates, *Long Shadow of Little Rock*, 224–25; *Defender*, "NAACP Attacks 'Moslem' Cult," August 15, 1959; *Jet*, July 6, 1961. See also Burns, *Nitty Gritty*, 175.

79. *Muhammad Speaks*, "Muhammad Sparks U.S. Muslim Movement," October–November 1961; "Muhammad Cites Three Basic Muslim Freedoms," October–November 1961.

80. *Muhammad Speaks*, "Muhammad Sparks U.S. Muslim Movement," October–November 1961.

81. Gomez, *Black Crescent*, 356. See also Essien-Udom, *Black Nationalism*, 71–72.

82. Malcolm X with Haley, *Autobiography*, 291; *Muhammad Speaks*, "ABC of Divine Knowledge," May 1962. For an image of Muhammad in the paper, see, for example, *Muhammad Speaks*, "The Muslim Program," July 31, 1962.

83. Clegg, *Original Man*, 117; Malcolm X with Haley, *Autobiography*, 241.

84. Lincoln, *Black Muslims*, 2. See also Malcolm X with Haley, *Autobiography*, 284, 286; Clarke, *Malcolm X*, 173. Another early study included Essien-Udom, *Black Nationalism*.

85. *Muhammad Speaks*, "Letters to Editor," April 1962; "Letters to the Editor," December 1961.

86. Muhammad Speaks Memorandum, April 17, 1962, MXC, box 11, fol. 4. Malcolm celebrated the paper's independence in a radio address. See MXC, box 6, fol. 8. See also Pride and Wilson, *History of the Black Press*, 242–46.

87. See Muhammad, *Supreme Wisdom*.

88. For more on Muhammad's religious beliefs, see, for example, "Elijah Muhammad (1897–1975) and the Absolutism of Black Particularistic Islam," in Curtis, *Islam in Black America*, 63–84; Curtis, *Black Muslim Religion*; Elijah Muhammad, *Message to the Blackman in America*; Malcolm X with Haley, *Autobiography*, 191–94.

89. *Muhammad Speaks*, "Search Made to Find Original Man!," May 1962; *Muhammad Speaks*, "Most Beautiful Woman in the World," December 1961. See also *Muhammad Speaks*, "Mr. Muhammad Speaks," May 1962; *Muhammad Speaks*, "Memo: From Desk of Muhammad To: The Original Black People!," September 11, 1964; *Muhammad Speaks*, "The Hallmark of Greatness," April 9, 1965.

90. *Muhammad Speaks*, "No History of White Man in Ancient Times," April 1962.

91. "Lazz" appears to have debuted in *Muhammad Speaks* in August 1962 and continued running through December 1962.

92. *Muhammad Speaks*, "Booker T. Washington Edict Is Carried Out," May 1962; *Muhammad Speaks*, "Tuskegee to Muhammad," October 22, 1965; *Muhammad Speaks*, "Marcus Garvey Said: 'A Messenger Will Follow Me!,'" June 5, 1964. See also *Muhammad Speaks*, "Letters to the Editor," October 23, 1964; *Muhammad Speaks*,

"March On under Messenger's Banner," February 5, 1965. The corresponding illustration parallels the famous statue on Tuskegee Institute's campus of Booker T. Washington unveiling freedom to black people. *Muhammad Speaks* even illustrated an imagined architectural redesigning of Tuskegee "as Muhammad Sees It," not unlike the paper's other projected designs of Nation-led cities and institutions. See also *Muhammad Speaks*, "Tuskegee Invites the Messenger!," October 22, 1965. See also Lomax, *When the Word Is Given*, 175, 178; Gomez, *Black Crescent*, 296. Muhammad insisted that Garvey's followers "should now follow me and co-operate with us in our work because we are only trying to finish up what those before us had started."

93. *Muhammad Speaks*, "Where Are Our Factories?," December 1961.

94. *Muhammad Speaks*, "White Man Destroyed Initiative," October–November 1961.

95. *Muhammad Speaks*, "Public Housing 'Prison without Bars' Say Inmates," September 25, 1964; *Muhammad Speaks*, "East Is East, West Is West," February 1962; *Muhammad Speaks*, "In the High Rent Tombs!," April 10, 1964; see also *Muhammad Speaks*, "Slums, Plus Fires Equals Destitution, Death," February 18, 1963; *Muhammad Speaks*, "The Ghetto: Breeder of Blighted Lives," March 4, 1963; *Muhammad Speaks*, "Frustration, Poverty Are Crime Breeders," August 16, 1963.

96. *Muhammad Speaks*, "Negro Leadership Blasted!," January 1962.

97. *Muhammad Speaks*, "Urban Renewals Are Tomorrow's Slums," April 1962; *Muhammad Speaks*, "Slum Removal . . . or Negro Removal," January 17, 1964; *Muhammad Speaks*, "Urban Renewal Becomes Loss for Negroes in Washington, DC," February 1962. Muhammad and the paper generally resisted many government-led initiatives to combat poverty. See also *Muhammad Speaks*, "War on Negro Outguns 'War on Poverty,'" February 5, 1965.

98. *Muhammad Speaks*, "Where Are Our Factories," December 1961; *Muhammad Speaks*, "Give the Poor So-Called Negroes a Chance to Do for Self!," February 1962.

99. *Muhammad Speaks*, "We Have Served You Well You Have Mistreated Us Well," April 1962; *Muhammad Speaks*, "Mobilize for Jobs or Face Destruction," April 1, 1963.

100. See, for example, *Muhammad Speaks*, "We Must Have Some of This Earth!," December 1961; *Muhammad Speaks*, "Blackman Our First Step to Success Is the Farm," December 10, 1965; *Muhammad Speaks*, "World under Islam," October 15, 1965; *Muhammad Speaks*, "Great Negro Business Centers," November 26, 1965; *Muhammad Speaks*, "Plan to Build Black Bank," September 11, 1964; *Muhammad Speaks*, "Let's Build Our Own House," September 25, 1864; *Muhammad Speaks*, "The Unity of 22 Million," October 9, 1964; *Muhammad Speaks*, "Prepare for the New World," July 2, 1965.

101. *Muhammad Speaks*, "Cleanliness Is Next to Godliness," July 1962; Malcolm X with Haley, *Autobiography*, 303, 235.

102. See *Muhammad Speaks*, "Visit Muhammad's Mosques of Islam," January 7, 1966, which listed the locations of many NOI mosques in cities across the country. See also Lincoln, *Sounds of the Struggle*, 41, 74; Lincoln, *Black Muslims*, 2, 18–21; Berg, *Elijah Muhammad and Islam*, 87–93.

103. *Muhammad Speaks*, December 1961; *Muhammad Speaks*, "The Muslim Program . . . What Do the Muslims Want?," July 31, 1962; a shorter version appears in the April 15, 1963, issue.

104. Clegg, *Original Man*, 115; Malcolm X with Haley, *Autobiography*, 229, 231. See, for example, *Defender*, "Off the Record," February 19, 1958, and *Defender*, "Moslem Set for Meeting February 23," February 22, 1958.

105. *Muhammad Speaks*, "'How to Sell 1,000 Papers per Week'—by One Who Knows," June 18, 1965; "Cleanliness Is Next to Godliness," July 1962.

106. See "Reading Bodies and Marking Race," in Johnson, *Soul by Soul*, 135–61. Here, I borrow from Johnson's interpretative frame in examining slave pens in Louisiana.

107. Muhammad, *Supreme Wisdom*, 3; MXC, box 11, fol. 6, and Elijah Muhammad to Abdul Basit Naeem, April 12, 1962, and November 13, 1962, box 11, fol. 4. *Muhammad Speaks*, "How Muhammad Transforms the Old into the New," July 30, 1965; Kelley, *Race Rebels*, 8–9. See also Clegg, *Original Man*, 289. He defines these terms as "the state of being unaware of the teachings of the Nation of Islam." See also "The Ethics of the Black Muslim Body," in Curtis, *Black Muslim Religion*, 95–130. For the significance of Naeem's support as a Pakistani Muslim, see, for example, Essien-Udom, *Black Nationalism*, 310–19.

108. *Muhammad Speaks*, "68-Yr.-Old Woman Laments Years Wasted before Embracing Messenger's Teachings," December 3, 1965.

109. Lomax, *Negro Revolt*, 176. See also Curtis, *Black Muslim Religion*, 127–30, 137.

110. *Muhammad Speaks*, October–November 1961; "Dressed for Leadership," August 15, 1962. For a good discussion of NOI grooming measures, see "The Ethics of the Black Muslim Body," in Curtis, *Black Muslim Religion*, 95–130. See also Lincoln, *Sounds of the Struggle*, 41, 45.

111. Curtis, *Black Muslim Religion*, 109–17; *Muhammad Speaks*, "Our Platform," October–November 1961. See also "Eager Beaver," July 1962; "You're a Muslim If You're Well-Dressed, Clean-Cut," June 1962. See also Curtis, *Black Muslim Religion*, 109–17.

112. *Muhammad Speaks*, "Disowned by Family, He Forges a Brighter Life," January 17, 1964.

113. White, *Inside the Nation of Islam*, 43. See also King, *Stride toward Freedom*, 222–23; Gertrude Samuels, "Two Ways: Black Muslim and N. A. A. C. P," in Meier and Rudwick, *Black Protest in the Sixties*, 44.

114. See, for example, Millerson, *Technique of Television Production*; Kellner, *Television and the Crisis of Democracy*, 50, 52–53. See also "'In a Crisis We Must Have a Sense of Drama': Civil Rights and Televisual Information," in Torres, *Black, White, and in Color*, 13–35. See also Mills, *Changing Channels*.

115. MacDonald, *Blacks and White TV*, 102, 85–89. See also Barnouw, *Tube of Plenty*, 260–65, 308, 325–27, 344; Leibman, *Living Room Lectures*; *Muhammad Speaks*, "Why We Have No TV Stations," May 1962.

116. Bodroghkozy, *Equal Time*, 2, 4–5, 57.

117. Barnouw, *Tube of Plenty*, 324; Malcolm X with Haley, *Autobiography*, 276, 278, 280–81. For examples of Malcolm's public speaking engagements, see MXC, box 5, fols. 11, 12, 15. See also Tuck, *Night Malcolm X Spoke*.

118. Gallen, *Malcolm X*, 59.

119. Malcolm X with Haley, *Autobiography*, 47, 61–62, 92, 243, 255, 248. See also Kelley, *Race Rebels*, 162, 165–67; Carol Tulloch, "'My Man, Let Me Pull Your Coat to Something': Malcolm X," in Bruzzi and Gibson, *Fashion Cultures*, 298–314.

120. Essien-Udom, *Black Nationalism*, 101; Gallen, *Malcolm X*, 131–32. For the interview with Kenneth B. Clark, see Clarke, *Malcolm X*, 168–81.

121. Gallen, *Malcolm X*, 59.

122. Gallen, 60, 65–66; Clarke, *Malcolm X*, 168.

123. Goldman, *Death and Life of Malcolm X*, 397.

124. Clarke, *Malcolm X*, 135, 179; see also Gallen, *Malcolm X*, 59–60; Abernethy, *Iconography of Malcolm X*, 96–103.

125. Malcolm X with Haley, *Autobiography*, 441–44.

126. Malcolm X with Haley, 445, 342; Clegg, *Original Man*, 178.

127. Malcolm X with Haley, *Autobiography*, 339, 99, 47–65, 114–16, 125, 126, 145, 155, 61, 330, 129, 51, 61–62, 125. Black participants in illicit economies had long been a sore spot of reformist-minded, respectability-driven black elites then and continued to be for groups like the NOI, which was steeped at once in radical, working-class, and respectability politics. See, for example, Wolcott, *Remaking Respectability*. See also "The Riddle of the Zoot: Malcolm Little and Black Cultural Politics During World War II," in Kelley, *Race Rebels*, 161–81; Curtis, *Black Muslim Religion*, 97.

128. Malcolm X with Haley, *Autobiography*, 330. For a discussion of the meaning and use of the "X" for Nation members, see, for example, Lomax, *When the Word Is Given*, 26.

129. Malcolm X with Haley, *Autobiography*, 342, 243, 290, 228, 244, 257, 342.

130. Clarke, *Malcolm X*, 139; Essien-Udom, *Black Nationalism*, 74.

131. Malcolm X with Haley, *Autobiography*, 332–33; Lomax, *Negro Revolt*, 17, 174.

132. Malcolm X with Haley, *Autobiography*, 275–83; Elijah Muhammad to Malcolm X, February 15, 1962, MXC, box 3, fol. 8; Elijah Muhammad to Malcolm X, September 18, 1962, box 3, fol. 8.

133. Malcolm X with Haley, *Autobiography*, 284; Lomax, *When the Word Is Given*, 73, 75, 80–81, 21–22. See also, for example, the transcripts of two of Malcolm's interviews in 1961 and 1963, in Clarke, *Malcolm X*, 149–81; Malcolm X with Haley, *Autobiography*, 282.

134. See, for example, Elijah Muhammad to Malcolm X, March 2, 1962, MXC, box 3, fol. 8. Other praise of Malcolm in the paper included *Muhammad Speaks*, "Oh, Ye Hypocrites! . . ." July 31, 1962; *Muhammad Speaks*, August 31, 1962; *Muhammad Speaks*, "Muslim Minister Rips 'Token Integration,'" September 15, 1962; *Muhammad Speaks*, "Muslim Minister Blast Press Bias," December 30, 1962; *Muhammad Speaks*, "MINISTER MALCOLM X," December 1961.

135. *Muhammad Speaks*, "Malcolm X, Rustin, Debating," March 1962; *Muhammad Speaks*, December 1961; *Muhammad Speaks*, "Kup, Tied Up . . . in Knots," April 1962.

136. *Muhammad Speaks*, "Muhammad Cites Awakening of Black Race, Old World Departing, New World Ahead," July 13, 1962.

137. Malcolm X with Haley, *Autobiography*, 305; Lomax, *When the Word Is Given*, 81.

138. Malcolm X with Haley, *Autobiography*, 442, 305; Elijah Muhammad to Malcolm X, September 21, 1962, MXC, box 3, fol. 8; Malcolm X to Elijah Muhammad, October 1, 1962, MXC, box 3, fol. 8.

139. Curtis, *Black Muslim Religion*, 7, 26–31, 118. "What Islam Has Done for Me" appears to have debuted in the paper on August 2, 1963, based on the paper's introduction of the section that day. "In view of the overwhelming testimonials coming from both Muslims and non-Muslims as to the effectiveness of the Messenger's teachings . . . *Muhammad Speaks* opens this page," it stated.

140. *Muhammad Speaks*, "What Islam Has Done for Me," May 22, 1964; *Muhammad Speaks*, "What Islam Has Done for Me," August 14, 1964; *Muhammad Speaks*, "What Islam Has Done for Me," November 6, 1964; *Muhammad Speaks*, "Islamic Teachings Saved Me from Treadmill of Evil," February 19, 1965.

141. *Muhammad Speaks*, "Who Profits from Narcotics? The Living Death," December 18, 1964. See also *Muhammad Speaks*, "The Cocaine Co-op: Of Junkies, Pushers and Policemen," January 1, 1965.

142. Garrow, *Bearing the Cross*, 281, 271, 283–84.

143. *Muhammad Speaks*, "It's Your Move," April 1962; "For Men Only," March 1962.

144. *Muhammad Speaks*, "Messenger's Demonstration of Love and Unity Brought Lost Soul to Islam," April 16, 1965.

145. *Muhammad Speaks*, "Messenger Leads Woman to Truth and Happiness," October 1, 1965. See also "Glad to Be an Original Woman," June 16, 1967.

146. *Muhammad Speaks*, "Accept Allah's Messenger and Help Self," January 1, 1965.

147. *Muhammad Speaks*, "68-Yr.-Old Woman Laments Years Wasted before Embracing Messenger's Teachings," December 3, 1965. See also *Muhammad Speaks*, "Muhammad Sparks U.S. Muslim Movement," October–November 1961.

148. *Muhammad Speaks*, "'I've Found Peace of Mind and Contentment in Islam,'" July 22, 1965; *Muhammad Speaks*, "Messenger's Demonstration of Love and Unity Brought Lost Soul to Islam," April 16, 1965; *Muhammad Speaks*, "Messenger Leads Woman to Truth and Happiness," October 1, 1965.

149. Quoted in Marable, *Malcolm X*, 238; *Muhammad Speaks*, "Clothing Factory Big Step Forward New Fashion Center Sets New Patterns," February 1962; *Muhammad Speaks*, "Good Grooming Goes from Head to Toe, Skin Out and All Around," August 15, 1962; *Muhammad Speaks*, "The Woman of Islam," October–November 1961; *Muhammad Speaks*, "Dress Should Identify Black Woman," July 1962; *Muhammad Speaks*, "Are Fashion and Beauty the Same?," April 1962; "Look Your Best!," "Dress Modestly," "Should Women Wear Pants or Dresses," "What Is Cultural Refinement," "Why No Makeup?," all in *Muhammad Speaks*, February 1962; *Muhammad Speaks*, "Beauty of Being Black," March 1962; Baldwin, *Fire Next Time*, 65. As Curtis has noted, discussions about appearance in the paper focused especially on women's dress. See Curtis, *Black Muslim Religion*, 28, 96–98, 109–12.

150. See also *Muhammad Speaks*, "For Men Only," March 1962; *Muhammad Speaks*, "Why Messenger's Program Benefits Black Womanhood," May 21, 1965. For

Malcolm's thoughts on women, see, for example, Malcolm X with Haley, *Autobiography*, 108, 266, 448. For more on histories of women in the NOI, see, for example, Gibson and Karim, *Women of the Nation*; Jeffries, *Nation Can Rise No Higher*; Taylor, *Promise of Patriarchy*; Farah Jasmine Griffin, "'Ironies of the Saint': Malcolm X, Black Women, and the Price of Protection," in Collier-Thomas and Franklin, *Sisters in the Struggle*, 214–229.

151. *Muhammad Speaks*, "1,000 Subscriptions Sold by 3 Salesladies," July 31, 1962. See also Malcolm X with Haley, *Autography*, 260; Jeffries, *Nation Can Rise No Higher*, 80.

152. Gomez, *Black Crescent*, 324–26.

153. See, for example, "Women's Features," May 1962; Curtis, *Black Muslim Religion*, 98–109, 146–53.

154. See, for example, *Muhammad Speaks*, "30 Minutes to Armageddon?," October–November 1961; *Muhammad Speaks*, "Anything by a Slave Boss," December 1961; *Muhammad Speaks*, "Blackwoman Beauty Is a Standard"; *Muhammad Speaks*, "Birth Control Death Plan," December 15, 1962; *Muhammad Speaks*, "The Twist and Twisted," January 1962; *Muhammad Speaks*, "Why No Makeup?," February 1962; *Muhammad Speaks*, "Destruction and Disaster Face Country," April 1962; *Muhammad Speaks*, "Still Last Hired and First Fired," July 5, 1963; *Muhammad Speaks*, "They Worship Force of Arms," November 6, 1964; *Muhammad Speaks*, "America Is Falling," December 4, 1964; *Muhammad Speaks*, "Invitation to Freedom," December 18, 1964; *Muhammad Speaks*, "Old World Dying, New World Coming," February 19, 1965; *Muhammad Speaks*, "Confused World," October 1, 1965.

155. Quoted in Lincoln, *Black Muslims*, 79–80.

156. See, for example, *Muhammad Speaks*, "Unity," October–November 1961. The paper said that "all Muslims are as one body."

157. See also *Muhammad Speaks*, "You're a Muslim If You're Well-Dressed, Clean-Cut," July 1962.

158. *Muhammad Speaks*, "Route of Ace Salesman from Marcus Garvey to the Messenger," October 9, 1964.

159. *Muhammad Speaks*, "'Islam Made a Man of Me,' Says Muslim from South," December 18, 1964.

160. Quoted in Curtis, *Black Muslim Religion*, 139.

161. *Muhammad Speaks*, "Brother Lopez Broke with Old Order, Joined Islam," February 19, 1965.

162. See, for example, Williams, *Politics of Public Housing*; Murch, *Living for the City*.

163. *Muhammad Speaks*, "1st Economic Program for Black America," July 3, 1964; *Muhammad Speaks*, "Economic Program," July 17, 1964; *Muhammad Speaks*, "Muhammad's 3-Year Plan to Fight Poverty, Want," August 28, 1964.

164. See "Making Home Life Measure Up," in Mitchell, *Righteous Propagation*, 141–72.

165. *Muhammad Speaks*, "Muhammad's 3-Year Plan to Fight Poverty, Want!," August 28, 1964.

166. *Muhammad Speaks*, "Unity of 22 Million to Win Land and Freedom," October 9, 1964.

167. See, for example, Wilson, *Urban Renewal*.

168. Garrow, *Bearing the Cross*, 442–43, 456–66. See *Muhammad Speaks*, "Tuskegee Invites the Messenger!," October 22, 1965.

169. See, for example, *Muhammad Speaks*, "Build New Business, Make New Jobs for Ourselves and for Others," July 15, 1962; *Muhammad Speaks*, "He Knows Islam Is 'Right Weapon' in War on Poverty," December 4, 1964. See also Malcolm X with Haley, *Autobiography*, 303, 235.

170. *Muhammad Speaks*, "Unity of 22 Million to Win Land and Freedom," October 9, 1964; *Muhammad Speaks*, "Muhammad's Plan for a Real War against Poverty," July 2, 1965.

171. *Muhammad Speaks*, "Economic Program," July 17, 1964.

172. Malcolm X with Haley, *Autobiography*, 243.

173. Collins with Bailey, *Seventh Child*, 97. For more on these class conflicts, see, for instance, "The Riddle of the Zoot Suit: Malcolm Little and Black Cultural Politics during World War II," in Kelley, *Race Rebels*, 161–81.

174. See, for example, *Muhammad Speaks*, "Their Business: Full-Time Sales of Muhammad Speaks," March 12, 1965. See also Lomax, *When the Word Is Given*, 69.

175. Malcolm X to Elijah Muhammad, October 1, 1962, MXC, box 3, fol. 8.

176. Perry, *Malcolm*, 220; Marable, *Malcolm X*, 121–22.

177. W. G. Lyons to Malcolm X, August 2, 1962, MXC, box 4, fol. 3.

178. Willa Ruth to Elijah Muhammad, October 8, 1962, MXC, box 3, fol. 8.

179. *Muhammad Speaks*, "Route to Ace Salesmen from Marcus Garvey to the Messenger," October 9, 1964; Perry, *Malcolm*, 221.

180. DeCaro, *On the Side of My People*, 185.

181. Curtis, *Black Muslim Religion*, 129.

182. "The Muslim-Islam Sect," May 11, 1962, MXC, box 11, fol. 6. See also Marable and Felber, *Portable Malcolm X Reader*, 203–4.

183. For more on the NOI's trouble with authorities, see, for example, Lincoln, *Black Muslims*, 3–4; Gardell, *In the Name of Elijah Muhammad*, 53; Clegg, *Original Man*, 259; Marable and Felber, *Portable Malcolm X Reader*, 221–22; Marable, *Malcolm X*, 135; Lincoln, *Sounds of the Struggle*, 74; and Curtis, *Black Muslim Religion*, 118. On NOI leaders' efforts to avoid police confrontations, especially like that of the Panthers, see McCartney, *Black Power Ideologies*, 170.

184. *Muhammad Speaks*, "Second Mass Protest Rally," May 20, 1962; "Muslims Will Protest Police Brutality in Times Square," February 13, 1963, MXC, box 11, fol. 18; Malcolm X to John F. Kennedy, February 16, 1963, MXC, box 11, fol. 18; Malcolm X to Frank Hogan, January 2, 1963, MXC, box 11, fol. 18.

185. Perry, *Malcolm*, 360, 371; *Muhammad Speaks*, "Freedom of Muhammad's Press Will Be Upheld," July 9, 1965.

186. For more on the murder of Stokes, see, for example, Evanzz, *Messenger*, 244–47; Clegg, *Original Man*, 170–75. See also *Muhammad Speaks*, "Stop Race Murders!," June 1962; *Muhammad Speaks*, "Eyewitness: 'Saw Cops Kill Muslim,'" June 1962; *Muhammad Speaks*, "Harlem to U Thant: Probe Stokes Murder!,"

July 1962; *Muhammad Speaks*, "The Prophetic Words of the Messenger," July 1962; *Muhammad Speaks*, "Muhammad to Speak at Boston Rally Protesting Cop Brutality," July 31, 1962; *Muhammad Speaks*, "Muslim Drive for Justice Stirs Nation," July 1962.

187. Marable, *Malcolm X*, 207–11; Lomax, *When the Word Is Given*, 47, 70.

188. *Muhammad Speaks*, "Muhammad Calls for United Black Front," June 1962; quoted in Terrill, *Malcolm X*, 94–95. See also MXC, "Muhammad Calls for . . . United Black Front," July 29, 1962, box 11, fol. 5.

189. *Muhammad Speaks*, "Coast-to-Coast Subscription Drive Underway," July 1962; Clegg, *Original Man*, 322n51; Malcolm X with Haley, *Autobiography*, 304.

190. Malcolm X with Haley, *Autobiography*, 453, 303, 287. See also the interview Malcolm did with WBAI radio on the shooting of Stokes in Gallen, *Malcolm X*, 102–43. For examples of the expansion of the media campaign, see *Muhammad Speaks*, "Muhammad's Nationwide Radio Schedule," December 1961; *Muhammad Speaks*, "On Television across the Nation," December 4, 1964; *Muhammad Speaks*, "The Voice . . . the Words . . . of Muhammad," June 25, 1965. See also *Muhammad Speaks*, "Muhammad Speaks," January 28, 1966; *Muhammad Speaks*, "Now on TV," January 7, 1966; *Muhammad Speaks*, "Urges All-Out Effort to Spread Truth via Newspaper, Messenger's Book, Records," December 15, 1967; see MXC, box 5, fol. 7 for some of the NOI and Malcolm's press releases. See also Malcolm X with Haley, *Autobiography*, 303, 287; Lomax, *When the Word Is Given*, 73; Lincoln, *Black Muslims*, 137.

191. *Muhammad Speaks*, April 1962. See also Lomax, *When the Word Is Given*, 19.

192. Malcolm X with Haley, *Autobiography*, 231, 259, 333, 268, 455, 336; Gallen, *Malcolm X*, 96.

193. Lomax, *When the Word Is Given*, 82; Gallen, *Malcolm X*, 96.

194. Rickford, *Betty Shabazz*, 153; Burnbow, *Tube of Plenty*, 314.

195. *New York Times*, "Malcolm X Scores U.S. and Kennedy," December 2, 1963; *Defender*, "Malcolm X Suspended! Muslim Head Drops Malcolm X in Rift," December 5, 1963. See also Lomax, *When the Word Is Given*, 91.

196. "The Chickens Coming Home to Roost," in Marable, *Malcolm X*, 269–96.

197. Malcolm X with Haley, *Autobiography*, 467. Malcolm did take some private interviews despite his silencing. See Lomax, *When the Word Is Given*, 169–80.

198. Lomax, *When the Word Is Given*, 179.

199. See "The March on Washington and a Peek into Racial Utopia" and "Selma in the 'Glaring Light of Television,'" in Bodroghkozy, *Equal Time*, 89–114, 115–52; Ogbar, *Black Power*, 56.

200. Elijah Muhammad was aware of the civil rights leaders' growing television presence, and even the Nation's own, among other mass media. See, for example, *Muhammad Speaks*, "The Revered Martin Luther King," April 9, 1965, and the illustration captioned, "Propaganda Will Not Avail against the Truth," March 12, 1965; *Muhammad Speaks*, "Dentist Defines Divine Mission of the Messenger," April 2, 1965; *Muhammad Speaks*, "Now on TV," November 5, 1965.

201. Malcolm X with Haley, *Autobiography*, 335, 309; Barnouw, *Tube of Plenty*, 314.

202. *Muhammad Speaks*, "On Television across the Nation," December 4, 1964; *Muhammad Speaks*, "Economic Program," July 17, 1964; *Muhammad Speaks*, "They've Changed the Name, but the Game Remains the Same," November 12, 1965.

203. Malcolm X with Haley, *Autobiography*, 333–34.

204. Malcolm X with Haley, 334. See also Breitman, *By Any Means Necessary*, 158. Louis E. Lomax noticed this too. See "The Black Muslims and the Negro Revolt," in Lomax, *When the Word Is Given*, 85–106. See also Marable and Felber, *Portable Malcolm X Reader*, 306–8.

205. Young, *Embodying Blackness*; Berrey, *Jim Crow Routine*, 35; Clark, *Final Speeches*, 21–22; Breitman, *By Any Means Necessary*, 158. In the same interview on January 18, 1965, in which he said the Nation was "dragging its feet," Malcolm explained further, "It didn't involve itself in the civil or civic or political struggles our people were confronted by. All it did was stress the importance of moral reformation—don't drink, don't smoke, don't permit fornication and adultery. When I found that the hierarchy itself wasn't practicing what it preached, it was clear that this part of its program was bankrupt. So the only way it could function and be meaningful in the community was to take part in the political and economic facets of the Negro struggle. And the organization wouldn't do that because the stand it would have to take would have been too militant, uncompromising, and activist, and the hierarchy had gotten conservative. . . . It was in a vacuum." See also Breitman, *Malcolm X Speaks*, 171. See also Raiford, *Imprisoned in a Luminous Glare*.

206. Malcolm X with Haley, *Autobiography*, 359–60, 346; Ogbar, *Black Power*, 57–61; Lomax, *Negro Revolt*, 174, 177. See also Terrill, *Malcolm X*.

207. Lomax, *When the Word Is Given*, 81–84. See also Lomax, *When the Word Is Given*, 179–80.

208. See also Marable, *Malcolm X*, 274–75, 277, 284; Evanzz, *Messenger*, 275; Malcolm X with Haley, *Autobiography*, 348.

209. For an example of the coverage, see Marable and Felber, *Portable Malcolm X Reader*, 306–8.

210. Marable, *Malcolm X*, 135; Clegg, *Original Man*, 113–14; Perry, *Malcolm*, 221–25.

211. Breitman, *By Any Means Necessary*, 2, 5, 62, 15.

212. See, for instance, Malcolm's comments at the founding rally of the Organization of Afro-American Unity on June 28, 1964, in Breitman, *By Any Means Necessary*, 67.

213. DeCaro, *On the Side of My People*, 227–29; quoted in DeCaro, *On the Side of My People*, 267. See also Malcolm X with Haley, *Autobiography*, 332–33, 339–41.

214. Goldman, *Death and Life of Malcolm X*, 409.

215. *Muhammad Speaks*, "Meet Some of the Ministers of Muhammad's Mosques of Islam," March 27, 1964; *Muhammad Speaks*, "'65, the Crucial Year," January 29, 1965. Some of the rank-and-file members also identified him by name. See, for example, *Muhammad Speaks*, "What Islam Has Done for Me," October 9, 1964, and July 31, 1964.

216. *Muhammad Speaks*, "Boston Minister Tells of Malcolm—Muhammad's Biggest Hypocrite," December 4, 1964. Consider, for instance, *Muhammad Speaks*,

"'I Am Teaching the Truth," March 12, 1965. The illustration that follows spoke to NOI leaders' awareness of the influence of radio, television, and newspapers, and their resistance to it as "Hysteria" and "Round-the-Clock Anti-Muslim Propaganda."

217. *Muhammad Speaks*, "Boston Minister Tells of Malcolm—Muhammad's Biggest Hypocrite," December 4, 1964; *Muhammad Speaks*, "Minister Who Knew Him Best—Part 1: Rips Malcolm's Treachery, Defection," May 8, 1964. See also *Muhammad Speaks*, "The Messenger Teaches: During Times of Pressure Only the Weak Shall Fade," March 26, 1965.

218. *Muhammad Speaks*, "Divine Messengers Must Be Obeyed," April 10, 1964.

219. *Muhammad Speaks*, "Biography of a Hypocrite by Two Muslim Brothers Who Knew Him Best," September 25, 1964; *Muhammad Speaks*, "Minister Exposed by Those Who Knew Him through Life," October 9, 1964. See also Marable, *Malcolm X*, 60–62.

220. *Muhammad Speaks*, "Facts Told on Role of Malcolm," April 10, 1964; Marable, *Malcolm X*, 75.

221. *Muhammad Speaks*, "New York Team Took Top Prize," June 19, 1964; *Muhammad Speaks*, "Why Hypocrites Fail to Wreck Muhammad's Work," November 26, 1965. See also *Muhammad Speaks*, "Freedom of Muhammad's Press Will Be Upheld," July 9, 1965; Breitman, *By Any Means Necessary*, 5. In interviews following the split, Malcolm was keen to make the point that "I am the founder of the paper, the originator of the paper. Few people realize it—I was the one who originated *Muhammad Speaks* newspaper. The initial editions were written entirely by me in my basement."

222. See Maureen Smith, "*Muhammad Speaks* and Muhammad Ali: Intersections of the Nation of Islam and Sport in the 1960s," in Magdalinksi and Chandler, *With God on Their Side*, 177–96; *Muhammad Speaks*, "When Lights Went Out He Sold Muhammad Speaks by Way of Candlelight," December 3, 1965. See also *Muhammad Speaks*, "Muhammad Speaks Meets with Champ Muhammad Ali," April 16, 1964; *Muhammad Speaks*, "Champ Credits Teachings of Messenger in Victory," June 4, 1965; Perry, *Malcolm*, 249; Curtis, *Black Muslim Religion*, 119; Abernethy, *Iconography of Malcolm X*, 63; Malcolm X and Haley, *Autobiography*, 353.

223. See, for example, Wallace with Gates, *Between You and Me*, 88, 90–91; Wallace and Gates, *Close Encounters*, 138; Clarke, *Malcolm X*, 106–13; Gallen, *Malcolm X*, 243–50; Malcolm X with Haley, *Autobiography*, ix, 443, 456, 459, 461–62, 465. See also Abernethy, *Iconography of Malcolm X*, 52, 59.

224. *Muhammad Speaks*, "Life of Muhammad the Prophet Like That of Messenger Muhammad Today," December 4, 1964.

225. *Muhammad Speaks*, "We Thank Allah for the Messenger," July 31, 1964.

226. *Muhammad Speaks*, "Cites 20-Year Association with Messenger of Allah," September 11, 1964.

227. *Muhammad Speaks*, "Muslim Minister Writes to Malcolm," July 3, 1964. See also *Muhammad Speaks*, "We Thank Allah for the Messenger," July 31, 1964; "An Open Letter to Malcolm Little," MXC, box 3, fol. 12.

228. *Muhammad Speaks*, "Minister Moves New York Mosque to New Heights Warns Muslims Against False 'Leaders,'" October 9, 1964; see also "An Open Letter to Malcolm Little," MXC, box 3, fol. 12; DeCaro, *On the Side of My People*, 227–29.

229. *Muhammad Speaks*, "Divine Messengers Must Be Obeyed," April 10, 1964. See also *Muhammad Speaks*, "Who Is He Kidding," February 12, 1965.

230. *Muhammad Speaks*, "Economic Program," July 17, 1964.

231. Malcolm X with Haley, *Autobiography*, 334–33.

232. *Muhammad Speaks*, "Life of Muhammad the Prophet Like That of Messenger Muhammad Today," December 4, 1964; *Muhammad Speaks*, "Muhammad Is the 'Magnet' Attracting the Multitudes," January 29, 1965.

233. *Muhammad Speaks*, "Life of Muhammad the Prophet Like That of Messenger Muhammad Today," December 4, 1964.

234. Malcolm X with Haley, *Autobiography*, 419–20. See also Estes, *I Am a Man!*, 104–5.

235. *Muhammad Speaks*, "Witness What Messenger Means to 'Outsiders,'" July 31, 1964. See also *Muhammad Speaks*, "The Hallmark of Greatness," April 9, 1965. Muhammad's size continued to grow in the paper. It declared that Muhammad "began to loom larger, growing through more than 30 years to Thor-like proportions while striding the horizons in the seven-league boots given him by divine proclamation."

236. See also *Muhammad Speaks*, "On the Fate of Hypocrites," January 15, 1965, and *Muhammad Speaks*, "Bible Parable Describes Attack on the Messenger," February 12, 1965; *Muhammad Speaks*, "As the Prophets Predicted the Maligning of a Modern Moses," July 31, 1964.

237. *Muhammad Speaks*, "Walk the Way of Free Men!," April 10, 1964; *Muhammad Speaks*, "On My Own," April 10, 1964.

238. *Muhammad Speaks*, "As the Prophets Predicted the Maligning of a Modern Moses," July 31, 1964; *Muhammad Speaks*, "Messenger's Divine Mission," December 4, 1964.

239. The *Defender* article was titled "Nation of Islam Warns Malcolm," published in December 1964. Clark, *Final Speeches*, 17–19; Malcolm X with Haley, *Autobiography*, 349, 356.

240. Malcolm X with Haley, *Autobiography*, 356, 365, 352, 435. See also Marable, *Malcolm X*, 423–27.

241. MXC, Malcolm X to Dr. Malik Badri, July 8, 1964, box 3, fol. 4. See also Byrd and Miri, *Malcolm X*; Leader, *Understanding Malcolm X*; Breitman, *Malcolm X Speaks*, 158.

242. Malcolm X with Haley, *Autobiography*, 357, 327–28; MXC, Warith (Wallace) Muhammad to Malcolm X, December 17, 1964, and December 25, 1964, box 3, fol. 9; Clarke, *Malcolm X*, 120; Clark, *Final Speeches*, 18; see also Evanzz, *Messenger*, 304, 328; Marable, *Malcolm X*, 429–30.

243. See Breitman, *By Any Means Necessary*, 67; Breitman, *Malcolm X Speaks*, 176–77; Estes, *I Am a Man!*, 104.

244. Malcolm X to Mr. Hussein El-Borai, January 7, 1965, MXC, box 3, fol. 4.

245. *Muhammad Speaks*, "On Television across the Nation," December 4, 1964. Perry, *Malcolm*, 323; Rickford, *Betty Shabazz*, 191; *Muhammad Speaks*, "Pakistani Muslim Blasts Handling of TV Interview with Messenger of Allah," January 1, 1965.

246. *Muhammad Speaks*, "New York Mosque to Host 'Night with the F. O. I.,'" January 1, 1965.

247. *Muhammad Speaks*, "'65, the Crucial Year," January 29, 1965.

248. Clarke, *Malcolm X*, 121.

249. See, for example, Breitman et al., *Assassination of Malcolm X*; Evanzz, *Judas Factor*.

250. Marable, *Malcolm X*, 454–56; DeCaro, *On the Side of My People*, 277–85.

251. See also Abernethy, *Iconography of Malcolm X*, 127–31.

252. *Defender*, "Views on Malcolm X Legacy of Malcolm X," March 11, 1965; Clarke, *Malcolm X*, 126.

253. Clarke, *Malcolm X*, 126–27. See also Malcolm X with Haley, *Autobiography*, 461. See also, *Muhammad Speaks*, "Letters to the Editor," February 1962. See also Davis's explanation of why he eulogized Malcolm in Clarke, *Malcolm X*, 128–31.

254. It should be noted that Muhammad did comment in a press conference the day after the assassination, however, denying involvement. See DeCaro, *On the Side of My People*, 275–76.

255. *Muhammad Speaks*, "Malcolm's Doom Decreed by God, Not the Messenger," August 27, 1965; *Muhammad Speaks*, "'Why, at Times, I Refused to Cooperate with Malcolm," August 20, 1965; *Muhammad Speaks*, "'Drop Past Events and Get On with the Work of Islam,'" March 12, 1965. See also *Muhammad Speaks*, "Pakistani Muslim Advises: March On under Messenger's Banner!," February 5, 1965; *Muhammad Speaks*, "Hypocrites Cannot Alter Muhammad's Divine Destiny," February 19, 1965; *Muhammad Speaks*, "Pakistani Muslim Looks at Demise of Malcolm," March 5, 1965; *Muhammad Speaks*, "Self-Publicity Motivated Malcolm, Not Devotion," August 13, 1965; *Muhammad Speaks*, "How the Late Malcolm X Misrepresented Himself and the Divine Messenger," August 5, 1965; *Muhammad Speaks*, "Malcolm's Doom Decreed by God, Not the Messenger," August 27, 1965; *Muhammad Speaks*, "Tells of Malcolm's Legacy: Lies, Mistruths, Falsehoods," December 10, 1965; *Muhammad Speaks*, "Rips Malcolm Statements Printed in Foreign Press," December 24, 1965.

256. Muhammad, *Message to the Blackman in America*; *Muhammad Speaks*, "Muhammad's Book Oct. 15," October 1, 1965. See also "Read Muhammad's Message to the Blackman in America," November 5, 1965; *Muhammad Speaks*, June 23, 1965; *Muhammad Speaks*, "Cleveland Opens Massive Sales Drive for Muhammad's 'Message to Blackman,'" December 17, 1965; Clegg, *Original Man*, 178–79.

257. Evanzz, *Messenger*, 342; Marable, *Malcolm X*, 465.

258. Alex Haley to Malcolm X, June 21, 1964, MXC, box 3, fol. 6.

259. "Out from the Shadow: Malcolm X," in Dudley, *My Father's Shadow*, 167–96; DeCaro, *On the Side of My People*, 199–261. It should be pointed out that many scholars have analyzed the autobiography also for the ways in which Haley shaped its narrative to fit his goals for the work, sometimes even against Malcolm's own wishes. See, for example, Abernethy, *Iconography of Malcolm X*, 80–92. It is interesting that one of the books published after Malcolm's death in 1965, featuring a collection of his speeches, was titled *Malcolm X Speaks*. See Breitman, *Malcolm X Speaks*.

260. Malcolm X with Haley, *Autobiography*, 283–84, 304, 273.

261. Malcolm X with Haley, 421–22, 431. See also "Communication and Reality," in Clarke, *Malcolm X*, 307–20. See also Breitman, *By Any Means Necessary*, 158. In

an interview on January 18, 1965, Malcolm said, "The press has purposely and skill-fully projected me in the image of a racist, a race supremacist, and an extremist." The interviewers asked, "What's wrong with this image? What do you really stand for?" "First, I'm not a racist," he answered. "I'm against every form of discrimina-tion. I believe in human beings, and that all human beings should be respected as such, regardless of their color." See also Perry, *Malcolm X*, 160, 164–65.

262. For more on Malcolm's new outlook, especially its religious dimensions, see, for example, "Malcolm," in Gomez, *Black Crescent*, 331–70.

263. Malcolm X with Haley, *Autobiography*, 349, 358.

264. "Highlights," May 30, 1964, MXC, box 14, fol. 3. See also "Press," MXC, box 14, fol. 3; Wallace Muhammad to Malcolm X, December 14, 1964, MXC, box 3, fol. 9. Wallace wrote Malcolm suggesting "the idea of consolidating our Islamic (reli-gious) interests. . . . We also need a publication no matter how cheaply put together." See also Malcolm X to David DuBois, December 17, 1964, MXC, box 3, fol. 13. Mal-colm stated to DuBois, "I am still rushing."

265. Clarke, *Malcolm X*, 336; MXC, box 14, fol. 7. The *Blacklash* issues appeared September 14, 1964, September 28, 1964, and November 9, 1964.

266. "Organization of Afro-American Unity," June 28, 1964, MXC, box 14, fol. 4; Malcolm X with Haley, *Autobiography*, 407, 431. Breitman, *By Any Means Necessary*, 2, 5, 62, 15. See also Tyner, *Geography of Malcolm X*.

267. Clarke, *Malcolm X*, 335–36, 339; Brietman, *By Any Means Necessary*, 38, 7, 48, 53, 55, 56, 62–63; DeCaro, *On the Side of My People*, 232–33.

268. Malcolm X to Alex Haley, March 19, 1964, Alex Haley Papers, box 3, fol. 1.

269. Malcolm X with Haley, *Autobiography*, 390; Malcolm X to Alex Haley, March 19, 1964, MXC, box 3, fol. 1; Lomax, *When the Word Is Given*, 59–60.

270. See also *Muhammad Speaks*, "The Truth," April 1, 1966; Essien-Udom, *Black Nationalism*, 136–38.

271. Malcolm X with Haley, *Autobiography*, 334. For more on the Panthers, see, for example, Murch, *Living for the City*; Bloom and Martin, *Black against Empire*; Joseph, *Waiting til the Midnight Hour*; Lazeron and Williams, *In Search of the Black Panther Party*; Self, *American Babylon*.

272. Ogbar, *Black Power*, 60–63, 82–85; Clegg, *Original Man*, 243. Interestingly, *Muhammad Speaks* featured an article by Eldridge Cleaver, titled "'As Crinkly as Yours, Brother." It was reprinted from another publication on June 12, 1962.

273. Rodger Streitmatter, "Black Panther Newspaper: A Militant Voice, a Salient Vision," in Vogel, *Black Press*, 229, 233; "Do-Nothing Terrorists and Other Problems" and "'Off the Pig,' 'Motherfucker,' and Other Terms," in Seale, *Seize the Time*, 365–69, 404–11; Murch, *Living for the City*, 127–31, 155; Bloom and Martin, *Black against Empire*, 34, 70, 212, 222; Foner, *Black Panthers Speak*, 273. For a discussion of their look, see, for example, Ongiri, *Spectacular Blackness*, 17, 73–74. See also Ogbar, *Black Power*.

274. Marable, *Malcolm X*, 403; Boyd et al., *By Any Means Necessary*, xvii. See, for example, *Black Panther*, May 15, 1967, and November 23, 1967.

275. "Do-Nothing Terrorists and Other Problems," in Seale, *Seize the Time*, 365–69; Bloom and Martin, *Black against Empire*, 376; Heath, *Off the Pigs!*, 26–28, 149;

Estes, *I Am a Man!*, 88, 106; Murch, *Living for the City*, 155; Ongiri, *Spectacular Blackness.* See also Abernethy, *Iconography of Malcolm X*, 131–35; "The Decline of the Black Muslims," in Cleaver and Scheer, *Eldridge Cleaver*, 13–17; Vogel, *Black Press*, 229, 233.

276. See also Evanzz, *Messenger*, 358–62. According to Evanzz, sometime in the 1970s, NOI and Panther members got into a fistfight in Atlanta over newspaper territory. In efforts to undermine both organizations, the FBI provoked some of the squabbles between the two.

277. Ogbar, *Black Power*, 121; Clegg, *Original Man*, 243; Ongiri, *Spectacular Blackness*, 19. For the nation's disagreements with young Black Power radicals, see, for example, Walker, *Islam and the Search*, 408–10. See also *Muhammad Speaks*, "Sees 'Black Power' Growing Influence of Muhammad," August 12, 1966; *Muhammad Speaks*, "Black Power Based on Muhammad's Program," August 4, 1967; *Muhammad Speaks*, "Finds 'Black Is Beautiful' Concept Inherent in the Messenger's Teachings," April 26, 1968.

278. *Muhammad Speaks*, "MS Cited as Key to Building Program," November 24, 1967; *Muhammad Speaks*, May 10, 1968.

Conclusion

1. Tinney and Rector, *Issues and Trends*, 102, 104.

2. "Fellow Publishers and Editors," ASFP, box 26, fol. 11. Sengstacke prepared a draft of the speech in 1978 or 1979.

3. Moynihan, *Negro Family*, 1. For more on the gendered implications of Moynihan's work, see also "The Moynihan Report," in Estes, *I Am a Man!*; "Strong Women and Strutting Men: The Moynihan Report," in Giddings, *When and Where I Enter*, 325–35.

4. Warren, *Who Speaks for the Negro?*, 267, 160–61, 261, 252, and "Foreword."

5. Fisher and Lowenstein, *Race and the News Media*, ix–x, 3, 5, 7.

6. Fisher and Lowenstein, *Race and the News Media*, 8–10, 132.

7. Cruse, *Crisis of the Negro Intellectual*, 563–65.

8. See Tinney and Rector, *Issues and Trends*, 9. It should be noted that a few studies at the time found that the *Defender* had grown conservative and avoided taking political stances. Other mainstream publications that tried to keep pace with the Black Power movement included *Negro Digest* and the *Carolina Times*. See James C. Hall, "On Sale at Your Favorite Newsstand: *Negro Digest/Black World* and the 1960s," in Vogel, *Black Press*, 188–206; Gershenhorn, *Louis Austin and the* Carolina Times, 183–207.

9. "The Negro Press in an Integrated Society," ASFP, box 25, fol. 4.

10. Illinois Academy of Criminology to Sengstacke, March 6, 1968, ASFP, box 25, fol. 9; Commission for Economic Development to John Sengstacke, May 8, 1968, ASFP, box 25, fol. 11. For more on the 1967 urban rebellions, see, for example, McLaughlin, *Long Hot Summer of 1967*.

11. Muhammad, *Message to the Blackman*, 313–14.

12. Richard M. Nixon to John Sengstacke, December 2, 1968, ASFP, box 29, fol. 68.

13. See, for example, John Sengstacke, "Riots and Their Impact on Race Relations," ASFP, box 24, fol. 50, p. 13. In a draft for a speech he wrote some time after the urban rebellions, Sengstacke asserted that "Black Power can be a constructive approach to the new life of freedom for black people in the Great Society. . . . The Black Revolution is the by-product of unfulfilled promises of democracy." The *Defender* also seemed to keep pace with Black Power. See, for example, *Defender*, "How to Build Black Pride," July 24, 1968.

14. *Report of the National Advisory Commission on Civil Disorders*, 1–2.

15. *Report of the National Advisory Commission on Civil Disorders*, 366, 384–85. See also Chiasso, *Press in Times of Crisis*, 172–74. See also Hrach, *Riot Report and the News*.

16. "A Businessman Looks at Riots," February 21, 1968, ASFP, box 25, fol. 9. See also "Jobs in the Ghetto," May 15, 1968, ASFP, box 25, fol. 11. Sengstacke delivered this speech before the Illinois commission for Economic Development. He mentioned Nixon's plans for "Black Capitalism." The speech reiterated themes from his speech before the Illinois Academy of Criminology, though in somewhat tempered forms. For more on Nixon, Black Capitalism, and black power, see, for instance, Hill and Rabig, *Business of Black Power*.

17. "A Businessman Looks at Riots," February 21, 1968, ASFP, box 25, fol. 9.

18. See also Michaeli, *Defender*, 475. Sengstacke shared with a reporter around this time, "I'd really like for people to leave me alone for a while. I've already got too much to do. After 40 years, I've been involved in too many things. It's not that I'm not interested. I'm just a little tired."

19. Tinney and Rector, *Issues and Trends*, 101–4, 115, 22. See also Buni, *Robert L. Vann*, 326. See also "John H. Sengstacke's Talk," May 14, 1965, ASFP, box 24, fol. 46.

20. Quoted in Michaeli, *Defender*, 475.

21. Quoted in Michaeli, 476.

22. Tinney and Rector, *Issues and Trends*, 104.

23. Tinney and Rector, 10.

24. Tinney and Rector, 107–10. See also "Difficulties of Covering Racial News" and "Past Deficiencies of Coverage," in Martindale, *White Press and Black America*, 32–52, 53–71. See also Wilson, *Black Journalists in Paradox*, 85–88. See also, "Into the White Newsroom," in Carrol, *Race News*, 180–206.

25. Cecelski, *Along Freedom Road*.

26. Tinney and Rector, *Issues and Trends*, 111.

27. Tinney and Rector, 102–5.

28. Tinney and Rector, 109, 104–5.

Bibliography

Archival Materials

Bentley Historical Library, University of Michigan, Ann Arbor
    Robert Franklin Williams Papers
Chicago Historical Society, Chicago, IL
    Claude A. Barnett Papers
Schomburg Center for Research in Black Culture, New York Public Library,
      New York, NY
    Alex Haley Papers
    The Malcolm X Collection
    Universal Negro Improvement Association Miscellaneous Collection
Vivian Harsh Collection, Chicago Public Library, Chicago, IL
    Abbott-Sengstacke Family Papers

Newspapers and Periodicals

Arkansas State Press
Atlanta Daily World
Black Panther
Chicago Daily Defender
Chicago Defender
Crisis
Crusader
Jet
Los Angeles Sentinel
Los Angeles Times
Muhammad Speaks
New York Amsterdam News
New York Times
Pittsburgh Courier
Washington Post and Times Herald

Published Primary Sources

Aptheker, Herbert, ed. *The Correspondence of W. E. B. DuBois*. 3 vols. Amherst:
    University of Massachusetts Press, 1973.
——. *A Documentary History of the Negro People in the United States*. New York:
    Carol Publishing Group, 1990.

——. *Writings in Periodicals Edited by W. E. B. Dubois, Selections from* The Horizon. New York: Kraus-Thomson, 1985.

Baldwin, James. *The Fire Next Time*. New York: Dial, 1963.

Bass, Charlotta. *Forty Years: Memoirs from the Pages of a Newspaper*. Los Angeles: Charlotta Bass, 1960.

Bates, Daisy. *The Long Shadow of Little Rock*. New York: David McKay, 1962.

Booker, Carol, ed. *Alone atop the Hill: The Autobiography of Alice Dunnigan, Pioneer of the National Black Press*. Athens: University of Georgia Press, 2015.

Booker, Simeon, with Carol McCabe Booker. *Shocking the Conscience: A Reporter's Account of the Civil Rights Movement*. Jackson: University Press of Mississippi, 2013.

Breitman, George. *By Any Means Necessary: Speeches, Interviews and a Letter by Malcolm X*. New York: Pathfinder, 1970.

——. *Malcolm X Speaks: Selected Speeches and Statements*. New York: Pathfinder, 1989.

Burns, Ben. *Nitty Gritty: A White Editor in Black Journalism*. Jackson: University Press of Mississippi, 1996.

Carson, Clayborne. *Malcolm X: The FBI File*. New York: Skyhorse, 2012.

——, ed. *The Papers of Martin Luther King, Jr.* Vol. 4. Berkeley: University of California Press, 2000.

Carson, Clayborne, David J. Garrow, Gerald Gill, Vincent Harding, and Darlene Clark Hine. *The Eyes on the Prize Civil Rights Reader*. New York: Penguin Books, 1991.

Clark, Steve, ed. *The Final Speeches: February 1965*. New York: Pathfinder, 1992.

Clarke, John Henrik, ed. *Malcolm X: The Man and His Times*. Toronto: Collier Books, 1969.

Cleaver, Eldridge, and Robert Scheer. *Eldridge Cleaver: Post-Prison Writings and Speeches*. New York: Ramparts Book, 1969.

Collins, Rodnell P., with Peter A. Bailey. *Seventh Child: A Family Memoir of Malcolm X*. Secaucus, NJ: Carol Publishing, 1998.

DuBois, W. E. B. *The Autobiography of W. E. B. DuBois; A Soliloquy on Viewing My Life from the Last Decade of Its First Century*. New York: International Publishers, 1968.

——. *Darkwater: Voices from within the Veil*. New York: Humanity Books, 2003.

——. *Dusk of Dawn: An Essay toward an Autobiography of a Race Concept*. New York: Harcourt, Brace, 1940.

Farrakhan, Louis. *The Meaning of F.O.I.* Chicago: Final Call, 1983.

Foner, Philip S., ed. *The Black Panthers Speak*. New York: Da Capo, 2002.

Frazier, Thomas R., ed. *Afro-American History: Primary Sources*. New York: Harcourt, Brace and World, 1970.

Gallen, David, ed. *Malcolm X: As They Knew Him*. New York: Carroll and Graf Publishers, 1992.

Garvey, Amy Jacques. *Garvey and Garveyism*. New York: Collier-Macmillan, 1970.

——. *Philosophy and Opinions of Marcus Garvey or Africa for the Africans*. Vol. 2. New York: Universal, 1926.

Hill, Robert A., ed. *The Marcus Garvey and Universal Negro Improvement Association Papers*. 10 vols. Berkeley: University of California Press, 1986.

King, Coretta Scott. *My Life, My Love, My Legacy*. New York: Henry Holt, 2017.

——. *My Life with Martin Luther King, Jr.* New York: Holt, Rinehart and Winston, 1969.

King, Martin Luther, Jr. *The Measure of a Man*. Philadelphia: Fortress, 1988.

——. *Stride toward Freedom: The Montgomery Story*. New York: Harper and Brothers, 1958.

Lomax, Louis E. *The Negro Revolt*. New York: Harper and Row, 1962.

——. *When the Word Is Given: A Report on Elijah Muhammad, Malcolm X, and the Black Muslim World*. New York: The World, 1963.

Marable, Manning, and Garett Felber. *The Portable Malcolm X Reader*. New York: Penguin Classics, 2013.

Marable, Manning, and Leith Mullings. *Let Nobody Turn Us Around: Voices of Resistance, Reform, and Renewal: An African American Anthology*. 2nd ed. New York: Rowman and Littlefield, 2009.

Meier, August, Elliot Rudwick, and Francis L. Broderick, eds. *Black Protest Thought in the Twentieth Century*. 2nd ed. Indianapolis: Bobbs-Merrill Educational Publishing, 1965.

Muhammad, Elijah. *The Supreme Wisdom*. Vol. 2. Chesapeake, VA: U. B. and U.S. Communications Systems, 1957.

Perry, Bruce, ed. *Malcolm X: The Last Speeches*. New York: Pathfinder, 1989.

Pohlmann, Marcus D. *African American Political Thought: Confrontation vs. Compromise: 1945 to the Present*. Vol. 2. New York: Routledge, 2003.

Schuyler, George S. *Black and Conservative: The Autobiography of George S. Schuyler*. New York: Arlington House, 1966.

Seale, Bobby. *Seize the Time: The Story of the Black Panther Party and Huey P. Newton*. New York: Random House, 1970.

Vincent, Theodore G. *Voices of a Black Nation: Political Journalism in the Harlem Renaissance*. Trenton, NJ: Africa World, 1990.

Voice of the Negro. Vol. 1, *1904*. New York: Negro Universities Press, 1969.

Wallace, Mike, and Gary Paul Gates. *Close Encounters*. New York: William Morrow, 1984.

Wallace, Mike, with Gary Paul Gates. *Between You and Me: A Memoir*. New York: Hyperion, 2005.

Washington, James M., ed. *A Testament of Hope: The Essential Writings and Speeches of Martin Luther King, Jr.* New York: Harper San Francisco, 1991.

Waters, Enoch P. *American Diary*. Chicago: Path, 1987.

Wilkins, Roy, with Tom Mathews. *Standing Fast: The Autobiography of Roy Wilkins*. New York: Viking, 1982.

Williams, Robert F. *Negroes with Guns*. New York: Marzani and Munsell, 1962.

X, Malcolm, with the Assistance of Alex Haley. *The Autobiography of Malcolm X*. New York: Ballantine Books, 1992.

Government Publications

The Chicago Commission on Race Relations. *The Negro in Chicago: A Study of Race Relations and a Race Riot.* Chicago: University of Chicago Press, 1922.

Moynihan, Daniel Patrick. *The Negro Family: The Case for National Action.* Washington, DC: US Department of Labor, Office of Policy Planning and Research, 1965.

Report of the National Advisory Commission on Civil Disorders. New York: E. P. Dutton, 1968.

Books, Articles, and Theses

Abernethy, Graeme. *The Iconography of Malcolm X.* Lawrence: University Press of Kansas, 2013.

Agnew, Jean-Christophe, and Roy Rosenzweig. *A Companion to Post-1945 America.* Malden, MA: Blackwell, 2002.

Aldama, Arturo J., ed. *Violence and the Body: Race, Gender, and the State.* Bloomington: Indiana University Press, 2003.

Allen, Robert L. *The Port Chicago Mutiny.* New York: Warner Books, 1989.

Anderson, Kevin R. *Agitations: Ideologies and Strategies in African American Politics.* Fayetteville: University of Arkansas Press, 2010.

Anderson, Sherwood. *Puzzled America.* New York: Charles Scribner's Sons, 1935.

Arsenault, Raymond. *Freedom Riders: 1961 and the Struggle for Racial Justice.* New York: Oxford University Press, 2006.

Asen, Robert, and Daniel C. Brouwer, eds. *Counterpublics and the State.* Albany: State University of New York Press, 2001.

Asukile, Thabiti. "Joel Augustus Rogers: Black International Journalism, Archival Research, and Black Print Culture." *Journal of African American History* 95, no. 3/4 (June 2010): 322–47.

Baker, Houston A., Jr. "Critical Memory and the Black Public Sphere." *Public Culture* 7, no. 1 (1994): 3–33.

Baldwin, Davarian L. *Chicago's New Negroes: Modernity, the Great Migration, and Black Urban Life.* Chapel Hill: University of North Carolina Press, 2007.

Barkan, Elazar. *The Retreat of Scientific Racism: Changing Concepts of Race in Britain and the United States between the World Wars.* New York: Cambridge University Press, 1992.

Barksdale, Marcellus. "Robert F. Williams and the Indigenous Civil Rights Movement in Monroe North Carolina, 1961." *Journal of Negro History* 69, no. 2 (Spring 1984): 73–89.

Barnouw, Erik. *Tube of Plenty: The Evolution of American Television.* New York: Oxford University Press, 1975.

Bassey, Magnus O. *Malcolm X and African American Self-Consciousness.* Lewiston, NY: Edwin Mellen, 2005.

Bates, Beth Tompkins. *Pullman Porters and the Rise of Protest Politics in Black America, 1925–1945.* Chapel Hill: University of North Carolina Press, 2001.

Bederman, Gail. *Manliness and Civilization: A Cultural History of Gender and Race in the United States, 1880–1917.* Chicago: University of Chicago Press, 1995.

Benton, Mark, and P. Jean Frazier. "The Agenda-Setting Function of Mass Media at Three Levels of Information-Holding." *Communication Research* 3 (1976): 261–74.

Berg, Herbert. *Elijah Muhammad and Islam.* New York: New York University Press, 2009.

Berrey, Stephen A. *The Jim Crow Routine: Everyday Performances of Race, Civil Rights, and Segregation in Mississippi.* Chapel Hill: University of North Carolina Press, 2015.

Best, Wallace. *Passionately Human, No Less Divine: Religion and Culture in Black Chicago, 1915–1952.* Princeton, NJ: Princeton University Press, 2005.

Biondi, Martha. *To Stand and Fight: The Struggle for Civil Rights in Postwar New York City.* Cambridge, MA: Harvard University Press, 2003.

Black Public Sphere Collective. *The Black Public Sphere: A Public Culture Book.* Chicago: University of Chicago Press, 1995.

Bloom, Joshua, and Waldo E. Martin Jr. *Black against Empire: The History and Politics of the Black Panther Party.* Berkeley: University of California Press, 2016.

Bodroghkozy, Aniko. *Equal Time: Television and the Civil Rights Movement.* Urbana: University of Illinois Press, 2012.

Boyd, Herb, et al. *By Any Means Necessary: Malcolm X: Real, Not Reinvented: Critical Conversations on Manning Marable's Biography of Malcolm X.* Chicago: Third World, 2012.

Bradley, Patricia. *Women and the Press: The Struggle for Equality.* Evanston, IL: Northwestern University Press, 2005.

Brandt, Nat. *Harlem at War: The Black Experience in WWII.* Syracuse, NY: Syracuse University Press, 1996.

Breitman, George, Herman Porter, and Baxter Smith. *The Assassination of Malcolm X.* New York: Pathfinder, 1976.

Broderick, Francis L. *W. E. B. DuBois, Negro Leader in a Time of Crisis.* Stanford, CA: Stanford University Press, 1959.

Brown, Tamara L., Gregory S. Parks, and Clarenda M. Phillips, eds. *African American Fraternities and Sororities: The Legacy and the Vision.* Lexington: University Press of Kentucky, 2005.

Brundage, W. Fitzhugh. *Lynching in the New South: Georgia and Virginia, 1880–1930.* Urbana: University of Illinois Press, 1993.

———, ed. *Booker T. Washington and Black Progress: Up from Slavery 100 Years Later.* Gainesville: University Press of Florida, 2003.

———, ed. *Under Sentence of Death: Lynching in the South.* Chapel Hill: University of North Carolina Press, 1997.

Bruzzi, Stella, and Pamela Church. *Fashion Cultures: Theories, Explorations and Analysis.* New York: Routledge, 2001.

Buckner, Timothy R., and Peter Caster, eds. *Fathers, Preachers, Rebels, Men: Black Masculinity in U.S. History and Literature, 1820–1945.* Columbus: Ohio State University Press, 2011.

Bullock, Cathy Ferrand. "'Freedom Is a Job for All of Us': The Arkansas *State Press* and Division in the Black Community during the 1957–59 School Crisis." *Howard Journal of Communications* 22 (2011): 83–100.

Buni, Andrew. *Robert L. Vann of the* Pittsburgh Courier: *Politics and Black Journalism.* Pittsburgh: University of Pittsburgh Press.

Butler, John Sibley. *Entrepreneurship and Self-Help among Black Americans: A Reconsideration of Race and Economics.* Albany: State University of New York Press, 1991.

Byrd, Dustin J., and Seyed Javad Miri, eds. *Malcolm X: From Political Eschatology to Religious Revolutionary.* Leiden: Brill, 2016.

Cairns, Kathleen A. *Front-Page Women Journalists, 1920–1950.* Lincoln: University of Nebraska Press, 2003.

Calloway-Thomas, Carolyn, and John Louis Lucaites, eds. *Martin Luther King, Jr., and the Sermonic Power of Public Discourse.* Tuscaloosa: University of Alabama Press, 1993.

Campbell, James T. *Middle Passages: African American Journeys to Africa, 1787–2005.* New York: Penguin, 2006.

Campbell, W. Joseph. *Yellow Journalism: Puncturing the Myths, Defining the Legacies.* Westport, CT: Praeger, 2001.

Carby, Hazel V. *Race Men.* Cambridge, MA: Harvard University Press, 1998.

Carle, Susan D. *Defining the Struggle: National Organizing for Racial Justice, 1880–1915.* New York: Oxford University Press, 2013.

Carrol, Fred. *Race News: Black Journalists and the Fight for Racial Justice in the Twentieth Century.* Urbana: University of Illinois Press, 2017.

Cecelski, David S. *Along Freedom Road: Hyde County, North Carolina, and the Fate of Black Schools in the South.* Chapel Hill: University of North Carolina Press, 1994.

Chiasso, Lloyd, Jr., ed. *The Press in Times of Crisis.* Westport, CT: Greenwood, 1995.

Clegg, Claude Andrew, III. *An Original Man: The Life and Times of Elijah Muhammad.* New York: St. Martin's, 1997.

Clifford, John, ed. *The Experience of Reading: Louise Rosenblatt and Reader-Response Theory.* Portsmouth, NH: Boynton/Cook, 1991.

Cloud, Barbara. *The Coming of the Frontier Press: How the West Was Really Won.* Evanston, IL: Northwestern University Press, 2008.

Cohen, Robert Carl. *Black Crusader: A Biography of Robert F. Williams.* Secaucus, NJ: Lyle Stuart, 1972.

Cole, Olen, Jr. *The African-American Experience in the Civilian Conservation Corps.* Gainesville: University Press of Florida, 1999.

Collier-Thomas, Bettye, and V. P. Franklin, eds. *Sisters in the Struggle: African American Women in the Civil Rights–Black Power Movement.* New York: New York University Press, 2001.

Collins, Rodnell P., with Peter A. Bailey. *Seventh Child: A Family Memoir of Malcolm X.* Secaucus, NJ: Carol, 1998.

Cooper, Brittney C. *Beyond Respectability: The Intellectual Thought of Race Women*. Urbana: University of Illinois Press, 2017.

Countryman, Matthew. *Civil Rights and Black Power in Philadelphia*. Philadelphia: University of Pennsylvania Press, 2006.

Cronon, E. David. *Black Moses: The Story of Marcus Garvey and the Universal Negro Improvement Association*. Madison: University of Wisconsin Press, 1969.

Cruse, Harold. *Crisis of the Negro Intellectual: A Historical Analysis of the Failure of Black Leadership*. New York: William Morrow, 1967.

Cunnigen, Donald, Rutledge M. Dennis, and Myrtle Gonza Glascoe, eds. *The Racial Politics of Booker T. Washington*. Oxford: Elsevier JAI, 2006.

Curtis, Edward E. *Black Muslim Religion in the Nation of Islam, 1960–1975*. Chapel Hill: University of North Carolina Press, 2006.

———. *Islam in Black America: Identity, Liberation, and Difference in African American Islamic Thought*. Albany: State University of New York Press, 2002.

Dann, Martin E., ed. *The Black Press 1827–1890, The Quest for National Identity*. New York: G. P. Putnam's Sons, 1971.

Davies, David R., ed. *The Press and Race: Mississippi Journalists Confront the Movement*. Jackson: University Press of Mississippi, 2001.

Davis, James C. *Commerce in Color: Race, Consumer Culture, and American Literature, 1893–1933*. Ann Arbor: University of Michigan Press, 2007.

DeCaro, Louis A., Jr. *On the Side of My People: A Religious Life of Malcolm X*. New York: New York University Press, 1996.

Denning, Michael. *The Cultural Front: The Laboring of American Culture in the Twentieth Century*. New York: Verso, 1998.

De Santis, Christopher C., ed. *Langston Hughes and the* Chicago Defender: *Essays on Race, Politics, and Culture, 1942–62*. Urbana: University of Illinois Press, 1995.

Detweiler, Frederick G. *The Negro Press in the United States*. Chicago: University of Chicago Press, 1922.

———. "The Negro Press Today." *American Journal of Sociology* (November 1938): 391–400.

DiPiero, Thomas. *White Men Aren't*. Durham, NC: Duke University Press, 2002.

Dowd, Jerome. *The Negro in American Life*. New York: Negro Universities Press, 1926.

Doyle, Bertram Wilbur. *The Etiquette of Race Relations in the South: A Study in Social Control*. New York: Schocken Books, 1971.

Drake, St. Clair, and Horace R. Cayton. *Black Metropolis: A Study of Negro Life in a Northern City*. New York: Harcourt, Brace, 1945.

Dubbert, Joe L. *A Man's Place: Masculinity in Transition*. Englewood Cliffs, NJ: Prentice-Hall, 1979.

DuBois, W. E. B. *The Philadelphia Negro: A Social Study*. Philadelphia: Published for the University, 1899.

———. *The Souls of Black Folk*. New York: Gramercy Books, 1994.

Dudley, David L. *My Father's Shadow: Intergenerational Conflict in African American Men's Autobiography*. Philadelphia: University of Pennsylvania Press, 1991.

Dudziak, Mary L. *Cold War Civil Rights: Race and the Image of American Democracy*. Princeton, NJ: Princeton University Press, 2000.

Durr, Robert. *The Negro Press: Its Character, Development, and Function*. Jackson: Mississippi Division, Southern Regional Council, 1947.

Edgerton, Robert B. *Hidden Heroism: Black Soldiers in America's Wars*. Boulder, CO: Westview, 2001.

Ellwood, Robert S. *The Fifties Spiritual Marketplace: American Religion in a Decade of Conflict*. New Brunswick, NJ: Rutgers University Press, 1997.

Essien-Udom, E. U. *Black Nationalism: A Search for an Identity in America*. Chicago: University of Chicago Press, 1962.

Estes, Steve. *I Am a Man!: Race, Manhood, and the Civil Rights Movement*. Chapel Hill: University of North Carolina Press, 2005.

Evanzz, Karl. *The Judas Factor: The Plot to Kill Malcolm*. New York: Thunder's Mouth, 1992.

———. *The Messenger: The Rise and Fall of Elijah Muhammad*. New York: Pantheon Books, 1999.

Ewing, Adam. *The Age of Garvey: How a Jamaican Activist Created a Mass Movement and Changed Global Black Politics*. Princeton, NJ: Princeton University Press, 2014.

Farr, Finis. *Black Champion; The Life and Times of Jack Johnson*. London: Macmillan, 1964.

Farrar, Hayward. *The* Baltimore Afro-American: *1892–1950*. Westport, CT: Greenwood, 1998.

Fehrenbacher, Don E. *The Dred Scott Case: Its Significance in American Law and Politics*. New York: Oxford University Press, 1978.

———. *Slavery, Law, and Politics: The Dred Scott Case in Historical Perspective*. New York: Oxford University Press, 1981.

Feimster, Crystal N. *Southern Horrors: Women and the Politics of Rape and Lynching*. Cambridge, MA: Harvard University Press, 2009.

Filene, Peter G. *Him/Her/Self: Gender Identities in Modern America*. Baltimore: Johns Hopkins University Press, 1975.

Finkle, Lee. *Forum for Protest: The Black Press during World War II*. Rutherford, NJ: Fairleigh Dickinson University Press, 1975.

Fisher, Paul L., and Ralph L. Lowenstein, eds. *Race and the News Media*. New York: Frederick A. Praeger, 1967.

Fleming, James G. "108 Years of the Negro Press." *Opportunity* 12 (March 1935), n.p.

Florette, Henri. *Black Migration: Movement North, 1900–1920*. New York: Anchor Press/Doubleday, 1975.

Foner, Phillip S. *American Socialism and Black Americans: From the Age of Jackson to World War II*. Westport, CT: Greenwood, 1977.

Forss, Amy Helene. *Black Print with a White Carnation: Mildred Brown and the Omaha Star Newspaper, 1938–1989*. Lincoln: University of Nebraska Press, 2013.

Forster, Stig, Wolfgang J. Mommsen, and Ronald Robinson, eds. *Bismarck, Europe, and Africa: The Berlin Africa Conference 1884–1885 and the Onset of Partition*. New York: Oxford University Press, 1988.

Foucault, Michel. *The Archaeology of Knowledge*. London: Tavistock, 1972.

———. *Discipline and Punish: The Birth of the Prison*. 2nd ed. New York: Vintage Books, 1995.

Fraser, Nancy. "Rethinking the Public Sphere." *Social Text* 25/26 (1990): 56–80.

Frazier, E. Franklin. *Black Bourgeoisie: The Rise of a New Middle Class*. New York: Free Press, 1957.

———. *The Negro Family in the United States*. Chicago: University of Chicago Press, 1966.

———. *The Negro in the United States*. New York: Macmillan, 1957.

Frederickson, George M. *The Black Image in the White Mind: The Debate on Afro-American Character and Destiny, 1817–1914*. New York: Harper and Row, 1972.

Freer, Regina. "L.A. Race Woman: Charlotta Bass and the Complexities of Black Political Development in Los Angeles." *American Quarterly* 56, no. 3 (September 2004): 607–32.

Friend, Craig Thompson. *Southern Masculinity: Perspectives on Manhood in the South since Reconstruction*. Athens: University of Georgia Press, 2009.

Gaines, Kevin K. *Uplifting the Race: Black Leadership, Politics, and Culture in the Twentieth Century*. Chapel Hill: University of North Carolina Press, 1996.

Gallon, Kim. "Silences Kept: The Absence of Gender and Sexuality in Black Press Historiography." *History Compass* 10, no. 2 (February 1, 2012): 207–18.

Gardell, Mattias. *In the Name of Elijah Muhammad: Louis Farrakhan and the Nation of Islam*. Durham, NC: Duke University Press, 1996.

Gardner, Eric. *Black Print Unbound: The Christian Recorder, African American Literature, and Periodical Culture*. New York: Oxford University Press, 2015.

Garrow, David J. *Bearing the Cross: Martin Luther King, Jr. and the Southern Christian Leadership Conference*. New York: Perennial Classics, 1986.

Gates, Henry Louis, Jr. "The Trope of a New Negro and the Reconstruction of the Image of the Black." *Representations* 24 (Autumn 1988): 129–55.

Geary, Daniel. *Beyond Civil Rights: The Moynihan Report and Its Legacy*. Philadelphia: University of Pennsylvania Press, 2015.

Gellman, Erik S. *Death Blow to Jim Crow: The National Negro Congress and the Rise of Militant Civil Rights*. Chapel Hill: University of North Carolina Press, 2012.

Gershenhorn, Jerry. *Louis Austin and the* Carolina Times: *A Life in the Long Black Freedom Struggle*. Chapel Hill: University of North Carolina Press, 2018.

Gibson, Dawn-Marie, and Jamillah Karim. *Women of the Nation: Between Black Protest and Sunni Islam*. New York: New York University Press, 2014.

Giddings, Paula. *In Search of Sisterhood: Delta Sigma Theta and the Challenge of the Black Sorority Movement*. New York: William Morrow, 1988.

——. *When and Where I Enter: The Impact of Black Women on Race and Sex in America*. Toronto: Bantam Books, 1984.

Gilmore, Glenda Elizabeth. *Defying Dixie: The Radical Roots of Civil Rights, 1919–1950*. New York: W. W. Norton, 2008.

——. *Gender and Jim Crow: Women and the Politics of White Supremacy in North Carolina, 1896–1920*. Chapel Hill: University of North Carolina Press, 1996.

Glasrud, Bruce A., and Cary D. Wintz, eds. *The Harlem Renaissance in the American West: The New Negro's Western Experience*. New York: Routledge, 2012.

Glisson, Susan M., ed. *The Human Tradition in the Civil Rights Movement*. New York: Rowman and Littlefield, 2006.

Gold, Matthew K. *Debates in the Digital Humanities*. Minneapolis: University of Minnesota Press, 2016.

Goldman, Peter. *The Death and Life of Malcom X*. New York: Harper and Row, 1973.

Gomez, Michael A. *Black Crescent: The Experience and Legacy of African Muslims in the Americas*. New York: Cambridge University Press, 2005.

Gordon, Eugene. "Negro Press." *American Mercury*, June 19, 1926.

Gore, Dayo F. *Radicalism at the Crossroads: African American Women Activists in the Cold War*. New York: New York University Press, 2011.

Gore, Dayo F., Jeanne Theoharis, and Komozi Woodard. *Want to Start a Revolution?: Black Women in the Black Freedom Struggle*. New York: New York University Press, 2009.

Gore, George W., Jr. *Negro Journalism: An Essay on the History and Present Conditions of the Negro Press*. Greencastle, IN: Journalism Press, 1922.

Grant, Colin. *Negro with a Hat: The Rise and Fall of Marcus Garvey*. New York: Oxford University Press, 2008.

Green, Adam. *Selling the Race: Culture, Community, and Black Chicago, 1940–1955*. Chicago: University of Chicago Press, 2007.

Greenberg, Cheryl Lynn. *"Or Does It Explode?": Black Harlem in the Great Depression*. New York: Oxford University Press, 1991.

Greenhaw, Wayne. *Fighting the Devil in Dixie: How Civil Rights Activists Took on the Ku Klux Klan in Alabama*. Chicago: Lawrence Hill Books, 2011.

Gregory, James. *The Southern Diaspora: How the Great Migrations of Black and White Southerners Transformed America*. Chapel Hill: University of North Carolina Press, 2005.

Grossman, James R. "Blowing the Trumpet: The *Chicago Defender* and Black Migration during World War I." *Illinois Historical Journal* 78, no. 2 (Summer 1985): 82–96.

——. *Land of Hope: Black Southerners and the Great Migration*. Chicago: University of Chicago Press, 1989.

Guzman, Richard R., ed. *Black Writing from Chicago: In the World, Not of It?*. Carbondale: Southern Illinois University Press, 2006.

Habermas, Jurgen. *The Structural Transformation of the Public Sphere: An Inquiry into a Category of Bourgeois Society*, trans. Thomas Burger, 1962. Cambridge, MA: MIT Press, 1991.

Hahn, Steven. *The Political Worlds of Slavery and Freedom.* Cambridge, MA: Harvard University Press, 2009.

Hall, Jacqueline Dowd. "The Long Civil Rights Movement and the Political Uses of the Past." *Journal of American History* 91 (March 2005): 1233–63.

Harper, Michael S. *The Collected Poems of Sterling A. Brown.* New York: Harper and Row, 1980.

Harper, Philip Brian. *Are We Not Men? Masculine Anxiety and the Problem of African American Identity.* New York: Oxford University Press, 1996.

Heath, G. Louis, ed. *Off the Pigs! The History and Literature of the Black Panther Party.* Metuchen, NJ: Scarecrow, 1976.

Heitner, Devorah. *Black Power TV.* Durham, NC: Duke University Press, 2013.

Helly, Dorothy O., and Susan M. Reverby, eds. *Gendered Domains: Rethinking the Public and Private in Women's History.* Ithaca, NY: Cornell University Press, 1992.

Henri, Florette. *Black Migration: Movement North, 1900–1920.* New York: Anchor Press/Doubleday, 1975.

Hill, Lance. *The Deacons for Defense: Armed Resistance and the Civil Rights Movement.* Chapel Hill: University of North Carolina Press, 2004.

Hill, Laura Warren, and Julia Rabig, eds. *The Business of Black Power: Community Development, Capitalism, and Corporate Responsibility in Postwar America.* New York: University of Rochester Press, 2012.

Hill, Roy L. *Who's Who in the American Negro Press.* Dallas: Royal, 1960.

Hine, Darlene Clark. *Hine Sight: Black Women and the Reconstruction of American History.* Brooklyn, NY: Carlson, 1994.

Hine, Darlene Clark, and Ernestine Jenkins, eds. *A Question of Manhood: A Reader in U.S. Black Men's History and Masculinity.* Bloomington: Indiana University Press, 1999.

Hine, Darlene Clark, and John McCluskey Jr., eds. *The Black Chicago Renaissance.* Urbana: University of Illinois Press, 2012.

Hogan, Lawrence D. *A Black National News Service: The Associated Negro Press and Claude Barnett, 1919–1945.* London: Fairleigh Dickinson University Press, 1984.

Holloway, Jonathan Scott. *Jim Crow Wisdom: Memory and Identity in Black America since 1940.* Chapel Hill: University of North Carolina Press, 2013.

Horne, Gerald. *The Rise and Fall of the Associated Negro Press: Claude Barnett's Pan-African News and the Jim Crow Paradox.* Urbana: University of Illinois Press, 2017.

Hornsby-Gutting, Angela. *Black Manhood and Community Building in North Carolina, 1900–1930.* Gainesville: University Press of Florida, 2009.

Hoven, Bettina van, and Kathrin Horschelmann, eds. "Introduction." In *Spaces of Masculinities.* New York: Routledge, 2005.

Howarth, David, and Jacob Torfing, eds., *Discourse Theory in European Politics: Identity, Policy, and Governance.* New York: Palgrave, 2005.

Hrach, Thomas J. *The Riot Report and the News: How the Kerner Commission Changed Media Coverage of Black America.* Amherst: University of Massachusetts Press, 2016.

Hutton, Frankie. *The Early Black Press in America, 1827–1960.* Westport, CT: Greenwood, 1993.

James, Winston. *Holding aloft the Banner of Ethiopia: Caribbean Radicalism in Early Twentieth-Century America.* New York: Verso: 1998.

Jeffries, Bayyinah S. *A Nation Can Rise No Higher Than Its Women: African American Muslim Women in the Movement for Black Self-Determination, 1950–1975.* Lanham, MD: Lexington Books, 2014.

Johnson, Walter. *Soul by Soul: Life inside the Antebellum Slave Market.* Cambridge, MA: Harvard University Press, 1999.

Jones, William P. *Tribe of Black Ulysses: African American Lumber Workers in the Jim Crow South.* Chicago: University of Illinois Press, 2005.

Jordan, William G. *Black Newspapers and America's War for Democracy, 1914–1920.* Chapel Hill: University of North Carolina Press, 2001.

Joseph, Peniel E., ed. *The Black Power Movement: Rethinking the Civil Rights–Black Power Era.* New York: Routledge, 2006.

———. *Waiting til the Midnight Hour: A Narrative History of Black Power in America.* New York: Henry Holt, 2006.

Karim, Benjamin, with Peter Skutches and David Gallen. *Remembering Malcolm.* New York: Carroll and Graf Publishers, 1992.

Kaye, Andrew M. "Colonel Roscoe Conkling Simmons and the Mechanics of Black Leadership." *Journal of American Studies* 37, no. 1 (2003): 79–98.

Kelley, Robin D. G. *Hammer and Hoe: Alabama Communists during the Great Depression.* Chapel Hill: University of North Carolina Press, 1990.

———. *Race Rebels: Culture, Politics, and the Black Working Class.* New York: Free Press, 1994.

Kellner, Douglas. *Television and the Crisis of Democracy.* Boulder, CO: Westview, 1990.

Kennedy, Stetson. *Jim Crow Guide to the U.S.A.: The Laws, Customs and Etiquette Governing the Conduct of Nonwhites and Other Minorities as Second-Class Citizens.* Westport, CT: Greenwood, 1959.

Kerlin, Robert T. *The Voice of the Negro 1919.* New York: E. P. Dutton, 1920.

Kimmel, Michael. *Manhood in America: A Cultural History.* New York: Oxford Press, 2006.

Kirby, John B. *Black Americans in the Roosevelt Era: Liberalism and Race.* Knoxville: University of Tennessee Press, 1980.

Kirk, John A. *Beyond Little Rock: The Origins and Legacies of the Central High Crisis.* Fayetteville: University of Arkansas, 2007.

Kirschke, Amy Helene, and Phillip Luke Sinitiere. *Protest and Propaganda: W. E. B. DuBois, the* Crisis, *and American History.* Columbia: University of Missouri Press, 2014.

Klarman, Michael. "How Brown Changed Race Relations: The Backlash Thesis." *Journal of American History* 81, no. 1 (June 1994): 81–118.

Kornweibel, Theodore, Jr. *"Investigate Everything": Federal Efforts to Compel Black Loyalty during World War I.* Bloomington: Indiana University Press, 2002.

——. *No Crystal Stair: Black Life and the Messenger, 1917–1928*. Westport, CT: Greenwood, 1975.

Korstad, Robert Rodgers. *Civil Rights Unionism, Tobacco Workers, and the Struggle for Democracy in the Mid-Twentieth-Century South*. Chapel Hill: University of North Carolina Press, 2003.

Kreiling, Albert Lee. "The Making of Racial Identities in the Black Press: A Cultural Analysis of Race Journalism in Chicago, 1878–1929." PhD diss., University of Illinois at Urbana, 1973.

Krugler, David F. *1919, the Year of Racial Violence: How African Americans Fought Back*. New York: Cambridge University Press, 2015.

Lacy, Michael G., and Kent A. Ono. *Critical Rhetorics of Race*. New York: New York University Press, 2011.

Lazeron, Jama, and Yohuru Williams, eds. *In Search of the Black Panther Party: New Perspectives on a Revolutionary Movement*. Durham, NC: Duke University Press, 2006.

Leader, Roland Edward. *Understanding Malcolm X: The Controversial Changes in His Political Philosophy*. New York: Vantage, 1993.

Leibman, Nina C. *Living Room Lectures: The Fifties Family in Film and Television*. Austin: University of Texas Press, 1995.

Lester, Julius, ed. *The Seventh Son: The Thought and Writings of W. E. B. DuBois*. New York: Random House, 1971.

Leuchtenburg, William E. *Franklin D. Roosevelt and the New Deal, 1932–1940*. New York: Harper and Row, 1963.

Lewis, David Levering. *W. E. B. DuBois: Biography of a Race, 1868–1919*. New York: Henry Holt, 1993.

——. *W. E. B. DuBois, 1919–1963: The Fight for Equality and the American Century*. New York: Henry Holt, 2000.

——. *When Harlem Was in Vogue*. New York: Penguin Books, 1997.

Lichtenstein, Nelson. *State of the Union: A Century of American Labor*. Princeton, NJ: Princeton University Press, 2002.

Lincoln, C. Eric. *The Black Muslims in America*. Grand Rapids, MI: W. B. Eerdmans, 1994.

Ling, Peter J., and Sharon Montieth, eds. *Gender and the Civil Rights Movement*. New Brunswick, NJ: Rutgers University Press, 1999.

Lippmann, Walter. *Public Opinion*. Mineola, NY: Dover, 2004.

Litwack, Leon F. *Trouble in Mind: Black Southerners in the Age of Jim Crow*. New York: Alfred A. Knopf, 1998.

Lochard, Metz P. "Phylon Profile XII: Robert S. Abbott—'Race Leader.'" *Phylon* 8 (1947): 124–32.

Logan, Rayford. *The Negro in American Life and Thought: The Nadir, 1877–1901*. New York: Dial, 1954.

MacDonald, J. Fred. *Blacks and White TV: African Americans in Television since 1948*. 2nd ed. Chicago: Nelson-Hall, 1992.

Magdalinksi, Tara, and Timothy J. L. Chandler. *With God on Their Side: Sport in the Service of Religion*. New York: Routledge, 2002.

Marable, Manning. *Malcolm X: A Life of Reinvention*. New York: Penguin, 2011.
———. *W. E. B. DuBois: Black Radical Democrat*. Boston: Twayne, 1986.
Martin, Tony. *Race First: The Ideological and Organizational Struggles of Marcus Garvey and the Universal Negro Improvement Association*. Westport, CT: Greenwood, 1976.
Martindale, Carolyn. *The White Press and Black America*. New York: Greenwood, 1986.
Maxwell, William J. *New Negro, Old Left: African-American Writing and Communism between the War Years*. New York: Columbia University Press, 1999.
McCartney, John T. *Black Power Ideologies: An Essay in African-American Political Thought*. Philadelphia: Temple University Press, 1992.
McDuffie, Erik S. *Sojourning for Freedom: Black Women, American Communism, and the Making of Black Left Feminism*. Durham, NC: Duke University Press, 2011.
McElvaine, Robert S. *The Depression and the New Deal: A History in Documents*. New York: Oxford University Press, 2000.
McEntee, James J. *Now They Are Men: The Story of the CCC*. Washington, DC: National Home Library Foundation, 1940.
McGuire, Danielle L. *At the Dark End of the Street: Black Women, Rape, and Resistance*. New York: Vintage Books, 2010.
McLaughlin, Malcolm. *The Long Hot Summer of 1967: Urban Rebellion in America*. New York: Palgrave Macmillan, 2014.
McMillan, John. *Smoking Typewriters: The Sixties Underground Press and the Rise of Alternative Media in America*. New York: Oxford University Press, 2011.
Meier, August, and Elliot Rudwick, eds. *Black Protest in the Sixties*. Chicago: Quadrangle Books, 1970.
Meier, August, Elliot Rudwick, and Francis L. Broderick, eds. *Black Protest Thought in the Twentieth Century*. 2nd ed. Indianapolis: Bobbs-Merrill Educational Publishing, 1965.
Menzise, Jeff, ed. *J. A. Rogers' Rambling Ruminations, Rare Writings from the Collection of Joel Augustus Rogers*. College Park, MD: Mind on the Matter Publishing, 2013.
Meriwether, James H. *Proudly We Can Be Africans: Black Americans and Africa, 1935–1961*. Chapel Hill: University of North Carolina Press, 2002.
Meyerowitz, Joanne, ed. *Not June Cleaver: Women and Gender in Postwar America, 1945–1960*. Philadelphia: Temple University Press, 1994.
Michaeli, Ethan. *The Defender: How the Legendary Black Newspaper Changed America*. Boston: Houghton Mifflin Harcourt, 2016.
Miller, Kelly. *Race Adjustment: Essays on the Negro in America*. New York: Neale, 1910.
Miller, Monica L. *Slaves to Fashion: Black Dandyism and the Styling of Black Diasporic Identity*. Durham, NC: Duke University Press, 2009.
Miller, Richard E. *The Messman Chronicles: African Americans in the U.S. Navy, 1932–1943*. Annapolis, MD: Naval Institute Press, 2004.

Millerson, Gerald. *The Technique of Television Production.* New York: Hastings House, 1961.

Mills, Kay. *Changing Channels: The Civil Rights Case That Transformed Television.* Jackson: University Press of Mississippi, 2004.

Mitchell, Michele. *Righteous Propagation: African Americans and the Politics of Racial Destiny after Reconstruction.* Chapel Hill: University of North Carolina Press, 2004.

Moore, Jack B. *W. E. B. DuBois.* Boston: Twayne, 1981.

Morgan, Iwan, and Philip Davies, eds. *From Sit-Ins to SNCC: The Student Civil Rights Movement in the 1960s.* Gainesville: University Press of Florida, 2012.

Morris, James McGrath. *Eyes on the Struggle: Ethel Payne, the First Lady of the Black Press.* New York: Amistad, 2015.

Moses, Wilson Jeremiah. *Black Messiahs and Uncle Toms: Social and Literary Manipulations of a Religious Myth.* University Park: Pennsylvania State University Press, 1993.

———. *Creative Conflict in African American Thought: Frederick Douglass, Alexander Crummell, Booker T. Washington, W. E. B. Du Bois, and Marcus Garvey.* New York: Cambridge University Press, 2004.

Muhammad, Elijah. *Message to the Blackman in America.* Chicago: Muhammad's Temple No. 2, 1965.

Muhammad, Khalil Gibran. *The Condemnation of Blackness: Race, Crime, and the Making of Modern Urban America.* Cambridge, MA: Harvard University Press, 2010.

Mullen, Bill V. *Popular Fronts: Chicago and African-American Cultural Politics, 1935–46.* Urbana: University of Illinois Press, 1999.

Murch, Donna Jean. *Living for the City: Migration, Education, and the Rise of the Black Panther Party in Oakland, California.* Chapel Hill: University of North Carolina Press, 2010.

Myrdal, Gunnar. *An American Dilemma: The Negro Problem and Modern Democracy.* New York: Harper and Row, 1962.

Naison, Mark. *Communists in Harlem during the Depression.* New York: Grove, 1983.

Nance, Susan. "Mystery of the Moorish Science Temple: Southern Blacks and American Alternative Spirituality in 1920s Chicago." *Religion and American Culture: A Journal of Interpretation* 12, no. 2 (Summer 2002): 123–66.

Nas, Peter J. M., and Annemarie Samuels, eds. *Hypercity: The Symbolic Side of Urbanism.* London: Kegan Paul, 2006.

Nerone, John. *Violence against the Press: Policing the Pubic Sphere in U.S. History.* New York: Oxford University Press, 1994.

Nesteby, James R. *Black Images in American Films, 1896–1954: The Interplay between Civil Rights and Film Culture.* Washington, DC: University Press of America, 1982.

Oak, Vishnu V. *The Negro Newspaper.* Yellow Springs, OH: Antioch, 1948.

Ogbar, Jeffrey O. G. *Black Power: Radical Politics and African American Identity.* Baltimore: Johns Hopkins University Press, 2004.

———, ed. *The Harlem Renaissance Revisited: Politics, Arts, and Letters.* Baltimore: John Hopkins University Press, 2010.

Ongiri, Amy Abugo. *Spectacular Blackness: The Cultural Politics of the Black Power Movement and the Search for a Black Aesthetic.* Charlottesville: University of Virginia Press, 2010.

Ottley, Roi. *The Lonely Warrior: The Life and Times of Robert S. Abbott.* Chicago: Henry Regnery, 1955.

———. *"New World A-Coming": Inside Black America.* Boston: Houghton Mifflin, 1943.

Ovington, Mary White. *Half a Man: The Status of the Negro in New York.* New York: Hill and Wang, 1969.

Painter, Nell Irvin. *Exodusters: Black Migration to Kansas after Reconstruction; The First Major Migration to the North of Ex-slaves.* New York: W. W. Norton, 1976.

Parker, Christopher S. *Fighting for Democracy: Black Veterans and the Struggle against White Supremacy in the Postwar South.* Princeton, NJ: Princeton University Press, 2009.

Payne, Charles. *I've Got the Light of Freedom: The Organizing Tradition and the Mississippi Freedom Struggle.* Berkeley: University of California Press, 1995.

Pegram, Thomas R. *One Hundred Percent American: The Rebirth and Decline of the Ku Klux Klan in the 1920s.* Chicago: Ivan R. Dee, 2011.

Penn, I. Garland. *The Afro-American Press and Its Editors.* Springfield, MA: Willey, 1891.

Perry, Bruce. *Malcolm: The Life of a Man Who Changed Black America.* Barrytown, NY: Station Hill, 1991.

Pride, Armistead. "Negro Newspapers: Yesterday, Today and Tomorrow." *Journalism Quarterly* 28 (Spring 1951): 179–88.

Pride, Armistead S., and Clint C. Wilson II. *A History of the Black Press.* Washington, DC: Howard University Press, 1997.

Protess, David L., and Maxwell McCombs, eds. *Agenda Setting: Readings on Media, Public Opinion, and Policymaking.* New York: Routledge, 1991.

Raiford, Leigh. *Imprisoned in a Luminous Glare: Photography and the African American Freedom Struggle.* Chapel Hill: University of North Carolina Press, 2011.

Ransby, Barbara. *Ella Baker and the Black Freedom Movement: A Radical Democratic Vision.* Chapel Hill: University of North Carolina Press, 2003.

Rauch, Basil, ed. *The Roosevelt Reader: Selected Speeches, Messages, Press Conferences, and Letters of Franklin D. Roosevelt.* New York: Rinehart, 1957.

Raymond, Emilie. *Stars for Freedom: Hollywood, Black Celebrities, and the Civil Rights Movement.* Seattle: University of Washington Press, 2015.

Reed, Christopher Robert. *Black Chicago's First Century.* Vol. 1, *1833–1900.* Columbia: University of Missouri Press, 2005.

———. *The Chicago NAACP and the Rise of Black Professional Leadership, 1910–1966.* Bloomington: Indiana University Press, 1997.

———. *The Rise of Chicago's Black Metropolis, 1920–1929.* Urbana: University of Illinois Press, 2014.

Reverby, Susan M., ed. *Tuskegee's Truths: Rethinking the Tuskegee Syphilis Study.* Chapel Hill: University of North Carolina Press, 2000.

Rice, Myiti Sengstacke. *Chicago Defender.* Charleston: Arcadia, 2012.

Rickford, Russel J. *Betty Shabazz: A Remarkable Story of Survival and Faith before and after Malcolm X.* Naperville, IL: Sourcebooks, 2003.

Roberts, Gee, and Hank Klibanoff. *Race Beat: The Press, the Civil Rights Struggle, and the Awakening of a Nation.* New York: Alfred A. Knopf, 2006.

Roberts, Randy. *Papa Jack: Jack Johnson and the Era of White Hopes.* New York: Free Press, 1983.

Rocksborough-Smith, Ian. "'Filling the Gap': Intergenerational Black Radicalism and the Popular Front Ideals of *Freedomways* Magazine's Early Years, (1961–1965)." *Afro-Americans in New York Life and History* 31, no. (1 (January 2007): 7–42.

Rolinson, Mary G. *Grassroots Garveyism: The Universal Negro Improvement Association in the Rural South, 1920–1927.* Chapel Hill: University of North Carolina Press, 2007.

Ross, Marlon B. *Manning the Race: Reforming Black Men in the Jim Crow Era.* New York: New York University Press, 2004.

Rotundo, E. Anthony. *American Manhood: Transformations in Masculinity from the Revolution to the Modern Era.* New York: Basic Books, 1993.

Rudwick, Elliot M. *W. E. B. DuBois: Propagandist of the Negro Protest.* New York: Atheneum, 1968.

Salmon, Lucy Maynard. *The Newspaper and the Historian.* New York: Oxford University Press, 1923.

———. *The Newspaper and Authority.* New York: Oxford University Press, 1923.

Salmond, John A. *The Civilian Conservation Corps, 1933–1942: A New Deal Study.* Durham, NC: Duke University Press, 1967.

Savage, Barbara Dianne. *Broadcasting Freedom: Radio, War, and the Politics of Race, 1938–1948.* Chapel Hill: University of North Carolina Press, 1999.

Scharff, Virginia J., ed. *Seeing Nature through Gender.* Lawrence: University Press of Kansas, 2003.

Scott, Emmett J. *Negro Migration during the War.* New York: Arno, 1969.

Self, Robert O. *American Babylon: Race and the Struggle for Postwar Oakland.* Princeton, NJ: Princeton University Press, 2003.

Simmons, Charles A. *The African American Press: A History of News Coverage during National Crises, with Special Reference to Four Newspapers, 1827–1965.* London: McFarland, 1998.

Sitkoff, Harvard. *A New Deal for Blacks: The Emergence of Civil Rights as a National Issue; The Depression Decade.* New York: Oxford University Press, 2009.

Sklaroff, Lauren Rebecca. *Black Culture and the New Deal: The Quest for Civil Rights in the Roosevelt Era.* Chapel Hill: University of North Carolina Press, 2009.

Smith, Jason Scott. *Building New Deal Liberalism: The Political Economy of Public Works, 1933–1956.* New York: Cambridge University Press, 2006.

Smock, Raymond W. *Booker T. Washington: Black Leadership in the Age of Jim Crow.* Chicago: Ivan R. Dee, 2009.

Solomon, William S., and Robert W. McChesney, eds. *Ruthless Criticism: New Perspectives in U.S. Communication History.* Minneapolis: University of Minnesota Press, 1993.

Spear, Allan H. *Black Chicago: The Making of a Negro Ghetto, 1890–1920.* Chicago: University of Chicago Press, 1967.

Stecopoulos, Harry, and Michael Uebel, eds. *Race and the Subject of Masculinities.* Durham, NC: Duke University Press, 1997.

Stein, Judith. *The World of Marcus Garvey: Race and Class in Modern Society.* Baton Rouge: Louisiana State University Press, 1986.

Stephens, Michelle Ann. *Black Empire: The Masculine Global Imaginary of Caribbean Intellectuals in the United States, 1914–1962.* Durham, NC: Duke University Press, 2005.

Stephens, Ronald J. "Narrating Acts of Resistance: Explorations of Untold Heroic and Horrific Battle Stories Surrounding Robert Franklin Williams's Residence in Lake County, Michigan." *Journal of Black Studies* 33, no. 5 (May 2003): 675–703.

Strain, Christopher B. *Pure Fire: Self-Defense as Activism in the Civil Rights Era.* Athens: University of Georgia Press, 2005.

Streitmatter, Rodger. *Raising Her Voice: African-American Women Journalists Who Changed History.* Lexington: University Press of Kentucky, 1994.

Strickland, Arvarh E. *History of the Chicago Urban League.* Columbia: University of Missouri Press, 2001.

Suggs, Henry Lewis. *P. B. Young, Newspaperman: Race, Politics, and Journalism in the New South, 1910–1962.* Charlottesville: University Press of Virginia, 1988.

Sugrue, Thomas. *Sweet Land of Liberty: The Forgotten Struggles for Civil Rights in the North.* New York: Random House, 2008.

Sullivan, Patricia. *Days of Hope: Race and Democracy in the New Deal Era.* Chapel Hill: University of North Carolina Press, 1996.

———. *Lift Every Voice: The NAACP and the Making of the Civil Rights Movement.* New York: New Press, 2009.

Summers, Martin. *Manliness and Its Discontents: The Black Middle Class and the Transformation of Masculinity, 1900–1930.* Chapel Hill: University of North Carolina Press, 2004.

Taylor, Ula Yvette. *The Promise of Patriarchy: Women and the Nation of Islam.* Chapel Hill: University of North Carolina Press, 2017.

———. *Veiled Garvey: The Life and Times of Amy Jacque Garvey.* Chapel Hill: University of North Carolina Press, 2002.

Terrill, Robert E. *Malcolm X: Inventing Radical Judgment.* East Lansing: Michigan State University Press, 2004.

Theoharis, Jeanne, and Komozi Woodard, eds. *Freedom North: Black Freedom Struggles Outside the South, 1940–1980.* New York: Palgrave Macmillan, 2003.

Tinney, James S., and Justine J. Rector. *Issues and Trends in Afro-American Journalism.* Washington, DC: University Press of America, 1980.

Tinson, Christopher M. *Radical Intellect: Liberator Magazine and Black Activism in the 1960s.* Chapel Hill: University of North Carolina Press, 2017.

Tolnay, Stewart E., and E. M. Beck. *A Festival of Violence: An Analysis of Southern Lynchings, 1882–1930.* Urbana: University of Illinois Press, 1995.

Torres, Sasha. *Black, White, and in Color: Television and Black Civil Rights.* Princeton, NJ: Princeton University Press, 2003.

Trotter, Joe William, Jr., ed. *The Great Migration in Historical Perspective: New Dimensions of Race, Class, and Gender.* Bloomington: Indiana University Press, 1991.

Tuck, Stephen. *The Night Malcolm X Spoke at the Oxford Union: A Transatlantic Story of Antiracist Protest.* Berkeley: University of California Press, 2014.

Tucker, Jed B. "Malcolm X, the Prison Years: The Relentless Pursuit of Formal Education." *Journal of African American History* 102, no. 2 (Spring 2017): 184–212.

Tuttle, William M. *Race Riot: Chicago in the Red Summer of 1919.* New York: Atheneum, 1970.

Tyner, James A. *The Geography of Malcolm X: Black Radicalism and the Remaking of American Space.* New York: Routledge, 2005.

Tyson, Timothy B. *The Blood of Emmett Till.* New York: Simon and Schuster, 2017.

———. *Radio Free Dixie: Robert F. Williams and the Roots of Black Power.* Chapel Hill: University of North Carolina Press, 1999.

Umoja, Akinyele Omowale. *We Will Shoot Back: Armed Resistance in the Mississippi Freedom Movement.* New York: New York University Press, 2013.

Verney, Kevern. *The Art of the Possible: Booker T. Washington and Black Leadership in the United States, 1881–1925.* New York: Routledge, 2001.

Vincent, Theodore G. *Black Power and the Garvey Movement.* New York: Ramparts, 1971.

Vogel, Todd, ed. *The Black Press: New Literary and Historical Essays.* New Brunswick, NJ: Rutgers University Press, 2001.

Von Eschen, Penny M. *Race against Empire: Black Americans and Anticolonialism, 1937–1957.* Ithaca, NY: Cornell University Press, 1997.

Walker, Dennis. *Islam and the Search for African-American Nationhood: Elijah Muhammad, Louis Farrakhan, and the Nation of Islam.* Atlanta: Clarity, 2005.

Wallace, Maurice O. *Constructing the Black Masculine: Identity and Ideality in African American Men's Literature and Culture, 1775–1995.* Durham, NC: Duke University Press, 2002.

Wallace-Sanders, Kimberly, ed. *Skin Deep Spirit Strong: The Black Female Body in American Culture.* Ann Arbor: University of Michigan Press, 2002.

Ward, Geoffrey C. *Unforgivable Blackness: The Rise and Fall of Jack Johnson.* New York: Alfred A. Knopf, 2004.

Warren, Robert Penn. *Who Speaks for the Negro?* New Haven, CT: Yale University Press, 2014.

Washburn, Patrick S. *The African American Newspaper, Voice of Freedom.* Evanston, IL: Northwestern University Press, 2006.

———. *A Question of Sedition: The Federal Government's Investigation of the Black Press during World War II.* New York: Oxford University Press, 1986.

Washington, Harriet A. *Medical Apartheid: The Dark History of Medical Experimentation on Black Americans from Colonial Times to the Present.* New York: Doubleday, 2006.

Watson, Steven. *The Harlem Renaissance: Hub of African-American Culture, 1920–1930.* New York: Pantheon Books, 1995.

Weiss, Nancy J. *Farewell to the Party of Lincoln: Black Politics in the Age of FDR.* Princeton, NJ: Princeton University Press, 1983.

———. *The National Urban League, 1910–1940.* New York: Oxford University Press, 1974.

Wendt, Simon. *The Spirit and the Shotgun: Armed Resistance and the Struggle for Civil Rights.* Gainesville: University Press of Florida, 2007.

Whalan, Mark. *The Great War and the Culture of the New Negro.* Gainesville: University Press of Florida, 2008.

White, Deborah Gray. *Too Heavy a Load: Black Women in Defense of Themselves, 1894–1994.* New York: W. W. Norton, 1999.

White, Vilbert L., Jr. *Inside the Nation of Islam: A Historical and Personal Testimony by a Black Muslim.* Gainesville: University Press of Florida, 2001.

Wiggins, David K. "Wendell Smith, the *Pittsburgh Courier-Journal*, and the Campaign to Include Blacks in Organized Baseball, 1933–1945." *Journal of Sport History* 10, no. 2 (Summer 1983): 5–29.

Wilder, Craig Steven. *In the Company of Black Men: The African Influence on African American Culture in New York City.* New York: New York University Press, 2001.

Williams, Chad L. *Torchbearers of Democracy: African American Soldiers in World War I Era.* Chapel Hill: University of North Carolina Press, 2010.

Williams, Oscar R. *George S. Schuyler: Portrait of a Black Conservative.* Knoxville: University of Tennessee Press, 2007.

Williams, Rhonda Y. *The Politics of Public Housing: Black Women's Struggles against Urban Inequality.* New York: Oxford University Press, 2004.

Wilson, Clint C., II. *Black Journalists in Paradox: Historical Perspectives and Current Dilemmas.* New York: Greenwood, 1991.

Wilson, James Q., ed. *Urban Renewal: The Negro and the Controversy.* Cambridge, MA: MIT Press, 1966.

Wilson, Jamie J. "'Come Down off the Cross and Get under the Crescent': The Newspaper Columns of Elijah Muhammad and Malcolm X." *Biography: An Interdisciplinary Quarterly* 36, no. 3 (Summer 2013): 494–506.

Wilson, Sondra Kathryn, ed. *The* Crisis *Reader: Stories, Poetry, and Essays from the N.A.A.C.P.'s* Crisis *Magazine.* New York: Modern Library, 1999.

———. *The Opportunity Reader: Stories, Poetry, and Essays from the Urban League's* Opportunity *Magazine.* New York: Modern Library, 1999.

———. *The Selected Writings of James Weldon Johnson.* Vol. 1. New York: Oxford University Press, 1995.

Wolcott, Victoria. "The Culture of the Informal Economy: Numbers Runners in Inter-War Black Detroit." *Radical History Review* 69 (Fall 1997): 46–75.

———. *Remaking Respectability: African American Women in Interwar Detroit.* Chapel Hill: University of North Carolina Press, 2001.

Wolseley, Roland E. *The Black Press, USA.* 2nd ed. Ames: Iowa State University Press, 1992.

Wolters, Raymond. *DuBois and His Rivals.* Columbia: University of Missouri Press, 2002.

———. *Negroes and the Great Depression: The Problem of Economic Recovery.* Westport, CT: Greenwood, 1970.

Wood, Amy Louise. *Lynching and Spectacle: Witnessing Racial Violence in America, 1890–1940.* Chapel Hill: University of North Carolina Press, 2009.

Wood, Joe, ed. *Malcolm X in Our Own Image.* New York: St. Martin's, 1992.

Woodard, Michael D. *Black Entrepreneurs in America: Stories of Struggle and Success.* New Brunswick, NJ: Rutgers University Press, 1997.

Woodley, Jenny. *Art for Equality: The NAACP's Cultural Campaign for Civil Rights.* Lexington: University Press of Kentucky, 2014.

Woods, Jeff. *Black Struggle Red Scare: Segregation and Anti-Communism in the South, 1948–1968.* Baton Rouge: Louisiana State University Press, 2004.

Woodson, Carter G. *A Century of Negro Migration.* New York: AMS Press, 1970.

Young, Consuelo Caldwell. "An Objective Reader Interest Study of the *Chicago Defender* Newspaper." Master's thesis, Northwestern University, 1943.

Young, Harvey. *Embodying Black Experience: Stillness, Critical Memory, and the Black Body.* Ann Arbor: University of Michigan Press, 2010.

Zackodnik, Teresa. *Press, Platform, Pulpit: Black Feminist Publics in the Era of Reform.* Knoxville: University of Tennessee Press, 2011.

Zuckerman, Phil, ed. *The Social Theory of W. E. B. DuBois.* Thousand Oaks, CA: Pine Forge Press, 2004.

Index

Gordon, Eugene, 81
Gottschalk, Arthur R., 231–32
Great Depression, 98–102, 106–13, 183, 270n61, 273n96
Great Migration: Abbott and, 33, 103; Chicago and, 33–34, 41; *Crisis* and, 28, 32; *Defender* and, 23–25, 28–29, 33–44, 251n146, 253n197; DuBois and, 32–33; masculinity and, 23–25, 38–39; mobility and, 39–40; in northern media, 21–22; "Red Summer" and, 52; in southern media, 21; winters and, 44–45; women and, 38–40
Great Northern Drive, 44
Greene, Percy, 171
Grey, Edgar, 69, 91
Griffin, Farah Jasmine, 282n119
Griffith, D. W., 28
Grossman, James, 44, 247n79, 251n144

Haley, Alex, 200, 217, 223
Half a Man (Ovington), 25
Hall, Rebecca, 64
Hamer, Fannie Lou, 154–55
Hampton Institute, 106, 114, 119
Harlem, 60–61, 65, 224
Harlem Renaissance, 58
Harper, Lucius C., 34, 130
Harris, Charles 19X, 217
Harrison, Hubert, 61–62, 73–74
"Hate that Hate Produced, The" (documentary), 181, 187–89, 199
Hearst, William Randolph, 33, 45–46
Herald Dispatch (newspaper), 187, 222
Herald-Examiner (newspaper), 45–46
Hine, Darlene Clark, 40
Honduras, 64
Horizon: A Journal of the Color Line (magazine), 26
Horton, Myles, 143
Houston Informer (newspaper), 14
Howard University, 118
Howe, David Ward, 130

How Rastus Got His Pork Chops (film), 27
Hue (magazine), 136

"If We Must Die" (McKay), 55, 77
"I Have a Dream" (King), 203
Internal Revenue Service (IRS), 122–23, 146–47
IRS. *See* Internal Revenue Service (IRS)

Jackson Advocate (newspaper), 171
Jacques, Amy. *See* Garvey, Amy Jacques
Jamaica, 57–58
James X, 217
Jeremiah X, 216
Jet (magazine), 136, 167
Jim Crow, 4–5, 22–23, 32, 36, 55, 99, 139. *See also* segregation
Johnson, Ethel Azalea, 156–57, 161
Johnson, Jack, 49
Johnson, James Weldon, 75
Johnson, John H., 136, 187
Johnson, Lyndon B., 208, 228
Johnson, Mordecai, 170
Joseph X, 216
Journal and Guide (newspaper), 5

Kansas City Call (newspaper), 4, 10–11, 79, 130, 147, 149
Kappa Alpha Psi, 127
Karriem, Isaiah, 217
Kemp, Walter 3X, 206
Kennedy, John F., 211
Kenya, 64
Kerlin, Robert T., 13, 18, 55
Kerner, Otto, 232
Kilroe, Edwin, 69, 91
Kimmel, Michael, 238n22, 241n47, 247n81, 275n164
King, Coretta Scott, 159, 166
King, Martin Luther, Jr., 11, 140–41, 144–45, 150, 154, 156–71, 175, 179–80, 193, 203, 283n147, 284n147
KKK. *See* Ku Klux Klan (KKK)

National Negro Press Association, 124

National Newspaper Publishers Association, 228

National Press Club, 136

National Urban League, 59, 133, 229, 254n5

Nation of Islam (NOI), 181–99, 204–5, 209–10, 223–24, 225–27, 287n15

NCNW. *See* National Council of Negro Women (NCNW)

Negro Daily Times (newspaper), 89

Negro Digest (newspaper), 304n8

Negroes with Guns (Williams), 178–79

Negro Family, The: The Case for National Action, 228–29

Negro Improvement Alliance, 89

Negro Newspaper Publishers Association (NNPA), 130, 133, 135, 152–53, 191, 228, 233–34

Negro Society for Historical Research, 62

Negro Spokesman (newspaper), 5

Negro World (newspaper), 2, 5; as Black Nationalist, 63; decline of, 107; *Defender* and, 65; founding of, 58; growth of, 59, 62, 64; Harlem and, 65; Harrison and, 73–74; Malcolm X and, 187; racial uplift and, 59; self-defense in, 162; sensationalism in, 63–64; Universal Negro Improvement Association and, 255n33; vision of racial advancement in, 61–62; women and, 63. *See also* Garvey, Marcus

New Deal, 110–12, 117, 273n96

New Negro, 50–51; Garvey and, 74–75, 79, 83–84; Great Depression and, 98; Harlem and, 60; Harlem Renaissance and, 58; masculinity and, 74–75, 79, 83–84; McKay and, 77; *Negro World* and, 58; racism and, 79–80; women and, 68

New Orleans Times-Picayune (newspaper), 145

"Newspapers Should Take Up Race Leadership" (Anderson), 1–2

Newton, Huey P., 225

New York Age (newspaper), 21, 26, 32, 34, 75

New York Amsterdam News (newspaper), 107, 170

New York News (newspaper), 21

New York Sun (newspaper), 56

New York Times (newspaper), 146, 198

New York World (newspaper), 31, 69–70, 75

Niagara movement, 25–26

Nigeria, 64

Nix, Robert, 148

Nixon, Richard, 232, 305n16

NNC. *See* National Negro Congress (NNC)

NNPA. *See* Negro Newspaper Publishers Association (NNPA)

NOI. *See* Nation of Islam (NOI)

nonviolent resistance, 145–46, 149–50, 155–56, 159–70, 172–73

Norfolk Journal and Guide (newspaper), 21, 31, 42, 72–73, 135

North Carolina Star of Zion (newspaper), 21

Nunn, William G., 175

OAAU. *See* Organization of Afro-American Unity (OAAU)

Ogbar, Jeffrey O. G., 61

Oklahoma City Black Dispatch (newspaper), 79

Old Mammy's Charge (film), 27

Omaha Star (newspaper), 12

Opportunity (magazine), 5, 59, 97–98

Organization of Afro-American Unity (OAAU), 218–19, 221, 223–24

Original Man, 194–96, 201, 217

Ottley, Roi, 54

Ovington, Mary White, 25

Owen, Chandler, 61, 73–74, 77–78

Panama, 57

Parker, Mack Charles, 150

Parks, Rosa, 168

Up from Slavery (Washington), 58
uplift. See racial uplift
Urban League, 45, 59, 133, 229, 254n5
urban renewal, 207

Vann, Robert L., 43, 126, 271n71
Vogel, Todd, 242n70, 255n11
Voice of the Negro (newspaper), 31
Voice of the Negro 1919, The (Kerlin), 55

Wagner Act, 117
Walker, Madame C. J., 48, 50
Walker, Wyatt Tee, 166
Wallace, Maurice O., 268n39
Wallace, Mike, 187–89, 215, 217–18, 221–22
Warner, Richard, 69, 91
War on Poverty, 208
Warren, Robert Penn, 229
Washington, Booker T., 11, 25, 30–31, 33, 35, 42, 58, 66, 72, 195, 246n68, 292n92
Washington Post (newspaper), 146, 156
Waters, Enoch P., 12, 15, 50, 124–25, 163, 269n42
Wells, Ida B., 23, 25, 31–32, 36–37, 238n19, 244n16
West End Post (newspaper), 112
Whip (newspaper), 5, 79, 88, 107
Whitcomb, Charlene, 197
White, Deborah Gray, 68, 128
White, Walter, 108, 254n209
"White Man's Heaven Is a Black Man's Hell" (Louis X), 211
Who Speaks for the Negro? (Warren), 229
Wilder, Susie, 68–69
Wilkins, Roy, 91–92, 147–51, 156, 180, 193, 203
Williams, Eugene, 52
Williams, Lorenzo X, 198
Williams, Mabel, 150–51
Williams, Robert F., 2, 18; Burroughs and, 148–49; civil rights movement and, 138–39, 153–55, 171–73;

criticisms of black press by, 175–76; in Cuba, 157; in Defender, 148, 173–74; in Detroit, 141; "Egos and Heroes," 171–72; Frazier and, 176; gender roles and, 159; King and, 140–41, 156, 165–67, 179–80, 283n147, 284n147; Malcolm X and, 181; masculinity and, 152–54; militancy and, 141–42, 178–80; Muhammad Speaks and, 181, 192; NAACP and, 138–39, 142–43, 146–48, 155–57, 285n172; as new kind of black publisher, 137, 151–52; racial advancement and, 139–40, 174, 180; self-defense and, 140–41, 153–61, 166, 173–74, 278n23; violence and, 142; Wilkins and, 147–48, 150–51; women and, 281n93
Wilson, Robert A., 51
Wolcott, Victoria, 271n82, 273n96
"Woman's Page," 12
women: civil rights movement and, 159–60; Garvey and, 67–69; gender roles and, 68, 99, 158; in Great Depression, 110, 271n82; Great Migration and, 38–40; as journalists, 12, 240n41; masculinity and, 68–69, 110–11; Nation of Islam and, 204–5; Negro World and, 63; prostitution and, 271n82; as publishers, 269n48; "Race Woman" concept and, 50–51, 76, 100; racism and, 4, 38; in Universal Negro Improvement Association, 67–68, 257nn67,70; violence against, 68, 154; Williams and, 281n93
Women's National Press Club, 136
Women's Political Council (WPC), 143, 154, 168
Woods, Jeff, 167–68
Woodson, Carter G., 52, 82, 109, 111
Woodville Times (newspaper), 29, 103, 112
Works Progress Administration (WPA), 273n96
World War I, 23, 47–48, 58, 66, 74, 107, 117, 162, 241n57

CPSIA information can be obtained
at www.ICGtesting.com
Printed in the USA
LVHW111933011118
595640LV00007B/120/P